Studies in the Scriptures

1947

Studies in the Scriptures
1947

Arthur W. Pink

THE BANNER OF TRUTH TRUST

THE BANNER OF TRUTH TRUST
3 Murrayfield Road, Edinburgh EH12 6EL
PO Box 621, Carlisle, Pennsylvania 17013, USA

★

© The Banner of Truth Trust
First published 1947
First Banner of Truth edition 1982
ISBN 0 85151 347 6

★

Printed in Great Britain by
Hazell Watson & Viney Ltd, Aylesbury, Bucks

CONTENTS

XXVI   JANUARY 1947   No. 1

STUDIES IN THE SCRIPTURES

"Search the Scriptures." *John v, 39*

Publisher and Editor—ARTHUR W. PINK,
29 Lewis Street,
Stornoway, Isle of Lewis,
Scotland.

GO FORWARD

Though the writer has passed the sixtieth milestone of life and completed a quarter of a century's hard but happy work on this magazine, yet he feels that "Go forward" (Ex. xiv, 15) is the Lord's clamant word unto him at this time. If he should have acquired any laurels, he certainly does not wish to rest upon them; nor does he—while health and strength are granted—intend to moderate his own studies or relax in his efforts. It has long been his desire to wear out rather than rust out, or, to express it in Scripture language, to "very gladly spend and be spent" (II Cor. xii, 15) in endeavouring to serve the Lord and minister to His beloved people. Nor could he warrantably look for any measure of realizing that desire if he slackened; rather should he seek to "Go forward" with increased earnestness and diligence—"redeeming the time, because the days are evil" (Eph. v, 16). The more evil the days, the grander the opportunity for proving the sufficiency of God's grace and the greater the privilege in serving His children.

"Go forward." Is not this a timely word for *each* of us as we enter a new year? a suitable motto for us to keep in mind as we journey through (if God permit) 1947? We need to clearly realize there is no such thing as remaining stationary in the spiritual life: if we do not progress, we inevitably retrograde. How that solemn fact should search our hearts! Christian friend, your history this year will be either one of going forward or backsliding. This new year will mark either an increased fruitfulness in your soul and life to the glory of Him whose name you bear, or increased leanness and barrenness to His reproach. It will witness either a growing in grace or a decline in your spirituality. It will record either an increased love for the Word, use of the Throne of grace, strictness of walk and closer communion with Christ, or a growing coldness and a following of Him afar off. O Christian reader, before reading any further, will you not now close your eyes and lift up your heart in earnest prayer for yourself *and* for all your brethren and sisters in Christ?

The historic occasion on which those words were uttered is noteworthy, and a brief consideration of the same the better enables us to make application of them unto ourselves. The situation confronting Israel was a hopeless one so far as they were concerned, and had not the Lord intervened they had undoubtedly perished. After their exodus from Egypt, Pharaoh at the

(continued on back page)

Important Notices

Please advise promptly of change in address, otherwise copies will be lost in the mails.

We are glad to send a sample copy to any of your friends whom you believe would be interested in this publication.

This magazine is published as " a work of faith and labour of love," the editor and his wife gladly giving their services free.   There is no regular subscription price, as we do not wish the poor of the flock to be deprived.   This does not mean that those looking for something for nothing may " help themselves."   Those getting this magazine who are financially able and who receive spiritual help from its pages, are expected to gladly contribute towards its expenses; otherwise their names are dropped from our list.

Will those forwarding International Money Orders please have them made out to us at Stornoway, Isle of Lewis, Scotland. Checks (Cheques—Eng.) made out on U.S.A. Banks are not negotiable here, so please do not send them.

All unsigned articles are by the Editor.

CONTENTS

THE PRAYERS OF THE APOSTLES

37. Colossians i, 9-12.

One chief reason why the Holy Spirit has placed on permanent record so many of the prayers of the apostles is that the saints of all succeeding generations might receive instruction therefrom.   The subject-matter of their petitions imply and denote the following things.   First, that what they requested for the saints are the particular things which Christians in all ages are to specially desire, prize and seek an increase of. Second, that God alone can impart, sustain and promote such blessings and graces.   Third, that we too should not only ask for. these favours, but must diligently strive after the realization of them.   Prayer was never designed to excuse apathy, nor to relieve us of the discharge of our responsibility. We are insincere if we cry unto God for certain things and do nothing ourselves to seek and secure them.   A healthy man who prayed for his daily bread and then remained idle would be mocking God.   To ask the Lord not to lead us into temptation but deliver us from evil, and then to carelessly trifle with sin and fellowship with the ungodly, is nothing but hypocrisy.   To make request for more light from the Word or a fuller understanding of the Divine will, and not continue diligently searching the Scriptures and meditating on its contents, is reprehensible.

It has been pointed out in the earlier articles that in each instance the substance of the apostle's prayer was regulated by the particular case or condition of each separate company of saints for which he made supplication —teaching us that one prayer is more pertinent and suitable to a Christian, or a group of Christians, at one time or circumstance than another. While having much in common, the various local churches of which we have any account in the New Testament differed in several respects: in their graces, trials and failures—as the apostles did from one another.   Though alike in essentials, they were dissimilar in circumstantials. The church at Colosse was no exception. Instead of its members being harassed by Judaisers, as were the Corinthians, they were in danger of being corrupted by the Gnostics. False teachers were seeking to rob the former of their *liberty* in Christ, while austere ascetics and subtle philosophers were endeavouring to deprive the latter of that *simplicity* which is in Christ. Indications of this are found in Colossians ii, 4, 8, 18, 20-23. Paul therefore prayed here more concerning the practical aspect of the Christian life.

There is no clear and direct Scriptural evidence that the apostle Paul was ever in Colosse, and still less that he founded the first Christian assembly there. The general testimony of antiquity favours the view that Epaphras, sent by Paul from Ephesus, was the one who carried the Gospel to that city and organized its church. As Matthew Henry well pointed out, " God is sometimes pleased to make use of the ministry of those who are of less note and lower gifts for doing great service to His Church. God uses what hands He pleases and is not tied to those of note, that the ' excellency of the power may appear to be of God ' (II Cor. iv, 7)." But the ancient opinion was considerably controverted during the past century, appeal being made to Acts xviii, 23—Colosse being in Phrygia But as the point is not one of any practical importance we shall not enter into any further discussion of it, except to say that we consider the apostle's statement, " for I would that ye know what great conflict I have for you, and them at Laodicea, and as many as have not seen my face in the flesh " (ii, 1), as far more decisive than the inference drawn from Acts xviii, 23.

Though Paul was not the planter of this church yet he was far from being indifferent to its welfare, nor did he make any difference between it and those which he had personally founded. Those who had been converted under others were as dear to him as were his own converts—O, for more of his large-heartedness. His deep solicitude for the Colossians is evinced by the trouble which he took in writing an epistle unto them. A careful reading of its contents makes it evident that it was penned in view of certain errors which extensively prevailed among the churches of that part of Asia Minor, and some knowledge—a general understanding at least—of those errors is necessary in order to correctly interpret some of the details of this epistle. Those errors consisted of a mixture of Grecian philosophy (ii, 4-8) and Jewish ceremonialism (ii, 16)—a type of Gnosticism which was really a Grecianized form of Oriental mysticism. The chief design of the apostle in this epistle was to assert the superior claims of Christianity over all philosophies, and its independence of the peculiar rites and customs of Judaism.

The best summary we have met with of this prayer is that furnished by Thomas Scott: " He especially requested that they might be ' filled ' or ' completely endowed with ' the knowledge of the will of God: both in respect of His method of saving sinners and their duties to Him and to all men as His redeemed servants; that they might understand the import and spiritual extent of His commandments, and how to obey them in the several relationships, situations and offices which they sustained in the church and in the community, and for the improvement of their different talents. That they might know how to apply general rules to their own particular cases, and so do the work of Christ assigned to each of them in the best manner, from the purest motives and with the happiest effect. Thus they would proceed ' in all wisdom and spiritual understanding,' with sagacity and prudent discernment of seasons and opportunities, distinguishing between real excellency and all deceitful appearances; wisely attending to their duties in the most inoffensive and engaging manner, without affording their enemies any advantage, or losing opportunities of usefulness out of timidity, or failing of success through want of caution and discretion.

"He was desirous of this especially, that they might habitually behave in a manner worthy of that glorious and holy Lord, whose servants and worshippers they were: not dishonouring Him or His cause by any inconsistency or impropriety of conduct, but acting as became persons so highly favoured and Divinely instructed; and that their conduct might in all respects be well-pleasing to Him, while fruitfulness in every kind of good work was connected with a still further increase in the knowledge of God, and of the glory and harmony of His perfections, and a happy experience of His consolations. The apostle and his helpers prayed also that the Colossians might be most abundantly strengthened in all the graces of the new nature with an energy suited to their utmost need, according to the glorious power of God by which He converted, upheld and comforted believers; that so they might be enabled to bear all their tribulations and persecutions with patient submission, persevering constancy, meekness of longsuffering, and joy in the Lord. While, amidst all trials, they gave thanks to the Father of our Lord Jesus, whose special grace had made them meet to partake of the inheritance provided for the saints in the world of perfect light, knowledge, holiness and happiness; at a distance from all ignorance, error, sin, temptation and sorrow."

Before considering it in detail, let us first give a brief analysis of this prayer. (1) Its *Address*. The majority of writers appear to regard this prayer as being one without an address, but this we consider is a mistake. It is true that none is found at the beginning of verse 9, but that was not necessary, since in verse 3 the apostle had said, "We give thanks to God and the Father of our Lord Jesus Christ, praying always for you." (2) Its *Supplicators*. In contrast with the "I" of Ephesians i, 15, and Philippians i, 9, 10, this proceeds from a "we"—Paul himself, Timothy (verse 1), Epaphras (verse 7), who was with him (Phile. 23), and possibly others. (3) Its *Occasion* or spring: "For this cause." Probably the saints at Colosse had sent their minister, Epaphras, to learn the apostle's mind on certain matters, a summary of which is intimated in this prayer. Moreover, the knowledge of their "love in the Spirit" unto them (verse 8) had drawn out their affections, which were now expressed in fervent supplications for them. (4) Its *Petitions*, wherein request is made that they might be intelligent Christians, pious, strong and thankful ones.

In regard to the character of those petitions we behold once more the breadth or comprehensiveness of the requests which Paul was wont to make for the saints. The "large petitions" which he spread before God were a marked feature in all his approaches unto the throne of grace on behalf of God's people, and it is one which we need to take to heart and emulate. For the saints at Rome he had prayed that God would "fill them with *all* peace and joy in believing, that ye may *abound* in hope" (xv, 5). For the Ephesians that they might be "filled with all the fullness of God" (iii, 19). For the Philippians that "their love might abound yet more and more" and be "filled with the fruits of righteousness" (i, 9, 11). So here: not merely that they might have a knowledge of God's will in wisdom, but "be *filled* with the knowledge of His will in *all wisdom*," etc.; not a bare and general request that their conduct should adorn the Gospel, but rather that they "might walk worthy of the Lord unto *all* pleasing, being fruitful in every *good* work." How different is this large-heartedness of the apostle from that cramped spirit which obtains in those quarters which pride themselves on being so "sound in the Faith"!

Once more we would press upon the reader the great importance of paying good heed to the order of their petitions if he would rightly apprehend and duly appreciate these prayers; and usually this is best accomplished by considering them in their *inverse order*. Let us do this with the one now before us. We are in no fit condition to be " giving thanks unto the Father for the inheritance of the saints in light "; yea, we lack an essential part of the evidence that *we* have been " made meet, to be partakers of it if we are not exercising " all patience and longsuffering with joyfulness " despite the difficulties and trials of the way. Nor will such graces as those be active except we first be " strengthened with all might, according to His glorious power." But that, in turn, is dependent upon our " increasing in the knowledge of God." Yet that will not be our happy experience except we " walk worthy of the Lord unto all pleasing, being fruitful in every good work." And how can we possibly do *that* unless, previously, we are filled with the knowledge of His will in all wisdom and spiritual understanding?

" For this cause [the declaration of their love] we also since the day we heard it, do not cease to pray for you [which is the most effective way of reciprocating Christian affection], and to desire [" make request for you "— R.V.] that ye might be filled with the knowledge of His will in all wisdom and spiritual understanding " (verse 9). As just intimated above, in order to discern and appreciate the force of this opening petition it is necessary to observe the relation which it bears to those that follow: it is related to them as cause to effect. As our being granted " a spirit of wisdom and revelation in the knowledge of God " (Eph. i, 17) is required in order to the eyes of our understanding being enlightened, that we may know what is " the hope of His calling "; as our being " strengthened with might by His Spirit in the inner man " (Eph. iii, 16) must precede Christ's dwelling in our hearts by faith, our being rooted and grounded in love, and our being filled with the fullness of God; and as their " love abounding yet more and more in all knowledge and judgment " (Phil. i, 10) is indispensable if we are to approve things that are excellent, and that we be " sincere and without offence," so to be " filled with the knowledge of His will in all wisdom and spiritual understanding " is essential if we are to " walk worthy of the Lord unto all pleasing and be fruitful in every good work."

" That ye might be filled with the knowledge of His will in all wisdom and spiritual understanding." For the Ephesian saints the apostle had prayed that they might " know the exceeding greatness of God's *power*," both as it worked in them and wrought for them; but here he asks for a knowledge of His *will*. To be without such knowledge is like the captain of a ship starting out on a long voyage without a chart, or for builders to erect a house or factory with no architectural plan to guide them. With rare exceptions, when we read in the Epistles of " the will of God," the reference is to His revealed and not His secret will, His authoritative and not His providential —His will as made known unto us in the Scripture of Truth. Neither his understanding, conscience, nor " new nature " is sufficient to serve the Christian as the director of his ways. It is in His *Word* that God's authoritative will is discovered to us: there and there alone do we have an all-sufficient and infallible Guide—a Lamp unto our feet, a Light unto our path. To be filled with a knowledge of the Divine will should not only be the main burden of our daily prayers but the principal quest of our lives: to obtain a better, closer, fuller knowledge of what God requires from us. Without that we can neither please nor glorify Him, nor shall we escape the innumerable pitfalls in our path.

At least three things are implied by the wording of this opening petition. First, that by nature we are *devoid* of such knowledge: before regeneration we are actuated only by self-will and Satanic suggestions—" we have turned every one to *his own way* " (Isa. liii, 6). Second, that to become " filled with the knowledge of God's will " is a gradual process, for the filling of a vessel is accomplished by degrees, by steady increase. And thus it is with the Christian: " precept upon precept, line upon line, here a little, there a little." Third, that it is our bounden duty to become so furnished, yet that constant recourse must be had to the throne of grace for Divine assistance therein. Ignorance is deplorable and inexcusable, yet wisdom cometh from Above and must be diligently sought. To be " filled with the knowledge of His will " imports a comprehensive and abundant knowledge, as well as a well-proportioned one. That for which the apostle here made request was something intensely *practical*: not speculations about the Divine nature, prying into the Divine decrees, nor inquisitive explorations of unfulfilled prophecy, but the knowledge of God's will as it respects the ordering of our daily walk in this world. As one has said, " The knowledge of our duty is the best knowledge." " That the soul be without knowledge is not good " (Prov. xix, 2).

It is a most serious mistake to suppose that at regeneration the understanding is enlightened once for all, that it is so completely illumined as to be in no further need of Divine assistance afterwards; as it is to imagine the surrender of our will unto God at conversion was so entire that it is unnecessary for the saint to daily renew his consecration unto Him. Such errors are manifestly refuted by that prayer of David's, " With my whole heart have I sought Thee: O let me not wander from Thy commandments " (Psa. cxix, 10). Though he had fully yielded himself unto the Lord and had made more than ordinary progress in godliness, yet he felt himself to be in deep need of perpetual quickening, directing and upholding, lest he lose the knowledge he already possessed and backslide from that course upon which he had entered. The truth is that the more experience we have of God's ways, the more sensible do we become of our deplorable proneness to wander from Him. On the other hand, the more we truly seek God with the whole heart, the more will our spiritual light be increased, for it is by a closer walking with Him that we obtain a clearer and fuller apprehension of His holiness, and that in turn makes us more conscious of our defects, for it is in His light we see light.

Such a longing after the knowledge of God's will as this prayer breathes is that of every healthy saint. The more knowledge he obtains of God's will the more aware does he become of his ignorance. And why is this the case? Because he has acquired a larger concept of his duty. At first, Christian consciousness of duty consists more in the general than in its details, more of the outward walk and the external acts of worship, more of quantity than of quality. But ere long he discovers that God requires him to regulate the inner man and subdue his soul unto Him; yea, he learns that this is the *principal task* assigned him—about which the majority of professors know nothing and care less, concerned only with the outward adornment of the sepulchre. It is as the believer more and more realizes the breadth of God's commandment (cxix, 96) and the exceeding spirituality of His Law (Rom. vii, 14) that he becomes painfully conscious of how far, far short he falls of discharging his responsibilities, and how sadly he has failed in this and that respect. Nevertheless, such a humbling discovery is evidence that his sense of duty has been enlarged, and that his own inability to perform it is the more apparent to him.

As a closer walking with God begets an enlarged sense of duty, so too it produces an increased realization of the difficulties attending the performance of it. As the natural man in his youth is full of vigour and hope, and in his inexperience and impetuosity rushes into engagements for which he is unqualified and is forward to rashly embark upon ventures which later he is sorry for; so the young Christian, all afire with affection and zeal, attempts tasks for which he is ill-fitted. and then is made to smart for acting presumptuously. But in the school of experience he discovers something of his ignorance, his weakness, the inconstancy of his heart, and learns to distinguish between the natural energy of the flesh and true spirituality. God has made him to know somewhat of "wisdom in the hidden part" (Psa. li, 6), which works in him self-diffidence and a holy fear. He becomes more dependent upon God, more diligent in mortifying his lusts, more humble in his approaches unto the throne of grace, more frequent in crying "Give me good understanding, and I shall keep Thy Law" (Psa. cxix, 34).

Thus, the babe in Christ will not advance very far along the Christian path before he realizes how perfectly suited unto his case is the opening petition of this prayer. To be filled with the knowledge of God's will becomes his ever-deepening desire, and that "in all wisdom and spiritual understanding." Those added words intimate, first, the sort of knowledge for which the Christian is to pray and strive: not merely a theoretical but an experimental, not simply in the letter but the power of it, an inward affectionate, operative knowledge wrought in the soul by God. As we saw when examining Philippians i, 9, light is needed to direct our graces, to instruct them that they may act judiciously. Heavenly wisdom is required that love may have a proper sense of the relative worth of objects, and suitable guidance in every instance of its exercise. Holy affections are no more all heat without light than are the rays of the sun, but are induced by some spiritual instruction received into the mind. The child of God is graciously affected when he perceives and understands something more than he did formerly of the character of God, the sufficiency of Christ, the glorious things exhibited in the Gospel. Such knowledge of those Objects is accompanied by and produces in him heavenly wisdom and spiritual understanding.

LIFE AND TIMES OF JOSHUA

17. The Ark.

In our November article we pointed out that in order to profit from its *practical* teaching—which should ever be our first quest and aim in the reading of God's Word—we need to view Israel's crossing of the Jordan as the Christian's surmounting of any formidable obstacle confronting him. In His providential dealings with us, God brings us into situations from which we are unable to extricate ourselves by any endeavours of our own wit or strength. Nor does He appear immediately for our deliverance, any more than He did for Israel's—who were required to gaze upon that unfordable river for three days before any solution of their dilemma was vouchsafed them. In like manner, the Lord so orders our affairs that at times we are brought to the end of our own resources and made conscious of our utter insufficiency. It is by such experiences that our pride is humbled and our faith developed, our own weakness realized and the sufficiency of Divine grace proved. It is on such occasions we discover that "the Lord is a very present help in trouble," and that the things which are impossible for us present no difficulty unto Him. It is only as we are brought to the end of ourselves that we learn to really look outside of ourselves and turn unto Him who never fails those who fully trust Him.

In our last we called the reader's attention to the fact that the Jordan is the symbol of death, and *that* must be passed through before Canaan can be entered—i.e. ere the Christian can experimentally enjoy his spiritual heritage in this life. That is accomplished by the exercise of faith and the operation of the spirit of obedience: faith appropriating the doctrinal declarations of Scripture, obedience being regulated by its precepts. Legally the saint *has* " passed from death unto life," for in the person of his Surety he received the wages of sin at the cross and came forth from the grave entitled to the reward of the Law. Thus all believers are informed, " For in that He died [as the Surety of His people], He died unto sin once, but in that He liveth, He liveth unto God "; and therefore they are bidden, " Likewise [by faith] reckon [account] ye also yourselves to be dead indeed unto sin, but alive unto God in Jesus Christ our Lord " (Rom. vi, 10, 11). That legal oneness of the believer with Christ in death and resurrection is to be made good practically, and what *that* entails is summed up in that word of His, " If any man will come after Me, let him deny himself, and take up his cross, and follow Me " (Matt. xvi, 24).

Self must be set aside ere Christ can be followed. Lusts have to be mortified ere graces become fruitful. We have to die unto self before we can live unto Christ. But what is meant by dying unto self? Giving it no place, denying it. To deny self is to repudiate our own righteousness, to distrust our own wisdom, to disown our own strength. To deny self is to renounce all self-will and self-pleasing. To " take up his cross " signifies much the same thing—the saint being required to order his life by the principle of self-sacrifice; and both of these are necessary in order to a real " following " of Christ—emulating His example, subject to His will, obeying Him in all things. The same truth is set before us again in II Corinthians v, 15: " He died for all, that they which live [legally and federally in Him their Head] should not henceforth live unto themselves [rather denying themselves], but [practically] unto Him which died for them and rose again." Said Paul, " For to me to live is Christ ": He is my Lord, my Object, my Portion. To be wholly ruled by Him, to be entirely devoted to Him, to promote His glory, is my ambition and endeavour.

It needs to be pointed out that only a regenerate soul is capacitated to meet the requirements of Matthew xvi, 24. First, because one who is yet dead in trespasses and sins has no love or desire for Christ. Second, because we ourselves must be on resurrection ground in order to " follow " a risen Christ, and before that can be, the soul must, by the supernatural and gracious operations of the Holy Spirit, pass from death unto life experimentally. Observe how this is typed out in Joshua iii: " And it came to pass, after three days, that the officers went through the host. And they commanded the people, saying, When ye see the ark of the covenant of the Lord your God, and the priests the Levites bearing it, then ye shall remove from your place, and go after it " (verses 2, 3). The ark was a figure of Christ, Israel's going after it adumbrated our " following " Him. But it was not until " after three days " they followed the ark dryshod across the Jordan, and " after three days " speaks of *resurrection* (Matt. xxvii, 63)!

" The ark " pointed to the Lord Jesus, but, as previously intimated, it is important that we should ascertain in what *particular character* Christ was here prefigured. The ark is mentioned first in Exodus xxv, 10-22, where detailed instructions were given for its manufacture, and concerning the mercy-seat which formed its lid. It was slightly over four and a half feet in length and about two and a half feet in breadth and height. The deep significance and sanctity of this holy vessel was signified unto Israel (and us) in various ways. When Jehovah gave instructions to Moses about the making of the tabernacle, He began with the ark: it came first in order because it was of the first importance. Before any details were communicated respecting the sanctuary itself, before a word was said about its court and chambers, its priesthood and ritual, its furniture and garniture, minute directions were given regarding the ark. Without the ark the whole service of the tabernacle had been meaningless and valueless, for it was upon it, as His throne, that God dwelt. The ark was the object to which the brazen altar pointed, the sacrifice of which gave right of access to the worshipper, who drew near unto the ark representatively in the person of the high priest.

The ark was the first of the holy vessels to be made and was made by Moses himself (Deut. x, 1-5), being the chest in which the tables of the Law were preserved. Its pre-eminence above all the other vessels was shown again in the days of Solomon, for the ark alone was transferred from the tabernacle to the temple. "It was the most sacred of all the instruments of the sanctuary; yea, the whole sanctuary was built for no other end but to be as it were a house, a habitation for the ark (see Ex. xxvi, 33). Hence, sanctification proceeded from all the parts of it, for, as Solomon observed, the places were holy whereunto the ark of God came (II Chron. viii, 11)"—Adolph Saphir. Now this pre-eminence of the ark is explained by the fact that it shadowed out *the person* of Christ. Each of the other vessels in the tabernacle pointed to some aspect of His work, or its effects, but the ark spoke of the blessed person of the God-man Mediator: they foreshadowed what He should do; this, what *He is*. The two natures in His theanthrophic person were adumbrated by the two materials of which the ark was made: its gold, His Divine glory; its shittim-wood, His holy and indestructible humanity. It was the ineffable person of Christ which gave value to His work.

In its emblematic significance the ark was, first of all, the witness of Jehovah's presence in the midst of His people: "there will I meet with thee, and I will commune with thee from above the mercy-seat, from between the two cherubim which are upon the ark of the testimony" (Ex. xxv, 22). That was Jehovah's throne, founded upon righteousness and mercy: "Thou that dwellest between the cherubim" was how the Psalmist thought of Him (Psa. lxxx, 1). Hence, when Jehovah departed from Israel, the ark was carried into captivity (I Sam. iii, 21; Psa. lxxviii, 60, 61). Second, it was the centre and means of Israel's communion with God, and it made known how He was to be worshipped and the manner in which He was to be approached by them (Lev. xvi, 12-14; Heb. ix, 11-14). Third, it was the symbol of Jehovah's relations with His people, inasmuch as by the richness of its composition and the supreme importance of its contents, together with its staves and rings (to be used when journeying), it embodied typically to Israel's faith the coming forth from heaven of God manifest in flesh, tabernacling among men. Fourth, it was the embodiment of the Lord's covenant with Israel, which was more especially made manifest in the sight of their enemies.

In the book of Exodus it is always called "the ark" or "the ark of testimony," in Leviticus it is mentioned but once—"the ark." But in Numbers x, 33-35, it is designated "the ark of the covenant." and, like all *first* mentionings, that one is worthy of special attention. "And they departed from the mount of the Lord three days' journey, and the ark of the covenant of the Lord went before them in the three days' journey, to search out a resting place for them " (verse 33). Very beautiful and blessed is that. Lovely type was it of the Good Shepherd going before His sheep (John x, 4), leading them into green pastures and making them to lie down beside the still waters. Observe the repeated reference unto the " three days' journey," for it is only on resurrection ground that such an experience is enjoyed, just as it is only there—and not in Egypt—that any can worship God acceptably (Ex. iii, 18). There is no " resting place " for any one in a world that lieth in the Wicked One and which is under the curse of the holy God: all is turmoil and travail there. None but their Covenant-head can lead God's people into peace, contentment and joy in this life; and none but He can bring them into their eternal rest—of which they have but an earnest and foretaste here.

But the preciousness of the above type is partly lost upon us unless we attend to the context in which it is found—the opening " and " of Numbers x, 33, calls to this. First, it should be duly noted that in Numbers ix, 18-23, reference is made to that notable instance of Jehovah's grace and faithfulness in having provided Israel with the cloud to guide them in their journey through the wilderness—the cloud pointing out the direction in which they were to go, intimating where they should encamp and when they should go forward again. Second, observe the failure of Moses. Forgetful of the Lord's promise to be their Guide, he desired to lean upon an arm of flesh, saying to his father-in-law, " Leave us not I pray thee, forasmuch as thou knowest how we are to encamp in the wilderness, and *thou* mayest be to us instead of eyes " (Num. x, 31). Alas, what is man, even the best of men! Then it was that the Lord intervened to maintain His glory, the ark of the covenant going before them in a three days' journey to search out a resting place for Israel. The keenest human eyes, the most mature human wisdom, is of no avail there.

There is only one other historical reference to " the ark of the *covenant* " in the Pentateuch, and that is in Numbers xiv, which chronicles one of the blackest chapters in Israel's chequered history, namely, their fatal unbelief and rebellion at Kadesh-barnea, when they refused to heed the counsel of Caleb and Joshua to go in and possess their inheritance; when they exclaimed, " would God we had died in the wilderness," and said one to another, " let us make a captain and let us return into Egypt " (verses 3, 5). " They kept not the covenant of God and refused to walk in His Law " (Psa. lxxviii, 10). For the benefit of new readers we must repeat what was pointed out in our last: Israel's breaking of the covenant at once released the Lord from making good unto *that* perverse generation His declarations unto Abraham, and therefore He told them, " your carcasses they shall fall in the wilderness, and your children shall wander in the wilderness . . . and ye shall know My breach of promise " (verses 32-34). Later, in their self-will, they determined to go up into Canaan, and, though told not to do so, they persisted (to their bitter cost), " nevertheless the ark of the covenant of the Lord, and Moses, departed not out of the camp " (verse 44)!

The forty years' wandering in the wilderness had expired with the death of Moses, and all whose sins occasioned that judgment had also died It was *the new* and younger generation of Israel over which Joshua was placed, and now a fresh chapter opened in the history of that nation. Joshua had received express promise that the Lord had given Canaan unto that generation (i, 2-5), and he had communicated the same unto the people (i, 11), yet that did not exempt them from the discharge of their duty—any more than the assurance " my God shall supply all your need " (Phil. iv, 19) provides a dispensation for us to be indolent or improvident. The guarantee that the Lord will fight for His people is designed to stir them up to be faithful and courageous. His promise to be our Shield and Defence would be grievously perverted if we deliberately trifled with sin and recklessly exposed ourselves to danger. If we would have the Lord show Himself strong in our behalf, then we must keep strictly to His "due order" (I Chron. xv, 13, and cf. Lev. x, 1). This comes out plainly in Joshua iii: implicit obedience from Israel was required before Jehovah put forth His mighty power and wrought a miracle for them.

"And it came to pass after three days that the officers went through the host and commanded the people, saying, When ye see the ark of the covenant of the Lord your God and the priests the Levites bearing it, then ye shall remove from your place and go after it. They were not left in ignorance nor any uncertainty of what was required from them. No carnal reasoning or scheming on their part was necessary. Definite instruction was given what to do and when to do it. They were bidden to fix their eyes upon the ark and regulate their actions by its movements. But note well the title by which it was here designated: not barely "the ark," but "the ark of the covenant of the Lord your God." *That* enforced their responsibility, for a "covenant" is a compact or engagement entered into between two or more parties (Gen. xxxi, 44; Luke xxii, 4, 5). Israel entered into a solemn agreement with the Lord at Sinai (Ex. xix, 1-6; xxiv, 1-8), which they bound themselves to keep, but which the first generation broke. The ten commandments were the *terms* of that covenant (Deut. iv, 13), and the ark was the seal and custodian of it.

Israel's being required to steadfastly eye and follow the ark through the Jordan signified, then, their dependence upon and confidence in the Lord, their subjection and obedience to His Law, their keeping of the covenant, and their eyeing of the propitiatory which formed the cover of the ark. Only as such graces were active, and as they were regulated by those principles could they, by God's intervention and blessing, enter into their heritage. The ark, as its name here connoted, was the token of the covenant, and also the pledge of Jehovah's protection so long as they walked in obedience to Him. It was not Israel who kept the ark, but the ark—or rather the God of the ark—who preserved them, as is quite clear from Numbers xiv, 44-46, for as soon as they acted in defiance of His revealed will, the symbol of His presence accompanied them not, and defeat and disaster was the consequence. The Holy One will not be the Patron and Guardian of a sinful people: rather than *that* He will surrender His manifestative glory into the hands of the enemy (I Sam. iii, 10-11), as He has suffered the apostate "churches" to become the laughing-stock of the world. So it is individually: I shall experience God's providential frowns rather than smiles if I follow a course of self-will and self-pleasing.

In the keeping of God's commandments "there is great reward" (Psa. xix, 11). No change of dispensation alters that basic fact: "that it may be well with us when we obey the voice of the Lord our God" (Jer. xlii, 6). "Godliness is profitable unto all things: having promise of the life that now is," as well as that which is to come (I Tim. iv, 8). "Whatsoever we ask we receive of Him, *because* we keep His commandments and do those things which are pleasing in His sight" (John iii, 22). There is no prosperity in his spiritual life and no experimental entering into his spiritual heritage until the Christian makes conscience of ordering his life by the Divine precepts. Unless he continues as he began and maintains that whole-hearted surrender to Christ which marked his conversion, then rest of soul will no longer be enjoyed by him, nor will the Lord put forth His power and subdue his enemies. We may dolefully sing, " Where is the blessedness I knew when first I saw the Lord? " but the answer thereto is not far to seek: there has been no change in Him! If that " blessedness " be no longer mine it is because I have changed, because I have departed from the Lord. To realize that, and mourn over it, will get you nowhere; the remedy is, " *Return* unto thy rest, O my soul " (Psa. cxvi, 7): take His yoke upon you afresh, and walk with Him in the paths of righteousness.

Ere proceeding farther, we must now do what lack of space prevented in the last two articles, namely, point out how the several details in this incident indicate how we may overcome any formidable obstacle or secure a passage through any " Jordon " that may confront us. (1) In order thereto we are required to gaze upon it until conscious of our utter insufficiency. (2) We are not to lean unto our own understanding or resort to any carnal expediency, but be regulated only by the Word of God. (3) The path of duty is clearly marked out for us, and if we recognize it not, the fault is ours. (4) We are to move forward in " newness of life," as regenerated persons. (5) Our eye is to be steadfastly fixed upon our covenant—God. (6) We are to act in implicit obedience unto His instructions. (7) We are to walk by faith, counting upon the Lord, expecting Him to put forth His wonder-working power on our behalf. In such case, He will not fail us and victory will be ours.

THE DOCTRINE OF REVELATION

1. Introduction

During the past fifteen years we have devoted nearly a quarter of this magazine to an expository unfolding of some portion of doctrinal truth, and were it possible to re-live those years we should not alter that plan. II Timothy iii, 16, 17, mentions some of the principal uses and values which the sacred Scriptures possess for us, and the first mentioned is that they are " profitable for *doctrine.*" There is an inseparable connection between doctrine and deportment: our convictions mould our characters, what we believe largely determines how we act—" as he thinketh in his heart, so is he " (Prov. xxiii, 7). To be soundly indoctrinated and to be well grounded in the Truth is one and the same thing, and nothing but the Truth operating in the soul will preserve from error, either theoretical or practical. Of the primitive Christians it is said, " They continued steadfastly [1] in the apostles' doctrine, and [2] fellowship, and [3] in breaking of bread, and [4] in prayers " (Acts ii, 42), which at once indicates that they esteemed soundness in the Faith as of first importance, and were of a radically different spirit from those who are so indifferent to the fundamentals of Christianity, insinuating if not openly saying, " It matters little what a man believes if his life be good."

The relation between sound doctrine and godly deportment is like unto that between the bones and flesh of the body, or between the tree and the fruit which it bears: the latter cannot exist without the former. The first epistle of the N.T. exemplifies our remark: three-fourths of it is occupied with a laying down of the essentials of Christianity, ere the apostle shows what is requisite for the adornment of the Christian character. The history of Christendom during the last four centuries strikingly illustrates our contention. Examine the writings of the Reformers, and what do you find? Why, that exposition of *doctrine* held the foremost place in their ministry: *that* was the light which God used to deliver so great a part of Europe from the popish ignorance and superstition which characterized "the dark ages"! The moral tendency upon the masses and the spiritual blessings communicated to God's people by doctrinal preaching appears in the time of the Puritans. Since that day, in proportion as the churches have departed from *their* doctrinal fidelity and zeal, has close walking with God, purity and uprightness before men, and morality in the masses, declined.

Each of our previous doctrinal discussions has taken one thing for granted, namely, that the Scriptures (to which we constantly appealed) are the inspired Word of God. Until recently the majority of our readers were residents of the U.S.A. and since there was available a book which we had had published there on that basic and vital subject, there was the less need for us to write thereon in these pages. Moreover, we were fully justified in taking a belief of that truth for granted, for the inerrancy and Divine authority of Holy Writ is a settled axiom with all true Christians, seeing that it constitutes the foundation of all their faith and the ground of all their hope. But since our book on the Divine Inspiration of the Scriptures is not at present obtainable by our British and Australian readers (for we decline to handle it while the disparity between the pound and the dollar persists), and since the tides of scepticism and infidelity continue to advance and constitute such a solemn menace unto the young, we feel moved to make an effort to show how strong and how sure are the foundations on which the faith of the Christian rests.

What we purpose doing in the next few articles of this series, namely, make a serious attempt to assist some of those who have inhaled the poisonous fumes of infidelity and been left in a state of mental indecision concerning sacred things, is something quite different from the course we usually follow in these pages. Yet in view of the bewilderment and uncertainty of many, and the shaken faith of others, it appears our duty to do so, and we trust our friends will make a point of reading these unto those of their children likely to need them, and that preachers will feel free to use portions of them in preparing special sermons or addresses for the young. Our principal object will be to set forth some of the numerous indications that the Bible is something far superior to any human production, but before doing that we must seek to establish the existence of its Divine Author. The later articles will be designed chiefly for preachers or older students of the Word, presenting as they will some of the rules which require to be heeded if the Scriptures are to be properly interpreted; and though their scope will go beyond the general title of "Divine revelation," yet they will complement and complete the earlier ones.

Under our present title, then, we purpose to treat (D.V.) of that revelation which God has given or that discovery which He makes of Himself unto the sons of men. If we were writing a comprehensive and systematic treatise on the whole subject, we should devote a proportionate space unto the manifestations which God has made of Himself, first, in creation, or the external world; second, in the moral nature—particularly the conscience—of man; third, in the controlling and shaping of human history by providence; fourth in His incarnate Son; fifth, in the sacred Scriptures; sixth, in the saving revelation which He makes of Himself unto the souls of His regenerate people; finally, in the beatific vision, when we shall "know as we are known." But, instead, we shall deal more briefly with the first four, and concentrate chiefly upon the Scriptures, presenting some of the evidences of their Divine Authorship, then pointing out some of the principles which govern their right interpretation, and then the application which is to be made of their contents. This is a considerable task to essay, rendered the more difficult because we desire to hold the interest of, and (under God) make these articles profitable unto, a considerable variety of readers—young and old, believers and unbelievers.

The present generation has, for the most part, been reared not only in an atmosphere of negative unbelief but of hostile unbelief. They live in a world where materialism and scepticism are rampant and dominant. In the great majority of homes the Sunday newspaper is the only thing read on the Lord's day. Doubt as to moral and spiritual truth is distilled through a score of channels. Our seats of learning are hotbeds of agnosticism. Our literature, with rare exceptions, makes light of God, and jokes about sacred things. The newspapers, the radio broadcasts, public utterances and private converse are steadily but surely removing the foundations of righteousness and destroying what little faith in spiritual things still remains. The vast majority in the English-speaking world are totally ignorant of the contents of the Bible, know not that it is a Divine revelation, yea, question whether there be any God at all. Yet modern scepticism is rarely candid, but is rather a refuge in which multitudes are sheltering from an accusing conscience. With such we are not here concerned, for where a prejudiced mind and a cavilling spirit obtain, argument is useless; and we can but leave them unto the sovereign mercy of the Lord.

Even those brought up in Christian homes are being corrupted by the paganism of modern education, are bewildered by the conflicting teachings they receive from parents and the school, and are harassed by doubts. Some of them are honestly seeking a resolving of their doubts, and it has become a pressing duty devolving upon the servant of God to recognize the mental conflict taking place in the minds of his youthful hearers, and seek to meet their more immediate need by presenting some of the " Christian evidences." It is therefore our desire and will be our endeavour in the earlier articles of this series to be of some help unto those who may have become entangled in Satan's snares, who have been seriously disturbed by the infidelity of this age, but are willing to carefully examine some of the " strong reasons " by which it is rational to believe in the existence of a living and personal God and to receive the Scriptures as an authoritative and inerrant revelation from Him, and that it is not only the most horrible impiety but the height of irrationality to doubt the one or call into question the other.

There are some likely to deem our present procedure as being needless if not actually wrong, considering that the existence of God and the authority of His Word are matters to be reverently believed and not argued; yet though we respect their conviction, we do not share the same. We fully agree that a rational discussion cannot produce anything but a rational faith, but even *that* should not be despised. Something has been accomplished if we can take away a stumbling block from the path of inquirers: the removal of weeds is necessary to prepare the garden for the seed. Though no external evidence, however weighty, can savingly convert the soul, it can carry conviction to the reason and conscience. Such arguments as we propose to submit are sufficient in themselves to beget in the mind a sober, intelligent and firm judgment that there is a God and that the Bible is His inspired Word. It is much to be thankful for if we can bring the serious minded to respect and read the Scriptures, waiting for a spiritual confirmation. Intellectual persuasives and motives of credibility are not the ground on which a spiritual faith rests, yet they often prove (under the Divine blessing) a paving of the way thereunto.

Nor is an appeal unto external evidences of the Truth, which address themselves to and are apprehended by the reasoning faculty of our minds, without value to the child of God. They are confirmatory of his faith, support it against the oppositions and objections of others, and relieve the mind under temptations to doubt. In such a day as this, the young Christian especially needs all the help he can obtain in order to withstand the assaults of the Enemy. Even older ones are prone to give way to doubting, and cannot be too strongly established in the fundamentals of the Faith. Moreover, such a course serves to exhibit the excellency of our profession and the impregnable rock on which it is founded. It enables us to perceive what good grounds and satisfactory confirmations we have for the Faith which we avow. Wisdom is justified of her children (Matt. xi, 19), and it behoves them to be equipped to justify their profession, if for no other reason than to close the mouths of gain-sayers. A Christian should be capable of knowing and giving expression to the distinct and special reasons why he believes in God and reveres His Word—that he has something more substantial and valuable than human " tradition " to appeal unto.

Before entering upon our immediate task it should be acknowledged that it is not possible to prove the existence of God by mathematical demonstration, for if such proof were procurable there would be no room left for the exercise of faith. Yet, on the other hand, it must be pointed out that it is equally impossible to demonstrate the non-existence of the Creator. But though we cannot prove to a demonstration that God is, yet we can adduce evidence so clear and weighty as must impel, if not compel us to accept His existence as a fact. Those evidences when carefully pondered, separately and together, afford the strongest possible ground for believing in the Divine Maker of heaven and earth: the probability actually amounting to the height of moral certainty. There are certain great facts of Nature which call for an explana-tion, such as the existence of matter, the existence of motion, and the existence of life. The heathen had sufficient perspicuity to realize " Ex nihilo nihil fit " —from nothing, nothing comes; and if we reject the truth that " the worlds were framed by the word of God " (Heb. xi, 3), then we are left in complete darkness, without any hope of obtaining any satisfactory explanation of either the noumenon or phenomenon of existence.

Most careful consideration ought to be given unto the alternative offered by unbelief. The great enigma which has confronted the human race through-out the centuries, and challenged its sages to supply a solution, is the problem of the universe: how it came to be; and within that macrocosm, the micro-cosm man—his origin, his intelligence, his destiny. Every explanation that has been advanced, save only the one provided by the Bible, fails to carry conviction to the mind, much less meets the longings of the heart. But the Bible supplies a solution of those problems, which has satisfied the reason and conscience of millions of people, yea, which has brought peace and joy to a countless number of souls. Sceptics have indeed rejected its explanation, but what have they offered in its place? Nothing but agnostic doubts and metaphysical vagaries so abstruse that none can understand them, or specula-tions so incredible and absurd that only those who prefer darkness to light will pay any heed unto them. Ponder well the immeasurable difference there is between Christianity and Infidelity, and despise not the former until you are quite sure the latter has something more solid and valuable to give you in its stead.

There is ample evidence both in the material and moral realm on which to base a rational and intelligent belief in the existence of God, and any one who seriously examines that evidence and then turns and carefully considers what infidelity has to offer as an alternative, should have no difficulty at all in perceiving which is the more convincing, adequate, and satisfying. As the author of *The Gordian Knot* rightly pointed out, " Scepticism is a restless sea on which any one who sails is tossed up and down and driven to and fro in endless uncertainty. There is *no solid ground* on which to stand until something true is found and believed." *That* is the alternative, the only one, for those who credit not the Scriptures. The infidel would take from you the Bible, young man, but what does he offer in its place but sneers and doubts! He scouts the idea of a personal Creator, but what explanation can he supply you of creation? He despises the Lord Jesus Christ, but to what other Redeemer does he point as being able to save you from your sins, and induct you into an inheritance that is incorruptible and undefiled, that fadeth not away, but will endure for all eternity in heaven?

2.   The Existence of God

First, *as manifest in creation.* The Bible opens with the words " In the beginning God." He was in the beginning because Himself *without* beginning: the uncaused, self-existent and self-sufficient One—" from everlasting to everlasting, Thou art God " (Psa. xc, 2). But the youthful yet intelligent inquirer will ask, And do *you* comprehend *that?* We candidly answer, Certainly not, for how could one who is finite comprehend the Infinite, a creature of time fully understand the Eternal One? Nevertheless, we believe it, being logically and rationally *obliged* to do so. There must of necessity be a First Cause, and if a *first* Cause, that Cause is obviously uncaused and self-existent. If that first Cause be the Originator of all other causes and effects, then it follows that Cause is not only self-existent but self-sufficient, or, in other words, all-mighty. Since we may ascertain something—often much— of the *nature* of a cause from the effects it produces, then from the effects perceptible to us in the visible universe, it is clearly evident that the First Cause must be endowed with life, with intelligence, with will, in a word, with Personality, and one infinitely superior to ours; which First Cause we recognize and own as God.

Though the opening words of the Bible take the existence of God for granted, yet what immediately follows supplies more than a hint where we may find irrefragable evidence that *He is:* " In the beginning God created the heaven and the earth." It has been truly said, " We need no other argument to prove that God made the world than the world itself—it carrieth in it and upon it the infallible tokens of its original " (John Owen). That is true if we consider it simply in the mass: how came it to be? Three theories have been put forward to account for the existence of matter by those who believe not in its creation. First, that matter is *eternal.* But that solves no difficulty, in fact it involves one much more perplexing than any which Genesis i, 1, can give rise to. In itself matter is both inert and unintelligent: whence then its motion and marks of design? Second, by *spontaneous generation.* But not only is there no proof to support such a view, but it is too self-evidently inadequate to merit discussion. Third, by *evolution:* concerning which we will now only point out, Push that hypothesis backward, stage by stage, till you come to the first molecule or protoplasm, and to the question, *How* did *it* originate? No answer is forthcoming. Something could not evolve from nothing!

Though the universe could not evolve from nothing, it could be created by an eternal and all-mighty Creator! Assuming the existence of God, our difficulty is at once resolved. But with the universe spread before our eyes we do not have to assume God's existence. " Because the things which may be known of God is manifest in them, for God hath showed it unto them. For the invisible things of Him from the creation of the world are clearly seen, being understood by the things that are made, even His eternal power and Godhead, so that they are without excuse " (Rom. i, 19, 20). God may be rationally inferred by reasoning back from effect to cause. Intelligent arrangement, wise contrivement, marks of design, argue an intelligent Designer. There are such palpable and innumerable impressions of Divine wisdom, power and goodness in the works of God that unprejudiced reason must necessarily conclude a Creator of whose perfections those impressions are the faint adumbrations. So true is this that atheists and all idolaters are left without any excuse. Thus it is apparent that the doubts of infidels are either affected or arise from the determination to rid themselves of the idea of accountableness. " The fool hath said in his heart—no God " (Psa. xiv, 1): it is moral depravity and not mental weakness which prompts such a desire.

" The heavens declare the glory of God and the firmament showeth His handiwork " (Psa. xix, 1). The universe proclaims God both by its very existence and its wondrous composition. From whence proceeded this vast system, with its exquisite order, its perfect balance, and its enduring strength? Every effect must have an adequate cause. If the heavens do *not* declare the existence of God and scintillate with the reflections of His glory, let the infidel tell us what they *do* bespeak. If the celestial bodies be nothing more than a fortuitous mass of atoms, flung together by unreasoning law or blind chance, then what has preserved them throughout the ages, what regulates their movements with more than clock-like precision? What invested the sun with light and actinic power? To put it on the lowest level, can scepticism furnish any answer to those questions which satisfies reason or appears adequate to common sense? If the thoughtful beholder of the stellar heavens perceives no evidence of a Divine Creator, then are we not obliged to sorrowfully exclaim, " None so blind as those who *will not* see "! It is true that a recognition of the Creator in His creation is no evidence of regeneration, for many who never open the Bible are convinced of the reality of His existence, yet such mental perception is much to be preferred to the stupidity of atheism or the darkness of agnosticism.

THE GREAT CHANGE

Those who have carefully read this magazine, if for only one year, must recognize that whatever be its faults and failings, it cannot fairly be charged with presenting a toned-down picture of a genuine Christian or that we hail as " Brother and Sister " all who style themselves such. More and more during the last ten years have we sought to expose windy professors and sweep away the sandy foundations on which so many of them rest their worthless hopes. Yet that does not warrant us going to the opposite extreme and cutting off those who are entitled to enjoy a Scriptural assurance, and when we see some doing so themselves, we deem it a duty to stretch forth a helping hand. It was in that spirit we wrote the three articles which have already appeared under our present title, for we know some who have concluded that the language of II Corinthians v, 17, prohibits them from regarding themselves as regenerated souls, and though others of God's little ones do not go so far as that, yet its terms have much perplexed their minds.

Having endeavoured to remove a stumbling-stone from the path of conscientious souls by showing that II Corinthians v, 13-21, does not describe the work of the Holy Spirit within God's people, but rather that which results legally from what Christ did for them, it seems needful that we should now seek to probe and search out a different class by considering what does take place in one who is supernaturally quickened. In other words, having dealt with the great *dispensational* change which the death and resurrection of Christ effected, we turn now to contemplate the great *experimental* change which, in due time, is wrought in each one of those for whom the Redeemer shed His precious blood. There are many in Christendom today who give no evidence that they have been made the subjects of such a change, who nevertheless are fully persuaded they are journeying heavenwards; while there are not a few souls perplexed because uncertain of what this great change consists of.

That which we now propose to treat of may perhaps be best designated "the miracle of grace." First, because it is produced by the supernatural operations of God. Second, because those operations are wholly of His sovereign benignity, and not because of any worthiness in those who are the favoured subjects of it. Third, because those operations are profoundly mysterious to human ken. Furthermore, that expression, "a miracle of grace," is sufficiently abstract and general as to include all such terms as being " born again," " converted," etc.—which really refer to only *one* phase or aspect of it. Moreover, it possesses the advantage of placing the emphasis where it properly belongs and ascribes the glory unto Him to whom alone it is due, for God is the sole and unassisted Author—whatever instruments or means He may or may not be pleased to use in the effectuation of the same—in a sinner's salvation. "It is not of him that willeth nor of him that runneth, but of God that showeth mercy" (Rom. ix, 16). By "a miracle of grace" we include *the whole* of God's work in His people, and not simply His initial act of quickening them.

Nothing short of a miracle of grace can change a " natural man " (I Cor ii, 14) into a " spiritual " one (I. Cor. ii, 15). Only the might of Omnipotence is able to emancipate a serf of Satan's and translate him into the kingdom of Christ. Anything less than the operations of the Holy Spirit is incapable of transforming a " child of disobedience " (Eph. ii, 2) into a " child of obedience " (I Pet. i, 14). To bring one whose carnal mind is enmity against God into loving and loyal subjection to Him is beyond all the powers of human persuasion. Yet being *supernatural* it necessarily transcends our powers to fully understand. Even those who have actually experienced it can only obtain a right conception thereof by viewing it in the light of those hints upon it which God has scattered throughout His Word: and even then, but a partial and incomplete concept. As our eyes are too weak for a prolonged gazing upon the sun, so our minds are too gross to take in more than a few scattered rays of the Truth. We see through a glass darkly, and know but in part. Well for us when we are made conscious of our ignorance.

The very fact that the great change of which we are here treating is produced by the miracle-working power of God implies that it is one which is more or less inscrutable. All God's works are shrouded in impenetrable mystery, even when cognizable by our senses. Life, natural life, in its origin, its nature, its processes, baffle the most able and careful investigator. Much more is this the case with spiritual life. The existence and being of God immeasurably transcend the grasp of the finite mind; how then can we expect to fully comprehend the process by which we become His children? Our Lord Himself declared that the new birth was a thing of mystery: " The wind bloweth where it listeth, and thou hearest the sound thereof, but canst not tell whence it cometh nor whither it goeth, *so* is every one that is born of the Spirit " (John iii, 8). The wind is something about which the most learned scientist knows next to nothing. Its nature, the laws which govern it, its causation, all lie beyond the purview of human inquiry. Thus it is with the new birth: it is profoundly mysterious, defying proud reason's diagnosis, insusceptible of theological analysis.

The one who supposes he has a clear and adequate comprehension of what takes place in a soul when God plucks him as a brand from the burning is greatly mistaken: " If any man think that he knoweth any thing, he knoweth nothing yet as he ought to know " (I Cor. viii, 2). To the very end of his earthly pilgrimage the best instructed Christian has reason to pray " that which I see not teach Thou me " (Job xxxiv, 32). Even the theologian and the Bible-teacher is but a learner and, like all his companions in the school of Christ, acquires his knowledge of the Truth gradually—" here a little, there a little " (Isa. xxviii, 10). He too advances slowly, as one great theme after another is studied by him and opened up to him, requiring him to revise or correct his earlier apprehensions and adjust his views on other portions of the Truth as fuller light is granted him on any one branch thereof. Necessarily so, for Truth is a unit, and if we err in our understanding of one part of it that affects our perception of other parts of it.

None should take exception to nor be surprised at our saying that even the theologian or Bible-teacher is but a learner and acquires his knowledge of the Truth gradually. " The path of the just is as the shining light, which shineth more and more unto the perfect day " (Prov. iv, 18). Like the rising of the sun, spiritual light breaks forth upon both preacher and hearer by degrees. The men who have been the most used of God in the feeding and building up of His people were not thoroughly furnished for their work at the outset of their careers, but only by dint of prolonged study did they make progress in their own apprehension of the Truth. Each preacher who experiences any real spiritual growth views most of his first sermons as those of a novice, and he will have cause for shame as he perceives their crudity and the relative ignorance which marked the production of them; for even if he was mercifully preserved from serious error, yet he will probably find many mistakes in his expositions of Scripture, various inconsistencies and contradictions in the views he then held, and which a fuller knowledge and maturer experience now enables him to rectify.

What has just been pointed out explains why the later writings of a servant of God are preferable to his earlier ones, and why in a second or third edition of his works he finds it necessary to correct or at least modify some of his original statements. Certainly this writer is no exception. Were he to re-write today some of his earlier articles and pieces, he would make a number of changes in them. Though it may be humiliating unto pride to have to make corrections, yet it is also ground for thanksgiving unto God for the fuller light vouchsafed which enables him to do so. During our first pastorate we were much engaged in combating the error of salvation by personal culture and reformation, and therefore we threw our main emphasis on the truth contained in our Lord's words, " ye must be *born again* " (John iii, 3, 5, 7), showing that something far more potent and radical than any efforts of our own were required in order to give admission into the kingdom of God; that no education, mortification, or religious adorning of the natural man could possibly fit him to dwell for ever in a holy heaven.

But in seeking to refute one error great care needs to be taken lest we land ourselves into another at the opposite extreme, for in most instances error is Truth perverted rather than repudiated, Truth distorted by failure to preserve the balance. Being " born again " is not the only way in which

Scripture describes the great change effected by the miracle of grace: other expressions are used, and unless they be taken into due consideration an inadequate and faulty conception of what that miracle consists of and effects will be formed. Our second pastorate was located in a community where the teaching of "Entire Sanctification" or sinless perfectionism was rife, and in combating it we stressed the fact that sin is not eradicated from any man's being in this life, that even after he is born again the "old nature" still remains within him. We were fully warranted by God's Word in so doing, though if we were engaged in the same task today we should be more careful in defining what we meant by "the old *nature*" and more insistent that a regenerate person has a radically different disposition sinwards from what he had formerly.

That a great change is wrought upon and within a person when God regenerates him is acknowledged by all His people—a change very different from that which is conceived of by many who have never personally experienced it. For example, it goes much deeper than a mere change of creed. One may have been brought up an Arminian, and later be intellectually convinced that such tenets are untenable; but his subsequent conversion to the Calvinistic system is no proof whatever that he is no longer dead in trespasses and sins. Again, it is something more radical than a change of inclination or taste. Many a giddy worldling has become so satiated with its pleasures as to lose all relish for the same, voluntarily abandoning them and welcoming the peace which he or she supposes is to be found in a convent or monastery. So too it is something more vital than a change of conduct. Some notorious drunkards have signed the pledge and remained total abstainers the rest of their days, and yet never even made a profession of being Christians. One may completely alter his mode of living and yet be thoroughly carnal, forsake a life of vice and crime for one of moral respectability, and be no more spiritual than he was previously. Many are deceived at this point.

Let not the reader infer from what has just been said that one may be the subject of a miracle of grace and yet it be unaccompanied by an enlightening of his understanding, a refining of his affections, or a reforming of his conduct. That is not at all our meaning. What we desire to make clear is that, that miracle of grace consists of something far superior to those superficial and merely *natural* changes which many undergo. Nor does that " something far superior " consist only in the communication of a new nature which leaves everything else in its recipient just as it was before: it is *the person* (and not simply a nature) who is regenerated or born again. "Except *a man* be born again he cannot see the kingdom of God" (John iii, 3) is an altogether different thing from saying "except a new nature be born *in* a man he cannot see the kingdom of God." Any deviation from Scripture is fraught with mischief, and if we reduce that which is personal to something abstract and impersonal we are certain to form a most inadequate—if not erroneous— conception of regeneration.

Those who have written upon God's work of grace in the soul, especially when treating of His initial act therein, have used a wide variety of terms— generally those most in vogue among the particular party to which they belonged. Each denomination has its own more or less distinctive nomenclature—determined by the portions of Truth it is wont to emphasize—and even when dealing with doctrine which is held by all the orthodox, does so with a certain characteristic pronunciation or emphasis. Thus, in some circles one would find "effectual calling" the term most frequently employed; in other places, where "the new birth" is substituted, few would understand what is meant by "an effectual call"; while "a change of heart" is how a third group would describe it. Others, who are looser in their terminology, speak of "being saved," by which some signify one thing, and others something quite different. As a matter of fact, each of those expressions is justifiable, and all of them need to be *combined* if we are to form anything approaching an adequate concept of the experience itself.

The better to enable our feeble understandings to grasp something of the nature of the great change which takes place in each of God's people, the Holy Spirit has employed a considerable variety of terms—figurative in character, yet expressing spiritual realities—and it behoves us to diligently collate or collect the same, carefully ponder each one, and regard *all of them* as being included in "the miracle of grace." Probably we are not capable of furnishing a full list, but the following are some of the principal verses in which experimental salvation is described. "The Lord thy God will *circumcise* thine heart, and the heart of thy seed, *to love* the Lord thy God with all thine heart" (Deut. xxx, 6): an operation painful to the soul, in removing its filth and folly—its love of sin—is necessary before the heart is brought to truly love God! This figure of circumcising the heart is found also in the New Testament: Romans ii, 29; Philippians iii, 3. "Thy people shall *be willing* in the day of Thy power" (Psa. cx, 3): omnipotence must be exercised ere the elect will voluntarily deny self and freely take Christ's yoke upon them.

"Then will I sprinkle clean water upon you, and ye shall be clean: from all your filthiness and from your idols will I cleanse you. A new heart also will I give you, and a new spirit will I put within you: and I will take away the stony heart out of your flesh, and I will give you a heart of flesh" (Ezek. xxxvi, 25, 26). We are not concerned here with the prophetic or dispensational bearing of this statement, but with its doctrinal import. Nor can we here attempt a full exposition of it. In our judgment those verses describe an essential aspect of that "miracle of grace" which God performs in His people. The "clean water" with which He sprinkles and cleanses them within is an emblem of His holy Word, as John xv, 3, Ephesians v, 26, make quite clear. The heart of the natural man is likened to one of "stone"—lifeless, insensible, obstinate. When he is regenerated, the heart of man becomes one "of flesh"—quickened into newness of life, warm, full of feeling, capable of receiving impressions from the Spirit. The change effected by regeneration is no superficial or partial one, but a great, vital, transforming, complete one.

"Make the tree good and his fruit good" (Matt. x, 32): the Husbandman's method of accomplishing this is shown in Romans xi, 17. "Except ye be converted and become as little children, ye shall not enter into the kingdom of heaven" (Matt. xviii, 3): to "be converted" is to experience a radical change, for pride to be turned into humility, and self-sufficiency into clinging dependence. "Of His fulness have all we received, and grace for grace" (John i, 16): the life of the Head is communicated to His members, and every spiritual grace that is found in Him is, in measure, reproduced in them. "No man can come to Me except the Father which hath sent Me draw him" (John vi, 44): to come to Christ is to receive Him as our Lord and Saviour—to abandon our idols and repudiate our own righteousness, to surrender to His government and trust in His sacrifice; and none can do that except by the power of God. "Purifying their hearts by faith" (Acts xv, 9, and cf. I Peter i, 22—"Ye have purified your souls by obeying the Truth"): the Christian does not have two hearts, but one which has been "purified"! "Whose heart the Lord opened, that she attended unto the things which were spoken " (Acts xvi, 14): the door of fallen man's heart is fast closed against God until He opens it.

" I have appeared unto thee for this purpose: to make thee a minister and a witness . . . to open their eyes, to turn them from darkness to light, and from the power of Satan unto God, that they might receive forgiveness of sins and inheritance among them which are sanctified by faith that is in Me " (Acts xxvi, 18). Here we have still another description of that miracle of grace which God performs within His people and wherein He is pleased to make use of the ministerial instrumentality of His servants. The faithful preaching of His Word is given an important place therein, though that preaching is only rendered effectual by the powerful operations of the Spirit. That miracle is here spoken of as the opening of our eyes, the reference being to the eyes of our understanding, so that we are enabled to perceive something of the spiritual meaning of the Gospel message and its bearing upon our own deep need. The soul which hitherto was engulfed in spiritual darkness is brought forth into God's marvellous light (I Pet. ii, 9) so that we now discover the perfect suitability of Christ unto our desperate case. At the same time the soul is delivered from the captivity of Satan, who is " the power of darkness " (Luke xxii, 53), and brought into a new relation with and knowledge of God, which produces faith in Him and issues in the forgiveness of sins.

CONVICTION OF SIN

(By the Holy Spirit, issuing in Conversion)

1. It is not the mere smiting of the natural conscience. Although man be utterly fallen, yet God has left natural conscience behind in every heart to speak for Him. Some men, by continual sinning, sear even the conscience as with a hot iron, so that it becomes past feeling; but most men have so much natural conscience remaining that they cannot commit open sin without their conscience smiting them. When a man commits murder or theft, no eye may have seen him, and yet conscience makes a coward of him. He trembles, fearing that God will take vengeance. Now that is a natural work which takes place in every heart, but conviction of sin is a supernatural work of the Spirit of God. If you have had nothing more than the ordinary smiting of conscience, then you have never been convicted of sin.

2. It is not any impression upon the imagination. Sometimes, when men have committed great sin, they have awful impressions of God's vengeance made upon their imaginations. In the night-time they almost fancy they see the flames of Hell burning beneath them; or they seem to hear doleful cries in their ears telling of coming woe; or they have terrible dreams, when they sleep, of coming vengeance. Now this is not the conviction of sin which the Spirit gives: it is altogether a natural work upon the natural faculties.

3. It is not a mere head knowledge of what the Bible says against sin. Many unconverted men read their Bibles, and have a clear knowledge that their case is laid down there. They know very well that they are in sin, and they know just as well that the wages of sin is death. One man lives a swearer, and he reads the words, and understands them perfectly: " The Lord will not hold him guiltless that taketh His name in vain." Another man lives in the lusts of the flesh, and he reads the Bible, and understands those words perfectly: " No unclean person hath any inheritance in the kingdom of Christ and of God." Another man lives in habitual forgetfulness of

God—never thinks of Him, and yet he reads: "The wicked shall be turned into Hell, and all the people that forget God." Now in this way most men have a head knowledge of their sin and of its wages, yet this is far from conviction of sin.

4. It is not to feel the loathsomeness of sin. This is what a child of God feels. A child of God has seen the beauty and excellency of God, and therefore sin is loathsome in his eyes. But no unconverted person has seen the beauty and excellency of God, and therefore sin cannot appear dark and loathsome in his eyes.

What, then, is this conviction of sin? It is a just sense of *the dreadfulness* of sin. It is not mere knowledge that we have many sins and that God's anger is revealed against them all; but it is a heart-feeling that we are under sin. It is a sense of the dishonour it does to God, and of the wrath to which it exposes the soul. Conviction of sin is no slight natural work upon the heart. It is all in vain that you read your Bibles and hear us preach, unless the Spirit uses the words to give feeling to your dead hearts. If we could prove to you, with the plainness of arithmetic, that the wrath of God is abiding on you, still you would sit unmoved. The Spirit alone can impress your heart.   R. M. M'CHEYNE.

<hr>

(continued from back page)

show Himself strong on our behalf. If we honour His precepts He will honour us. "Go forward," then, in complete subjection to His revealed will, walking according to His Word.

"Go forward." Third, this was *a command to advance*. It was so to Israel; it is so unto us. Onward Christian soldiers! Steadfastly persevere along the path of duty, walking in that narrow way which the Divine precepts have marked out for us. No matter what be your condition and circumstances, what obstacles may confront you, what Red Sea of difficulty or danger be before you, "Go forward" is your marching orders. Raise no objections. "The slothful man saith, There is a lion without, I shall be slain in the streets" (Prov. xxii, 13); let no such idle excuse issue from your lips. Rather say, "I can do all things through Christ which strengtheneth me" (Phil. iv, 13). When your heart fails, when your soul is well-nigh overwhelmed by the problem or task facing you, panic not, lift up the eyes of faith unto the Lord, realize He it is who bids you advance, go forward depending on His promise, and you will not be confounded.

Christ's oft-repeated "follow Me" is but another form of "Go forward." So too is every exhortation for us to "grow in grace and in the knowledge of the Lord." We are ever in need of such a word, for we are prone to relax and take things easy—the more so as old age creeps upon us. Rest not satisfied with your present knowledge and apprehension of the Truth, but seek for a deeper and fuller one. Be not content with your present attainments, for "there remaineth yet very much land to be possessed" (Josh. xiii, 2). The manna you gathered yesterday will not suffice for today. "Be not weary in well doing" (II Thess. iii, 13). "No man having put his hand to the plough, and looking back, is fit for the kingdom of God" (Luke ix, 62). Let the prayerful resolve of each of us be, "forgetting those things which are behind, and reaching forth unto those things which are before, I press toward the mark for the prize of the high calling of God in Christ" (Phil. iii, 13, 14). Beg God to write this word in your heart.

head of a great military force pursued and overtook them. With impassable obstacles on either side, the Red Sea in front, and the enemy in the rear, that company of ex-slaves with their wives and children were in a truly desperate plight, and death was all they expected (Ex. xiv, 10, 12). Then it was that Moses said, "Fear ye not, stand still, and see the salvation of the Lord, which He will show you today; for the Egyptians whom ye have seen today, ye shall see them again no more forever. The Lord shall fight for you, and ye shall hold your peace" (verses 13, 14).

Those words, "stand still and see the salvation of the Lord," have been grossly carnalized and grievously wrested by those who foster a fatalistic inertia. "Stand still" obviously has the force here of "be not dismayed, do not panic, keep calm," as the "hold your peace" shows. Then followed "and see the salvation [deliverance] of the Lord," which signified, Lift up your hearts and eyes in the exercise of *faith*. But faith must have a foundation to rest upon, even the Word of Him that cannot lie, and hence the sure promise was given, "which He will show you today . . . the Lord shall fight for you." Previously they had "lifted up their eyes and beheld the Egyptians" (verse 10), and in consequence were sore afraid. But there was something else and some One else for faith to "see," namely, the promised salvation or deliverance of Jehovah—not yet visible to outward sight! If their faith were steadfastly occupied with *that*, their trembling hearts would be stilled and strength obtained for the performance of duty or the discharge of their responsibility.

Then came the Divine order to Moses, "Speak unto the children of Israel that they go forward" (verse 15). That was *a challenge to faith*. To carnal reason, compliance appeared suicidal. To "Go forward" meant walking into the Red Sea, which at that time presented an unbroken mass of water. Ah, but they had been promised Divine deliverance. Yes, but God required them to lay hold of that promise and act on it. And they did: "*By faith* they passed through the red sea, as by dry land" (Heb. xi, 29). If "by faith" then certainly not 'by sight," the two things being opposed the one to the other (II Cor. v, 7). Not until they stepped out with confidence in God's Word did He appear for them and begin to open the waters, and as they continued onward He continued to open a way for them. It is in response to the actings of faith that God works, for He never sets a premium on unbelief. Here, then, is the first signification of this word for us: "Go forward" with your heart resting on the sure promises of God and with the eyes of faith steadfastly fixed upon Him.

"Go forward." Second, this was *a call to obedience*, namely, "the obedience of faith" (Rom. i, 5). There was a command annexed to the promise: to prove them and show whether or no they had received the promise sincerely. There are certain grand benefits which God gives to His people without imposing any condition, such as the providing of a Redeemer, who took our nature, fulfilled the Law, satisfied God's provoked justice on our behalf, and merited grace sufficient for our salvation. But having laid this glorious foundation, God treats with us as moral agents, propounds to us a covenant which requires *our* cordial consent or agreement. Repentance and faith are required of us in order to the forgiveness of our sins. All through the Christian life our concurrence is necessary. God requires from us faith in each of His promises and obedience to the commands annexed to them. Obedience is the path He has appointed and in which His blessing is to be found. We must follow the course He has prescribed if we would have Him

(continued on preceding page)

XXVI   FEBRUARY 1947   No. 2

STUDIES IN THE SCRIPTURES

"Search the Scriptures." John v, 39

Publisher and Editor—ARTHUR W. PINK,
29 Lewis Street,
Stornoway, Isle of Lewis,
Scotland.

LOOK UPWARD

This brief message is designed as the sequel unto the opening one in the January issue, for certain it is that we shall only be able to *go forward* as we steadfastly look upward for all-needed grace. Faith is to the soul what the eye is to the body, namely, that which enables its possessor to look outside of himself and steadfastly fix his gaze on an external object. And hence it is that the exercise and act of faith is so often referred to in the Word under the figure of "lifting up the eyes" and "looking unto the Lord." Look upward! Was not that the very first thing which the blessed Spirit taught you, dear friend, after He had revealed to you your lost condition and made you realize you were a guilty, polluted, and undone sinner? As the serpent-bitten Israelites were bidden to look up to the brazen serpent upon the pole, so you were taught to look upon the crucified Saviour as the One who was willing and able to meet your dire need. "Look unto Me and be ye saved all the ends of the earth" (Isa. xlv, 22).

Now, as you commenced, so you must continue (Col. ii, 6). Christ enthroned in glory is henceforth to be the grand Object of your contemplation and adoration. Look up to Him daily and view Him by faith as the eternal Lover of your soul, as the Lord your righteousness, as the Bread of life to feed upon. Contemplate Him as "full of grace and truth" (John i, 14). However cold, dull and corrupt you feel to be in yourself let your very consciousness of the same serve to drive you more and more out of yourself, to rest wholly on what He did and suffered for you, and what *He now is to you.* Since He is your Saviour, who loved you and gave Himself for you, make use of Him. Live by faith upon Him, and thereby you will please and honour Him. Look by faith within the veil and take a view of what your great High Priest is there doing for you: He has all your concerns before Him, and is making all things work together for your good. Let that encourage you to cast all your care upon Him and entrust all your concerns to Him.

Now it is Satan's chief business to hinder Christ's redeemed from so doing, for not only does he hate Christ, but he knows he cannot prevail with you while you be believingly and lovingly absorbed with Him and drawing strength from Him. Therefore he will do everything in his power to keep you from this "one thing needful." He did so when you were under conviction of sin. He sought to get you occupied entirely with your guilt and defilement, telling

(continued on back page)

Important Notices

Please advise promptly of change in address, otherwise copies will be lost in the mails.

We are glad to send a sample copy to any of your friends whom you believe would be interested in this publication.

This magazine is published as " a work of faith and labour of love," the editor and his wife gladly giving their services free.   There is no regular subscription price, as we do not wish the poor of the flock to be deprived.   This does not mean that those looking for something for nothing may " help themselves."   Those getting this magazine who are financially able and who receive spiritual help from its pages, are expected to gladly contribute towards its expenses; otherwise their names are dropped from our list.

Will those forwarding International Money Orders please have them made out to us at Stornoway, Isle of Lewis, Scotland.   Checks (Cheques—Eng.) made out on U.S.A. Banks are not negotiable here, so please do not send them.

All unsigned articles are by the Editor.

CONTENTS

THE PRAYERS OF THE APOSTLES

38.   Colossians i, 9-12

" That ye might be filled with the knowledge of His will in all wisdom and spiritual understanding " (verse 9). This opening petition was for something very much more than a bare notional acquaintance with the Divine will— an increase of their intellectual information; rather was it a request that the saints should be brought into a fuller and more acceptable *obedience*. It is God's preceptive and authoritative will which is in view, and the " knowledge " thereof is a practical and operative one, which is to be evidenced in a worthy walk. The babe in Christ has the *principle* of obedience in his heart (Divinely communicated grace and holiness) but it needs feeding, strengthening, quickening, illuminating, directing, so that that principle of obedience may act aright and perform those things which God has appointed, and not those which human tradition has invented, or which natural sentiment or personal inclination may dictate. We saw that *this* came first in the prayer of Ephesians i: " give unto you the spirit of wisdom and revelation in the knowledge [and " acknowledgment," margin] of Him " (verse 17). So also was it made the opening petition for the Philippian saints: " that your love may abound yet more and more in knowledge and in all judgment " (verse 9). Thus we see the prime importance of this blessing.

In our last we pointed out that this petition has respect unto an affectionate and operative knowledge, which is increased as the child of God is favoured with a better understanding of Divine objects. The clearer and fuller be his views of them, the more is his heart drawn out unto them. The more we perceive the ineffable beauty of Divine things, the more is the soul sensibly influenced by them. Those things which are the objects on which the Christian's love is to be acted, particularly the Divine precepts, must be discerned in their true nature and excellence before there can be spiritual delight in them. While there be no spiritual understanding of spiritual things there can be no spiritual pleasure in them. We are quite deceived if we suppose our love for God's commandments is increasing unless there be a growing realization of their *worth*. There can be no growth of spiritual love without an increase of spiritual knowledge. The more a Christian knows the importance and value of his Rule, the more will he be taken with it. Herein lies the defect of much modern religion: either an attempt to stir the emotions by sentimental appeals, or exhorting unto the exercise of love without presenting those things which feed love and spontaneously draw it forth.

Faith is fed by knowledge and works by love, and therefore the fuller and deeper be the soul's experimental acquaintance with God and the more his affections be drawn out unto and centred upon Him, the more will faith and love produce that obedience which is honouring unto Him. As it is a spiritual knowledge of the Lord as He is revealed to the heart that causes us to put our trust in Him (Psa. ix, 10), as it is a believing sight in Him as our suffering Surety which opens the floodgates of evangelical repentance (Zech. xii, 10), so it is a sense of our deep indebtedness to Him, a spirit of gratitude, which issues in acceptable obedience. The more we apprehend God's infinite worthiness, the more shall we strive to walk worthily before Him. The more we behold His excellency, the more will our hearts be inflamed toward Him. The more intimate and constant be our communion with Him, the more shall we delight ourselves in Him, and the more tender shall we be of those things which grieve Him. So too the more we perceive of the high sovereignty and majesty of God, the more shall we be awed by and be amenable to His authority, and the more diligent shall we be in cleaving to that path in which alone fellowship with Him can be enjoyed.

There are many today who have a most inadequate and defective idea of what fellowship with God consists of. They regard it as an especial luxury which is only enjoyed occasionally, whereas it should be so regularly. They imagine it is experienced only when their souls are ecstatically elevated by some uncommonly powerful sermon, during some season of unusual liberty in prayer, or when meditating on some precious portion of the Word. But *that* is more a time when the soul is sensible of the Lord's having drawn nigh unto and lifted up the light of His countenance upon him, favouring him with a special love-token. But it is something else we now have in mind. It is one of the great errors of Romanists that intimate fellowship with God can be enjoyed only in the cloister: it can be had equally by the housewife while engaged in her domestic tasks and by her husband as he works for his daily bread. God graciously communes with each of His people while they are about their daily callings if their secular duties be discharged in obedience to Him—thankful to be engaged in making an honest living, thankful also for the health and strength which enables them to do so.

What we particularly have in mind, and what is exactly parallel with the first two petitions of that prayer we are here considering, are those words, " He will teach us of His ways and we will walk in His paths " (Isa. ii, 3). To teach us of His ways is for God to fill us with " the knowledge of His will," and for us to walk in His paths is to " walk worthy of the Lord unto all pleasing." A well-known hymn expresses this desire: " O for a closer walk with God." Well, my reader, there is only one way in which that longing can be realized, and that is by cleaving more exactly to the paths which He has marked out for us. God holds communion with us in " His Ways " and in none other, namely, " the paths of righteousness." We cannot walk with God in a way of self-will and self-pleasing, nor in the broad road trodden by the world. Every step we take in the right way—the one of God's revealed will—is one of obedience, and God accompanies us therein. But the moment we forsake the path of duty, and wander into what Bunyan styles "By-path meadow," we turn away from God, and leave the only place wherein fellowship with Him may be had.

"In all wisdom and spiritual understanding." Those added words not only intimate the sort of "knowledge" for which the Christian is to pray and endeavour, but also what is necessary in order for him to employ such knowledge unto advantage. In this superficial age knowledge and wisdom are often confounded, yet they are far from being synonymous. There are many learned fools in the world: frequently the almost illiterate exercise more natural intelligence than does the average university graduate. "Wisdom" is the capacity to make a right and good use of knowledge. Even when we have considerable knowledge of God's will, much wisdom and spiritual understanding is required in order to go in the path of His commandments. Sometimes it is the Christian's duty to admonish an erring brother, yet he is likely to do him more harm than good unless he speaks discreetly. There is a time and a season to every thing, but good judgment and spiritual discernment are requisite in order to recognize the same. Much prudence is called for to rightly distinguish between relative duties: to deliberately neglect secular duties in order to feast upon spiritual things, to deprive my family of things which they urgently need in order to give more liberally to the Lord's cause, to forsake my wife in the evenings to engage in religious activities, betrays an absence of spiritual understanding.

How the believer needs to pray "Make me to understand the way of Thy precepts" (Psa. cxix, 37), to be taught how to walk in each duty and every detail of conduct! It is not sufficient to have a general and notional knowledge of the Word: it must be translated into practice, and for that, spiritual insight is required, so that we may perceive when and where and how to perform each action. Some are wise in the general who err sadly in particular details. Only that wisdom which cometh from above will enable us to order our lives in every relation and situation according to the revealed will of God. "Give me understanding, and I shall keep Thy Law" (Psa. xxxiv and cf. verses 73, 144, 169). See how often David repeated that petition! Many times God's children are placed in a dilemma, when they have to choose between duty and duty—duty to God, to their family, to their neighbours—and wisdom and spiritual understanding are required to show them when the one is to be dispensed with and the other performed, when the inferior is to yield to the superior. Circumstances have to be observed as well as actions, that we may know when to "stand still" and when to "go forward." We are not to act on impulse but be regulated by principle.

"That ye might walk worthy of the Lord unto all pleasing, being fruitful in every good work, and increasing in the knowledge of God." This is the second thing Paul requested for the saints and there is an inseparable connection between them, for this cannot be realized except the first be actualized. The walk and works of a person are determined, both in quality and quantity, by his ignorance or knowledge of God's will and by the measure of his wisdom and spiritual understanding. Or to state it another way: here we are shown the use to which such knowledge is to be put. As another said in a different connection, "Our aim in getting an understanding of God's Word is not that we may wrangle about questions, but direct and order our conversation. The Word was not given us to try the acuteness of our wits in disputing, but the readiness of our obedience in performing" (T. Manton). As we pointed out in our last, that knowledge of God's will for which the Christian should pray and labour consists not of a prying into God's secret decrees, speculating about the personal relations between the three Persons in the Trinity, or the eternal destiny of those who are cut off in infancy, nor in theorizing about the future history of this world under the guise of studying prophecy, but rather in learning what God requires from us and how we may be enabled to meet those requirements.

"That ye might walk worthy of the Lord." That is, of "Christ, the Lord" (Luke ii, 11), as is always the case, except in two or three passages like Acts iv, 29; Revelation xi, 15. "Walking" is a term which is applied in Scripture to the conduct or behaviour of persons. It points to the active rather than the passive side of the Christian's life. It expresses not only motion but voluntary motion, in contrast with being carried or dragged. It imports progressive motion or going forward, an advancing in holiness. It signifies the fixing and holding of a steady course in our journey heavenward. As "walking" is in contrast with sitting and lying down, so also from an aimless meandering—a keeping to the way which God has marked out for us. But what is meant by "walking *worthily*," as it should be rendered, and is so in the R.V.? Certainly not meritoriously, as the Papists teach, for it is impossible for the creature to do anything to make God his Debtor or entitle him to reward as a matter of justice—"When ye have done all those things which are commanded you, say, We are unprofitable servants: we have done that which was our duty to do" (Luke xvii, 10). But no Christian ever did all that he was commanded, and even if he had, so imperfectly, it would be unacceptable to God were it not for the mediation of the Redeemer.

But it may be rejoined, Are we not told "Worthy is the Lamb" (Rev. v, 12) and is not that the same term? Yes, save that it is in its adjectival form. The Lamb is indeed worthy, infinitely worthy, but no mere creature is so, no, not even the holy angels, as this very same passage expressly declares. When the question was asked, "Who is worthy to open the book to loose the seals thereof?" we are informed "And no man [Greek "no one"] in heaven nor in earth, neither under the earth, was able to open the book, neither to look thereon. And I wept much because no one was found worthy to open and read the book," which decisively and for ever disposes of the Romish fiction. But there is a worthiness of congruity (fitness) as well as a worthiness of condignity (deservingness), and it is the former which is here in view. To "walk worthily of the Lord" signifies to conduct ourselves as becometh saints, to act in accordance with the character of the One whose name we bear and whose followers we profess to be. To walk worthily of the Lord means to comport ourselves suitably and agreeably to our relation and indebtedness unto Him, to carry ourselves meetly as those who are not their own—the same Greek word is rendered "as becometh" in Romans xvi, 2, and Philippians i, 27.

"As obedient children, not fashioning yourselves according to your former lusts in your ignorance: but as He which hath called you is holy, so be ye holy in all manner of conversation "or "conduct" (Peter i, 14, 15) serves to interpret what has just been before us. Let the livery of your daily lives make manifest your change of masters. Formerly you served your lusts, but that was in the days of your ignorance, when you were strangers to God. Now that you have enlisted under the banner of the Lord Jesus and have the "knowledge of God's will," evince it in a practical way: "walk becomingly of the Lord." How? "Let this mind be in you which was also in Christ Jesus" (Phil. ii, 5). And what was that? The mind of self-abnegation—vailing His glory and taking upon Him the form of a servant. The mind of self-abasement—making Himself "of no reputation." The mind of voluntary subjection and unreserved surrender—" He became obedient unto death, even the death of the cross." How? By the life of Christ being reproduced in us, so far as our measure and capacity admits—that we " may grow up into Him in all things " (Eph. iv, 15). How? By making Him our Exemplar—" Because Christ also suffered for us, leaving us an example that ye should follow His steps " (I Peter ii, 21). Only in proportion as we do shall we " walk worthily of the Lord."

To " walk worthily of the Lord " is the great task which is assigned the Christian, and it is to be attempted with the utmost seriousness as his principal care, and attended to with unwearied diligence as a matter of the utmost importance. To honour that blessed One whose we are and whom we serve, to so conduct myself that fellow saints " glorify God in me " (Gal. i, 24), to " adorn the doctrine of God our Saviour in all things " (Titus ii, 10), should be my supreme quest and business, one which is never to be forgotten or laid aside. The Christian ought to be even more earnest in endeavouring to approve himself unto God than they are who contend so zealously for the honours of this world and those who devote all their energies unto the acquirement of its riches. We should make it our constant employ to bring no reproach upon the name of Him who loved us and gave Himself for us. Otherwise we cannot magnify Him nor His cause here upon earth. It is not our talk but our walk that most furthers His interests. People soon forget what we say, but they long remember Christlike conduct. Actions speak louder than words. The Lord has called us out of darkness into His marvellous light that we should " *show forth* His praises " or " virtues " (I Peter ii, 9).

If we be not walking worthily of the Lord, we lack evidence of our title to heaven. Of Enoch it is said that " before his translation [to heaven] he had this testimony, that he pleased God " (Heb. xi, 5). That looks back to Genesis v, 24, where we are told that " Enoch walked with God." Therein he " pleased Him," and that testimony bore witness to his eternal inheritance. Only as holiness is our care do we have a token and an earnest that heaven is our portion, for without holiness " no man shall see the Lord " (Heb. xii, 14). It is indeed the merits of Christ which alone give any one title to the Inheritance, yet personal holiness confirms that title unto us. There is no good hope toward Christ where there is no sincere effort to honour Him: " Hereby we do know that we know Him, if we keep His commandments " (I John ii, 3). Only those are meet to live with Him hereafter who make conscience of walking with Him here: at death we change our place, but not our company. " They shall walk with Me in white, *for* they are worthy " (Rev. iii, 4)—fitly disposed and prepared to do so. On the other hand, " Know ye not that the unrighteous shall not inherit the kingdom of God. Be not deceived " (I Cor. vi, 9, 10)—those who gratify the flesh are necessarily excluded.

Unless we give the utmost attention unto our daily walk and the ordering of it by the revealed will of God, we break that covenant which we solemnly entered into with Him at our conversion. It was then that we renounced all other lords, forsook our idols, surrendered ourselves to the righteous claims of the Lord and promised that henceforth we would love Him with all our hearts and serve Him with all our strength. It was then that we voluntarily and deliberately entered upon a course of obedience to Him, " choosing the things that please Him," and thereby " taking hold of His covenant " (Isa. lvi, 4). Consequently, to return unto the pleasing of self, or to seek the favour of men or the applause of the world, is a denial of the covenant and a throwing-off of the yoke of Christ which formerly we took freely upon us. It is a practical denial that we are not our own but bought with a price. Such deplorable backsliding will issue in having a conscience which is no longer " void of offence " but rather one that accuses and condemns us. The joy of salvation is then lost, the light of God's countenance is then hid from us, that peace which passeth all understanding is no longer our portion. Instead, darkness and doubts possess the heart, the rod of Divine chastisement falls heavily upon us, our prayers remain unanswered, relish for the Word is gone.

We cannot enjoy conscious communion with Him unless we walk worthily of the Lord. We cannot have the comfort of His presence in every company or in all conditions. If we consort with the ungodly the Lord is grieved and will evince His displeasure. If we turn to the pleasures of this world for satisfaction, His smile will be withheld from us. If we indulge the lusts of the flesh, it will be said to us as it was to His people of old, " your iniquities have *separated* between you and your God " (Isa. lix, 2). It is the one who hath Christ's commandments and keepeth them who proves his love to Him, and to whom He says, " and I will love him and will manifest Myself to him." And again, " If a man love Me, he will keep My words, and My Father will love him and We will come unto him and make Our abode with him " (John xiv, 21, 23). Nor can we otherwise even enjoy the creature or the things of this life: " Go thy way, eat thy bread with joy and drink thy wine with a merry heart [when?]; *for* God now accepteth thy works " (Eccl. ix, 7). When our walk be right then are our earthly comforts satisfying, for we taste God's love in them and can use them as His blessings with thankfulness and cheerfulness. Contrariwise, He sends a curse upon our blessings (Mal. ii, 2).

But let us strike a higher note and, rising above necessity, the requirements of duty, and personal expediency, come to *holy privilege*. The Christian has been " called unto the fellowship of God's Son, Jesus Christ our Lord " (I Cor. i, 9). What an inestimable favour is that! How highly it should be valued, how tenderly cherished! And " fellowship," be it remembered, is a joint affair, a mutual thing, and therefore is that searching question put to each of us who bear His name, " Can two walk together except they be agreed? " (Amos iii, 3): that is, except they be one in disposition, desire and aim. He is the Holy One, and if I forsake the highway of holiness, then I turn from His presence. The root idea of fellowship is partnership—one having in common with another. In His wondrous love and amazing condescension the Lord Jesus deigned to make the interests of His people His own. That was unspeakable grace on His part, and what does it call for from us? Surely that deepest gratitude should now make His interests ours, that we should exercise the utmost circumspection in avoiding everything which would injure His interests, and that we should now exert ourselves to the utmost in promoting the honour of His name on earth. Love so amazing, so Divine, demands my love, my life, my all. What can I render unto the Lord for all His benefits, but earnestly endeavour to walk worthily of Him.

LIFE AND TIMES OF JOSHUA

The Ark

" And they commanded the people, saying, When ye see the ark of the covenant of the Lord your God, and the priests the Levites bearing it, then ye shall remove from your place, and go after it. Yet there shall be a space between you and it, about two thousand cubits by measure: come not near unto it, that ye may know the way by which ye must go; for ye have not passed this way heretofore " (iii, 3, 4). Keeping in mind the principal things which have already been before us: that this was a new generation of Israel which was about to enter into their heritage; that that heritage prefigured the portion and privileges which should—in this life—be enjoyed by the Christian; that the ark was an outstanding type of the person of Christ; that the particular name by which it is here designated intimates the special character in which Christ is to be viewed and followed by the believer; that Israel's crossing of the Jordan and entrance into Canaan is fraught with the most important practical instruction for us today; let us proceed.

The ark was the sacred chest in which the two tables of stone were deposited, and thus it pointed to Christ as our Lawgiver (Psa. xl, 8; John xiv, 15). The ten commandments were the terms of the covenant which was mutually entered into between Jehovah and Israel at Sinai (Ex. xxxiv, 28), and it was on the basis of their compliance or non-compliance with that solemn pact that the Lord agreed to deal with Israel and make good His promises to Abraham. Hence the name by which the ark is called throughout Joshua iii and iv. Thus the ark here prefigured Christ as the believer's *Covenant-head*, the meaning of which, though of the first moment, is alas little understood today. It is in the Gospel that Christ is tendered unto us as such, and it is by our complying with its terms that the soul enters into a covenant with Him. "Incline your ear, and come unto Me: Hear, and your soul shall live; and I will make an everlasting covenant with you, even the sure mercies of David" or "the Beloved" (Isa. lv, 3). That is the Gospel offer or proposal, and our acceptance thereof is a "joining ourselves to the Lord, to serve Him and to love the name of the Lord" and is a "taking hold of His covenant" (Isa. lvi, 6).

That which will best enable us to grasp the basic truth which we are here concerned with is the *marriage contract*, for marriage is a covenant voluntarily, lovingly, and solemnly entered into between two parties, wherein each gives himself or herself unto the other, disowning all rivals, pledging unending fidelity, vowing to make the interests and welfare of the other his or her own. Nothing less than is what the Lord requires from man. The evangelist calls upon his hearers to throw down the weapons of their enmity against Him, forsake all illicit lovers, and unite themselves with those who declare, "Come, and let us join ourselves to the Lord in a perpetual covenant that shall not be forgotten." (Jer. l, 5). Thus it was in that wondrous and blessed foreshadowment in Genesis xxiv, where Abraham (figure of the Father) sent forth his servant Eliezer (figure first of the Holy Spirit, yet principally of the evangelist through whom He works) to seek and woo a wife (emblem of the Church collectively and of the believer individually) for his son Isaac—Christ; the whole of which sets before us a most instructive picture of the preaching of the Gospel, both from the standpoint of God's sovereign grace and the enforcing of human responsibility—though, as usual, the latter is ignored by most Calvinistic writers thereon.

As the figure of the evangelist we may note how Eliezer received most specific instructions from Abraham concerning his mission and how that servant obediently complied therewith (Gen. xxiv, 10). Then we observe how Eliezer betook himself unto prayer, asking the Lord to grant him "good speed" and success on his errand (verse 12)—an unmistakably plain intimation that Eliezer is not to be regarded solely as a type of the Holy Spirit. When Abraham's servant encountered the object of his quest he presented her with tokens of his good will (verse 22), and extolled the excellency of his master (verse 35). Then we behold how she was required to make a personal decision: "Wilt thou go with this man?" (verse 58): she had to choose for herself, freely and deliberately. Such a decision, personal and definite, is required from the sinner as the terms of the Gospel are presented unto him, for they are addressed to him as a moral agent, testing and enforcing his responsibility. " And she said, I will go." She was willing and ready to turn her back upon the old life, and forsake her family to become the wife of Isaac. ",And she became his wife" (verse 67), and never regretted her decision. And that is the grand type and picture of a soul entering into an everlasting covenant with the Lord Jesus, the eternal Lover of His people —made willing in the day of His power.

In full accord with the striking type of Genesis xxiv we find our Lord Himself speaking of the Gospel-order thus: " The kingdom of heaven is like unto a certain King which made a *marriage* for His Son " (Matt. xxii, 2), upon which Matthew Henry rightly averred, " The Gospel covenant is a marriage covenant betwixt Christ and the believer, and it is a marriage of God's making. This branch of the similitude is only mentioned, and not prosecuted here "; by which he meant that the wedding feast and its guests is what is mainly dwelt upon in the sequel. Concerning the force of the " marriage " figure itself, Thomas Scott aptly said, " The union of the Son of God with man by assuming human nature; the endeared relationship into which He receives His Church and every member of it; the spiritual honours, riches and blessings to which they are advanced by this sacred relation; the comforts they receive from His condescending and faithful love, and from communion with Him; and the reciprocal duties of their relation to Him are all intimated by the metaphor." True, yet, with their accustomed partiality and lack of balance, most preachers have dwelt considerably upon the first four of these analogies, but have been criminally silent upon the " reciprocal duties " which that relation involves, and which we are here insisting upon.

The same lopsidedness is seen again in the explanations given of Matthew xxii, 11: " When the King came in to see the guests, He saw there a man which had not on a wedding garment." Thomas Scott is right in saying, " This denotes that some who are not true believers appear as willing and welcome guests at the Gospel feast and intrude into its most sacred ordinances." but it seems to us he quite missed the point when he added, " It is not material whether we understand the wedding garment to mean the imputed righteousness of Christ, or the sanctification of the Spirit; for both are alike necessary and they always go together." This parable is not treating so much of the Divine side of things, but rather the testing of human *responsibility* and the disclosing of its failures. Verses 3, 5 and 6 exhibit man's obstinacy and enmity, while verse 11 depicts the exposure of an empty profession. " If the Gospel be the wedding feast, then the wedding garment is a frame of heart and a course of life agreeable to the Gospel and our profession of it " (Matthew Henry). Many take up a profession of the Gospel and claim to be united to Christ without any newness of heart and life. They lack a disposition and conduct suited to Christ and His precepts: they are devoid of habitual and practical holiness. They have no marriage " certificate "!

Now none can enter into and enjoy the heritage which God has provided for His people save those who have personally and experimentally passed from death unto life, who have entered into definite and solemn covenant with Him, and who cleave unto and conduct themselves by the commandments of Christ—the anti-typical Joshua. That is the great and grand truth portrayed here in Joshua iii and iv, and it is because it is such a momentous one, and yet so little apprehended today, that we are labouring it so much in our comments upon this passage. It is at regeneration that the soul passes from death unto life, when by a sovereign act of God's power—wherein we are entirely passive—we are spiritually quickened and thereby capacitated to turn unto Him. This miracle of grace is made manifest by the understanding of its subject being enlightened to perceive his awful enmity against God, by his conscience being convicted of his guilty and lost condition, by his affections being turned against sin so that he now loathes it, by his will being inclined Godwards; all of which issues in a genuine conversion or right-about-face—a forsaking of his wicked ways, an abandoning of his idols, a turning away from the world, and a taking of Christ to be his absolute Lord, all-sufficient Saviour, and everlasting Portion.

Such a conversion—and none other is a saving one—is an entering into covenant with God in Christ, and a being married or united unto Him. Hence we find the conversion of the Corinthians described thus: they " first gave their own selves to the Lord and unto us, by the will of God " (II Cor. viii, 5): that is, they willingly yielded and gladly dedicated themselves unto the Lord—acknowledging the just requirements of His proprietorship and authority, and responding to the claims of His redeeming love as the only suitable acknowledgment of that debt which can never be repaid; and gave up themselves unto His servants to be directed by them; which is ratified in baptism, when we *openly* give up ourselves to be His people. Hence, under a slightly varied figure Paul reminded those who had been thus converted under his preaching, " I have espoused you to one Husband, that I may present you as a chaste virgin to Christ " (II Cor. xi, 2). The apostle had been the instrument in forming a connection between them and Christ like that of the marriage union, the obligations of which are devotedness, fidelity, loving obedience; and unto the preservation and promotion thereof the apostle laboured with a godly jealousy for them.

At regeneration the Spirit vitally unites us to Christ; at conversion we personally and practically give up ourselves unto Him. Conversion is when we accept Christ to be our Husband and Lord, to be cherished and ruled by Him. It is an entering into a covenant-engagement with Him, for Him to be our only God, and for us to be His faithful people. That the covenant relationship *is* a marriage union is clear from Jeremiah xxxi, 32, Hosea ii, 18, 19 (and cf. Jer. ii, 2; Ezek. xvi, 60); and that is why Israel's idolatry was commonly spoken of as (spiritual) adultery—unfaithfulness to Jehovah, going after other gods. Since conversion be our entering into covenant with God in Christ, the great business of the Christian life is to " *keep* His covenant " (Psa. xxv, 10): that is, to be regulated at all times by its terms. Or, since conversion be a marriage union with Christ, the whole aim of the Christian life is to be as a loving and dutiful wife should unto her husband. All of which is summed up in that comprehensive word, " As ye have therefore received Christ Jesus the Lord, so walk ye in Him " (Col. ii, 6): continue as you began, be actuated by the same motives and principles now as when you first surrendered to Him, let your Christian life be a perpetuation of your conversion, be wholly devoted to Him.

What we have endeavoured to set before the reader above as a definition and description of the true and normal Christian life is that which is typically portrayed in Joshua iii and iv. The ark was a figure of Christ; the " ark of the covenant of the Lord your God " pointed to Him as our Covenant-head, the One with whom we entered into a solemn compact and engagement at our conversion, to be henceforth and for ever only His. Israel's *following* of that ark pictured our *keeping* of the covenant, our being in practical subjection to Christ as our Lord and Lawgiver, our being faithful to the marriage relationship, ever seeking to please and promote the interests of the eternal Lover of our souls. Just in proportion as we conduct ourselves *thus* will Israel's experiences become ours. As they submitted unto Joshua's orders, as they obediently followed the ark of the covenant, God put forth His mighty power on their behalf, they entered into a present " rest " (Heb. iv, 3), He subdued their enemies, and a land flowing with milk and honey became their actual portion. And if *such* experiences be not those of the writer, or the reader, it is just because he is failing to conduct himself as Israel did here.

Having entered so fully into an attempt to explain the fundamental principles underlying this incident and the main lessons to be learned from it, there will be the less need to spend much time on its details. " There shall be a space between you and it about two thousand cubits by measure: come not near unto it " (verse 4). That was parallel with the solemn prohibition given unto Irael when the Lord was about to enter into covenant with their fathers, and make known unto them the terms of that covenant: " the third day the Lord will come down in the sight of all the people upon mount Sinai. And thou shalt set bounds unto the people round about, saying, Take heed to yourselves that ye go not up into the mount or touch the bound of it. Whosoever toucheth the mount shall be surely put to death " (Ex. xix, 12). The spiritual application of both unto us is set forth in that word, " God is greatly to be feared in the assembly of the saints and to be had in reverence of all them that are round about Him " (Psa. lxxxix, 7). Or, to express the same in New Testament language, " Let us have grace whereby we may serve God acceptably with reverence and godly fear: for our God is a consuming fire " (Heb. xii, 28, 29).

The natural and local reason why the ark of the covenant should proceed so far in advance was that it could readily be seen by all the vast multitude: had there been no space between it and them, those who followed closely behind it would obscure the view of the others—only those in the first few ranks had been able to behold it. But being borne by the priests half a mile in the van, the ark would be visible to the whole multitude. But typically and spiritually the lessons inculcated were: First, we should ever bear in mind that by nature we are sinners, and as such far removed from the Holy One. Second, that as sinners we are to look off unto Christ as our Sin-bearer, of which the mercy seat or propitiatory (which formed the lid of the ark) spoke. As the uplifted serpent on the pole (emblem of Christ bearing the curse for His people) was visible to all the congregation, so the ark in the foreground. Third, that as saints we need to keep our eyes steadfastly fixed upon Him, " looking off unto Jesus the Author and Finisher of faith " (Heb. xii, 2), for it is a life of faith unto which He has called us, strength for which is to be found in Him alone.

Fourth, Christ's leaving His people an example that they should " follow His steps." for " when He putteth forth His sheep, He goeth before them and the sheep follow Him " (John x, 4): our duty is to " follow the Lamb whithersoever He goeth " (Rev. xiv, 4). Fifth, the immeasurable superiority of Christ above His people—" that in all things He should have the pre-eminence " (Col. i, 18), He being the Head. we. but members of His body. This must ever be borne in mind by them, for though He be their Kinsman-Redeemer and is not ashamed to call them " brethren," nevertheless He is their Lord and their God, and to be owned and worshipped as such—" that all should honour the Son even as they honour the Father " (John v, 23). Sixth, that we must conduct ourselves toward the Lord our God with proper decorum and not with unholy familiarity.   Seventh, that He entered the anti-typical Canaan in advance, to take possession of heaven on our behalf: " whither the Forerunner is *for us* entered " (Heb. vi, 20)—there is both a present and future, an initial and a perfect occupying of our heritage.

THE DOCTRINE OF REVELATION

2.   The Existence of God.

In our last it was pointed out that the origin of three essential things in Nature call for explanation from the attentive observer: matter, motion and life.   Having considered the alternative solutions for the first-mentioned, let us now contemplate the others.   Concerning them we cannot do better than present to the reader a summary of what we deem a singularly able and convincing discussion by John Armour in his unique work (out of print), *Atonement and Law.*

As we contemplate the wondrous movement of bodies in the solar system, measuring time for us with absolute exactness, and as we rise to the conception of the harmonious motion of all bodies in space, measuring duration for all created beings, we cannot but be actuated with an intense desire to know the cause of this wondrous *motion.*   But the question, what is the cause of the motion of the heavenly bodies in space? naturally resolves itself into the more general question: what is the cause of all motion?   The ready, the only answer is *force.*   But this raises the real question: what is the origin of force?   Every investigation of that subject leads to the profound conviction that all force is traceable to *life.*

In the entire vegetable kingdom we have perpetual demonstration of the intimate and necessary relations of motion, force and life.   Even the least instructed, who have no conception of the real activity or of the observable motion in all growing plants, cannot but know also that the mighty forests are built up by vital force operating tirelessly century after century, cannot but know that the whole world is covered over with the countless, varied and marvellous products and proofs of the mysterious, universally recognized but invisible vital power.   But only those who have patiently and perseveringly gazed into that limitless world into which the microscope is the only door, and have witnessed the amazing activity of vital force in plant life, can have any idea of the manner in which the entire vegetable kingdom testifies of the intimate relations of motion, force and life.

Let anyone spend but a few hours in watching the rapid and incessant motion in a small leaf (such as that of the *Anacharis Alsinastrum*) under one of the best microscopes art has been able to furnish, the field being less than ten thousandths part of an inch.   In that small field can be distinctly seen twelve rows of cells with an average of five cells in each row.   The current can be seen flowing rapidly along appropriate channels, like rivers with broken ice on the surface, while in each of the sixty oblong cells the fluids are seen circulating like eddies or whirlpools in a rushing stream.   But for the perfection which microscopic art has attained, this amazing activity would never have been suspected or credited.   Witnessing this activity in the ten-thousandth part of an inch of the surface of a small leaf, what would be the impression upon the mind could we look upon a single tree, discerning the activity of vital force in *every* part of it with the same degree of clearness?   While we cannot do this, imagination can transfer what we have seen in the leaf under the microscope to all the leaves of the forest, to all vegetation on the globe, for in every cell of every living plant there is substantially the same vital activity.

Whether we look upon forest or field the eye of the mind should discern, not merely motionless forms of life, but everywhere intensely active vital power. Were we capable of seeing the real activity of the vital force in the living tree, it would be to us scarcely less wonderful than the " great sight " which Moses turned aside to see; nor could it fail to produce in us a sense of the Divine presence not unlike that which he experienced. This vital action, which man and all created intelligences must ever strive to behold, and may ever more and more clearly discover, God Himself alone sees as it is.

The same line of remark might be followed out at length in regard to force and motion in every department of the animal kingdom. Here also the Life is the force and force that never ceases to produce activity. In the *ova* vitalized, and from that instant, on and on through all vicissitudes, motion is demonstrably uninterrupted till death, or rather the cessation of motion *is* death. The only absolute test of life is vital action. When this has ceased it is proof that vital force has ceased—that vitality is extinct. Nor is there the slightest ground to believe that this vital action, having ceased for an instant, can start again of itself. Vital activity can no more begin in plant or animal organism in which it has once ceased than in matter in which it never existed. The animal kingdom, then, is a witness, and in all its extent, with myriad voices in perfect unison, it declares, " All motion is from vital force." The testimony of these two kingdoms is both positive and negative. Their witness agrees: " In us all motion is from vital force "; " With us all motion ceases when vital force ceases."

When we come, however, to *man*, and consider the motion traceable to him, we have to deal with a very different problem, and unless we give special attention we shall probably leave out of the estimate the vastly greater part of the evidence in this case. For man, unlike all other living beings on earth, or at least infinitely beyond other beings on earth, has the power to produce motion, not merely by force of muscle without skill, but he has the power to originate and sustain motion on a grand scale by means of the vital force of brain as well. The savage who should cast a stone a little way into the sea by strength of arm, or from a sling, or shoot an arrow from his bow, or propel his little barque a few miles from the shore in a calm sea, would give proof of the extent of his power. Clearly, in each case, from that of the stone which could be hurled but a few rods to that of the vessel which might be propelled perhaps as many miles, the motion would be wholly attributable to vital force of muscle and brain, or to skill and strength.

The civilized man who constructs and launches the ocean steamer that ploughs its furrow through the sea, in calm and storm, for thousands of miles gives proof of his power to produce motion by skill and strength. The ocean steamer that circumnavigates the globe, displacing the water and defying the storm, is, as one might truthfully say, hurled around the world; and its motion, in that entire revolution, is as clearly traceable to vital force of hand and brain in the civilized man, as is that of the stone from the hand, or the arrow from the bow, of the savage. Let an honest inquirer light upon the ocean steamer at any stage of its long journey. Let him search the vessel from keel to top-mast. Finding no life in hull or rigging, no life in coal or fire, no life in water or steam, no life in engine or propeller, shall he say, " This vessel does not owe its force and motion to life at all." If he so determine he is not a philosopher but a fool. For every part of the vessel, from keel to top-mast, is eloquent in its testimony to the vital force of combined skill and strength of man in its construction. And this we may recognize with all the confidence with which, on approaching an eight-day clock in the middle of the week, we recognize its onward movement as the vital force of the constructor of the clock, combined with the vital force of the person who wound it up; for not only is the vital force of the hand that wound the clock as truly the cause of its continued motion as though that hand had never for an instant been withdrawn, but the vital force of the contriver and the actual constructor, though he may have passed away centuries ago, is as clearly prolonged as would be the vital force of the hand that wound the clock, though the very next hour it were cold and motionless in death. I have ventured to dwell longer on this illustration because of the argument it furnishes in favour of the recognition of vital force as the cause of other and infinitely grander movements.

We come now to a stage in our investigations in which, unless we exercise the utmost vigilance, we shall utterly fail to interpret the transcendent scene where there is an aggregate of motion in comparison with which all we have hitherto considered is but as the small dust of the balance; where, as to rapidity, the swiftest we have as yet contemplated is as that of the snail; where, as to vastness of orbit, even that of the ocean steamer around the globe is but as the " finger ring of a little girl "—as we contemplate motion on a scale so grand, motion of bodies so vast and so numerous, motion in orbits a scarcely perceptible arc of which has been traversed since man appeared on earth, motion which highest created intelligences must regard with never-ending wonder and admiration, shall we begin to *detach*, in our conception, motion from force, or force from that which lives? If we do, how can we any longer pretend that we are consistent, scientific or philosophical? All motion hitherto considered has been traceable to that which lives. Why at this stage begin to question whether that which moves is moved by force or whether force proceeds from life? Motion on a small scale we have found is from vital force. All the motion that man has ever been able to trace to its source he has found to proceed from life. There is not a shred of trustworthy evidence that any visible thing on earth has the power to originate motion. And the invisible power that causes all the motion we can at all trace to its source is always vital power.

We have traced force and motion from that in the smallest seed in plant and that of the *ova* in animal life, and have found force and motion ever proceed from that which lives. Why then, when we stand in the presence of the most wondrous motion—motion that speaks of force beyond all conception—do we, all at once, lapse from the conviction that motion must proceed from force and that force must proceed from life? Doubt comes in where evidence is most abundant. A stone seen moving through the air we believe was hurled by some lad, though we see him not; a cannon ball crossing the bay we do not doubt was sent by persons having skill and power; an ocean steamer driven around the world we know owes its force and motion to skill and power of living beings. When we see mighty orbs moving in space, why do we raise any question regarding the origin of motion and force? The only shadow of reason that can be imagined is that we cannot readily conceive of a Being infinite, ever-present, and all-mighty, the Source of all motion, all force producing all motion in the universe. In a vastly higher sense than that in which the motion of the steamship in mid-ocean is to be attributed to man, all motion in the universe, including that produced *in* and *by* vital organisms in this world and in all worlds, is to be attributed to the

Infinite, the Ever-living, the Almighty. In the presence of the moving universe may we not exclaim: *" Power belongeth unto God "*?

Why should we hesitate to accept the conclusions thus reached? The data furnished to all men leave them without excuse. The soundness of the reasoning by which I have undertaken to prove that motion, mere motion, as recognized everywhere in the universe, since it assures us of the universality of law, is to us direct proof of the existence of the Ever-living, Ever-present Lawgiver is confidently submitted to the judgment of candid and competent reasoners.

The great timepiece of the universe in its surpassing grandeur and glory may continue to move with absolute exactness and utmost harmony from age to age and century to century; the multitudes of mankind may continue to look upon it mainly to see what time of day it is, as indicated upon the broad dial-plate that meets their gaze, and never reflect that this grand time-measurer, like every poor imitation of it man has ever constructed, measures time by means of motion, and motion sustained by force, this force in its turn necessarily from the living, traceable to the living. Yet there may be those who shall find time, even in this busy age, to look with prolonged and steadfast gaze, with awakened and quickened powers, and with intensest interest upon the ever-present and never-exhausted wonders of that aggregate of motion before which all effort towards estimate is perfectly powerless; and when favourably situated therefor, the truly evidential nature of God's glorious work may flash out even as the noonday itself, so that, before this one surpassing demonstration of the power and presence of God, all doubts shall be driven away, even as night itself is chased around our globe by the glorious king of day; so that thenceforward, even to life's close, they shall live in the noonday splendour of unquestioning faith—faith, not vision, for God gives everywhere and in all things not merely proof that He is, but that He is and must be for ever more the Invisible.

But though invisible, God is neither the Incredible nor the Unknowable, for He has set before all men " the invisible things of Him " and these " are clearly seen, being understood by the things that are made, even His eternal power and Godhead, so that they are without excuse." Among the visible things of Him which are clearly seen, that is, clearly and fully recognized by all men, motion, force and life have place; for by these are made known the universality of law, the presence, power and glory of the Ever-living, Ever-present Lawgiver.

Not only does the existence of matter, of motion, and of life, testify that God is, but the magnitude and magnificence of creation announce the same grand truth: the work reveals the Workman. " The massive dome of St. Peter's fane, rising four hundred feet, and ablaze with the masterpieces of Italian art, declares an architect and artist—some one who planned, builded, decorated it. This is a thought in stone and tells of a thinker. It did not grow of itself, or come to be by some mysterious ' evolution ' or ' development.' Atoms never could arrange themselves in such harmonious relations, or fall accidentally into such marvellous combination. Blind chance never built that cathedral in Rome. There must have been a controlling intelligence— an intelligent control. Yet some would have us believe that the vaster Dome of Heaven, with its millions of starry lamps, surmounting a grander Temple of Creation, had neither Architect to plan nor Builder to construct! The author of the epistle to the Hebrews indulged in no mere poetic rhapsody when he wrote: ' Every house is builded by some one: but He who built all things is God.'

" The thoughtful observer must feel that in the heavens there is not only a testimony to a Creator, but a partial revelation of His character and attributes. Such a work and workmanship not only reveal a Workman, but hint what sort of workman He is. For example, as no bounds have ever been found in the universe, it is natural to infer an *infinite* Creator. The vast periods discovered by astronomy suggest His eternity. The forces of the universe, displaying stupendous power, bespeak His omnipotence. Waste, everywhere going on and needing perpetual resupply, demands omnipresence. The exact proportion and wise adaptation of every part to each other, and of all to the great whole, tell of omniscience, which includes both infinite knowledge and wisdom. The Being who survives and guides all the changes of this universe must Himself be immutable; and He who lavishes upon His work such wealth of splendour and variety of beauty must be both infinitely rich in resources and versatile in invention. So also the universal harmony, by which the whole mechanism is regulated, indicates a character of infinite perfection in harmony with itself. Thus, seen from no higher point of view than the scientific and philosophical, the dome of the sky bears, wrought on its expanse, in starry mosaics, ' *There is a God* ' " (*The Gordian Knot*).

Descending from the heavens to the planet on which we reside, here too we are confronted with phenomena, both in the general and the particular, both in nature and number, for which no explanation is adequate save that of an all-mighty, benevolent, and infinitely wise Creator. Upon the surface of this earth are incalculable hosts of creatures, varying in size from gnats to elephants, each requiring its regular food, the total amount of which for a single day defies human computation if not the imagination. Those creatures are not set down in a dwelling place where the table is bare, but where there is abundance for them all; nor are they furnished merely with a few necessities, but, instead, with a great variety of luxuries and dainties. From whence proceed such ample and unfailing supplies? From Nature, says the materialist. And what or whom endowed Nature to bear so prolifically and ceaselessly? To which no intelligent reply is forthcoming. Only one answer satisfactorily meets the case: *from the living God!* " *He* causeth the grass to grow for the cattle and herb for the service of men: the earth is full of Thy riches. These all wait upon Thee, that Thou mayest give them meat in season. *Thou* openest Thy hand, they are filled with good* " (Psa. civ).

The continuous fertility of the earth after six thousand years of incessant productiveness can only be satisfactorily explained by attributing the same unto the riches and bounty of its Maker. That one generation of creatures is succeeded by another, in endless procession, upon its surface, to find such an illimitable store of food available for them, is nothing but a stupendous miracle, the marvel of which is lost upon us either through our thoughtlessness or because of its unfailing and regular repetition. The constant supplies which God causes the earth to yield for such myriads of beings is just as remarkable as the original production of the place in which they were to live, for the annual re-fertilization of the earth is actually a *continuous creation*. To quote again from Psalm civ: as the reverent beholder contemplates the revived countenance of Nature in the springtime, he cannot but turn his eyes unto the living God and exclaim, " *Thou* renewest the face of the earth " (verse 30). Beholding as he does the barren fields, the leafless trees, the frozen ground, and often the sunless skies, during the dreary months of winter, and seeing everything mantelled in white, it appears that the earth has grown old and died, that a pall of snow has fallen to hide its forbidding features. And what could man do, what could all the scientists in the world do, if winter should be prolonged month after month, and year after year? Nothing, but slowly yet surely die of starvation.

But the Creator has declared, " While the earth remaineth, seedtime and harvest shall not cease " (Gen. viii, 22), and therefore He makes good that promise each year, by causing winter to give place to spring and " renewing the face of the earth." The world is as full of creatures today as though none had ever died, for as soon as one generation passes from it, it is at once replaced by another, coming to a larder already well filled for it. And again we insist, *that* was made possible and actual only by God's having " renewed the face of the earth." And what a marvellous thing that is, yea, a series of marvels. That such a variety of food, so perfectly adapted to the greatly varying digestive organs of insects, animals and men, so replete with nourishment, so attractive in appearance, should be produced by *soil,* than which nothing is more insipid, sordid, and despicable. What a pleasing variety of fruits the trees bear: how beautifully coloured, elegantly shaped, and admirably flavoured! Shall we be struck most with agreeable astonishment at the Cause of such effects or at the manner of bringing them into existence.

THE GREAT CHANGE

Continuing our review of the numerous passages wherein the Holy Spirit has described His work of regeneration, and wherein He has used such a great variety of figures and terms the better to enable us to form something more than a one-sided conception thereof, we turn next to Romans v, 5, where we read, " the love of God is shed abroad in our hearts by the Holy Spirit which is given unto us." By nature no man has any love for God. To those Jews who contended so vehemently for the unity of God and abhorred all forms of idolatry, and who in their mistaken zeal sought to kill the Saviour because of " making Himself equal with God," He declared, " I know you, that ye have not the love of God in you " (John v, 18, 42). Not only loveless, the natural man is filled with enmity against God (Rom. viii, 7). But when a miracle of grace is wrought within him by the Holy Spirit, his heart experiences a great change Godwards, so that the One he formerly dreaded and sought to banish from his thoughts is now the Object of his veneration and joy, the One upon whose glorious perfections he delights to meditate, and for whose honour and pleasure he now seeks to live.

That great change which is wrought within the regenerate does not consist in the annihilation of the evil principle, " the flesh," but in freeing the mind from its dominion, and in the communication of a holy principle which conveys a new propensity and disposition to the soul: God is no longer hated but loved. That freeing of the mind from the evil dominion of the flesh is spoken of in Ezekiel xxxvi, 26, as God's taking away " the stony heart," and that shedding abroad of His love within the heart by His Spirit is termed giving them " a heart of flesh." Such strong figurative language was used by the prophet to intimate that the change wrought is no superficial or transient one. Through regarding too carnally (" literally ") the terms used by the prophets, dispensationalists and their adherents have created their own difficulty and failed to understand the purport of the passage. It is not that an inward organ or faculty is removed and replaced by a different one, but rather that a radical change for the better had been wrought upon the original faculty—not by changing its essential nature or functions, but by bringing to bear a new and transforming influence upon it.

It ought not to be necessary for us to labour what is quite simple and obvious to the spiritually-minded, but in view of the fearful confusion and general ignorance prevailing, we feel that a further word (for the benefit of the perplexed) is called for. Perhaps a simple illustration will serve to elucidate still further. Suppose that for a long time I have cherished bitter animosity against a fellow creature and treated him with contempt, but that God has now made me realize I have been grievously wronging that person and brought me to repent deeply of the injustice I have done him, so that I have humbly confessed my sin to him, and henceforth shall esteem him highly and do all in my power to amend the wrong I did him; surely no one would have any difficulty in understanding what was meant if I said that I had undergone a real "change of heart" toward that person, nor would it be misleading to say that a "heart of bitterness" had been removed from me and "a heart of good will" given to me. Though we do not pretend to explain the *process*, yet something very much like that are the *nature* and *effect* of God's taking away the heart of stone and giving a heart of flesh, or freeing the mind of enmity against God and shedding abroad His love in the heart.

"But God be thanked, that ye were the servants of sin, but ye have obeyed from the heart that form of doctrine which was delivered you ["whereunto ye were delivered"—margin]. Being then made free from [the guilt and dominion of] sin, ye became the servants of righteousness" (Rom. vi, 17, 18). In this passage the Holy Spirit is describing that wondrous transformation whereby the servants of sin become the servants of righteousness. That transformation is effected by their being delivered unto that form of doctrine which requires hearty obedience. To aid our feeble understanding another similitude is used. "The Truth which is after godliness" (Titus i, 1) is called "that form ["type or impress," Young; rendered "fashion, pattern" in other passages] of doctrine" or "teaching": the figure of a mould or seal being used wherein the hearts of the regenerate (softened and made pliable by the Holy Spirit) are likened to molten metal which receives and retains the exact impress of the mould into which it is poured, or as melted wax is cast into the impress of a seal, answering to it line for line, conformed to the shape and figure of it. The quickened soul is "delivered unto" (the Greek word signifies "given over to," as may be seen in Matthew v, 25; xi, 27; xx, 19) the Truth, so that it is made answerable or conformable unto it.

In their unconverted state they had been the willing and devoted servants of sin, uniformly heeding its promptings and complying with its behests, gratifying their own inclinations without any regard to the authority and glory of God. But now they cordially yielded submission to the teaching of God's Word whereunto they had been delivered or cast into the very fashion of the same. They had been supernaturally renewed into or conformed unto the holy requirements of Law and Gospel alike. Their minds, their affections, their wills had been formed according to the tenor of God's Standard. Thus, from still another angle, we are informed of what the great change consists: it is God's bringing of the soul from the love of sin to the love of holiness, a being transformed by the renewing of the mind—such a transformation as produces compliance with the Divine will. It is an inward agreement with the Rule of righteousness into which the heart is cast and after which the character is framed and modelled, the consequence of which is an obedience from the heart—in contrast with forced or feigned obedience which proceeds from fear or self-interest.

"For I was alive without the Law once: but when the commandment came, sin revived, and I died " (Rom. vii, 9). As the last-considered passage describes the positive side of the great change experienced in the child of God, this one treats more of its negative aspect. The commentators are generally agreed that in Romans vii, 7-11, the apostle is narrating one of the experiences through which he passed at his conversion. First, he says, there had been a time when he was " without the Law "—words which cannot be taken absolutely. In his unregenerate days he had been a proud pharisee. Though he had received his training under the renowned rabbi, Gamaliel, where his chief occupation was the study of the Law, yet being totally ignorant of its spirituality he was, vitally and experimentally speaking, as one " without " it—without a realization of its design or an inward acquaintance of its power. Supposing that a mere external conformity unto its requirements was all that was necessary, and strictly attending to the same, he was well pleased with himself, satisfied with his righteousness, and assured of his acceptance with God.

Second, " but when the commandment came ": verse seven informs us it was the tenth commandment which the Holy Spirit used as the arrow of conviction. When those words, " thou shalt not covet," were applied to him, when they came in the Spirit's illuminating and convicting power to his conscience, the bubble of his self-righteousness was pricked and his self-complacency was shattered. Like a thunderbolt out of a clear sky that Divine prohibition, " thou shalt not [even] desire that which is forbidden," brought home to his heart with startling force the strictness and spirituality of the Divine Law. As those words, " thou must have no self-will," pierced him, he realized the Law demanded inward as well as outward conformity to its holy terms. Then it was that " sin revived ": he was conscious of his lusts rising up in protest against the holy and extensive requirements of the Divine Rule. The very fact that God has said " thou shalt not lust " only served to aggravate and stir into increased activity those corruptions of which previously he was unconscious, and the more he attempted to bring them into subjection the more painfully aware did he become of his own helplessness.

Third, " and I died ": in his own apprehensions, feelings, and estimate of himself. Before he became acquainted with his inward corruptions and was made to feel something of the plague of his heart, living a morally upright life and being most punctilious in performing the requirements of the ceremonial law, the apostle deemed himself a good man. He was in his own opinion " alive "—uncondemned by the Law, having no dread of punishment and judgment to come. But when the tenth commandment smote his conscience, he perceived the spirituality of the Law and realized that hitherto he had only a notional knowledge of it. Convicted of his inward depravity, of his sinful desires, thoughts and imaginations, he felt himself to be a condemned criminal, deserving eternal death. That is another essential element in the great change—which we should have introduced much earlier had we followed a theological order rather than tracing out the various references to it as recorded in the Scriptures. That essential element consists of a personal conviction of sin, of one's lost estate, and such a conviction that its subject completely despairs of any self-help and dies to his own righteousness.

" And such were some of you: but ye are washed, but ye are sanctified, but ye are justified in the name of the Lord Jesus and by the Spirit of our God," (I Cor. vi, 11). The " such were some of you " refers to the licentious and vicious characters mentioned in verses nine and ten, of whom Matthew Henry said they were " very monsters rather than men. Note, some that are eminently good after conversion have been as remarkable for wickedness before." What a glorious alteration does grace effect in reclaiming persons from sins so debasing and degrading! That grand transformation is here described by three words: " washed, sanctified, justified." It may appear very strange to some of our readers to hear that quite a number of those who regard themselves as the champions of orthodoxy, if they do not explicitly repudiate the first, yet give it no place at all in their concept of what takes place at regeneration. They so confine their thoughts to that which is newly created and communicated to the Christian that any change and cleansing of his *original* being is quite lost sight of. God's children are as truly " washed " as they are sanctified and justified. Literally so? Yes; in a material sense? No, *morally*.

" But ye are washed " was the fulfilment of that Old Testament promise, " Then will I sprinkle clean water upon you, and ye shall be clean; from all your filthiness and your idols will I cleanse you " (Ezek. xxxvi, 25). Titus iii, v, makes it clear that the new birth consists of something more than the communication of a new nature, namely, " the washing of regeneration " —cf. Ephesians v, 26. It is further to be noted that the " ye are washed " is distinct from " justified," so it cannot refer to the removal of guilt. Moreover, it is effected by the Spirit and therefore must consist of something which He does *in* us. The foul leper is purged: by the Spirit's agency he is cleansed from his pollutions and his heart is made " pure " (Matt. v, 8). It is a moral cleansing or purification of character from the love and practice of sin. First, " washed," then " sanctified " or set apart and consecrated to God as vessels meet for His use. Thereby we obtain evidence of our justification— the cancellation of guilt and the imputation of righteousness to us. Justification is here attributed to the Holy Spirit because He is the Author of that faith which justifies a sinner.

" But we all with open [it should be " with *unveiled* "] face beholding as in a glass [better " mirror "] the glory of the Lord, are changed into the same image from glory to glory, as by the Spirit of the Lord " (II Cor. iii, 18). In the " unveiled face " there is a double reference and contrast. First, to the veil over the face of Moses (verse 13), which symbolized the imperfection and transitoriness of Judaism: in contrast, Christians behold God as He is fully and finally revealed in the person and work of His Son. Second, to the veil which is over the hearts of unconverted Jews (verse 16): in contrast with them, those who have turned to the Lord have the blinding effects of error and prejudice removed from them, so that they can view the Gospel without any medium obscuring it. The " glory of the Lord," the sum of His perfections, is revealed and shines forth in the Word, and more particularly in the Gospel. As His glory is beheld by that faith which is produced and energized by the Spirit, its beholder is changed gradually from one degree to another into the " same image," becoming more and more conformed unto Him in character and conduct. The verb " changed " (" meta-morphoo ") is rendered " transformed " in Romans xii, 2, and " transfigured " in Matthew xvii, 2!

The " mirrors " of the ancients were made of burnished metals, and when a strong light was thrown on them they not only reflected images with great distinctness but the rays of light were cast back upon the face of one looking into them, so that if the mirror were of silver or brass a white or golden glow suffused his or her countenance· The " mirror " is the Scriptures in which the glory of the Lord is discovered, and as the Spirit shines upon the soul and enables him to act faith and love thereon, he is changed into the same image. The glory of the Lord is irradiated by the Gospel, and as it is received into the heart is reflected by the beholder, through the transforming agency of the Spirit. By the heart's being occupied with Christ's perfection, the mind's meditating thereon, the will's subjection to His precepts, we drink into His spirit, become partakers of His holiness, and are conformed to His image. As our view of Christ is imperfect, the transformation is incomplete in this life: only when we " see Him " face to face shall we be made perfectly " like Him " (I John iii, 2).

" For God, who commanded the light to shine out of darkness, hath shined in our hearts, unto the light of the knowledge of the glory of God in the face of Jesus Christ " (II Cor. iv, 6). Had we been following a strictly logical and theological order, this is another aspect of our subject we should have brought in earlier, for the spiritual illumination of the understanding is one of the first works of God when He begins to restore a fallen creature. By nature he is in a state of complete spiritual ignorance of God, and therefore of his own state before Him, sitting in " darkness " and " in the region and shadow of death " (Matt. iv, 16). That " darkness " is something far more dreadful than a mere intellectual ignorance of spiritual things: it is a positive and energetic " power " (Luke xxii, 53), an evil principle which is inveterately opposed to God, and with which the heart of fallen man is in love (John iii, 19), and which no external means or illumination can dispel (John i, 5). Nothing but the sovereign fiat and all-mighty power of God is superior to it, and He alone can bring a soul " out of darkness into His *marvellous* light."

As God commanded the light to shine out of that darkness which enveloped the old creation (Gen. i, 2, 3), so He does in the work of new creation within each of His elect. That supernatural enlightenment consists not in dreams and visions, nor in the revelation to the soul of anything which has not been made known in the Scripture of Truth, for it is " The entrance of Thy words [which] giveth light " (Psa. ccviv, 130). Yes, the *entrance*: but ere that takes place, the blind eyes of the sinner must first be miraculously opened by the Spirit, so that he is made capable of receiving the light: it is only in God's light we " see light " (Psa. xxxvi, 9). The shining of God's light in our hearts partially and gradually dissipates the awful ignorance, blindness, error. prejudice, unbelief of our souls, thereby preparing the mind to (in measure) apprehend the Truth and the affections to embrace it. By this supernatural illumination the soul is enabled to see things as they really are (I Cor. ii, 10-12), perceiving his own depravity, the exceeding sinfulness of sin, the spirituality of the Law, the excellency of truth, the beauty of holiness, the loveliness of Christ.

We repeat: the Spirit communicates no light to the quickened soul which is not to be found in the written Word, but removes those obstacles which precluded its entrance, disposes the mind to attend unto the Truth (Acts xvi, 14) and receive it in the *love* of it (II Thess. ii, 10). When the Divine light shines into his heart the sinner perceives something of his horrible plight, is made conscious of his guilty and lost condition, feels that his sins are more in number than the hairs of his head. He now *knows* that there is " *no* soundness " (Isa. i, 6) in him, that all his righteousnesses are as filthy rags, and that he is utterly unable to help himself. But the Divine light shining in his heart also reveals the all-sufficient remedy. It awakens hope in his breast. It makes known to him " the glory of God " as it shines in the face of the Mediator, and the sun of righteousness now arises upon his benighted soul with healing in His wings or beams. Such knowledge of sin, of himself, of God, of the Saviour, is not obtained by mental effort but is communicated by the gracious operations of the Spirit.

"For the weapons of our warfare are not carnal, but mighty through God to the pulling down of strongholds; casting down imaginations, and every high thing that exalteth itself against the knowledge of God, and bringing into captivity every thought to the obedience of Christ" (II Cor. x, 4, 5). The apostle is here alluding to his ministry: its nature, difficulties, and success. He likened it unto a conflict between truth and error. The "weapons" or means he employed were not such as men of the world depended upon. The Grecian philosophers relied upon the arguments of logic or the attractions of rhetoric. Mohammed conquered by the force of arms. Rome's appeal is to the senses. But the ambassadors of Christ use nought but the Word and prayer, which are "mighty through God." Sinners are converted by the preaching of Christ crucified, and not by human wisdom, eloquence, or debate. The Gospel of Christ is the power of God unto salvation (Rom. i, 16).

Sinners are here pictured as sheltering in "strongholds." By hardness of heart, stubbornness of will, and strong prejudices they have fortified themselves against God and betaken themselves to a "refuge of lies" (Isa. xxviii, 15). But when the Truth is effectually applied to their hearts by the Spirit those strongholds are demolished and their haughty imaginations and proud reasonings are cast down. They no longer exclaim, "I cannot believe that a just God will make one a vessel unto honour and another to dishonour," or "I cannot believe a merciful God will consign any one to eternal torments." All objections are now silenced, rebels are subdued, lofty opinions of self cast down, pride is abased, and reverential fear, contrition, humility, faith and love take their place. Every thought is now brought into captivity to the obedience of Christ: they are conquered by grace, taken captives by love, and Christ henceforth occupies the throne of their hearts. Every faculty of the soul is now won over to God. Such is the great change wrought in a soul who experiences the miracle of grace: a worker of iniquity is made a loving and loyal child of obedience.

HOLINESS AND PRAYER

"If thou wert pure and upright, surely now He would awake for thee" (Job viii, 6). Holy persons are fit for holy duties, and only they. Sin is our separation from God, and holy duties are acts of communion with Him: how then shall sin and duty stand together? Make thy supplication unto God, but be thou pure and upright. What have unholy persons to do about holy things? God cannot like the services of those who are unlike Him. Prayer purifies, yet purifying must be a preparative to prayer. "If I regard iniquity in my heart, the Lord will not hear" (Psa. lxvi, 18). We are commanded to pray, "lifting up holy hands" (I Tim. ii, 8). "When ye spread forth your hands, I will hide Mine eyes from you; yea, when ye make many prayers I will not hear: your hands are full of blood" (Isa. i, 15). As He speaks out the fullness of His grace ("come now and let us reason together, though your sins be as scarlet," etc.), so also the necessity of gracious purity in man: "Wash ye, make you clean."

The prayers of the pure and upright are prevailing prayers. "The effectual fervent prayer of a righteous man availeth much" (James v, 16). Fervency of prayer effects nothing, unless the person praying be righteous. God is not melted into compassion by the heat of our words, but by the holiness of our hearts. In the prayer of a righteous man there is prevailing strength, such as God Himself yields to. " As a prince hast thou power with God, and has prevailed," said He to Jacob when He wrestled with him.

It is in no way contrary to the doctrine of free grace to say we must be holy if we desire to be heard. Bildad's doctrine is an excellent piece of divinity. Though he said before, " Thou must seek unto God and make supplication to Him, that out of His free grace He would bestow a blessing," yet he adds, " if thou wert pure and upright." Though we are not heard because we are pure and upright, yet none can come with a warrantable confidence to be heard in their impurity and hypocrisy: if they do, God will reject their confidences. It is impudence, not confidence, to make supplication to God with a reserve, or a resolve in secret to go on in sin. The greatest sinners in the world may come to God, they that are most impure and filthy, and may find favour; yet every man that cometh unto God must come with this desire—to have his impurities removed and his backslidings healed. " Unto the wicked God saith, What hast thou to do to declare My statutes, or that thou shouldest take My covenant in thy mouth? seeing thou hatest instruction and casteth My words behind thee " (Psa. l, 16, 17). It no way crosses the doctrine of grace when in the same breath we say that God will do us good freely for His own name's sake, and that we must be pure and upright who come to God. " With the pure Thou wilt show Thyself pure, and with the froward Thou wilt show Thyself froward " (Psa. xviii, 26). But doth the Lord take colour from everyone He meets, or change His temper as the company changes? He cannot do so, being without variableness or shadow of turning. God is pure and upright with the unclean and hypocritical, as well as with the pure and upright, and His actions show Him to be so. Though there be nothing in purity and sincerity which deserveth mercy, yet we cannot expect mercy without them. Our comforts are not grounded upon our graces, but our comforts are the fruits of them.

JOS. CARYL (1647).

(continued from back page)

which includes a great variety of blessings. Let us conclude with a short " Bible reading " which will serve to open the meaning of this " help " and at the same time set forth the different favours *for which* it is the Christian's privilege to *look upward*. 1. For a daily supply of grace: " In the morning will I direct my prayer unto Thee, and will look up " (Psa. v, 3). 2. For wisdom: " Neither know we what to do; but our eyes are upon Thee " (II Chron. xx, 12). 3. For deliverance from temptations: " Mine eyes are ever toward the Lord, for He shall pluck my feet out of the net " (Psa. xxv, 15). 4. For illumination and transformation: " They looked unto Him and were lightened " (Psa. xxxiv, 5). 5. For directions: " As the eyes of servants look unto the hand of their masters, . . . so our eyes wait upon the Lord " (Psa. cxxxiii, 2). 6. For comfort: " Mine eyes are unto Thee . . . leave not my soul destitute " (Psa. cxl, 8). 7. For the awing of the heart: " Lift up your eyes on high, and behold who hath created these things " (Isa. xl, 26). 8. For courage: " Not fearing the wrath of the king, for he endured as seeing Him who is invisible " (Heb. xi, 27). 9. For perseverance: " Let us run with patience the race that is set before us, looking unto Jesus " (Heb. xii, 1, 2). 10. For the appearing of Christ, " Looking for that Blessed Hope " (Titus ii, 13).

N.B. We need scarcely point out that the last paragraph contains " seed thoughts " which will furnish suitable material, if he develops them, for the sermonizer.

you your case was hopeless and trying to drive you to despair. When you were half delivered from that snare, he set you to work trying to save yourself by a process of reformation and religious exercises. But you found there was no relief for your lacerated conscience and burdened heart until you looked away from self and beheld " the Lamb of God " taking your place and suffering the Just for the unjust. Only as you turned the eye of a feeble and flickering faith unto the atoning Redeemer did your burden roll away and peace surpassing all understanding fill your soul.

But Satan is very persistent. Even though you did find pardon and peace at the Cross, he will not abandon his efforts to entangle you afresh, rob you of peace and joy, and bring you into darkness and bondage. He will now seek to get you absorbed with self, to dwell unduly upon your failings (instead of confessing them to Christ), and push you down into the slough of despond. If that succeeds not, he will endeavour to get you occupied with your graces and attainments, telling you what wonderful progress you have made, and puffing you up with pride. Or he will absorb your mind with your " service for Christ," your evangelistic zeal and love for souls, and try and persuade you of being an eminent Christian. We are not ignorant of his devices (II Cor. ii, 11), or, at any rate, we ought not to be so with God's Word in our hands, and therefore we should " resist the devil " (James iv, 7) and refuse to be ensnared by him—constantly looking upward to the Lord.

Many of God's children are ensnared by Satan today by quite a different device from those mentioned above, namely, by getting them unduly concerned with what is happening in the world. He persuades them that it is their duty to be well informed upon current events. That it is necessary for them to " keep up with the times " and take an intelligent interest in what is occurring in different parts of the earth, and particularly with the political and social conditions in their own country. He would fix their minds on the sensational items recorded in the newspapers, devoting much time to reading and listening-in to the news of the day. And what good is accomplished thereby? Your concern over the doings of the Kremlin and your dismay at the successes of the Vatican will not affect either of them one iota. No, but it will injuriously affect you! It will get you absorbed with carnal things and take the edge off your appetite for spiritual things. Look upward and contemplate the Divine Throne. God is ruling this world, working out His eternal purpose, having " His way in the whirlwind and in the storm " (Nah. i, 3).

Then emulate the Psalmist: said he, " I will lift up mine eyes unto the hills, from whence cometh my help," and then, turning from poetic language to plain prose, added, " My help cometh from the Lord " (cxxi, 1, 2). For the benefit of young preachers, let us say that were we sermonizing this verse our divisions would be: 1. A definite decision—" I will." 2. A right resolve—" I will lift up mine eyes." 3. An obvious object—" unto the hills " (the Lord). 4. An eager expectation—" from whence cometh [not " possibly may come "] my help." It was the look of faith and hope, and such a look is never put to confusion. It was the opposite of slothful inertia or fatalistic apathy. He did not say " I will wait until I feel moved by the Spirit," but determined upon discharging his own responsibility. He had no right to expect unless he sought it—sought it definitely, resolutely, earnestly, believingly. " Therefore will the Lord wait that He may be gracious unto you " (Isa. xxx, 18), and He often waits for our importunate waiting upon Him, for only then do we really value His gracious supplies.

" Mine help cometh from the Lord." That is a very comprehensive word

(continued on preceding page)

XXVI	MARCH 1947	No. 3

STUDIES IN THE SCRIPTURES

"Search the Scriptures." *John v, 39*

Publisher and Editor—ARTHUR W. PINK,
29 Lewis Street,
Stornoway, Isle of Lewis,
Scotland.

SPIRITUAL CONVERSE

" Let your speech be always with grace, seasoned with salt " (Col. iv. 6). What a noble faculty is speech! Man, alone of all the creatures of the earth, possesses it. Equally with the power of reasoning, it is one of the things which set man high above the animals, for there is no comparison between the chatter of the ape or the prattle of the parrot and the articulated language of man. What an influential faculty is speech! What we say is capable of eternally affecting those who hear us, and therefore the Bible ranks our words with our works. How often has the oratory of a single man swayed a whole nation! We know not how deeply impressed, helped or injured another may be by a single utterance. Speech is capable of high and wide service. Man is never more majestic than when he speaks with dignity, authority and power. Speech is indeed a blessed gift, but it is also a responsible charge. God will yet hold us to strict account for the use we make of our tongues: " Every idle word that men shall speak, they shall give account thereof in the Day of Judgment. For by thy words thou shalt be justified, and by thy words thou shalt be condemned " (Matt. xii, 36, 37). What an unspeakably solemn consideration is that!

While capable of producing much good, the tongue is also a power for much evil. This valuable gift from the Creator is frequently perverted, yea, generally put to an evil use. What guilt is acquired, what havoc is wrought, by profanity, by filthy talk, by slander, by angry and cruel utterances, by tale-bearing! How each of us needs to cry daily unto God, " Set a watch, O Lord, before my mouth; keep the door of my lips " (Psa. cxli, 3). What a fearful amount of gossip or idle talk the children of God are guilty of! In early English the word gossip was " God sip," meaning *related to God*; but, alas, gossip is now far more akin to the Devil. How few there are who make conscience of engaging in or encouraging (by listening to it!) profitless conversation! Far better to be dumb, and counted dull by our fellows, than to prostitute this faculty by pouring out a stream of empty and useless prattle which is worse than profitless, for " in the multitude of words there wanteth not *sin*, but he that refraineth his lips is wise " (Prov. x, 19). Even when an instructive and edifying subject of conversation *is* introduced, how quickly the average hearer seeks to turn it into a lower channel!

(continued on back page)

Important Notices

Please advise promptly of change in address, otherwise copies will be lost in the mails.

We are glad to send a sample copy to any of your friends whom you believe would be interested in this publication.

This magazine is published as "a work of faith and labour of love," the editor and his wife gladly giving their services free. There is no regular subscription price, as we do not wish the poor of the flock to be deprived. This does not mean that those looking for something for nothing may "help themselves." Those getting this magazine who are financially able and who receive spiritual help from its pages, are expected to gladly contribute towards its expenses; otherwise their names are dropped from our list.

Will those forwarding International Money Orders please have them made out to us at Stornoway, Isle of Lewis, Scotland. Checks (Cheques—Eng.) made out on U.S.A. Banks are not negotiable here, so please do not send them.

All unsigned articles are by the Editor.

CONTENTS

THE PRAYERS OF THE APOSTLES

39. Colossians i, 9-12.

"That ye might walk worthily of the Lord unto all pleasing, being fruitful in every good work" (verse 10). Having already pointed out the relation of this petition and its dependence upon the former one, and having explained what we conceive to be the meaning of " walk worthily of the Lord," we turn now to the next clause. Those added words, " unto all pleasing," serve both to define and amplify the previous sentence, informing us *how* we are to walk worthily and the *entirety* of that duty and privilege. We are to pray and strive to walk worthily of the Lord unto *all* pleasing. Not merely on the Sabbath, but every day; not simply comport ourselves reverently in the house of prayer, but conduct ourselves becomingly in the outside world. Our aim and endeavour must be to approve ourselves unto Christ, and please Him not only in those things which are esteemed by common consent, nor those which commend themselves unto and are agreeable to us, but also in those things which cross our wills and pinch the flesh. Nothing short of universal and uniform obedience is what is required from us. Christ died to deliver His people from the curse of the Law, but not from the duty of practising its precepts. He died, not to free His people from the service of God, but rather that they might be enabled to serve Him acceptably and with peace of conscience and joy of heart.

There are but two classes of people in the world, namely, those who are offensive unto God, and those who are esteemed by Him: the one are self-pleasers, the other self-deniers. Therein lies the essential difference between sincere souls and hypocrites: the former honestly endeavour to please Christ, and are regarded by Him as " the excellent of the earth " (Psa. xvi, 3); the latter seek the approbation of men and live to gratify self, and therefore are they unto God as " vessels wherein is no pleasure " (Hos. viii, 8). There is no other alternative possible but either living to please self or please the Lord. No matter what may be their pretensions, what name they go under, what be their creed, how highly regarded by their fellows, if self be their " God," they are hateful unto the Holy One. Those in whom God delights are the ones who are regulated by His will, who live for His glory, whose daily walk honours Him, who are fruitful in good works. How that simple but discriminating classification serves to expose the empty profession all around us! Tens of thousands call themselves by the name of Christ, but they wear not His yoke, take not up their cross (the principle of self-abasement and sacrifice), follow not His example.

Unless we have fully given ourselves up to God and are genuinely seeking to please Him in all that we do, then our supposed conversion was merely a delusion. If the gratifying of our natural desires be our chief pleasure, we are yet in our sins. If we be sowing to the flesh, we shall of the flesh reap corruption. Make no mistake, dear reader, whoever you be: the Omniscient One cannot be imposed upon, neither will He accept a divided heart. No man can serve two masters. If you think to placate God by acting piously on the Sabbath, while thoroughly worldly through the week, then you are woefully mistaken. God will not be served with any reserve or limitation, but requires us to love Him with all our hearts, soul and strength. In order to please Him we have to shun whatever He hates: mortify the flesh, separate from the world, resist the Devil. The Lord will not be served with that which costs us nothing (II Sam. xxiv, 2). Those who detest such strictness and look upon puritans as idiots, will discover in the day to come who were the ones that played the fool and trifled with their souls.

But is it possible that a mere creature of the earth, and a fallen and sinful one at that, can please the great and holy God? Certainly it is. Of Enoch it is recorded that " he pleased God " (Heb. xi, 15). That must not be carnalized as though He were subject to emotions; neither must it be emptied of all meaning. The Lord is so infinitely above us that no analogy can be found in human relations. But to aid our feeble perceptions, take a tutor who has gone to particular pains in instructing one of his scholars: is he not gratified when he sees him at the top of his class? or when parents behold their children putting into practice those precepts which they have so lovingly and earnestly instilled into them, do they not rejoice? So, when we act as becometh His people, we are " approved unto God." Said David, ' He delivered me [from enemies] because He delighted in me " (II Sam. xxii, 20). " Such as are upright in the way are His delight " (Prov. xi, 20). ' The Lord taketh pleasure in them that fear Him, in them that hope in His mercy " (Psa. cxlvii, 11). " The prayer of the upright is His delight " (Prov. xv, 8). In reality, it is God approving *His own* handiwork, esteeming that which His Spirit has wrought in us; nevertheless, we are not passive therein, but determine and perform as He works in us both to will and to do of His good pleasure.

As there are degrees in wickedness and obnoxiousness unto God, so there are of bringing delight unto Him. That for which Christians are here taught to pray—and therefore to diligently and constantly strive after—is to " walk worthily of the Lord unto *all* pleasing," which includes to " walk not in the counsel of the ungodly " (Psa. i, 2), to " walk in the Law of the Lord " (Psa. cxix, 1), to " walk in newness of life " (Rom. vii, 4), to " walk by faith and not by sight " (II Cor. v, 7), to " walk in the spirit " (Gal. v, 17), to " walk in love " (Eph. v, 2), to "walk circumspectly " (Eph. v, 15). As an aid thereto, observe the following rules. First, be ever on your guard in avoiding everything that is grievous to God, and in order to that, cultivate a sense of His *presence.* If you are on your best behaviour when in the company of cherished friends, how much more so should you be in the presence of your heavenly Friend ! If the knowledge of human lookers-on restrains you from acts of sin, much more should a respect for the Holy One. That was what governed Joseph: " How then can I do this great wickedness, and sin against God? " (Gen. xxxix, 9).

Second, be diligent in choosing those things which God esteems. When Solomon sought wisdom that he might rule Israel righteously, we are told it " pleased the Lord that Solomon had asked that thing " (I Kings iii, 10). The more our hearts be set upon things above, and the more we aim at God's glory, the greater pleasure will He have in us. Third, be whole-hearted in your devotedness to the Lord. There must be no picking and choosing among His precepts: no in with one duty and out with another. The whole scope of the Christian life should be a studying to show oneself approved unto God: the understanding perceiving what is due to Him, the conscience swayed by His authority, the affections drawn out in adoring homage, the will surrendered to Him. Caleb was one who greatly pleased the Lord, and of him it is recorded that " he *wholly* followed the Lord God " (Josh. xiv, 14). Fourth, meditate in God's Law day and night (Psa. i, 2): make it your constant concern how to serve and honour Him, remembering that He is more pleased with obedience than with your worship and free-will offerings (I Sam. xv, 22). Fifth, maintain a steady dependence upon the Lord, for you have no strength of your own: He must be daily sought unto for the needed wisdom and power. Frequent the throne of grace that there you may "find grace to help in time of need."

Further: if we are to be approved by God, it is by no means sufficient that "we make clean the outside of the cup and platter," yet many suppose that is all that matters. " Cleanse *first* that which is *within* " (Matt. xxiii, 26) is our Lord's command, whereas in this degenerate day such a task is not merely relegated to the second place, but it is given none at all. It is the Devil who seeks to persuade people that they are not responsible for the state of their hearts, and can no more change them than they can alter the stars in their courses. Such a lie is very agreeable unto those who think to be carried to heaven on downy beds of ease, and there are few left to disillusion them. But no regenerate soul, with God's Word before him, will credit such a falsehood. The Divine demand is plain: " Keep thy heart with all diligence, for out of it are the issues of life " (Prov. iv, 23). That is the principal task set us, for it is at *the heart* God ever looks, and there can be no pleasing of Him while it be unattended to ; yea, woe be unto those who disregard it. He who makes no honest endeavour to cast out sinful thoughts and evil imaginations, and does not mourn over their presence, is a moral leper. He who makes no conscience of the workings of unbelief, the cooling of his affections, the surgings of pride, is a stranger to any work of grace in his soul.

Not only does God bid thee to keep thy heart, but He requires thee to do it "with all diligence": that is, to make it your main concern and constant care. The Hebrew word for "keep" signifies *to guard.* Watch over thine heart (the soul or inward man) as a precious treasure, of which thieves are ever ready to rob thee. Guard it as a garrison into which enemies will enter if you be not on the alert. Attend to it as a garden in which the Lord would regale Himself (Song vi, 2), removing all weeds and keeping its flowers and spices fragrant: that is, be diligent in mortifying your lusts and in cultivating your graces. The devotions of your lips and the labours of your hands are unacceptable to the Lord if your heart be not right in His sight. What husband would appreciate the domestic attentions of his wife if he had good reason to believe her affections were alienated from him? God takes note not only of the matter of our actions, but the springs from which they proceed, the motives actuating them, as also the manner in which they are done and our design in the same. If we become slack and careless in any of these respects it shows that our love has cooled and that we have become weary of God.

The One with whom we have to do "is a God of knowledge, and by Him actions are weighed" (Sam. ii, 3) in the balances of righteousness and truth, and whatever is "found wanting" or is deficient is rejected by Him. Nay more, we are told that "all the ways of a man are clean in his own eyes; but the Lord weigheth *the spirits*" (Prov. xvi, 2): i.e. that which lies behind the actions, which colours as well as prompts them. Self-love may blind our judgment and make us partial in our own cause, but we cannot deceive the Omniscient One. God not only brings our actions to the test and standard of holiness but the frames of our spirits which inspired them. "The Lord God trieth the hearts and the reins" (Psa. vii, 9): that is, the inward principles from which our conduct proceeds. He scrutinizes our affections and motives, whether we be sincere or no. The Lord God is "He that pondereth the heart" (Prov. xxiv, 12), observing all its motions: its most secret intentions are open unto Him. He perceives when your contributions to His cause are made cheerfully or graudgingly. He knows whether your alms-deeds are done in order to be seen of men and admired by them, or whether they issue from disinterested benevolence. He knows whether your expressions of good will and love toward your brethren are feigned or genuine.

Since the Lord looketh on and pondereth the heart, should not we do so too? Since from the heart proceed the issues of life, should not we make it our chief concern and care? Out of the heart proceed all the evils mentioned by our Lord in Mark vii, 21, 22. But it is equally true that out of the heart proceed the fruit described in Galatians v, 22, 23: "a good man out of the good treasure of the heart bringeth forth good things" (Matt. xii, 35), but the good man will *not* do so unless he diligently resists his inward corruptions and tends and nourishes his graces. If we are to walk worthily of the Lord "unto all pleasing" we must frequently "search and try our ways" (Lam. iii, 40), take our spiritual pulse, and ascertain whether all be well within. We must heed that injunction, "Stand in awe, and sin not: commune with your own heart upon your bed, and be still" (Psa. iv, 4) that ye may ascertain your spiritual condition. We must daily attend to that precept, "Little children, keep yourselves from idols" (I John v, 20), lest anything be allowed that place in our affections which belongs alone to Christ. We must constantly examine our motives and challenge our aims and intentions, for *they* are what count most with God. We must "cleanse ourselves from all filthiness of the spirit as well as of the flesh" (II Cor. vii, 1).

Alas, how sadly has the standard been relaxed! How little is now heard, even in the centres of orthodoxy, of "walking worthily of the Lord unto all pleasing"! How very few today are being informed that God requires them to keep their *hearts* with all diligence, and to work out their own salvation with fear and trembling. Will not the Lord yet say unto many an unfaithful occupant of the modern pulpit (and editors of religious magazines), "You have not spoken of Me the thing that is right"? You did not make known the high requirements of My holiness, nor teach My people those things which would most "adorn the doctrine" they profess. You have been tithing mint and anise and cummin, but omitting "the weightier matters": concerned with politics, wrangling over forms of church government, speculating about prophecy, but failing to insist on practical godliness. No wonder the "churches"—Calvinistic, equally with others—are in such a low state of spirituality. But the failure of those in the pulpit does not excuse those in the pew. The individual Christian still has access to God's Word, and even if there were none others left on earth who respect it, *he* is responsible to be regulated by its elevated and exacting teachings. O Christian reader, whatever others do or do not, see to it that *you* turn Colossians i, 10, into daily prayer, and strive to translate it into practice.

It is for the glory of God and your own good that you do so. If you be careless about your walk, and indifferent as to whether the state of your heart be pleasing or displeasing unto the Lord, then His ear will be closed to your prayers! And that is something else about which little is preached today, even in those quarters which style themselves "places of truth." Yet the Scriptures are explicit thereon: "Whatsoever we ask, we receive of Him, *because* we keep His commandments and do those things which are *pleasing* in His sight" (I John iii, 32): that cannot be "legalistic," for those are the words of the Holy Spirit. It is not because our obedience is in anywise meritorious, but because this is the *order* of things which Divine holiness has established. God has appointed an inseparable connection between the acceptableness of our conduct and of our petitions. If we would have His ear then we must attend unto His voice. We cannot expect God to grant our requests while we ignore what He requires of us. Not that our obedience ingratiates us into God's favour, but that it is a necessary adjunct to our receiving favours at His hand. We must delight ourselves in the Lord if we would have Him grant us the desires of our heart (Psa. xxxvii, 4).

As the prohibitions ever imply the performance of the opposites—as "thou shalt not kill" signifies thou shalt use all lawful means to preserve life, and "thou shalt not commit adultery" involves thou shalt live chastely— so each positive precept argues its negative, as I John iii, 22, also imports we shall not receive from God those things we ask of Him if we keep not His commandments and do not those things which are pleasing in His sight. Should any uncertainty remain in this point, then Proverbs xxviii, 9, at once removes it: "He that turneth away his ear from hearing the Law, even his prayer shall be abomination." God has appointed an inseparable connection between the performance of duty and the enjoyment of privilege. Psalm lxvi, 18, is yet more searching, showing again what God requires within as well as without: "If I regard iniquity in my *heart*, the Lord will not hear me." If I countenance and secretly foster any sin, even though I practise it not; if I view it favourably or even palliate and excuse it, His ear is closed against me. Unsorrowed and unconfessed sins prevent many a prayer from being answered. The Holy One will not connive at sin "For God to accept our devotions while we are delighting in sin, would make Him the God of hypocrites " (Spurgeon).

If we are to " walk worthily of the Lord unto all pleasing " then we must be most attentive in the cultivation of *faith*, " for without faith it is impossible to please Him " (Heb. xi, 6). The more fully and constantly we trust Him, the more we walk by faith, the more will the Lord delight in us. Does not a husband, a wife, a parent, a friend, like to be confided in? In an infinitely higher sense God is pleased when we cling to Him in the darkness, look to Him for the fulfilling of His promises, count upon His loving kindness. But He is displeased when we doubt His word or suspect His love. Faith in God, in His precepts, in His promises, is the grand and distinguishing principle which is to actuate all our conduct, for it is that which honours and magnifies Him. Abraham was " strong in faith, giving glory to God," being fully assured that He would—despite all appearances to the contrary—make good His word (Rom. iv, 20, 21). To give glory to God is to regard Him as being what He really is—all-mighty, faithful. It is to show by our conduct that we give Him full credit (so to speak) that He can and will do what He has said.

" By Him therefore let us offer the sacrifice of praise to God continually . . . giving thanks to His name. But to do good and to communicate forget not: for with such sacrifices God is well pleased " (Heb. xiii, 15, 16). Then let us not be backward in offering them. God loves to hear the songs of His children. The " sweet Psalmist of Israel " is how He designated David. " Whoso offereth praise glorifieth Me " (Psa. l, 23). If our walk be regulated by the Rule God has given us, then our praise will be acceptable unto Him, for it is the breathing of love and joy, rendering to Him His due. Yea, more it will—as it is the spontaneous, hearty, grateful tribute of the heart—*glorify* Him. Praise is an exalting of God's name, a proclaiming of His excellency, a publishing of His renown, an adoring of His goodness, a breaking open the box of our ointment, and therefore it is a " sweet savour " unto Him. " I will magnify Him with thanksgiving . . . this shall *please* the Lord better than an ox " (Psa. lxix, 30, 31)—how comforting was that for the one who was unable to bring Him a costly offering! If God deems it an honour to be well pleased with our praises and condescends to accept them as an offering from us, let us be frequently engaged in this delightful exercise and act like spiritual larks.

But let it not be concluded that it is only in the *devotional* side of our lives that we may give delight unto God. Different by far is the teaching of His Word. The Lord not only takes notice of our attitude toward and actions unto Himself, but also of our conduct and dealings with our fellows. We may please Him—and it should be our diligent aim so to do—in the shop, the office, the factory, the home. " A false balance is abomination to the Lord, but a just weight is His delight " (Prov. xi, 1). Under that word " balance " we are to include all weights and measures, descriptions of articles and profits therefrom. Such a verse as that should be carefully pondered and kept constantly in mind by all who are engaged in any form of business, whether they be employers or employees, making conscience of all their words and deeds. To misrepresent a piece of merchandise, to overcharge, or to deliberately short-change a customer, is a grievous sin, which, though it may escape the notice of men, is recorded against us by the Holy One, and we shall be made to pay dearly for the same. Contrariwise, to be fair and honest in our trading is pleasing unto God: "such as are upright in their way are His delight" (Prov. xi, 20).

Not only does God take notice of and record the sins of those who are guilty of unjust and fraudulent practices, but He refuses the hypocritical homage of all such. There is no bribing of the Divine Judge, nor can He be imposed upon by a pious demeanour in those who wrong their fellows. They who grind the faces of the poor through the week, and equally those who fail to supply a fair day's work for a fair day's pay, only mock the Lord when they sing His praises and make an offering to His cause on the Sabbath day. "The sacrifice of the wicked is an abomination unto the Lord: but the prayer of *the upright* is His delight" (Prov. xv, 8). The external acts of worship of those whose business dealings are corrupt are an offence unto the Most High, and it is the bounden duty of the pulpit to announce it. "He that turneth away his ear from hearing the Law [which enjoins loving our neighbour as ourself], even his prayer shall be abomination" (Prov. xxviii, 9). We do but deceive ourselves if we imagine God hearkens to our petitions while our every-day lives give the lie to our devotions. On the other hand, "The righteous Lord loveth righteousness: His countenance doth [favourably] behold the upright" (Psa. vii, 11). Everything we do either pleases or displeases God.

LIFE AND TIMES OF JOSHUA
19.   The Ark.

"Yet there shall be a space between you and it, about two thousand cubits by measure: come not near unto it, that ye may know the way by which ye must go; for ye have not passed this way heretofore" (iii, 4). Having pointed out some of the probable reasons why the ark was to proceed so far in advance of the people, we must now turn to consider the meaning of the last clause of this verse. Personally, we consider the commentators and sermonizers have quite missed the force of the "for ye have not passed this way heretofore" when they explain it is signifying "For ye are about to march over *unfamiliar* ground." Admittedly the Hebrew, and at first glance this English rendering, appears to decidedly favour such a view, yet a careful weighing of this clause in the light of its whole setting seem to require a different interpretation of it, understanding it to mean "for ye have not marched in this *manner* hitherto." Nor is that by any means a wresting of the text, for though the Hebrew word "derek" be translated "way" in the vast majority of instances, yet it is rendered "manner" eight times—as, for example, in Genesis xix, 31; Isaiah x, 24, 26).

To give as the reason why the children of Israel should follow the ark on this occasion as "because ye are about to tread new and strange ground" seems to possess little or no point, for had not *that* been equally true on most of their journeying across the wilderness! But, it will be asked, to what else is the reference? We answer, something entirely different from what had marked their marches previously, as the "heretofore" indicates. The immediate context is concerned with the informing of Israel as to when they were to advance: "when ye see the ark of the covenant of the Lord your God, and the priests the Levites bearing it, *then* ye shall remove from your place and go after it" (verse 3). Hitherto, it was only when the cloud moved that they did so too (see Ex. iii, 21, 22, xl, xxxviii); "whether it was by day or by night that the cloud was taken up, they journeyed " (Num. ix, 21, and cf. xiv, 14). During the whole of the preceding forty years Israel had been led by that supernatural " pillar of cloud," but now and henceforth that cloud was no longer to be with them. It was a visible token of Jehovah's presence, especially granted unto Moses, and with his death it disappeared.

A different arrangement was now made, a new means for recognizing God's will concerning their journeyings was now revealed unto Israel, another symbol of Jehovah's presence should henceforth strike terror into the hearts of His enemies. The ark of the covenant now took, in an important sense, a new position. Formerly, when journeying the ark had been carried in the midst of the host. It had indeed gone before Israel on one previous occasion " to search out a resting place for them " (Num. x, 33), yet the very next verse informs us " and the cloud of the Lord was upon them by day, when they went out of the camp "; and, as we have seen, the immediate sequel was the fatal apostasy of that generation. The cloud had moved above the ark (cf. Lev. xvi, 2), where all the people could see it easily and follow the ark without inconvenience; but now the cloud was no longer with them—the ark becoming their visible guide.. Another indication of this new arrangement appears in the ones who bore the ark. A specific command had been given that the ark should be carried by the sons of Kohath (Num. iii, 30, 31; iv, 15), but here " the priests " were appointed as its bearers.

Thus, in keeping with this new venture by the new generation, a different order of procedure was appointed—" ye have not travelled in this manner before." The first generation of Israel had been a lamentable and utter failure, but there can never be any failure with the Lord God, nor in the accomplishment of His eternal counsels. God always takes care of His own glory and of the full and final blessing of His people according to His purpose; yea, He never suffers them to be divorced or pass out of His own hands. In His wondrous wisdom and amazing grace God has inseparably united the two, and therefore does He make all things work together for the accomplishment of each alike, for He has made His people and their blessing a constituent part of His glory—" Israel My glory " (Isaiah. xlvi, 13). Thus we see how fitting it was that the ark of the covenant went in advance of the twelve tribes on their entrance into Canaan, which the Lord had chosen to be the place where He would make a full display of Himself in the midst of His people. As the Lord had magnified Himself before Pharaoh and his hosts in Egypt and at the Red Sea in connection with Israel's exodus, so now He would magnify Himself in the sight of the Canaanites as He bared His arm on behalf of His people.

This is indeed a marvellous and blessed truth that God has bound up the good of His people with His own manifestative glory, that at the same time that He furthers the one He promotes the other also. It is a truth which ought to exercise a powerful influence upon our hearts and lives, both in strengthening holy confidence and in preventing unholy conduct. It furnishes us with an invincible plea when praying for the prosperity of God's cause on earth or for our own individual fruitfulness: " grant it, O Lord, for the honour of Thy great name." It was on *that* ground Moses, in a sore crisis, presented his petition (Num. xiv, 15-17), so Joshua (vii, 9), Hezekiah (II Kings xix, 19), Joel (ii, 17). But One far greater than any of those prayed " Father, the hour is come, glorify Thy Son, that Thy Son also may glorify Thee " (John xvii, 1). And should not each Christian say, " Father undertake for me, that Thy child may—in his measure—glorify Thee"! Yet this wondrous truth has a bearing on duty as well as privilege. Since my good and God's glory be inseparably united, how careful I should be in avoiding everything which would bring reproach upon His name! How diligent in seeking to tread that path where communion with Him is alone to be had! How zealous in "doing all things to the glory of God" (I Cor. x, 31).

"And Joshua said unto the people, Sanctify yourselves, for tomorrow the Lord will do wonders among you" (iii, 5). The word "sanctify" is one of the most difficult terms to define that is used in Scripture: partly because of the great variety of objects to which it is applied; partly because it has so many different shades of meaning; partly because doctrinally and experimentally considered there is both a Divine and a human side to sanctification, and few find it easy to adjust those two sides in their minds. With their customary partiality Calvinistic writers and preachers confine themselves almost entirely to the Church's sanctification by the Father (setting her apart from the non-elect by His eternal decree), by the Son (who cleansed her from her sins and adorned her by His merits), and by the Holy Spirit (by her regeneration and daily renewing), and say little or nothing upon the necessity and duty of the Christian's *sanctifying himself*. Whereas Arminian writers and preachers dwell almost exclusively on the human side of things, as the believer's dedication of himself unto God and His service, and his daily cleansing of himself by the Word. Since the days of the Puritans few indeed have made a full-orbed presentation of this important truth.

The first time the term occurs in Holy Writ is Genesis ii, 3, and, as is invariably the case, this *initial* mention at once indicates its essential meaning and content: "And God blessed the seventh day and sanctified it," which obviously means that He separated it from the other six days and set it apart for His own particular use—such is the underlying and root idea in all its subsequent occurrences where *God* Himself is the Agent or Actor. The next reference is Exodus xiii, 2: "Sanctify unto Me all the firstborn: whatsoever openeth the womb among the children of Israel, of man or beast: it is Mine": that was something which the Lord required *from them*, namely, to dedicate and devote the firstborn entirely unto Him. The third occurrence is in Exodus xix: "And the Lord said unto Moses, Go unto the people and sanctify them today and tomorrow, and let them wash their clothes. And be ready against the third day, for the third day the Lord will come down in the sight of all the people upon mount Sinai" (verses 10, 11, and see verse 15). There the word "sanctify" manifestly has reference unto a personal cleansing by the Israelites themselves, to fit them for the approach of the thrice Holy One.

Now it is quite clear that the injunction which Joshua gave unto Israel in verse 5 was of precisely the same import as that which Moses received for the people in Exodus xix. The Lord was about to appear on their behalf, and they were required to be in a meet condition. When God bade Jacob go to Bethel and make there an altar unto Him, we are told that the patriarch said unto his household, "Put away the strange gods that are among you and be clean, and change your garments" (Gen. xxxv, i, 2)—idols and the worship of the Lord do not accord. Unto the elders of Bethlehem the prophet said, "I am come to sacrifice unto the Lord: sanctify yourselves, and come with me to the sacrifice" (I Sam. xvi, 5). In each case the reference was first unto the removal of ceremonial defilement, the putting away of all outward pollution, and then to bringing their hearts into a suitable frame towards the One with whom they had to do, for God has never been satisfied with mere external purification and punctiliousness of formal worship (Isa. xxix, 13, 14). Sacred duties call for diligent preparation on the part of those who would discharge them. Holy things are not to be touched with unholy hands nor approached with hearts filled by the world (Psa. xxvi, 6; I Tim. ii, 8).

Christians are bidden to draw near unto God, " having their hearts sprinkled from an evil conscience [i.e. all known sin forsaken and confessed] and their bodies washed with pure water "—their daily walk regulated and purified by the Word (Heb. x, 22), for we must not insult Him by carelessness and moral unfitness. In order thereto we need to give constant heed to that precept, " Let us cleanse ourselves from all filthiness of the flesh and spirit, perfecting holiness in the fear of God " (II Cor. vii, 1). And be it carefully noted that " cleanse ourselves " is as much a part of the inspired Word of God as is " the blood of Jesus Christ His Son cleanseth us from all sin," and that that latter statement is qualified by (though scarcely ever quoted!) " If we walk in the light as He is in the light." The Holy One requires us to sanctify ourselves both internally and externally, and if we do not, our worship is unacceptable. " If a man purge himself from these [the things which " dishonour "] he shall be a vessel unto honour, sanctified, and meet for the Master's use, prepared unto every good work " (II Tim. ii, 21). " Every man that hath this hope in him *purifieth himself* even as He is pure " (I John iii, 3). How? By mortifying his lusts and cultivating his graces, by daily repentings and renewings of his consecration.

" Sanctify yourselves," then, has been an imperative requirement of God upon His people in all generations. The only difference which the change of covenant has made is that, under the old, their sanctification of themselves consisted chiefly in a ceremonial and external purification, while that of the new is principally a moral and internal one, and where *that* obtains the outward life will be adjusted to our Rule. No servant of Christ declares " all the counsel of God " who fails to press that imperative requirement of God's upon His people, and if he be silent thereon he " withholds " that which is " profitable for them." *We* must " draw nigh to God " if we would have Him draw nigh unto us (James iv, 8), and, as that verse goes on to tell the careless and those with unexercised consciences, in order to draw near unto Him aright we must " cleanse our hands and purify our hearts "! " Who shall ascend into the hill of the Lord? or who shall stand in His holy place? " which in New Testament language means, Who shall be received by God as an acceptable worshipper? The inspired answer is, " He that hath clean hands and a pure heart, who hath not lifted up his soul unto vanity, nor sworn deceitfully " (Psa. xxiv, 3, 4). Alas that so little heed is now given to such verses.

" And Joshua said unto the people, Sanctify yourselves, for tomorrow the Lord will do wonders among you." That was an enforcing of their moral responsibility. It was a call for them to cleanse themselves and dedicate themselves unto the Lord their God. It was a bidding of them to prepare themselves by prayer and meditation, to recall God's gracious interventions in the past, to ponder His ineffable holiness, awful majesty, mighty power and abundant mercy, and thereby bring their hearts into a fit frame, so that with faith, reverence and admiration they might behold the great work which Jehovah was about to do for them. They must be in a suitable condition in order to witness such a manifestation of His glory: their hearts must be "perfect toward Him"—sincere and upright, honest and holy—if He was to "show Himself strong in their behalf" (II Chron. xvi, 9). Have we not here the explanation why God is *not* now performing marvels in the churches?—they are too carnal and worldly! And is not this the reason why a way is not being made through our personal "jordans"? And why we receive not wondrous and blessed discoveries of His glory—we are not "sanctified" in a practical way nor sufficiently separated from the world.

"And Joshua said unto the people, Sanctify yourselves, for tomorrow the Lord will do wonders among you." Observe the positive and confident language of Joshua: there was no doubt whatever in his mind that their covenant God would perform a miracle on their behalf, and therefore he assured them accordingly. What an example for Christ's servant to follow! He has no right to expect that his flock will wax valiant in fight if their shepherd be full of unbelief and fear. And, too, when urging upon them the duty of self-sanctification, he should fail not to add the encouragement, "the Lord will do wonders," for sure it is that the more we shun that which defiles, and devote ourselves unto God's service and glory, the more will He work mightily in us, for us and through us. It is quite possible that on this occasion Joshua had in mind that word, "And it came to pass when the ark set forward that Moses said, Rise up, O Lord, and let Thine enemies be scattered" (Num. x, 35), for certain Joshua was that when the ark should now advance the waters of the Jordan would recede.

"And Joshua spake unto the priests, saying, Take up the ark of the covenant and pass over before the people. And they took up the ark of the covenant and went before the people" (verse 6). Having directed the people what to do, Joshua now gives instruction unto the priests. Thereby he acted in strict accord with his own personal commission ("do according to all that is written in this book of the Law" (i, 8)—i.e. the Pentateuch), for in preparation of Jehovah's descent upon Sinai Moses had given express charge to the priests as well as to the people (Ex. xix, 22). In the charge here given to the priests we see how their subjection to the revealed will of God was put to the proof, how their faith and courage were tested, and how their reverence for the symbol of the Lord's presence was to be manifested. Corresponding unto them today are the ministers of the Gospel, concerning whom T. Scott well said, "They are especially required to set before the people an example of obedience, patience, and unshakable confidence in God, by abiding in their perilous position or difficult stations which He has assigned them, when others fear to pass that way; and in so doing they may expect peculiar support and protection."

The people were commanded to follow the priests as far as they carried the ark, but no farther, and God's children today are responsible to heed and obey His servants (Heb. xiii, 7, 17) only while they set forth and honour Him of whom the ark was a figure. Namely, Christ; yet not simply as a Saviour, but in the fullness of His threefold office: as our Prophet or Teacher (the Law within the ark), our Priest (the propitiatory upon it), our King and Lord ("the ark of *the covenant*"). But the minister of the Gospel is required to do more than faithfully preach Christ, namely *live* Him: "Be thou an example of the believers in word, in conversation, in love, in spirit, in faith, in purity" (I Tim. iv, 12); "In all things showing thyself a pattern of good works" (Titus ii, 7; and cf. I Thess. ii 10; I Peter v. 3). The minister is to set before his people a godly example. Unless he takes the lead in enduring hardships and facing dangers (not showing more concern for his own ease and safety), then his exhortations unto self-denial and courageous action will have no power upon his hearers.

THE DOCTRINE OF REVELATION

3. The Existence of God.

" The heavens declare the glory of God, and the firmament showeth His handiwork " (Psa. xix, 1). The stellar heavens proclaim the attributes of their Maker, bespeaking not only His existence but His excellency; while the atmospheric heavens exhibit His unique skill, revealing to us both their Author and His wondrous wisdom. Upon the former many have descanted, but the latter has received very much less notice. The " firmament " signifies " the expanse " and, as distinct from the sphere of the more distant planets, refers to the atmosphere surrounding the earth—the air in which the clouds are seen. The Hebrew verb rendered " showeth " means to " place before " for our thoughtful inspection, as challenging our most serious and reverent contemplation. Though the atmosphere be not an object of our sight, and for that reason is little regarded, yet it is a most remarkable contrivance or apparatus, a source of many advantages to us, and one which richly repays those who carefully consider it and take pleasure in " seeking out " the works of the Lord (Psa. cxi, 2).

The atmospheric pressure upon a person of ordinary stature is equal to the weight of fourteen tons, and it scarcely needs to be pointed out that the falling upon him of a very much lighter object would break every bone in his body and drive all breath out of his lungs. Why then is it that we suffer no inconvenience from it, nay, thrive therein and enjoy it? Here is a phenomenon which, if thus viewed, is not unlike that which so awed Moses of old when he beheld the miracle of the burning bush—the combustible substance all aflame and yet not consumed. And by what means are we preserved from that which, considered abstractly, is such a deadly menace? By the Creator's having so devised that the air permeates the whole of our body, and by its peculiar nature pressing equally in all directions, all harm and discomfort is prevented—" the heads of the thigh and arm bones are kept in their sockets by atmospheric pressure " (International Encyclopedia).

The air, commissioned by its benign Author, performs many offices for the good of mankind. While it covers us without any conscious weight, the air reflects, and thereby increases, the life-giving heat of the sun. The air does this for us much as our garments supply additional heat to our bodies. If the reader has, like the writer, climbed a mountain and reached a point thirteen thousand feet above sea level, then he has proved for himself how considerably the solar warmth is diminished as the quality of the air becomes more attenuated. At its base the clime was comfortably warm, but had we remained a night on its summit, death by freezing would have been the outcome. What reason have we, then, to bless the Disposer of all things for placing us at a level where we suffer no ill or inconvenience from the atmosphere, for the combined wisdom of men could no more moderate it than regulate the actions of the ocean.

The air co-operates with our lungs, thereby ventilating the blood and refining the fluids of the body, stimulating the animal secretions, and attempering our natural warmth. We could live for months without the light of the sun or the glimmering of a star, but if deprived of air for a very few minutes we quickly faint and die. Not to us alone does this " universal nurse " (as Hervey eloquently styled her) minister: it is this gaseous element enveloping the earth which both sustains and feeds all vegetable life. Again, the air conveys to our nostrils those minute particles (effluvia) which are emitted by odiferous bodies, so that we are both refreshed by the sweet fragrance of flowers and warned by offensive smells to withdraw from a dangerous situation or beware of injurious food. So, by the undulating motions of the air, all the diversities of sound are conducted to the ear, for if you were placed in a room from which all air had been withdrawn and a full orchestra (wearing artificial respirators) played at fortissimo, not a sound would you hear.

Not only does the air waft to our senses all the charming modulations of music and the elevating influences of refined and edifying conversation, but it also acts as a seasonable and faithful monitor. For example, should I be walking along the road, my eyes looking off unto some object or my mind so absorbed that I am completely off my guard, and a vehicle be bearing down upon me from behind, though my eyes perceive not my danger, yet my ear takes alarm and informs me of my peril, even while it be some distance away, and with kindly if clamorous importunity bids me act for my safety. Let us then inquire, what is it that has endowed the atmosphere with such varied and beneficient adaptations, so that it diffuses vitality and health, retains and modifies solar heat, transmits odours and conveys sound? Must we not rather ask " Whom? " and answer, " This also cometh from the Lord of hosts, which is wonderful in counsel and excellent in working " (Isa. xxviii, 29).

" Hearken unto this, O Job: Stand still and consider the wondrous works of God. Dost thou know when God disposed them [i.e. the winds and clouds, the thunder and lightning, the frost and rain], and caused the light of His cloud to shine? Dost thou know the balancing of the clouds, the wondrous works of Him who is perfect in knowledge " (Job xxxvii, 14-16). The same queries are addressed unto each of us, and call for calm and quiet reflection. " Stand still and consider the wondrous works of God " which appear in the firmament. That is, cease for an hour from your feverish activities and devote yourself, as a rational creature, to serious reflection, and compose yourself for thoughtful contemplation. " Consider " what is brought forth in, by and from the atmosphere, and then be filled with reverent wonderment and awe. Ponder well the fact that water is much denser and far heavier than the air, and yet it rises into it, makes a way through it, and takes up a position in its uppermost regions! One would just as soon expect the rivers to run backward to their source; yet Divine wisdom has contrived a way to render it not only practicable but a matter of continual occurrence.

There in the firmament we behold an endless succession of clouds fed by evaporation from the ocean, drawn thither by the action of the sun. The clouds are themselves a miniature ocean, suspended in the air with a skill which as far transcends that of the wisest man as his knowledge does that of an infant in arms. It is because so very few " stand still and consider " the amazing fact of millions of tons of water being suspended over their heads and sustained there in the thinnest parts of the atmosphere, that such a prodigy is lost upon them. The writer recalls the impressions made upon him over thirty years ago as he was driven around the Roosevelt Dam in Arizona and inspected that great engineering feat: probably some of our readers have experienced similar ones as they have beheld some huge reservoir of human contrivance. But what are *they* in comparison with the immeasurably vaster quantities of water which, without any conduits of stone or barriers of cement, are suspended in the clouds, and kept there in a buoyant state!

The clouds, as another pointed out, " travel in detached parties, and in the quality of itinerant cisterns round all the terrestial globe. They fructify by proper communications of moisture the spacious pastures of the wealthy and gladden with no less liberal showers the cottager's little garden. Nay, so condescending is the benignity of the great Proprietor that they satisfy the desolate and waste ground, and cause, even in the most uncultivated wilds, the bud of the tender herb to spring forth, so that the natives of the lonely desert, those savage herds which know no master's stall, may nevertheless experience the care and rejoice in the bounty of an all-supporting Parent " (Jas. Hervey). But what most fills us with wonderment is that these celestial reservoirs, so incalcuably greater than any of human construction, should be *suspended in the air*. This it was which so evoked the admiration of both Job and Eliphaz: " He [saith the former] bindeth up the waters in His thick clouds, and the cloud is *not rent* under them " (Job xxvi, 8)— notwithstanding their prodigious weight.

One of the things attributed to God in Holy Writ is that He has fixed " the bound of the sea by a perpetual decree, that it cannot pass it; and though the waves thereof toss themselves, yet they cannot prevail; though they roar, yet can they not pass over it " (Jer. v, 22). If it be not its Maker whose mandate had determined the bounds of the sea, *who has* fixed its limits? Certainly not man, for he who cannot control himself is scarcely competent to issue effective orders to the ocean. That was made fully evident in the days of Noah, when for the first and last time God gave the waters their full freedom, and dire was the consequence, for the whole human race was helpless before them. Without that Divine decree the impetuous sea would again overflow the earth, for such is its natural propensity. But by the mere fiat of His lips God immutably controls this turbulent element. On some coasts high cliffs of rock serve as impregnable ramparts against the raging main, but in others—to evince God is confined to no expedients, but orders all things according to the counsel of His own will—He bids a frail bank of earth curb the fury of its angry waves.

But wonderful as it is that, by the Divine ordinance, a narrow belt of contemptible sand should confine the sea to its appointed limits, yet to us it seems even more remarkable that such immense volumes of water are held in the air within the compass of the clouds. Writing thereon, one of the ablest of the Puritans pointed out: " There are three things very wonderful in that detention of the waters. First, that the waters, which are a fluid body and love to be continually flowing and diffusing themselves, should yet be stopped and stayed together by a *cloud*, which is a thinner and so a more fluid body than the water. It is no great matter to see water kept in conduits of stone or in vessels of brass, because these are firm and solid bodies, such as the water cannot penetrate nor force its way through; but in the judgment of nature, how improbable is it that a thin cloud should bear such a weight and power of waters, and yet not rend nor break under them! This is one of the miracles in Nature, which is therefore not wondered at because it is so common, and which because it is constant is not inquired into.

"Second, as it is a wonder that the cloud is *not* rent under the weight of water, so that the cloud *is* rent at the special order and command of God. At His word it is that the clouds are locked up, and by His word they are opened. As in spiritual things so in natural: ' He openeth, and no man shutteth; He shutteth, and no man openeth.' Third, this also is wonderful that when at the word of God the cloud rents, yet the waters do not gush out like a violent flood all at once, which would quickly drown the earth, but descend in moderate showers, as water through a colander, drop by drop. God carrieth the clouds up and down the world, as the gardener does his watering-can, and bids them distil upon this or that place as Himself directeth. The clouds are compared to " bottles " in Job xxxviii, 27, and those God stops or unstops, usually as our need requires, and sometimes as our sin deserves. ' I have withholden the rain from you ' (Amos iv, 7), and He can withhold it till the heavens above us shall be as brass and the earth under us as iron. ' I will also command the clouds that they rain no rain upon it ' (Isa. v, 6) " (Jos. Caryl, 1643).

There were still other features of the handiwork of God in the firmament which Job was enjoined to stand still and consider, namely, that God " caused the light of His cloud to shine," and " the balancing of the clouds," which are denominated " the wondrous works of Him which is perfect in knowledge " (xxxvii, 15, 16). Upon the expanse of ether overhead we behold scenes infinitely more exquisite than any which a Turner or a Raphael could produce: sights so delicately coloured, so subtle in texture, so vast in extent, they could do no justice unto in their attempts to reproduce. What artist's brush can begin to portray the splendours of the eastern sky as the monarch of the day emerges from his rest, or the entrancing magnificence of the western horizon as he retires to slumber? The Hebrew verb for " shine " in Job xxxvii, 15, means to shine in an illustrious manner, as in Deuteronomy xxxii, 1 (and cf. Psa. l, 1; lxxx, 1), and " the light of the cloud " refers to the light of the sun's reflection from or upon a watery cloud, producing that wonderful phenomenon the rainbow, which is so conspicuous and beautiful, so desirable and attractive, so mysterious and marvellous.

" Dost thou know the *balancings* of the clouds?" Canst thou explain how such prodigious volumes of water are suspended over thine head and held there in the thinnest parts of the atmosphere? Canst thou tell what it is which causes those ponderous lakes to hang so evenly and hover like the lightest down? What poises those thick and heavy vapours in coverings so much lighter and thinner than themselves, and prevents their rushing down more impetuously than a mountain torrent? Must we not again employ the personal pronoun, and answer, "HE bindeth up the waters in His thick clouds, and the cloud is not rent under them " (Job xxvi, 8). Who puts the clouds, as it were, into scales, and so orders their weight that one does not overpower another, but rather hang evenly? This is another of the wondrous works of God, who makes the clouds smaller or larger, higher or lower, according to the service He hath appointed and the use He makes of them: nothing but the Divine wisdom and power can satisfactorily account for such a prodigy.

Yes, " He *bindeth up* the waters in His thick cloud." Those masses of water do not remain stationary in the firmament of themselves, nor could they, for, being so much heavier than the air, they would naturally fall of their own weight and power at once in disorder and ruin to the land beneath. It is God who makes them behave and perform His bidding. By some secret power of His own, God fetters them so that they cannot move until He permits. And though these waters be of such mighty bulk and weight, they do not rend the fleecy filament which contain them. " The thick cloud is not *rent* under them ": the same Hebrew word is rendered " divided " in Psalm lxxviii, 13, where the reference is to the Almighty cleaving a way for His people through the Red Sea. There is a natural tendency and power in those waters *to* rend the clouds, but until God bids them they are held in place, delicately poised, mysteriously but perfectly balanced.

" Which doeth great things and unsearchable, marvellous things without number. Who giveth rain upon the earth, and sendeth waters upon the fields " (Job v, 9, 10). Observe the tense of the verb in the first sentence: it is not only that God " hath done " or that He " will do " great things, though both be true, but that He *now* " doeth " as a present and continued act, for us to take notice of today. Among those stupendous and inscrutable wonders is His sending of the rain, which, though an almost daily provision, is something which men can neither manufacture nor regulate its supply. We do not have far to go in order to inquire or actually see these " marvellous things ": they are near to hand, of frequent occurrence, and, if closely looked into, every shower of rain discovers the wisdom, power and goodness of God. Nature works not without the God of nature, and its common blessings are not dispensed without a special providence. The course of nature only moves as it is turned by the hand of its Maker and directed by His counsels. The heaviest clouds distil no water until they receive commission from God to dissolve.

" For He maketh small the drops of water: they pour down rain according to the vapour thereof, which the clouds do drop and distil upon man abundantly " (Job xxxvi, 27, 28). " Rain is the moisture of the earth drawn up by the heat of the sun into the middle region of the air, which being there condensed into clouds is afterward, at the will of God, dissolved and dropped down again in showers " (Jos. Caryl). Though an ordinary and common work of God, yet it is a very admirable one. The Psalmist tells us " God *prepareth* rain for the earth " (cxlvii, 18). He does so by the method just described, and then by " making small " its drops, for unless He did the latter it would pour down in a flood. That too is a work of His power and mercy, for the earth could not absorb solid volumes of water at once.

" Also can any understand the *spreadings* of the clouds? " (Job xxxvi, 29). Fully so? No, as the diverse and inadequate theorizings of men go to show. It is almost amusing to examine the various answers returned by philosophers and scientists to the question. What holds the clouds in position? The heat of the sun, say some. But if that were the case rain would fall during the night only, whereas the fact is that as many clouds break and empty themselves in the daytime as during the hours of darkness. By the winds, which keep them in perpetual motion, say others. But how can that be, for sometimes the clouds unburden themselves when a hurricane is blowing, and at others in a dead calm. By their sponginess, which permits their being permeated by the air, thus holding them in place, say others. Then why do light and heavy clouds alike move and evaporate? We are logically forced to rise higher, to the will and power of *God*. It is also of His mercy that the clouds serve as a cool canopy over our heads and break the fierce heat and glare of the sun.

Let us pause here and make practical application of what has been before us. These wonders of nature, so little considered by the majority of our fellows, should speak loudly to our hearts. They should awe us, humble us, bow us in wonderment before the Author of such works. But it is more especially the children of God we now have in mind, and particularly those who are in straits and trouble, whose way is hedged up, whose outlook appears dark and foreboding. As we have contemplated such marvels of Divine wisdom and power should not our faith be strengthened, so that we look upward with renewed confidence unto our heavenly Father? Must we not, in view of such prodigies, join with the prophet in exclaiming, " There is nothing too hard for Thee " (Jer. xxxii, 17)? Cannot He who has commissioned the very atmosphere to perform so many useful and benevolent offices for thy good, relieve thy temporal distress? Cannot He who sustains such mighty volumes of water over thy head, also support and succour thee? Cannot He who paints the glorious sunrise shine into thy soul and dissipate its gloom? Consider the rainbow, not only as a mystery and marvel of nature, but also as a sacramental sign, as a token of God's covenant faithfulness.

That is the use we should make of " the wondrous works of Him who is perfect in knowledge." That is how we should " consider " them, and the conclusion we should draw from them. There is no limit to the power of that One who in the beginning made heaven and earth, and who throughout the centuries has preserved them in being. When we are confronted with difficulties which seem insurmountable, we should look above, around, below, and beholding the marvellous handiwork of God commit ourself and our case into His hands with full assurance. When Hezekiah was confronted with the formidable hosts of Sennacherib he sought refuge in the Divine omnipotence, spreading that king's haughty letter before the Lord and appealing to Him as " Thou hast made heaven and earth " (II Kings xix, 15) and therefore canst vanquish for us our enemies. So too the apostles, when forbidden by the authorities to preach the Gospel, appealed to God as the One who " made heaven and earth, and the sea, and all that in them is " (Acts iv, 24, 29). Rest then in this blessed and stimulating truth, that " nothing is too hard " for Him who hath loved thee with an everlasting love!

THE GREAT CHANGE

" My little children, of whom I travail in birth again until Christ be formed in you " (Gal. iv, 19). In the past the apostle had laboured hard in preaching the Gospel to the Galatians, and apparently his efforts had met with considerable success. He had plainly set before them " Christ crucified " (iii, 1) as the sinner's only hope, and many had professed to receive Him as He was offered in the Gospel. They had abandoned their idolatry, seemed to be soundly converted, and had expressed great affection for their spiritual father (iv, 15). For a time they had " run well," but they had been " hindered " (v, 7). After Paul's departure, false teachers sought to seduce them from the Faith and persuade them that they must be circumcised and keep the ceremonial law in order to salvation. They had so far given ear unto those Judaisers that Paul now stood in doubt of them (iv, 20), being fearful lest after all they had never been truly regenerated (iv, 11). It is to be carefully noted that he did not take refuge in fatalism and say, If God has begun a good work in them He will certainly finish it, so there is no need for me to be unduly worried. Very much the reverse.

No, the apostle was much exercised over their state and earnestly solicitous about their welfare. By this strong figure of speech " I travail in birth again," the apostle intimated both his deep concern and his willingness to labour and suffer ministerially after their conversion, to spare no pains in seeking to deliver them from their present delusion and get them thoroughly established in the truth of the Gospel. He longed to be assured that the great change had taken place in them, which he speaks of as " Christ be formed in you." By which we understand that they might be genuinely evangelized by a saving knowledge of Christ. First, that by spiritual apprehension of the Truth He might be revealed in their understandings. Second, that by the exercise of faith upon Him, He might " dwell in their hearts " (Eph. iii, 17): faith gives a subsistence and reality in the soul of that object on which it is acted (Heb. xi, 1). Third, that He might be so endeared to their affections that neither Moses nor any one else could be admitted as a rival. Fourth, that by the surrender of their wills He might occupy the throne of their hearts and rule over them. Christ thus " formed in " us is the proof of His righteousness imputed to us.

" For we are His workmanship, created in Christ Jesus unto good works, which God hath before ordained that we should walk in them " (Eph. ii, 10). In those words the apostle completes the blessed declaration he had made in verses 8 and 9, thereby preserving the balance of Truth. Verses 8 and 9 present only one side of the Gospel and ought never to be quoted without adding the other side. None so earnest as Paul in proclaiming sovereign grace; none more insistent in maintaining practical godliness. Has God chosen His people in Christ before the foundation of the world? It was that they " should be holy " (Eph. i, 4). Did Christ give Himself for us? It was that " He might redeem us from all iniquity and purify unto Himself a peculiar people zealous of good works " (Titus ii, 14). So here, immediately after magnifying free grace, Paul states with equal clearness the moral results of God's saving power, as they are exhibited with more or less distinctness in the lives of His people. Salvation by grace is evidenced by holy conduct: unless our lives are characterized by " good works " we have no warrant to regard ourselves as being the children of God.

" We are His workmanship ": He, and not ourselves, has made us what we are spiritually. " Created in Christ Jesus " means made vitally one with Him. " In Christ " always has reference to union with Him: in Ephesians i, 4, to a mystical or election union; in I Corinthians xv, 22, to a federal or representative one; in I Corinthians vi, 17, and II Corinthians v, 17, to a vital or living one. Saving faith (product of the Spirit's quickening us) makes us branches of the living Vine, from whom our fruit proceeds (Hos. xiv, 8). " Created in Christ Jesus unto good works " expresses the design and efficacy of God's workmanship, being parallel with " This people have I formed for Myself: they shall show forth My praise " (Isa. xliii, 21). God fits the thing for which He creates it: fire to burn, the earth to yield food, His saints to walk in good works—God's work in their souls inclining and propelling thereunto. He creates us in Christ or gives us vital union with Him that we should walk in newness of life, He being the Root from which all the fruits of righteousness proceed. United to the Holy One, holy conduct marks us. Those who live in sin have never been savingly jointed to Christ. God saves that we may glorify Him by a life of obedience.

" Put on the new man, which after God is created in righteousness and true holiness " (Eph. iv, 24). Those words occur in the practical section of the epistle, being part of an exhortation which begins at verse 22, the passage as a whole being similar to Romans xiii, 12-14. Its force is, Make it manifest by your conduct that you are regenerate creatures, exhibiting before your fellows the character of God's children. That which most concerns us now is the particular description which is here given of the great change effected in the regenerate, namely, " a new man which after God is created in righteousness and true holiness." With our present passage should be carefully compared the parallel one in Colossians, for the one helps to explain and supplements the other. There we read " And have put on the new man, which is renewed in knowledge after the image of Him that created him." In both we find the expression " the new man," by which we are *not* to understand that a new individual has been brought into existence, that a person is now brought forth who previously had no being. Great care needs to be taken when seeking to understand and explain the meaning of terms which are taken from the material realm and applied to spiritul objects and things.

A regenerated sinner is the same individual he was before, though a great change has taken place in his soul. How different the landscape when the sun is shining than when darkness of a moonless night is upon it—the same landscape and yet not the same! How different the condition of one who is restored to fullness of health and vigour after being brought very low by serious illness—yet it is the same person. How different will be the body of the saint on the resurrection morning from its present state—the same body which was sown in the grave, and yet not the same! So too with those saints alive on earth at the Redeemer's return: " Who shall change our vile body that it may be fashioned like unto His glorious body " (Phil. iii, 21). Thus it is, in measure, at regeneration: the soul undergoes a Divine work of renovation and transformation: a new light shines into the understanding, a new Object engages the affections, a new power moves the will. It is the same individual, and yet not the same. " Once I was blind, but now I see " is his blessed experience.

In Ephesians iv, 24, we read of the new man " which after God is created in righteousness and true holiness," while in Colossians iii, 10, it is said " which is renewed in knowledge after the image of Him that created him." i.e. originally. By comparing the two passages, we understand the " which after God " to signify in conformity to Himself, for it is parallel with " after the image of Him." That the new man is said to be " created " denotes that this spiritual transformation is a Divine work in which the human individual plays no part, either by contribution, co-operation, or concurrence. It is wholly a supernatural operation, in which the subject of it is entirely passive. The " which is *renewed* " of Colossians iii, 10, denotes that it is not something which previously had no existence, but the spiritual quickening and renovating of the soul. By regeneration is restored to the Christian's soul the moral image of God, which image he lost in Adam at the fall. That " image " consists in " righteousness and true holiness " being imparted to the soul, or, as Colossians iii, 10, expresses it, in the spiritual " knowledge " of God. God is now known, loved, revered, loyally served. It is now fitted for communion with Him.

" Being confident of this very thing, that He which hath begun a good work in you will finish it " (Phil. i, 6). This verse contains a manifest warning, if an indirect or implied one, against our pressing too far the figure of a " new creation." " Creation " is an act and not a " work," a finished or completed object and not an incomplete and imperfect one. God speaks and it is done, wholly and perfectly done in an instant. The very fact that the Holy Spirit has employed such figures as " begetting " and " birth " to describe the saving work of God in the soul, intimates that the reference is only to the *initial* experience of Divine grace. A new life is then imparted, but it requires nurturing and developing. In the verse now before us we are informed that the great change produced in us is not yet fully accomplished, yea, that it is only just begun. The work of grace is called " good " because it is so in itself and because of what it effects: it conforms us to God and fits us to enjoy God. It is termed a " work " because it is a *continuous process,* which the Spirit carries forward in the saint as long as he is left in this scene.

This good work within the soul is commenced by God, being wrought neither by our will nor our agency. That was the ground of the apostle's persuasion or confidence: that He who had begun this good work would perform or finish it—had it been originated by man, he could have had no such assurance. Not only did God initate this good work, but He alone continues and perfects it—were it left to unto us, it would quickly come to nought. " Will finish it until the day of Jesus Christ " tells us it is not complete in this life. With that should be compared " them that believe to the saving of the soul " (Heb. x, 39): observe carefully, not " have believed " (a past act) to the salvation (a completed deliverance) of the soul, but " who believe [a present act] to the *saving* of the soul "—a continuous process. As Christ ever liveth to make intercession for us, so the Spirit ever exercises an effectual influence within us. The verb for " finish " is an intensive one, which means to carry forward unto the end. " The Lord *will perfect* that which concerneth me " (Psa. cxxxviii, 8) enunciates the same promise.

" According to His mercy He saved us by the washing of regeneration and renewing of the Holy Spirit, which He shed on us abundantly through Jesus Christ " (Titus iii, 5, 6). If we followed our inclination, we should essay an exposition of the whole passage (verses 4, 7), but unless we keep within bounds and confine ourself to what bears directly on our present theme, these articles will be extended too much to suit some of our readers. In this passage we are shown how the three Persons of the Godhead co-operate in the work of salvation, and that salvation itself has both an experimental and legal side to it. Here we are expressly said to be " saved by " the effectual operations of the Holy Spirit, so that the Christian owes his personal salvation unto *Him* as truly as he does unto the Lord Jesus. Had not the blessed Spirit taken up His abode in this world, the death of Christ would have been in vain. It is by the meditation and merits of His redemptive work that Christ purchased the gift and graces of the Spirit, which are here said to be " shed on us abundantly *through* Jesus Christ our Saviour."

The will of the Father is the originating cause of our salvation, the worth of the Son's redemption its meritorious cause, and the work of the Spirit its effectual cause. Experimental salvation is begun in the soul by " the washing of regeneration," when the heart is cleansed from the prevailing love and power of sin and begins to be restored to its pristine purity. And by the " renewing of the Holy Spirit," that is, the renewing of the soul in the Divine image: or, more particularly, " the renewing of the mind " (Rom. xii, 2), or, more expressly still, the " renewing of the *spirit of* the mind " (Eph. iv, 23), that is, in the *disposition* of it. The whole of which is summed up in the expression, God has given us " a sound mind " (II Tim. i, 7), " an understanding, that we may know Him " (I John v, 20). The mind is renovated and reinvigorated, so that it is capacitated to " spiritually discern " the things of the Spirit, which the natural man cannot do (I Cor. ii, 14), no matter how well he be educated or religiously instructed.

But that to which we would specially direct the attention of the reader is the present tense of the verbs: " the washing and renewing [not " renewal "] of the Holy Spirit." Like II Corinthians iii, 18, and Philippians i, 6, this is another verse which shows the great change is not completed at the new birth, but is a *continual process*, in course of effectuation. The " good work " which God has begun in the soul, that washing and renewing of the Holy Spirit, proceeds throughout the whole course of our earthly life, and is not consummated until the Redeemer's return, for it is only then that the saints will be perfectly and eternally conformed to the image of God's Son. God says of His heritage, " I the Lord do keep it: I will *water it every moment* " (Isa. xxvii, 3): it is only by the continuous and gracious influences of the Spirit that the spiritual life is nurtured and developed. The believer is often conscious of his need thereof, and under a sense of it cries, " quicken me according to Thy Word." And God does: for " Though our outward man perish, yet the inward is renewed day by day " (II Cor. iv, 16). That " inner man " is termed " the hidden man of the heart " (I Peter iii, 4).

" For this is the covenant that I will make with the house of Israel after those days, saith the Lord. I will put My laws into their minds, and I will write them in their hearts " (Heb. viii, 10—quoted from Jer. xxxi, 31-34). Without entering into the prophetic bearings of this passage (about which none should speak without humble diffidence), suffice it to say that by the " house of Israel " we understand " the Israel of God " (Gal. vi, 16), the whole election of grace, to be here in view. The " I will put " and " I will write " refer to yet another integral part of the great change wrought in God's people, the reference being to that invincible and miraculous operation of the Spirit which radically transforms the favoured subjects of it. " God. articles with His people. He once wrote His laws *to* them, now He writes His laws *in* them. That is, He will give them understanding to know and believe His laws, memories to retain them, hearts to love and consciences to revere them; He will give them courage to profess and power to put them into practice: the whole habit and frame of their souls shall be a table and transcript of His laws " (Matthew Henry).

" I will put My laws into their minds, and I will write them in their hearts." We are here shown how rebels are made amenable to God. " God calls to us without effect as long as He speaks to us in no other way than by the voice of man. He indeed teaches us and commands what is right, but He speaks to the deaf; for when we seem to hear aright, our ears are only struck by an empty sound, and the heart, being full of depravity and perverseness, rejects every wholesome doctrine. In short, the Word of God never penetrates into our hearts, for they are iron and stone until they are softened by Him; nay they have engraved on them a contrary law, for perverse passions reek within, which lead us to rebellion. In vain then does God proclaim His Law by the voice of men until He writes it by His spirit on our hearts, that is, until He frames and prepares us for obedience " (Calvin).

" And I will write them in their hearts." The " heart," as distinguished from the " mind," comprises the affections and the will. This is what renders actually effective the former. The heart of the natural man is alienated from God and opposed to His authority. That is why God wrote the Ten Words upon tables of stone: not so much to secure the outward letter of them, as to represent the hardness of heart of the people unto whom they were given.

But at regeneration God takes away " the heart of stone " and gives " a heart of flesh " (Ezek. xxxvi, 26). Just as the tables of stone received the impression of the finger of God, of the letter and words wherein the Law was contained, so " the heart of flesh " receives a durable impression of God's laws, the affections and will being made answerable unto the whole revealed will of God and conformed to its requirements: a principle of obedience is imparted, subjection to the Divine authority is wrought in us.

Here, then, is the grand triumph of Divine grace: a lawless rebel is changed into a loyal subject, enmity against the Law (Rom. viii, 7) is displaced by love for the Law (Psa. cxix, 97). The heart is so transformed that it now loves God and has a genuine desire and determination to please Him. The renewed heart " delights in the Law of God " and " serves the Law of God " (Rom. vii, 22, 25), it being its very " nature " to do so! Let each reader sincerely ask himself, is there now that in me which responds to the holy Law of God? Is it truly my longing and resolve to be wholly regulated by the Divine will? Is it the deepest yearning of my soul and the chief aim of my life to honour and glorify Him? Is it my daily prayer for Him to " work in me both to will and to do of His good pleasure "? Is my acutest grief occasioned when I feel I sadly fail to fully realize my longing? If so, the great change has been wrought in me.

(continued from back page)

It may be only the quoting of a single precept or promise, but often that means much to a fellow pilgrim who is discouraged and cast down by the difficulties of the way. " A word spoken in due season, how good is it! " (Prov. xv, 23): yes, just a word if it be prompted by the Holy Spirit. " A word fitly spoken [out of a compassionate heart and with grace] is like apples of gold in pictures of silver " (Prov. xxv, 11)—like luscious oranges with their glistening leaves for background. Only the day to come will reveal how many a traveller on life's highway went forth with renewed courage and strength after receiving an uplifting word from a humble Christian, as it will also reveal how many a golden opportunity we missed of uttering such a word! Of our Saviour it is recorded, " Grace is poured into Thy lips " (Psa. xlv, 2), and even His enemies were obliged to admit " Never man spake like this Man." Then seek to learn of Him and become more like Him.

If Christians be in a healthy state of soul they should never be at a loss for matter of spiritual conversation when they meet one another. Then should each of them have occasion to say, " I will bless the Lord at all times, *His* praise shall be continually in my mouth. O magnify the Lord with me, and let us exalt His name *together*" (Psa. xxxiv, 1, 3). Then will we be employing our tongues to good purpose. " I will speak of the glorious honour of Thy majesty and of Thy wondrous works. I will declare Thy greatness. They shall abundantly utter the memory of Thy great goodness. They shall speak of the glory of Thy kingdom and talk of Thy power " (Psa. cxlv). What themes suited to the lips of the redeemed are these! They are indeed appropriate subjects for spiritual converse which will edify one another. Instead of dwelling upon the evanescent trivialities which engage the thoughts of the unregenerate, exercise your mind and tongue upon those ineffable and eternal verities which the angels delight to contemplate. As you do so, the hearts of your hearers will burn within them, their souls will rejoice, and your Master will be magnified. Such spiritual converse is registered on high (Mal. iii, 16), for nothing concerning Christ can be lost or miss its reward.

A person's speech is a sure index to his character, for " out of the abundance of the heart the mouth speaketh " (Matt. xii, 34). One does not have to pass condemnatory judgment upon his fellow when he listens to his vain and vulgar, or silly and senseless, chatter, for he plainly proclaims what he is by his own lips. " The mouth of fools poureth out foolishness (Prov. xv, 2): water will not rise above its own level, neither will a foul well yield that which is fit to drink. " They are of the world, *therefore* speak they of the world, and the world heareth them " (I John iv, 5). Then how many whitewashed or respectable worldlings are there in the " churches," for their everyday talk is about little or nothing else than some phase of this world. As a man's nature, so is his discourse. The portion of a natural man is a temporal one, and, as his interests are confined thereto, neither his aspirations, thoughts nor speech rise any higher. Where a man's treasure is, there is his heart also, and since the treasure of the unregenerate be limited to the things of time and sense, and his heart is absorbed with them, his speech is about them.

The power of speech is a blessed privilege, but it entails a solemn responsibility. How am I, how are you, using this talent? Since it be a Divine gift, ought it not to be consecrated to God? Yet how few, even among His children, seem to realize it is both their duty and privilege to definitely dedicate their tongues unto the Lord. " I beseech you therefore, brethren, by the mercies of God, that ye present your bodies a living sacrifice, holy, acceptable unto God, which is your reasonable service " (Rom. xii, 1). That is, your body as a whole and in all its parts: " yield yourselves unto God as those that are alive from the dead, and your *members* as instruments of righteousness unto God " (Rom. vi, 13); and one of the most important and influential of those members is the *tongue*! It is no longer your own, but " bought with a price." Christians should be distinguished from non-Christians by their converse—as in everything else. Their calling (Heb. iii, 1), their citizenship (Phil. iii, 20), their inheritance (I Peter i, 4), is each a heavenly one; and ought not their speech to be so too? " A wholesome tongue is a tree of life " (Prov. xv, 4), ministering refreshment, wholesome and nourishing instruction unto others. Seek to make your converse spiritually profitable unto your fellows.

" Let your speech be always with grace, seasoned with salt," especially when conversing with God's children. *That is how* we ought to employ our tongues, and how the Lord has bidden us to use them: our speech should be seasoned with true piety, savouring of heavenly things, elevating to the spiritual ear, such as will be " edifying, that it may minister grace unto the hearers " (Eph. iv, 29). Surely the one whose affections are set upon things above will find it a delight to speak about them to a responsive soul. If Christ be " the Chiefest among ten thousand " unto you, then must you not perforce extol Him? Perhaps you say, I would love to, but I do not possess the tongue of the learned. " Learning " is not necessary, nor are you called upon to address a learned congregation. But if the Word of Christ dwells in you richly, when you meet one of His own, will you not spontaneously speak of His excellency? It is indeed useless to turn on the tap if a barrel be empty, but if your heart be really occupied with the One who is " altogether " lovely," then out of the abundance of your heart your mouth will speak.

Not that every Christian is competent to preach a whole sermon even to his most intimate friend, but he should, whenever he meets a member of the Household of Faith, be able to say something which will help and cheer him.

(*continued on preceding page*)

XXVI   APRIL 1947   No. 4

STUDIES IN THE SCRIPTURES

"Search the Scriptures." John v, 39

Publisher and Editor—ARTHUR W. PINK,
29 Lewis Street,
Stornoway, Isle of Lewis,
Scotland.

SPIRITUAL SINGING

Does not one have to be in the right mood for singing, either to engage in it personally or to enjoy that of others? Such is the idea which prevails generally among professing Christians. From one standpoint it is of course true, but from another it is not so. But surely no one sings when he is thoroughly miserable—unless he forces himself to do so. Ah, is not that exactly what the worldling would say? It is; and, sad to say, the great majority of church members hold the same view, which only evidences the carnality of their conceptions. Are the children of God in no better case than the children of the Devil? Are they too "creatures of circumstances," swayed by the situation in which they find themselves, a prey to their feelings? But must not one be in a cheerful frame in order to really sing? Yes, to sing naturally. But does not the saint require to be on the mountain ere he can break forth into spiritual song? Such questions indicate how unscriptural are the thoughts of most people on this subject: they reduce singing to a mere physical exercise, an outburst of their *natural* emotions.

Christians are bidden to delight themselves in the Lord, and if they really do so, songs of praise are bound to spring up in their hearts. That it is not God's will His children should be miserable is clear from the fact that the service of song is an ordinance of worship, both under the old covenant (I Chron. vi, 31) and the new (Eph. v, 19). It is an act by which the soul renders homage and the heart adores the glorious One: "Praise the Lord with harp, sing unto Him with the psaltery" (Psa. xxxiii, 2). Singing is expressive of contentment and joy: "my heart greatly rejoiced, and with my song will I praise Him" (Psa. xxviii, 7). "Is any merry? let him sing psalms" (James v, 13). Such expressions of spiritual gladness are both honouring and pleasing to Him: "I will praise the name of God with a song and will magnify Him with thanksgiving. This also shall please the Lord *better than* an ox" (Psa. lxix, 30, 31)—the most costly of the oblations appointed by Him under the Mosaic economy.

"The morning stars sang together and all the sons of God shouted for joy" (Job xxxviii, 7). The reference there is to the angelic hosts celebrating the creation of this world. For the next twenty-five centuries Scripture records no further singing! Why? Because sin had come in and defiled the fair

(continued on back page)

Important Notices

Please advise promptly of change in address, otherwise copies will be lost in the mails.

We are glad to send a sample copy to any of your friends whom you believe would be interested in this publication.

This magazine is published as " a work of faith and labour of love," the editor and his wife gladly giving their services free. There is no regular subscription price, as we do not wish the poor of the flock to be deprived. This does not mean that those looking for something for nothing may " help themselves." Those getting this magazine who are financially able and who receive spiritual help from its pages, are expected to gladly contribute towards its expenses; otherwise their names are dropped from our list.

Will those forwarding International Money Orders please have them made out to us at Stornoway, Isle of Lewis, Scotland. Checks (Cheques—Eng.) made out on U.S.A. Banks are not negotiable here, so please do not send them.

All unsigned articles are by the Editor.

CONTENTS

THE PRAYERS OF THE APOSTLES

40. Colossians i, 9-12.

" That ye might walk worthily of the Lord unto all pleasing, being fruitful in every good work " (verse 10). To walk worthily means to conduct ourselves becomingly, to act agreeably to the Name we bear, to live as those who are " not their own." To walk " worthily of the Lord unto all pleasing " is for our obedience to be uniform and universal, taking no step without the warrant of God's Word, seeking His approbation and honour in every department and aspect of our lives. " Being fruitful in every good work " is a further extension of the same thought, evincing again how high and holy is the Standard at which we should continually aim. Grace is no enemy unto good works, but is the promoter and enabler of them. It is utterly vain for us to speak and sing of the wonders of Divine grace if we are not plainly exhibiting its lovely fruits. Grace is a principle of operation, a spiritual energizer which causes its possessor to be active in good works and makes him a fruitful branch of the Vine. It is the empty professor who is viewed as a barren tree, a cumberer of the ground. By the miracle of regeneration God makes His people " good trees " and they bear " good fruit." It is their privilege and duty to be " fruitful in *every* good work," and in order thereto they must constantly endeavour to " walk worthily of the Lord unto all pleasing."

Saints are " trees of righteousness," the planting of the Lord, and their graces and good works are their fruit. There is some confusion in the minds of hyper-Calvinists on this subject, for in their zeal to ascribe all glory unto the heavenly Husbandman they virtually reduce the Christian to an automaton. We must distinguish between the fruit-Producer and the fruit-bearer. We are first made trees of the Lord, and then we receive grace from Him, and then by grace we ourselves really do bring forth fruit. We must indeed thankfully own the truth of our Lord's words, " from Me is thy fruit found " (Hos. xiv, 8), but while freely acknowledging that all is of His ordination and gracious enablement, yet it must not be overlooked that even here God Himself terms it "*thy* fruit": because it is of His origination, that alters not the fact it is also of our co-operation. While there be many who make far too much of man, there are others who make too little of him—less than Scripture does; repudiating his moral agency. We must be careful lest we press too far the figure of the "branch": the branch of a tree has neither rationality, spirituality, nor responsibility—the Christian has all three. God does not produce the fruit independently of us. We are more than pipes through which His energy flows.

The very fact that Paul here prays that the saints *might be* "fruitful" clearly imports these two things: they could not be so without God's enabling; it was their privilege and duty to be such. We do but mock God unless we ourselves diligently strive after those spiritual enlargements for which we supplicate Him; as we dishonour Him if we suppose we can attain unto them in our own strength. When God has renewed a person, He does not henceforth treat with him as though he were merely a mechanical entity: rather does he communicate to him a gracious willingness to act, stirs him into action, and then *he* actually performs the good works. In fruit-bearing we are not passive but active. It is not fruit tied on to us, but fruit growing out of us, which makes manifest that we have been engrafted into Christ. If the believer's personal and practical holiness were not the outflowing of his renewed heart, then it would be no evidence (as it *is*) that spiritual life has been imparted to his soul. Perhaps the surest evidence that, in one sense, the fruits and good works which I bear are *mine*, is that I am *dissatisfied* with and grieve over them—that my love is fickle, my zeal unstable, my best performances defective; whereas if they were God's fruits and works, independent of me, they would be *perfect*!

When God in His sovereign benignity communicates grace unto a person, it is for the purpose of equipping him to the better discharge of his responsibility: that is to say, it is given to animate and actuate all the faculties of his soul—and what *He* works in *we* are to work out (Phil. ii, 12, 13). Having imparted life to His people, they are required to walk in newness of life. Having bestowed faith upon them, theirs is for that faith to be active in producing good works. Or, following the order of this prayer, if we have been "filled with the knowledge of His will in all wisdom and spiritual understanding," it is in order "that ye might walk worthily of the Lord unto all pleasing, being fruitful in every good work." Those last words express both variety and abundance. It is not fruitfulness of one kind only, but of every sort. The Christian is to be like unto that "tree" in the Paradise of God which "bears twelve manner of fruits and yieldeth her fruit every month" (Rev. xxii, 2). Said the Lord Jesus, "Herein is My Father glorified: that ye bear *much fruit*" (John xv, 8). Alas that any of His children should be content if they can but be persuaded they bear a little fruit and thereby be convinced they belong to His family—setting more store on their own peace than upon their glorifying of Him. Little wonder their assurance is so feeble.

That word of Christ's, "Herein is My Father glorified that ye bear much fruit," supplies further confirmation of what we have pointed out above: in a very real sense it is their fruit—"ye bear." Though it is indeed by Divine energizing, notwithstanding it is by their own activity. But observe too and admire the strict accuracy of Scripture: not that "ye *produce* much fruit," for God is both the original and efficient Cause of it. Mark too the beautiful harmony of the two verses: "walk worthily of the Lord unto all *pleasing,* being fruitful in every good work," " Herein is My Father *glorified* that ye bear much fruit "—by so doing you exhibit the power and reality of His transforming grace, display the lineaments of His image, reflect the beauty of His holiness. That " much fruit " involves and includes the exercise of all holy affections: not merely some acts of holiness, but the putting forth of every grace in all the variety of their actings; not only inwardly, but outwardly as well, labouring to abound in the same; and this not spasmodically and only for a season, but steadfastly as long as we be left on earth, bringing forth fruit " with patience " (Luke viii, 15), persevering in the same.

" Being fruitful in every good work and increasing in the knowledge of God." Observe that those two things are not separated by a semi-colon, but are linked together by an " and," the latter being closely connected with and dependent upon the former. " Increasing in the knowledge of God " is the *reward* of " walking worthily of the Lord unto all pleasing, being fruitful in every good work." Or, if some of our readers prefer the expression, it is the *effect* thereof, though they should not object against the former when Scripture itself declares that " in keeping of them [the Divine statutes] there is great reward " (Psa. xix, 11)—a considerable part of which consists in a growing acquaintance with and a deeper delight in the Lord. Said our Saviour, " I am the light of the world, he that followeth Me shall not walk in darkness, but shall have the light of life " (John viii, 12), and what is it to *follow* Christ but to yield to His authority, practise His precepts, and keep before us His example. The one who does so shall be no loser, but the gainer: he shall be delivered from the power and misery of sin, and made the recipient of spiritual wisdom, discernment, holiness and happiness; or, in a word, he shall enjoy the light of God's countenance. So the consequence of a sincere endeavour to please the Lord and glorify Him by bearing much fruit will be an increase in our experimental knowledge of God.

Note well, dear reader, it is not simply an increase in " knowledge " which is here spoken of, but " increasing in the knowledge *of God*," which is a vastly different thing. This is a kind of knowledge for which the wise of this world have no relish, and it is one unto which the empty professor is a total stranger. There are many who are keen " Bible students " and eager readers of a certain class of expository and theological works—which explain types, prophecies, doctrine, but contain little or nothing that searches the heart and reproves carnality—and they become quite learned in the letter of Scripture and in the intellectual apprehension of its contents, yet have no personal, saving and transforming knowledge of God. A merely theoretical knowledge of God has no effectual influence upon the soul, nor does it exert any beneficial power upon one's daily walk. Nothing but a vital knowledge of God will produce the former, and only a practical knowledge of Him secures the latter. A vital and saving knowledge of God is His personal revelation of Himself to a soul in quickening power, whereby He becomes an awe-inspiring but blessed reality: all uncertainty as to *whether* He is or as to *what* He is, is now at an end. That revelation of God creates in the soul a panting after Him, a longing to know more of Him, a yearning to be more fully conformed unto Him.

It is not so much an increasing in the vital or even the devotional knowledge of God of which our text speaks, but rather of what that issues in, which, for want of a better term, we designate the *practical knowledge* of God. What is here before us in Colossians i, 10, is very similar to that word of Christ's, " If any man will do His will, he shall know of the doctrine "

(John vii, 17), or, as the Interlinear so much more lucidly renders it, " If any one desires His will to practise, he shall know the teaching whether from God it is." As the Christian makes conscience of walking becomingly of the Lord, and as he is diligent in performing good works, he discovers by practical experience the wisdom and kindness of God in framing such a Rule for him to walk by: he obtains personal proof of " that good, and acceptable, and perfect will of God " (Rom. xii, 2), he is brought into a closer and more steady communion with Him, and procures a deeper appreciation of His excellency. " Then shall we know, if we follow on to know the Lord " (Hos. vi, 1). This is both the appointed way and means for such attainment: if we perform the prescribed duty, we shall receive the promised blessing; if we tread the path of obedience, we shall be rewarded by an increasing and soul-satisfying knowledge of the excellency of our Master.

This is not a knowledge which can be acquired by art or taught us by men: no, not even by the ablest " Bible teachers." It can be learned nowhere but in the school of Christ, by practising His precepts and being fruitful in every good work. Yet let it be pointed out that this increase in the knowledge of God does not follow automatically upon our performing of good works, but only as God Himself be sought unto in them—a matter of the first moment, though frequently overlooked. As there were those who followed Christ during the days of His flesh for the loaves and fishes or because they were eager to witness His miracles, and not because their hearts were set upon Him, so there are some in the religious world today who are (relatively speaking) active in various forms of good works, yet are they not performed out of love for or gratitude unto Christ. The good works of the Christian must not only be wrought by a faith which worketh by love, but his aim in them must be the seeking unto *God* in the doing of them. That should be our chief design and end in all duties and ordinances—in the reading of the Word or in hearing it preached, in prayer, and in every act of obedience: not to rest in the good works, but to learn more of God in them, through them, and from them.

As it is his greatest need, so it is the genuine longing of every regenerate soul to increase in the knowledge of God; yet most of them are slow in discovering the way in which their longing may be realized. Too many turn from the simple and practical to bewilder themselves by that which is mystical and mysterious. It should be obvious to even the babe in Christ that if he forsakes the paths of rightousness he is forsaking God Himself. To know God better we must cleave more to Him, walk closer with Him. Communion with God can only be had in the highway of holiness. The previous clauses of Colossians i, 10, reveal what is required from us in order to an increasing knowledge of God. If we be diligent and earnest in seeking to walk worthily of the Lord unto all pleasing, being fruitful in every good work, the outcome will be a more intimate fellowship with Him, a better acquaintance with His character, an experimental realization that " His commandments are not grievous," daily proofs of His tender patience with our infirmities, and fuller discoveries of Himself unto us. " He that hath My commandments and keepeth them, he it is that loveth Me . . . and I will love him and *manifest Myself* to him " (John xiv, 21). God manifests His delight towards those who delight in Him.

This increasing in the practical knowledge of God is more an intensive thing than an extensive one: that is to say, it is not an adding to our store of information about Him, but the soul becoming more experimentally acquainted and being more powerfully affected with what is already known of Him. It consists not in further discoveries of God's perfections, as in a livelier appreciation of them. As the Christian earnestly seeks to walk with Him in His ways, he obtains a growing acquaintance with God's grace in inspiring him, His power in supporting, His faithfulness in renewing, His mercy in restoring, His wisdom in devising, and His love in appointing a course wherein such pleasure is found and whose paths all are peace. This is indeed a practical and profitable knowledge. The more we know of God in *this* way, the more shall we love Him, trust in Him, pray to Him, depend upon Him. But such knowledge is not acquired in a day, nor fully attained unto in a few short years. We grow into it gradually, little by little, as we make use of both the Divine precepts and promises, and from a desire to please and glorify Him, and with the design of having communion with Him therein.

"Strengthened with all might, according to His glorious power, unto all patience and longsuffering with joyfulness" (verse 11). This is the third petition of the prayer, and we will begin our remarks upon it by pointing out *its relation* to those preceding it. In their brief comments neither Matthew Henry, Gill nor Scott makes any attempt to show the connection between this request and the two foregoing. In the short exposition supplied by Ellicott only this general analysis is given: "This is a prayer for our full knowledge of God's will, and it is emphatically connected with a practical walking in that will. Manifested first by fruitfulness in every good work, second by enduring afflictions, third by the thankful acceptance of God's call to the inheritance (verse 12). Thus this 'knowledge of His will' is *tried* by the three tests of obedience, patience or endurance, and thankful humility." That is good so far as it goes, and as a broad tracing out of the order of thought of this prayer probably cannot be improved upon.

While Ellicott has indicated the general relation of verse 11 to verse 9, let us now consider its closer connection with verse 10. First, it seems to us that whereas verse 10 treats more of the *active* side of the Christian life, verse 11 has more definitely in view its *passive* side. Or, to express it in another way, whereas the former intimates the use we should make of communicated grace in a way of *doing*, this teaches us how to improve that grace in a way of *suffering*. And is not this usually the order in which Divine providence affords the saint occasion to discharge each of those responsibilities? While the Christian is young and vigorous, those graces which are expressed in the performing of good works are afforded their fullest opportunity. But as natural strength and youthful zeal abate, as trials and infirmities increase, there is a call for another set of graces to be exercised, namely, patience and longsuffering. Even in old age, yea, while lying upon a bed of sickness and helplessness, the Christian walks worthily of the Lord unto all pleasing if he meekly bears his appointed lot and murmurs not. And certainly he is bearing fruit to the glory of God if he endures his trials cheerfully and is "longsuffering with joyfulness."

But may we not trace a yet closer relation between the two verses. If by grace the child of God be enabled to walk worthily of the Lord unto all pleasing, being fruitful in every good work, what is certain to be the consequence? Why this: not only will he increase in the practical knowledge of God, but he will also incur the hatred of his fellows. The closer he cleaves to the Standard set before him, the more conscience he makes of "wholly following the Lord," the more will he stir up the enmity of the flesh.

the world, and the Devil. The more he endeavours to deny self and be out and out for Christ, the more opposition will he encounter, especially from empty professors, who detest none so much as those whose uncompromising strictness exposes and condemns their vain pretensions. Yes, young Christian, you must be fully prepared for this and expect nothing else. The closer you walk with Christ, the more will you be persecuted. And what does such opposition, such hatred, such persecution and affliction call for from us? What will enable us to stand our ground and keep us from lowering the banner? What but being " strengthened with all might, according to God's glorious power, unto all patience and longsuffering with joyfulness "?

Finally, a still closer link of connection may be seen in the closing clause of verse 10 and what follows in verse 11: " increasing in the knowledge of God: strengthened with all might according to His glorious power, unto all patience and longsuffering with joyfulness." This will be the more apparent as we bear in mind the particular kind of " knowledge of God " which is there spoken of: not one that is obtained by theological study and reasoning, nor even by meditative devotions, but rather one which is acquired *through obedience* unto His precepts. The order of the Greek—" increasing in the knowledge of God: with all might being strengthened "—makes this yet clearer: the latter follows upon the former. Those who have habituated themselves to heed God's commandments will find it far easier than others do to submit themselves unto His providential will. Those who have lived to please God rather than themselves are the ones least likely to be stumbled by afflictions and are the last to sink into despair under them. Those who are zealous of good works will possess their souls with patience in adversity, and cheerfully endure when the enemy rages against them.

We are greatly the losers if we do not pay the closest attention to the *order* of the petitions in the prayers of the apostles (equally so with the Family prayer in Matt. vi, 9-13, and the High Priestly one of Christ in John xvii) and the *relation* of one petition to the other; for not only do we fail to perceive their real import, but we miss valuable lessons for our spiritual lives. Those who cursorily scan them, instead of giving the same prolonged meditation, rob their own souls. How many Christians bemoan their lack of " patience " under affliction, and must be startled if not staggered by a weighing of this expression, "longsuffering with joyfulness"; yet how very few of them are aware of the cause *why* they are strangers to such an experience! Yet that cause is here plainly revealed: it is due to the fact that they have been so little " strengthened with all might according to His glorious power." And that, in turn, is because they have " increased " so little " in the knowledge of God," i.e. that personal *proving* of the goodness, the acceptableness, and the perfection of the " will of God " (Rom. xii, 1), which is obtained through an obedient walking with Him, making conscience of " pleasing Him " in all things, and being " fruitful in every good work." It is failure in the *practical* side of our Christian lives which explains why our " experience " is so unsatisfactory.

LIFE AND TIMES OF JOSHUA
20. The Miracle.

" And the Lord said unto Joshua, This day will I begin to magnify thee in the sight of all Israel, that they may know that as I was with Moses so I will be with thee. And thou shalt command the priests that bear the ark of the covenant, saying, When ye are come to the brink of the water of Jordan ye shall stand still in Jordan " (Jos. iii, 7, 8). Before his death it had been revealed to Moses by the Lord that Joshua should be his successor as the leader of His people, and unto that office he had been solemnly set apart (Num. xxvii, 18-23). Moses had also announced unto Israel that Joshua " should cause them to inherit the Land " (Deut. i, 38), and " the children of Israel hearkened unto him, and did as the Lord commanded Moses " (Deut. xxxiv, 9). After the death of Moses the people had avowed their willingness to do whatever Joshua commanded them and to go whither he should send them, and expressed the desire that Divine assistance would be granted him: " the Lord thy God be with thee, as He was with Moses " (i, 16, 17). In the interval the two spies had reconnoitred Jericho at his orders, the people had followed him from Shittim to the Jordan (iii, 1), and had remained there three days. Now the time had come for the Lord to more fully authenticate His servant.

Joshua had duly discharged his duty and now he was to be rewarded. He had set before the people a noble example by acting faith on God's word, had confidently expressed his assurance that God would make good His promise (i, 11, 15), and now the Lord would honour the one who had honoured Him. Joshua had been faithful in a few things and he should be made ruler over many. Devotedness unto God never passes unrecognized by Him. The Lord would now put signal honour upon Joshua in the sight of Israel as He had done upon Moses at the Red Sea and at Sinai. " The Lord said unto Moses, Lo, I come *unto thee* in a thick cloud that the people may hear when I speak unto thee, and *believe thee* for ever " (Ex. xix, 9): thus did He honour and authenticate Moses. And here at the Jordan he magnified Joshua by the authority which He conferred upon him, and attested him as His appointed leader of Israel. The result of this is stated in iv, 15, " on that day the Lord magnified Joshua in the sight of all Israel, and they feared [revered and obeyed] him as they feared Moses, all the days of his [Joshua's] life."

But we must be careful lest we overlook something far more glorious than what has just been pointed out. Surely those words, " This day will I begin to magnify thee in the sight of all Israel," should at once turn our thoughts to One infinitely superior to Joshua: that what God did here for His servant was a foreshadowment of what later He did to His Son at this same Jordan. No sooner was our blessed Lord baptized in that river than, " Lo, the heavens were opened unto Him and he saw the Spirit of God descending like a dove, and lighting upon Him: And, lo, a voice from heaven, saying, This is My beloved Son, in whom I am well pleased " (Matt. iii, 16, 17). Then was *He* " made manifest to Israel " (John i, 31). Then was He authenticated for His great mission. Then did God " begin to magnify Him." Still more wonderful is the type when we observe at what part of the Jordan this occurred: " These things were done in Beth-abara " (John i, 28), which signified " the place of passage " (John i, 28), so that Christ was attested by the Father at the very place where Israel passed through the river and where Joshua was magnified!

Solemn indeed was the contrast. By what took place at the Jordan Israel knew that Joshua was their Divinely appointed leader and governor, and therefore they " feared him . . . all the days of his life " (iv, 15), rendering implicit and undeviating obedience unto his orders: " And Israel served the Lord all the days of Joshua " (xxiv, 31). But after the anti-typical Joshua had been far more illustriously magnified at the Jordan, identified as the Son of God incarnate, and owned by the Father as the One in whom He delighted, what was Israel's response? Did they love and worship Him? Did they fear and obey Him? Very far otherwise: " He came unto His own, and His own received Him not " (John i, 11). Their hearts were alienated and their ears closed against Him. Though He spake as never man spake, though He went about doing good, though He wrought miracles of power and mercy, they " despised and rejected Him," and after a brief season cried " Away with Him, crucify Him." Marvel, dear Christian reader, that the Lord of glory endured such humiliation " for us men and our salvation." Wonder and adore that He so loved us as not only to be willing to be hated of men but smitten of God that our sins might be put away.

" And thou shalt command the priests that bear the ark of the covenant, saying, When ye are come to the brink of the water of Jordan, ye shall stand still in Jordan " (verse 8). What anointed eye can fail to see here again a shadowing forth of a greater than Joshua! Next after this mention of God's beginning to magnify Joshua in the sight of the people, we find him exercising high authority and giving orders to the priests; and almost the first public act of Christ's after the Father had attested and honoured Him at the Jordan is what is recorded in Matthew v—vii. In that sermon on the mount we behold our Saviour doing the very same thing: exercising high authority, as He evinced by His frequently repeated " I say unto you," and issuing orders to His disciples, who, under the new covenant, correspond to the priests under the old; and it is very striking to see how the twofold application of that term and the type appear in that sermon. As we pointed out in our last, the " priests," when bearing the ark of the covenant, were figures of the ministers of the Gospel in their official character, but looked at as those privileged to draw near unto God. The " priests " were types of all the redeemed of Christ (I Peter ii, 5, 9).

Now in the opening verses of Matthew v, it was His servants whom " Christ taught " (verses 1, 2, 13-16), and to whom He issued commandments, for " His disciples " there are to be understood as " apostles "—as in x, i, 2, and xxviii, 16-20. Yet as we continue reading that wondrous discourse we soon perceive that it cannot be restricted unto ministers of the Gospel, but is addressed to the whole company of His people. Therein we learn what is required from the redeemed by the One who is their Lord, possessed of Divine authority: namely, entire subjection unto Him, unreserved conformity to His revealed will. As the priests of Israel must order their actions by the instructions which they received from Joshua, so must the ministers of the Gospel take their orders from their Divine Master, and so also must the whole company of His redeemed be regulated wholly by the injunctions of the Captain of their salvation. Nothing less is due unto Him who endured such shame and suffering on their behalf; nothing else becomes those who owe their all unto Him who died for them. It is in *this* way that their gratitude and devotion is to be manifested: " If ye love Me, keep My commandments " (John xiv, 13).

" And thou shalt command the priests that bear the ark of the covenant, saying, When ye are come to the brink of the water of Jordan, ye shall stand still in Jordan." What a testing of their faith and obedience was that! The swollen and unfordable river before them, and they ordered to advance unto the very edge thereof, yea, to stand still in it! How senseless such a procedure unto carnal reason! Such too appears the policy and means appointed by God in the Gospel: " For after that in the wisdom of God the world by wisdom knew not God, it pleased God by the foolishness of preaching to save them that believe" (I Cor. i, 21). And the preaching of Christ crucified, my ministerial friends, is entirely a matter of faith and obedience, for to our natural intellect and perceptions it appears to be utterly inadequate to produce eternal fruits. And even when we *have* preached Christ to the best of our poor powers, it often seems that our efforts are unavailing, and we are perhaps sorely tempted to act contrary unto that word, "the weapons of our warfare are not carnal, but spiritual." Seek grace, then, to heed the lesson pointed by the above verse: discharge your responsibility to the utmost extent and trustfully leave the issue with God, as did the priests.

But there is not only a much-needed message contained in verse 8 for the discouraged servants of Christ, but there is one too for the rank and file of God's people, especially those of them who may be sorely tried by present circumstances. Their faith and obedience must be tested—that its reality may appear. Some of the Lord's commandments present less difficulty, for they are embodied in the laws of our land and respected by all decent people. But there are others of His precepts which are most trying to flesh and blood and which are scoffed at by the unregenerate. Nevertheless, our course is clear: there can be no picking and choosing—"whatsoever He saith unto you, do" (John ii, 5). Yes, but when I *have* sought to obey to the best of my ability I find circumstances all against me, a situation beyond my powers to cope with, a "jordan" too deep and wide for me to pass through. Very well, here is the word exactly suited to your case: come to "the brink of the water" and then "stand still in it": proceed to your utmost limits in the path of duty and then count upon the omnipotent One to undertake for you.

"And Joshua said unto the children of Israel, Come hither, and hear the words of the Lord your God" (verse 9). Once more our minds are carried beyond the type to Antitype, who said unto Israel, "My doctrine is not Mine, but His that sent Me" (John vii, 16), and again, "the Father which sent Me, He gave Me a commandment what I should say and what I should speak" (John xii, 49). And therefore the most diligent heed is to be given and the most unquestioning obedience rendered unto Him. "And Joshua said, Hereby ye shall know that the living God is among you, and that He will without fail drive out from before you the Canaanites, and the Hittites, and the Hivites, and the Perizzites, and the Girgashites, and the Amorites, and the Jebusites" (verse 10). That title, "the living God," is used in the Scriptures to point a contrast with the inanimate idols of the heathen (II Kings xix, 4; I Thess. i, 9), and doubtless was employed by Joshua on this occasion for the purpose of accentuating the impotency and worthlessness of all false gods, who were utterly incapable of rendering aid, still less of performing prodigies, for their deluded votaries; a warning also to Israel against the sin of idolatry to which they ever were so prone. As Joshua owned Jehovah as "the living God" so also Christ acknowledged the One who had sent Him as the "living Father" (John vi, 57).

"And Joshua said, Hereby ye shall know that the living God is among you" (verse 10). Note carefully the statement which immediately follows: "and that He will without fail drive out from before you the Canaanites," etc. We had naturally expected Joshua to say in this connection, God will open a way for you to pass through this Jordan, but instead he gives assurance of the conquest of the "seven nations in the land of Canaan" (Acts xiii, 19). And why? To assure Israel that the miracle of the Jordan was a Divine earnest, a certain guarantee, that the Lord *would continue* to show Himself strong in their behalf. And similarly He assures His people today. " Being confident of this very thing: that He which hath begun a good work in you, will finish it " (Phil. i, 6). Israel's supernatural journey through Jordan was a figure of our regeneration, when we pass from death unto life, and that experience ensures that the living God will *perfect* that which concerneth us " (Psa. cxxxviii, 8). In a word, regeneration is an infallible earnest of our ultimate glorification. But as Israel concurred with God, and were themselves active in driving out the Canaanites, *so we* have to mortify our lusts and overcome the world in order to possess our inheritance.

Yes, replies the reader, but that is much easier said than done. True, yet, not only is it indispensable that we should do so, but if due attention be paid to the passage before us and its spiritual application unto ourselves, valuable instruction will be found herein as to the secrets of success. Not to anticipate too much what yet remains to be considered in detail, let us summarize the leading points so far as they bear upon what was just said above. First, Israel was required to act with implicit confidence in God: so must we, if we are to be successful in our warfare, for it is " the good fight *of faith* " which we are called upon to wage. Second, Israel must render the most exact obedience to God's revealed will: so we can only prevail over our lusts and possess our possessions by walking in the path of His precepts. Third, Israel had to fix their eyes upon " the ark of the covenant ": so we are to be subject unto Christ in all things, and make daily use of His cleansing blood—the propitiatory which formed the lid of the ark. Fourth, " The Lord of all the earth "—God in His unlimited dominion—was the particular character in which Israel here viewed God: so we must rely upon His all-mighty power and count upon Him making us more than conquerors.

" Behold, the ark of the covenant of the Lord of all the earth passeth over before you into Jordan. Now therefore take you twelve men out of the tribes of Israel, out of every man a tribe. And it shall come to pass, as soon as the soles of the feet of the priests that bear the ark of the Lord, the Lord of all the earth, shall rest in the waters of Jordan, that the waters of Jordan shall be cut off from the waters that come down from above; and they shall stand upon a heap " (verses 11-13). In those words Joshua now specifically announced and described one of the most remarkable of the miracles recorded in Holy Writ. The priests were to proceed unto the edge of the water and then stop—that it might be the more evident that the Jordan was driven back at the presence of the Lord. As Matthew Henry wrote, " God could have divided the river without the priests, but they could not without Him. The priests must herein set a good example and teach the people to do their utmost in the service of God, and trust Him for help in time of need." Note how the opening word of verse 11 emphasized yet again that attention was to be concentrated upon *the ark*, which, as we have previously pointed out, was made for the Law and not the Law for it—typifying Christ, " made under the Law " (Gal. iv, 4), magnifying and making it honourable (Isa. xlii, 21).

Remember too that the propitiatory formed the lid of the ark: it was not only a cover for the sacred coffer, but a *shield* between the Law and the people of God. The central thing within it was the Law (I Kings viii, 9), and between the cherubim on its mercy seat Jehovah had His throne (Psa. xcix, 1). That is why all through Joshua iii and iv it is termed " the ark of the covenant," for when Moses went up upon Sinai the second time we are told that " he wrote upon the tables the words of the covenant, the ten commandments" (Ex. xxxiv, 28). It should be carefully borne in mind that even under the old covenant the *promise* preceded the giving of the Law (Ex. iii, 17; xii, 25), yet the fulfilment thereof was not to be without the enforcing of their accountability. In like manner the ten commandments themselves were prefaced by " I am the Lord thy God which have brought thee out of the land of Egypt," manifesting His " goodness " to them and His " severity " upon their enemies—that was the testimony of His character who entered into covenant with them.

It is to be duly noted that the particular designation given to Jehovah in connection with the ark of the covenant in verse 11 is repeated in verse 13, which at once intimates it is one of special weight and significance. This title, " the Lord of all the earth," is not found in the Pentateuch, occurring here in Joshua iii for the first time, its force being more or less indicated by what is said in verse 10 and the nature and time of the miracle then wrought. The reference here is unto God the Father, and signifies His absolute sovereignty and universal dominion—the Proprietor and Governor of the earth which He created, the One whom none can successfully resist. This title occurs in the Scriptures seven times! Twice in Joshua iii, then in Psalm xcvii, 5, Micah iv, 15, Zechariah vi, 5. In Zechariah iv, 14, we behold the three Persons of the Godhead in their covenant characters: " these are the two Anointed Ones [Christ and the Holy Spirit] that stand before the Lord of all the earth." But in Isaiah liv, 5, we see the incarnate Son, " the Lord of hosts is His name, and thy Redeemer the Holy One of Israel, the God of all the earth shall He be called "—a prophetic intimation of the taking down of the " middle wall of partition," when Jew and Gentile alike should own Him as their *God*.

THE DOCTRINE OF REVELATION

4. The Existence of God.

" *The sea* is His and He made it " (Psa. xcv, 5). The ocean and its inhabitants present to our consideration as many, as varied, and as unmistakable evidences of the handiwork of God as do the stellar and atmospheric heavens. If we give serious thought to the subject it must fill us with astonishment that it is possible for any creatures to live in such a suffocating element as the sea, and that in waters so salty they should be preserved in their freshness; and still more so that they should find themselves provided with abundant food and be able to propagate their species from one generation to another. If *we* were immersed in that element for a few minutes only, we should inevitably perish. Were it not for our actual observation and experience, and had we but read or heard that the briny deep was peopled with innumerable denizens, we should have deemed it an invention of the imagination, as something utterly impracticable and impossible. Yet by the wisdom and power of God not only are myriads of fishes sustained there, but the greatest of all living creatures—the whale—is found there. In number countless, in bulk matchless, yet having their being and health in an element in which *we* could not breathe!

As it is with us in the surrounding air, so it is with the fish in their liquid element: the principle of the equal transmission of pressure enables their frail structures to bear a much greater pressure and weight than their own without being crushed—the air and the fluids within them pressing outward *with a force as great* as the surrounding water presses inward! Moreover,

" They are clothed and accoutred in exact conformity to their clime. Not in swelling wool or buoyant feathers, nor in flowing robe or full-trimmed suit, but with as much compactness and with as little superfluity as possible. They are clad, or rather sheathed, in *scales,* which adhere closely to their bodies, and are always laid in a kind of natural oil; than which apparel nothing can be more light, and at the same time so solid, and nothing so smooth. It hinders the fluid from penetrating their flesh, it prevents the cold from coagulating their blood, and enables them to make their way through the waters with the greatest possible facility. If in their rapid progress they strike against any hard substance, this their scaly doublet breaks the force of it and secures them from harm " (Jas. Hervey).

Being slender and tapering the shape of fishes fits them to cleave the waters and to move with the utmost ease through so resisting a medium. Their tails, as is well known, are extremely flexible, consisting largely of powerful muscles, and act with uncommon agility. By its alternate impulsion the tail produces a progressive motion, and by repeated strokes propels the whole body forward. Still more remarkable is that wonderful apparatus or contrivance, the air-bladder, with which they are furnished, for it enables them to increase or diminish their specific gravity, to sink like lead or float like a cork, to rise to whatever height or sink to whatever depths they please. As these creatures probably have no occasion for the sense of hearing, for the impressions of sound have very little if any existence in their sphere of life, to have provided them with ears would have been an incumbrance rather than a benefit. Is that noticeable and benignant distinction to be ascribed to blind chance? Is it merely an accident that fishes, that need them not, are devoid of ears which *are* found in all the animals and birds? The cold logic of reason forbids such a conclusion.

A spiritually minded naturalist has pointed out that almost all flat fish, such as soles and flounders, are white on their underside but tinctured with darkish brown on the upper, so that to their enemies they resemble the colour of mud and are therefore more easily concealed. What is still more remarkable, Providence, which has given to other fishes an eye on either side of the head, has placed both eyes on the same side in *their* species, which is exactly suited unto the peculiarity of their condition. Swimming as they do but little, and always with their white side downward, an eye on the lower part of their bodies would be of little benefit, whereas on the higher they have need of the quickest sight for their preservation. Admirable arrangement is that! Where nothing is to be feared, the usual guard is withdrawn; where danger threatens their guard is not only placed, but doubled! Now we confidently submit that such remarkable adaptations as all of these argue design, and that, in turn, a designer, and a Designer too who is endowed with more than human wisdom, power and benignity.

" One circumstance relating to the natives of the deep is very peculiar, and no less astonishing. As they neither sow nor reap, have neither the produce of the hedges nor the gleanings of the field, they are obliged to plunder and devour one another for necessary subsistence. They are a kind of licensed banditti that make violence and murder their professed trade. By this means prodigious devastations ensue, and without proper, without *very extraordinary* recruits, the whole race would continually dwindle and at length become totally extinct. Were they to bring forth, like the most prolific of our terrestrial animals, a dozen only or a score, at each birth, the increase would be unspeakably too small for consumption. The weaker species would be destroyed by the stronger, and in time the stronger must perish, even by their successful endeavours to maintain themselves. Therefore to supply millions of assassins with their prey and millions of tables with their food, yet not to depopulate the watery realms, the issue produced by every breeder is almost incredible. They spawn not by scores or hundreds, but by thousands and tens of thousands. A single mother is pregnant with a nation. By which amazing but most needful expedient, a periodical reparation is made proportionable to the immense havoc " (Jas. Hervey).

" Speak to the earth, and it shall teach thee; and the fishes of the sea shall declare unto thee " (Job xii, 8). Mute though the fishes be, yet they are full of instruction for the thoughtful inquirer. Study them intelligently and thy mind shall be improved and thy knowledge increased. And *what is it* that the dumb fishes declare unto us? Surely this: that there is a living God, who is " wonderful in counsel and excellent in working " (Isaiah xxviii, 29); that the creature is entirely dependent on the Creator, who fails not to supply all its needs; that ready obedience to the Divine will becometh the creature, and is rendered by all save rebellious man. In exemplification of that last fact, let us call attention to that amazing phenomenon of countless multitudes of finny visitors crowding upon our shores at the appointed season of the year, and in an orderly succession of one species after another. What is equally remarkable, though less known, is the fact that as they approach, the larger and fiercer ones—who would endanger the lives of the fishermen and drive away the ones which provide us with food—are restrained by an invisible Hand and impelled to retire into the depths of the ocean. As the wild beasts of the earth are directed by the same over-ruling Power to hide themselves in their dens, so the monsters of the deep are laid under a providential interdiction!

If we survey with any degree of attention the innumerable objects which the inhabitants of this *earth* present to our view we cannot but perceive unmistakable marks of design, clear evidences of means suited to accomplish specific ends, and these also necessarily presuppose a Being who had those ends in view and devised the fitness of those means. Order and harmony in the combined operation of many separate forces and elements point to a superintending Mind. Wise contrivances and logical arrangements involve forethought and planning. Suitable accommodations and the appropriate and accurate fitting of one joint to another unquestionably evinces intelligence. The mutual adjustment of one member to another, especially when their functions and properties are correlated, can no more be fortuitous than particles of matter could arrange themselves into the wheels of a watch. The particular suitability of each organ of the body for its appointed office comes not by accident. Benevolent provision and the unfailing operation of law, logically imply a provider and a lawgiver. The fitting together of parts and the adoption of means to the accomplishment of a definite purpose can only be accounted for by reference to a designing Will. Thus, the argument from design may be fairly extended so as to include the whole range of creation and the testimony it bears in all its parts to the existence of the Creator.

Forcibly did Professor John Dick argue, " If we lighted upon a book containing a well-digested narrative of facts, or a train of accurate reasoning, we should never think of calling it a work of chance, but would immediately pronounce it to be the production of a cultivated mind. If we saw in a wilderness a building well proportioned and commodiously arranged and furnished with taste, we should conclude without hesitation and without the slightest suspicion of mistake that human will and human labour had been employed in planning and erecting it. In cases of this kind, an atheist would reason precisely as other men do. Why then does he not draw the same inference from the proofs of design which are discovered in the works of creation? While the premises are the same, why is the conclusion different? Upon what pretext of reason does he deny that a work, in all the parts of which wisdom appears, is the production of an intelligent author? And attribute the universe to chance, to nature, to necessity, to anything, although it should be a word without meaning, rather than to God ? "

"He that planted the ear, shall He not hear? and He that formed the eye, shall He not see? " (Psa. xciv, 9). The manifest adaptedness of the ear to receive and register sounds, and of the eye for vision, argues an intelligent Designer of them. The infidel will not allow that conclusion, but what alternative explanation does he offer? This: there may be adaptation without design, as there may be sequence without causation. Certain things he tells us, are adapted to certain uses, but not made *for* certain uses: the eye is capable of vision, but had no designing author. When he be asked, How is this striking adaptation to be accounted for apart from design, he answers, Either by the operation of law, or by chance. But the former explanation is really the acknowledgment of a designer, or it is mere tautology, for that law itself must be accounted for, as much as the phenomena which come under it. The explanation of "chance" is refuted by the mathematical doctrine of probability. The chance of matter acting in a certain way is not one in a million, and in a combination of ways, not one in a trillion. According to that theory, natural adaptation would be more infrequent than a miracle, whereas the fact is that adaptation to an end is one of the most common features of nature, occuring in innumerable instances.

When the Psalmist said, "I am fearfully and wonderfully made" (Psa. cxxxix, 14), he gave expression to a sentiment which every thoughtful person must readily endorse. Whether that statement be taken in its widest latitude as contemplating man as a composite creature—considering him as a material, rational and moral being—or whether it be restricted to his physical frame, yet it will be heartily confirmed by all who are qualified to express an opinion thereon. Regarding it in its narrower scope, the composition and construction of the human body is a thing of amazing workmanship. To what extent David was acquainted with the science of anatomy we know not, but in view of the pyramids and the Egyptians' skill in embalming the body (and "Moses was learned in all the wisdom of the Egyptians"—Acts vii, 22—and doubtless passed on much of the same unto his descendants) and the repeated statement of Holy Writ that "there is nothing new under the sun," we certainly do not believe the ancients were nearly so ignorant as many of our inflated moderns wish to think. But be that as it may, the outward structure of the body, the ordering of its joints and muscles for the service of its tenant, the proportion of all its parts, the symmetry and beauty of the whole, cannot but strike with wonderment the attentive student of the human frame.

This living temple has aptly been termed "the masterpiece of creation." Its sinews and muscles, veins and blood, glands and bones, all so perfectly fitted for their several functions, are a production which for wisdom and design, the adaptation of means to ends, not only far surpasses the most skilful and complicated piece of machinery ever produced by human art, but altogether excels whatever the human imagination could conceive. That the nutritive power of the body should be working perpetually and without intermission replacing waste tissue, that there should be a constant flowing of the blood and beating of the pulses, that the lungs and arteries (comprised of such frail and delicate substances) should move without cessation for seventy or ninety years—for nine hundred years before the Flood!—presents a combined marvel which should fill us with astonishment and awe, for they are so many miracles of omniscience and omnipotence. But turning to the more obvious and commonplace, the human hand and eye, let us conclude this article with a rather longer quotation than usual from *The Gordian Knot*, for it calls attention to features which, though equally remarkable, the most untrained are able to appreciate.

"The human *hand* was obviously meant to be the servant of the entire body. It is put at the extremity of the arm, and the arm is about half the length of the body, and, as the body can bend almost double, the hand can reach any part of it. The hand is at the end of an arm having three joints, one at the shoulder, one at the elbow, one at the wrist, and each joint made on a different pattern so as to secure together every conceivable motion—up and down, sidewise, backward and forward, and rotary. The hand is made with four fingers and an opposing thumb, which secures a double leverage, without which no implement or instrument could be securely grasped, held, or wielded, and so strangely are the fingers moulded of unequal lengths that they exactly touch tips over a spherical surface, such as a ball or the round handle of a tool.

"There are two hands—opposite and apposite to each other in position and construction, so that they exactly fit each other and work together without interference, making possible by joint action what neither could accomplish alone. Montaigne, referring to one only of the hand's many capacities—gesture—says: 'With the hand we demand, promise, call, dismiss, intreat, deny, encourage, accuse, acquit, defy, flatter, and indicate silence; and with a variety and multiplication that almost keep pace with the tongue.' The hand is so strikingly capable of being used to express conceptions and execute designs that it has been called 'the intellectual member.'

"The human *eye* is perfect in structure and equally perfect in adaptation. It is placed in the head like a window just under the dome, to enable us to see farthest; placed in front, because we habitually move forward; shielded in a socket of bone, for protection to its delicate structure, yet protected from that socket by a soft cushion; provided with six sets of muscles, to turn it in every direction; with lids and lashes, to moisten, shut it in, protect it and soothe it; with tear duct, to conduct away excess of moisture; and having that exact shape—the only one of all that might have been given—to secure distinct vision by refracting all rays of light to a single surface, which is known in science as the ellipsoid of revolution.

"By a wonderful arrangement of iris and pupil it at once adapts itself to near and far objects of vision and to mild or intense rays of light, and, most wonderful of all, the human eye is 'provided in some inscrutable manner with the means of expressing the mind itself, so that one may look into its crystal depths and see intellectuality, scorn, and wrath, and love, and almost every spiritual state and action' (Dr. E. F. Burr).

"The eye of man has taught us the whole science of optics. It is a camera obscura, with a convex lens in front, an adjustable circular blind behind it; a lining of black to prevent double and confusing reflections; humors, aqueous and vitreous, to distend it; a retina or expansion of the optic nerve, to receive the images of external objects; with minute provision for motion in every direction; and, most wonderful of all, perhaps, perfect provision against the spherical and chromatic aberration which would produce images and impressions ill defined and false coloured. Yet the microscope shows these lenses themselves to be made up of separate folds, in number countless, the folds themselves composed of fibers equally countless, and toothed so as to interlock. And with all this, perfect transparency is preserved!

"It is in the *minutiae* of creation, perhaps, that the most surprising marvels, mysteries and miracles of creative workmanship are often found. It is here also that the works of God so singularly differ from the works of man. However elaborate man's work it does not bear minute microscopic investigation. For instance, the finest cambric needle becomes coarse, rough and blunt under the magnifying lens, whereas it is only when looked at with the highest power of the microscopic eye that Nature's handiwork really begins to reveal its exquisite and indescribable perfection. Where the perfection of man's work ends the perfection of God's work only begins.

"The proofs of this perfection in *minutiae are lavishly abundant.* When a piece of chalk is drawn over a blackboard, in the white mark on the board, or the powder that falls on the floor, are millions of tiny white shells, once the home of life. The dust from the moth's wing is made up of scales or feathers, each as perfect as the ostrich plume. The pores of the human skin are so closely crowded together that seventy-five thousand of them might be covered by a grain of sand. The insect's organ of vision is a little world of wonders in itself. In the eye of a butterfly thirty-four thousand lenses have been found, each perfect as a means of vision. The minute cells in which all life, vegetable and animal, reside present as true an evidence of the mysterious perfection of individual workmanship and mutual adaptation as the constellations that adorn the sky, and equally with them declare the glory of God! How it speaks of a *Creator* who can lavish beauty even on the stones, and who carries the perfection of His work into the realm of the least as well as the greatest!"

THE GREAT CHANGE

"According as His Divine power has given unto us all things that pertain unto life and godliness, through the knowledge of Him that hath called us by glory and virtue. Whereby are given unto us exceeding great and precious promises, that by these ye might be partakers of the Divine nature, having escaped the corruption that is in the world through lust" (II Peter i, 3, 4). That is more of a general description of experimental salvation than a delineation of any particular part thereof, yet since there be in it one or two expressions not found elsewhere, it calls for a separate consideration. The opening "According as" should be rendered "Forasmuch as" or "Seeing that" (R.V.), for it indicates not so much a standard of comparison, as that verses 3 and 4 form the ground of the exhortation of verses 5 to 7. First, we have their spiritual enduement. This was by "Divine power," or as Ephesians i, 19, expresses it, "the exceeding greatness of His power to usward, who believe according to the working of His mighty power," for nothing less could quicken souls dead in trespasses and sins or free the slaves of sin and Satan.

That Divine power " hath given unto us [not merely offered them in the Gospel, but hath graciously bestowed, actually communicated] all things that pertain unto life and godliness ": that is, whatever is needful for the production, preservation and perfecting of spirituality in the souls of God's elect. Yet though the recipients be completely passive, yea, unconscious of this initial operation of Divine grace, they do not continue so, for, second, their enduement is accompanied by and accomplished " through the knowledge of Him that hath [effectually] called us by glory and virtue " or " energy." That " knowledge of Him " consists of such a personal revelation of Himself to the soul as imparts a true, spiritual, affecting, transforming perception of and acquaintance with His excellency. It is such a knowledge as enables its favoured recipient in adoring and filial recognition to say, " I have heard of Thee by the hearing of the ear; but now mine eye seeth Thee " (Job xlii, 5). God has now become an awe-producing, yet a living and blessed reality to the renewed soul.

Third, through that spiritual " knowledge " which God has imparted to the soul is received all the gracious benefits and gifts of His love: " Whereby are given unto us exceeding great and precious promises, that by these ye might be partakers," etc. The " whereby " has reference to " His glory and virtue," or better " His glory and energy " or " might." The " promises " are " given unto us " not simply in words but in their actual fulfilment: just as the " by His glory and might " is the same thing as " His Divine power " in the previous verse, so " are given unto us exceeding great and precious promises, that by these ye might be partakers of the Divine nature " corresponds with " hath given unto us all things that pertain unto life and godliness," the one amplifying the other. The " exceeding great and precious promises " were those made in the Old Testament—the original (Gen. iii, 15), fundamental, central, and all-pervading one being that of a personal Saviour; and those made by Christ, which chiefly respected the gift and coming of the Holy Spirit, which He expressly designated as " *the* promise of the Father " (Acts i, 4).

Now those two promises—that of a Divine Saviour and that of a Divine Spirit—were the things that the prophets of old " ministered not unto themselves, but unto us " (I Peter i, 12), and they may indeed most fitly be termed " exceeding great and precious promises," for they ' who are given this Saviour and this Spirit do in effect receive " all things that pertain unto life and godliness," for Christ becomes their Life and the Spirit their Sanctifier. Or, as verse 3 expresses it, the end for which this knowledge (as well as its accompanying blessings) are bestowed is first " that by these [i.e. the promises as fulfilled and fulfilling in your experience] ye might be partakers of the Divine nature." Here we need to be on our guard against forming a wrong conclusion from the bare sound of those words: " Not the essence of God, but His communicable excellencies, such moral properties as may be imparted to the creature, and those not considered in their absolute perfection, but as they are agreeable to our present state and capacity " (Thos. Manton).

That " Divine nature," or " moral properties," is sometimes called " the life of God " (Eph. iv, 18), because it is a vital principle of action; sometimes the " image of Him " (Col. iii, 10), because they bear a likeness to Him— consisting essentially of " righteousness and true holiness " (Eph. iv, 24); or in verse 3, " life and godliness "—spiritual life, spiritual graces, abilities to perform good works. It is here called " the Divine nature " because it is the communication of a vital principle of operation which God transmits unto

His children. The second end for which this saving knowledge of God is given is expressed in the closing words: " having escaped the corruption which is in the world through lust." Personally we see no need for taking up this expression *before* " partakers of the Divine nature " as that eminent expositor Thos. Manton did, and as did the most able John Lillie (to whom we are indebted for part of the above), for the apostle is not here enforcing the human-responsibility side of things (as he *was* in Rom. xiii, 12; Eph. iv, 22-24), but treats of the Divine operations and their effects.

It is quite true that *we* must put off the old man before we can put on the new man in a practical way, that we must first attend to the work of mortification ere we can make progress in our sanctification, but this is not the aspect of Truth which the apostle is *here* unfolding. When the Gospel call is addressed unto our moral agency the promise is " that whosoever believeth in Him should not perish, *but have* eternal life " (John iii, 15, 16). But where spiritual things are concerned, the unregenerate man never discharges his moral agency. A miracle of grace must take place before he does that, and therefore God in a sovereign manner (unsought by us) imparts life, that he may and will believe (John i, 12, 13; I John v, 1)—the " sanctification of the Spirit " precedes the saving " and belief of the Truth " (II Thess. ii, 13)! In like manner, our becoming " partakers of the Divine nature " precedes (not in time, but in order of nature and of actual experience, though not of consciousness) our escaping " the corruption that is in the world through lust."

Let not the young preacher be confused by what has been pointed out in the last paragraph. His marching orders are plain: when addressing the unsaved he is to enforce their responsibility, press upon them the discharging of their duties, bidding them forsake their " way " and " thoughts " *in order to* pardon (Isa. lv, 7), calling upon them to " repent " and " believe " if they would be saved. But if God be pleased to own his preaching of the Word and pluck some brands from the burning, it is quite another matter (or aspect of Truth) for the preacher (and, later on, his saved hearer, by means of doctrinal instruction) to understand something of the nature of that miracle of grace which God wrought in the hearer, which caused him to savingly receive the Gospel. It is *that* which we have endeavoured to deal with in the above paragraphs, namely, explain something of the operations of Divine grace in a renewed soul, so far as those operations are described in II Peter i, 3, 4.

" Having escaped the corruption that is in the world through lust." First, by the Divine operation, and then by our own agency, for it is ever " God which worketh in you both *to* will and *to* do of His good pleasure " (Phil. ii, 13). Indwelling sin (depravity) is here termed " corruption " because it blighted our primitive purity, degenerated our original state, and because it continues both in its nature and effects to pollute and waste. That " corruption " has its source, or is seated in, our " lusts "—depraved affections and appetites. This " corruption " is what another apostle designated " evil concupiscence " (Col. iii, 5), for it occupies in the heart that place which is due alone unto the love of God as the Supreme Good. " Lust " always follows the " nature ": as is the nature, so are its desires— if corrupt, then evil; if holy, then pure. All the corruption that is in the world is " through lust," i.e. through inordinate desire: lust lies at the bottom of every unlawful thought, every evil imagination.

The world could harm no man were it not for "lust" in his heart—some inordinate desire in the understanding or fancy, a craving for something which sets him a-work after it. The fault is not in the gold, but in the spirit of covetousness which possesses men; not in the wine, but in their craving to excess. "But every man is tempted when he is drawn away of *his own* lust" (James i, 14)—the blame lies on us rather than Satan! It is remarkable that when the apostle explained his expression "all that is in the world," he defined it as "the lust of the flesh, and the lust of the eye, and the pride of life" (I John ii, 16). Now of Christians our passage says, "having escaped the corruption that is in the world through lust," and that by the interposition of the Divine hand, as Lot escaped from Sodom; yet not through a simple act of omnipotence, but by the gracious bestowments which that hand brings, by that holiness which He works in the heart, or, as a passage already reviewed expresses it, "by the washing of regeneration and renewing of the Holy Spirit." We escape from the dominion of inward corruption by the "Divine nature in us" causing us to hate and resist our evil lusts.

Thus it is by adhering closely to the Divine order of this passage that we are enabled to understand the meaning of its final clause. When we become partakers of "the Divine nature," that is, when we are renewed after the image of God, a principle of grace and holiness is communicated to the soul, which is called "spirit" because "born of the Spirit" (John iii, 6), and that principle of holiness (termed by many "the new nature") is a vital and operating one, which offers opposition to the workings of "corruption" or indwelling sin, for not only does the flesh lust against the spirit, but "the spirit lusteth against the flesh" (Gal. v, 17). The "Divine nature" has wrought "godliness" in us, drawing off the heart of its recipient from the world to heaven, making him to long after holiness and pant for communion with God. Herein lies the radical difference between those described in II Peter i, 3, 4, and the ones in II Peter ii, 20—nothing is said of the latter being "partakers of the Divine nature"! Their "escaping from the pollutions of the world" was merely a temporary reformation from *outward* defilements and gross sins, as their *turning again* to the same makes clear (verse 22).

"We know that we have passed from death unto life because we love the brethren" (I John iii, 14). Here is set before us still another criterion by which the Christian may determine whether the great change has been wrought in him. First, let us point out that it seems to be clearly implied here (as in other places in this epistle: e.g. ii, 3; iv, 13) that the miracle of grace is *not* perceptible to our senses at the moment it occurs, but is cognizable by us afterward from its effects and fruits. We cannot recall a single statement in Scripture which expressly declares or even plainly implies that the saint is conscious of regeneration during the moment of quickening. There are indeed numbers (the writer among them) who can recall and specify the very hour when they were first convicted of sin, realized their lost condition, trusted in the atoning blood, and felt the burden of their hearts roll away. Nevertheless, they knew not when life was imparted unto their spiritually dead souls—life which prompted them *to* breathe, feel, see, hear and act in a way they never had previously. Life must be present before there can be any of the functions and exercises of life. One dead in sin cannot savingly repent and believe.

Now it is one of the designs for which the first epistle of John was written that the regenerate may have assurance that eternal life has been imparted to them (v, 13), several different evidences and manifestations of that life being described in the course of the apostle's letter. The one specified in iii, 14, is " love for the brethren." By nature we were inclined to hate the children of God. It could not be otherwise: since we hated God, and that because He is holy and righteous, we despised those in whom the image of His moral perfections appeared. Contrariwise, when the love of God was shed abroad in our hearts and we were brought to delight ourselves in Him, His people became highly esteemed by us, and the more evidently they were conformed unto His likeness, the more we loved them. That " love " is of a vastly superior nature from any natural sentiment, being a holy principle. Consequently, it is something very different from mere zeal for a certain group or party spirit, or even an affection for those whose sentiments and temperaments are like our own. It is a Divine, spiritual and holy love which goes out unto the whole family of God: not respect to this or that brother, but which embraces " the brethren " at large.

That of which I John iii, 14, treats is a peculiar love for those saved by Christ. To love the Redeemer and His redeemed is congenial to the spiritual life which has been communicated to their renewed souls. It is a fruit of that holy disposition which the Spirit has wrought in them. It must be distinguished from what is so often mis-termed " love " in the natural realm, which consists only of sentimentality and amiability. The regenerate " love the brethren " not because they are affable and genial, or because they give them a warm welcome to their circle. They " love the brethren " not because they deem them wise and orthodox, but because of their *godliness*, and the more their godliness is evidenced the more will they love them; and hence they love *all* the godly—no matter what be their denominational connections. They love those whom Christ loves, they love them for His sake —because they belong to Him. Their love is a spiritual, disinterested and faithful one which seeks the good of its objects, which sympathizes with them in their spiritual trials and conflicts, which bears them up in their prayers before the throne of grace, which unselfishly shows kindness unto them, which admonishes and rebukes when that be necessary.

But that to which we would here direct particular attention is the language employed by the Spirit in describing the great change, namely, " passed from death unto life." The same expression was used by our Lord in John v, 24, though there its force is rather different. " Verily, verily, I say unto you, He that heareth [with an inward or spiritual ear] My word, and [savingly] believeth on Him that sent Me, *hath everlasting life* [the very fact he so heareth and believeth is proof he has it] and shall not come into condemnation, but is passed from death unto life." The " shall not come into condemnation " brings in the forensic side of things, and therefore the " hath passed from death unto life " (which, be it duly noted, is in addition to " hath everlasting life " in the preceding clause) is *judicial*. The one who has had " everlasting life " sovereignly imparted to him, and who in consequence thereof " hears " or heeds the Gospel of Christ and savingly believes, has for ever emerged from the place of condemnation, being no longer under the curse of the Law, but now entitled to its award of " life," by virtue of the personal obedience or meritorious righteousness of Christ being imputed unto him; for which reason he is exhorted " reckon ye also yourself to be dead indeed unto sin but alive unto God through [in] Jesus Christ our Lord " (Rom. vi, 11).

But I John iii, 14, is not treating of the forensic or legal side of things, but the experimental, that of which God's elect are made the subjects of in their own persons. Here it is not a relative change (one in relation to the Law), but an actual one that is spoken of. They have " passed from " that fearful state in which they were born—" alienated from the life of God " (Eph. iv, 18): a state of unregeneracy. They have been supernaturally and effectually called forth from the grave of sin and death. They have entered " into life," which speaks of the state which they are now in before God as the consequence of His quickening them. They have for ever left that sepulchre of spiritual death in which by nature they lay, and have been brought into the spiritual sphere to " walk in newness of life." And " love for the brethren " is one of the effects and evidences of the miracle of grace of which they have been the favoured subjects. They evince their spiritual resurrection by this mark: they love the beloved of Christ; their hearts are spontaneously drawn out unto and they earnestly seek the good of all who wear Christ's yoke, bear His image and seek to promote His glory. I John iii, 14, is not an exhortation but a factual statement of Christian experience.

Now let the reader most diligently note that in I John iii, 14, the Holy Spirit has employed the figure of *resurrection* to set forth the great change, and that *it* also must be given due place in our thoughts as we endeavour to form something approaching an adequate conception of what the miracle of grace consists. Due consideration of this figure should check us in pressing too far that of the new birth. The similitude of resurrection brings before us something distinct and in some respects quite different from that which is connoted by " new creation," " begetting " (Jas. i, 18) or being " born again " (I Peter i, 23). Each of the latter denotes the bringing into existence of something which previously existed not; whereas " resurrection " is the quickening of what is there already. The miracle of grace consists of far more than the communication of a new life or nature: it also includes the renovation and purification of the original soul. Because it is a " miracle," an act of omnipotence, accomplished by the mere fiat of God, it is appropriately likened unto " creation," yet it needs to be carefully borne in mind that it is not some *thing* which is created in us: for " we [ourselves] are His workmanship created in Christ Jesus " (Eph. ii, 10). It is the person himself, and not merely a nature, which is born again.

We have now reviewed not less than twenty-five passages from God's Word, wherein a considerable variety of terms and figures are used to set forth the *different aspects of* the great change which takes place in a person when the miracle of grace is wrought within him; all of which passages, in our judgment, treating of the same. We have not sought to expound or comment upon them at equal length, but, following our usual custom, have rather devoted the most space in an attempt to explain those which are least understood, which present the most difficulty to the average reader, and upon which the commentators often supply the least help. A comparison of those passages will at once show that what theologians generally speak of as " regeneration " or " the effectual call " is very far from being expressed by the Holy Spirit in uniform language, and therefore that those who restrict their ideas to what is connoted by being born again, or, even on the other hand, " a change of heart," are almost certain to form a very one-sided, inadequate and faulty conception of what experimental salvation consists. Regeneration is indeed a new birth, or the beginning of a new life; but that is not *all* it is—

there is also something resurrected and renewed, and something washed and transformed!

The Bible is not designed for lazy people. Truth has to be *bought* (Prov. xxiii, 23), but the slothful and worldy minded are not willing to pay the price required. That " price " is intimated in Proverbs ii, 1-5: there must be a diligent applying of the heart, a crying after knowledge, a seeking for an apprehension of spiritual things with that ardour and determination as men employ when seeking for silver; and a searching for a deeper and fuller know-ledge of the Truth as men put forth when searching for hid treasures— persevering until their quest is successful; if we would really understand the things of God. Those who complain that these articles are " too difficult " or " too deep " for them, do but betray the sad state of their souls and reveal how little they really value the Truth; otherwise they would ask God to enable them to concentrate, and re-read these pages perseveringlv until they made its contents their own. People are willing to work and study hard and long to master one of the arts or sciences, but where spiritual and eternal things are concerned it is usually otherwise.

(continued from back page)

if faith be engaged with its Beloved and ravished with His perfections it will evoke song unto Him, about Himself, as it did from the bleeding and manacled apostles in the Philippian dungeon (Acts xvi)!

" Sing unto the Lord O ye saints, and give thanks at the remembrance of His holiness " (Psa. xxx, 4). The Divine holiness is indeed an attribute which inspires deepest awe, yet it also evokes praise from those enabled to discern its supernatural beauty. " Holy, holy, holy! " is the song of the seraphim, and in it the saints should join, as Israel did at the Red Sea when they adored Jehovah for being " glorious in holiness " (Ex. xv, 1): " My tongue shall sing aloud of Thy righteousness " (Psa. li, 14): can it be otherwise when the soul is assured His righteousness is imputed unto Himself! " I will sing of Thy power " (Psa. lix, 16): we must do so if we realize that power is not against but is " to usward " (Eph. i, 19). " I will sing of the mercies of the Lord " (Psa. lxxxix, 1): it was not merely that the Psalmist was then in " a happy frame," but that his faith was exercised on its Object! " Thy statutes have been my songs in the house of my pilgrimage " (cxix, 54): " Happy is the heart which finds its joy in God's commands and makes obedience its recreation " (Spurgeon).

Observe well, my reader, that one thing is most conspicuous by its absence from the above passages: there is nothing whatever in those songs about man's experiences, not a word about *his* peace, *his* joy, *his* assurance, *his* progress. Again we say, what a contrast from the sickly rubbish which now passes as " hymns." The theme of Israel's song at the Red Sea, of Isaiah's, of the Psalmist's, were the perfections of *the Lord*: HIS holiness, righteousness, power, mercy, statutes. And when *that* be the theme, the song needs neither musical instruments as an " accompaniment " nor a trained choir to " render " it! The only song acceptable unto God is that which issues from a renewed soul, which is prompted by faith, and is directed by love. You may, dear friend, be cut off from other saints, unable to mingle your voice with theirs in public worship, yet in the privacy of your own room you can be engaged in " singing and making melody *in your heart* to the Lord " (Eph. v, 19), and thereby anticipate Heaven.

handiwork of God, and sin and crying, rather than sin and singing, more fitly accompany one another. It is salvation from sin which constitutes both the suitable occasion and the appropriate theme for song. Hence it is we read in Exodus xv, 1. " Then sang 'Moses and the children of Israel this song unto the Lord." That was in most blessed contrast from what had characterized them while they toiled amid the brick kilns of Egypt. There were no joyful strains upon the lips of the Hebrews while they laboured under the taskmasters of Pharaoh: instead we read, that " the children of Israel sighed by reason of the bondage, and they cried . . . and God heard their groaning " (Ex. ii, 23, 24).

" *Then* sang Moses and the children of Israel " (Ex. xv, 1). When? The closing verses of xiv tell us: " the Lord *saved* Israel that day out of the hand of the Egyptians, and Israel saw the Egyptians dead upon the sea shore. And Israel saw that great work which the Lord did . . . and *believed* the Lord." Ah, it is faith, and not unbelief, which evokes the spiritual song: a faith which perceived " Thou in Thy mercy hast led forth the people which Thou hast *redeemed* " (xv, 13). It was the song of redemption which issued from the hearts of an emancipated people. Conscious of being freed from their bondage, they fervently praised their Deliverer. And *what* did they sing about? Entirely of Jehovah: " I will sing unto the Lord for He hath triumphed gloriously " (verse 1). There was nothing about themselves: it was wholly concerning Him. The word " Lord " occurs no less than twelve times in eighteen verses, while the pronouns " He, Him, Thy, Thee, Thou " are found no less than thirty-three times! " I will exalt *Him* " (verse 2) expressed their design, as it must that of every truly spiritual song. If the Lord engage our hearts and minds there will be less groaning and more singing!

" Now will I sing a song to my Wellbeloved, a song of my Beloved " (Isa. v, 1). Not only is He the Object of that song but its Theme too. How different this from modern hymnology! The majority of the hymns (if such they are entitled to be called) of the past fifty years are full of maudlin sentimentality instead of Divine adoration. They announce *our* love to God, instead of His to us. They recount our experiences instead of His excellencies. They describe human attainments far more than they do Christ's atonement. Sad index to the lack of spirituality in the churches. While the jingling tunes to which they are set and the irreverent speed at which they are sung witness only too plainly unto the low state of present-day religion. Christian singing has been *carnalized* both in its conception and its execution. Singing, like anything else which is acceptable unto the Father, must be " in spirit and in truth," and not a musical performance of the flesh.

The singing which the Scriptures inculcate is not a thing of the senses but of faith. It is not an outburst of emotional exuberance but an expression of the heart's adoration. God is the Object of faith, and when that grace be in exercise the soul is absorbed with His perfections and melodious praise fills it. " I will pray with the spirit and I will pray with the understanding also. I will sing with the spirit [not merely the throat] and I will sing with the understanding [not the emotions] also " (I Cor. xiv, 15): how that lifts those holy exercises above the plane of our natural feelings! Unless the Christian's singing proceeds from the " spirit " or new nature it is but lip service. Faith rises above nature and triumphs over all circumstances. No matter how distressing our situation, how low we may be in our feelings,

(continued on preceding page)

XXVI   MAY 1947   No. 5

STUDIES IN THE SCRIPTURES

"Search the Scriptures." *John v, 39*

Publisher and Editor—ARTHUR W. PINK,
29 Lewis Street,
Stornoway, Isle of Lewis,
Scotland.

THE GOLDEN RULE

" Therefore all things whatsoever ye would that men should do to you, do ye even so to them: for this is the Law and the Prophets" (Matt. vii, 12). The "therefore" points back to the foregoing section of our Lord's sermon (verses 7-11), and it intimates three things. First, that privileges and duties must not be separated: blessing from God is designed to enable us the better to discharge our responsibilities unto men. Second, otherwise our future praying will be hindered. "We cannot expect to receive good things from God if we do not fair things and that which is lovely and of good report among men. We must not only be devout, but honest, else our devotion is but hypocrisy." (Matt. Henry.) Third, much Divine grace is required by us in order to our performing the duty here enjoined, and such must be sought diligently and daily at the throne of grace. In what follows that opening "therefore" our Lord has given us a brief but comprehensive rule for the regulating of our conduct unto our fellows, the carrying out of which plays no small part in evidencing the genuineness of our profession and the suitable adorning of the same. That golden rule embodies in an abridged form the teaching of the Law and the Prophets on this subject, and proves that Christianity enforces *their* requirements.

"All things whatsoever ye would that men should do to you, do ye even so to them." There is a special need to press this injunction upon God's people today. This is a generation which is characterized by gross selfishness, when the law of decency has been displaced by the lawlessness of the savage, when good manners are a thing of the past, when human beings conduct themselves more like hogs at the trough or hungry dogs fighting for a bone. There is no regard for the rights of others, and therefore no concern for the comforts of others. It is every man for himself, whether scrambling into a train or bus, or turning on his radio full blast without any consideration for his neighbours. In the past it was customary for those who preached or wrote on this text to say, The rule by which too many act is, Do unto others *as they* do unto you. But this generation has sunk lower than that: no matter what consideration be shown them, they exercise none unto their fellows. Courtesy is answered by rudeness, kindness by meanness. If you treat people decently and generously, they take a despicable advantage of what they regard as weakness.

(continued on back page)

Important Notices

Please advise promptly of change in address, otherwise copies will be lost in the mails.

We are glad to send a sample copy to any of your friends whom you believe would be interested in this publication.

This magazine is published as "a work of faith and labour of love," the editor and his wife gladly giving their services free. There is no regular subscription price, as we do not wish the poor of the flock to be deprived. This does not mean that those looking for something for nothing may "help themselves." Those getting this magazine who are financially able and who receive spiritual help from its pages, are expected to gladly contribute towards its expenses; otherwise their names are dropped from our list.

Will those forwarding International Money Orders please have them made out to us at Stornoway, Isle of Lewis, Scotland. Checks (Cheques—Eng.) made out on U.S.A. Banks are not negotiable here, so please do not send them.

All unsigned articles are by the Editor.

CONTENTS

THE PRAYERS OF THE APOSTLES

41. Colossians i, 9-12

"Strengthened with all might according to His glorious power, unto all patience and longsuffering with joyfulness" (verse 11). It will appear unto some of our readers that we are drawing out these articles to a wearisome length, but others will be thankful to find in them something more profitable than the brief and superficial generalizations which characterize most of the religious literature of this day. Our aim in them is to do something more than furnish bare expositions of the passages before us, namely, foster a spirit of devotion and provide that which will be of practical use in the daily life of the Christian. Take this present verse as an example. It is indeed important that the reader should obtain a correct idea of the terms used in it, yet he needs much more than that. To supply a full and lucid definition of what patience is, and then exhort one who is in acutely trying circumstances to exercise that grace, will be of little real help. To bid him pray for an increase of it, is saying nothing more than he already knows. But to point out how patience is wrought and increased in us, what are the means for the development of it and the things which hinder—in short, what God requires from us in order to increase its growth—will surely be more to the point.

First, the apostle prays that the saints might be "strengthened with all might according to His glorious power." Such language implies that it was no ordinary strength for which he here supplicated, such as in his general deportment does commonly assist the Christian unto holy exercises and acts, but rather that an unusual, yea, "glorious power," was required for the particular task in view. His language argues that he had in mind an exercise of grace more difficult than any other, one from which our constitutions are so naturally remote that more than ordinary diligence and earnestness must be put forth by us at the Mercy-seat in the obtaining of this urgently needed supply. Every act of grace by us must needs have an act of Divine power going before it to draw it forth into exercise. As "the work of faith" is "with power" (II Thess. i, 11), so the work of patience to bear afflictions requires a Divine strengthening of the soul, and to acquit ourselves with "all patience and longsuffering with joyfulness" necessitates that we be "strengthened with all might according to God's glorious power."

To be "strengthened with all might" signifies to be mightily strengthened, to be given a supply of grace amply sufficient unto the end in view. It means spiritual energy proportioned unto whatever was needed, with all they would have occasion for, to enable them to discharge their duty and carry themselves in a manner pleasing and honouring to God. "According to His glorious power" imports both the excellency and sufficiency of it. The glory of God's power is most seen when it appears as an *overcoming* power, when victory attends it: as when we read that "Christ was raised up from the dead by the *glory* of the Father" (Rom. vi, 4). Thus the apostle sets over against our utter weakness the "all might" of Divine grace, and "His glorious power" against our sinful corruption. The special use to which this strength was to be put is "unto all patience," that is, sufficient for the enduring of all trials; "and longsuffering" would be patience drawn out to its greatest length; "with joyfulness," not only submitting unto trials without repining, but doing so gladly, rejoicing in the Lord alway. This third petition, then, was for such a supply of grace as would enable the saints to bear all trials with meek subjection, persevering constancy, and cheerfulness of spirit.

Again we see what an exalted standard of conduct is the one set before us, yet at the same time what blessed supplies of help are available. Say not such a standard is utterly unattainable by poor me, when the Lord declares "My grace is sufficient for thee"—sufficient not only to enable thee to endure "a thorn in the flesh, the messenger of Satan, to buffet," but also to make you resolve "Most gladly therefore will I rather glory in my infirmities that the power of Christ may rest upon me." Look not in unbelief upon either the number and might of your enemies or upon thine own weakness, but in the confidence of a humble but expectant faith say, "I can do all things through Christ which strengtheneth me" (Phil. iv, 13). And is not this "glorious strength" indeed, which enables its recipients to persevere in the path of duty notwithstanding much opposition, to bear up manfully under trials, yea, to rejoice in tribulations? What a glorious power is that which is proportioned unto all we are called upon to do and suffer, enabling us to resist the corruptions of the flesh, the allurements of the world, and the temptations of the Devil; which keeps us from either sinking into abject despair or making shipwreck of the faith; causing us to hold on our way unto the end.

And how is this "all might" secured? Some will answer: By no endeavour of ours; we in our helplessness can do no more in the obtaining of grace for the soul than the parched ground can cause refreshing showers to descend from heaven; we must submit to God's sovereign determination and hope for the best. But that is a denial of the Christian's responsibility. God indeed asks nothing from the ground, for it is an inanimate and irrational creature, but different far is it with moral agents, the more so when He has regenerated them. "For unto whomsoever much is given, of him shall be much required" (Luke xii, 48). And much *has* been given unto the one born of God: Christ is his in the forgiveness of sins, the Holy Ghost indwells him, life has been communicated to his soul, faith imparted to his heart; and therefore much may justly be required of him. Grace is not some mysterious influence which fortuitously descends and enters into the Christian's heart irrespective of how he acts. The opening word of our verse intimates the contrary, for "strengthening" implies God's blessing upon our use of suitable means—whether it be the strengthening of the body, the mind, or the spiritual life. Observe, the first (though not the only) means is an earnest and importunate crying unto God.

It is both our privilege and our duty to come boldly (or "freely") unto the throne of grace, that we may obtain mercy (for past failures) and find grace to help in time of need. Oft-times we have not because we ask not, or because we ask amiss. Grace must be sought believingly, fervently, perseveringly, as Paul himself sought in II Cor. xii. Moreover, there has to be a daily feeding upon "the Word of His grace" (Acts xx, 32) if the soul is to be "nourished up in the words of grace" (I Tim. iv, 6). If we neglect our daily bread, fail to meditate upon and appropriate a regular supply of manna, we soon become feeble and faint. Further, exercise is essential: we must *use* the grace already given us if we would obtain more (Luke viii, 18). Spiritual strength is not given to release us from the fight of faith, but to furnish and fit us for the same. Grace is not bestowed upon the Christian in order that heaven may be won without engaging in a fierce conflict, as many seem to think, but in order that he may be "strong in the Lord and in the power of His might," and thereby to put on the whole armour of God, and thus "be able to stand against the wiles of the Devil." So in our text: we are strengthened with all might "unto [for this end] all patience."

We must now inquire into the nature of "patience," or, more specifically, the particular kind of patience which is here in view. It is a steady persisting in duty, which keeps one from being deterred by opposition or fainting under suffering. Actively, it finds expression in perseverance or refusing to quit the race because of the difficulties or length of the course. Passively, it appears in a meek and quiet spirit, which endures afflictions without repining. Primarily, though perhaps not exclusively, it is the latter that is spoken of here, namely, that frame of heart which bears submissively whatever trials and tribulations the Lord calls upon one to pass through. It is very much more than a placidity of temper which it not unduly provoked by the common irritations of life, for often that is more a matter of healthy nerves than a virtuous exercise of the mind and will. Grace is more potent than nature: it can make the timid courageous, cool the most hot-headed, quieten the impetuous. Grace works submissiveness in the most impulsive. It is a making our hearts calm when outward circumstances are tempestuous, and though God lets loose His winds upon us, He can keep us from being discomposed by them and lay the same command upon our passions as upon the angry waves—"Peace, be still."

We will now particularize a little, both negatively and positively, in order that it may more clearly appear what this grace of patience is. It is not a stoical apathy under the Divine dispensations. It is no narcotic virtue to stupefy us and take away the sense and feeling of afflictions. If it had any such opiate quality, then there would be nothing commendable or praiseworthy in it. That is no suffering which is not felt; and if patience deprived us of the feeling of sorrow, it would cease to be patience. During the past few years we have witnessed the mass of our fellows stupefied and insensible under the hand of God, taking no notice of Him when His judgments fell heavily upon them, enduring them with stolidity, or rather moral stupidity; but the senseless boast, "we can take it," was no more to be accounted patience than is the non-writhing of a block of wood when it is sawn and planed. Patience quickens the sufferings of a saint, for he refers them unto his deserts; consciousness of his sins in provoking God pierces his conscience and brings pain to his inner man also. But the wicked look only upon *what* they suffer, and make no reflection upon their deserts.

Nor does the grace of patience stifle all modest complaints and moderate sorrow. A patient Christian is permitted this vent through which his grief may find relief. Grace does not destroy but regulates and corrects nature. God allows His children to shed tears, so long as the course of them does not stir up the mud of their sinful passions and violent affections. It is not wrong to complain of what we suffer, so long as we complain not against God from whom we suffer. We may lawfully, and without any breach of patience, express our grief in all outward and natural signs of it, so long as that agitation exceeds not its due bounds and measures. Holy Job, who is commended to us as the great example of patience, when he received the sad news of the loss of his estate and of his children, "rent his mantle and fell down upon the ground" (i, 20); and that we might not regard this as a display of impatience, the Spirit has added, "In all this Job sinned not, nor charged God foolishly." The disciples made "great lamentation" over Stephen (Acts viii, 2), though by his martyrdom he had greatly glorified God. It is not grief, but the excess of it which is disallowed.

Nor does patience oblige us to continue under afflictions when we may warrantably free ourselves from them. As an eminent Puritan rightly pointed out: "When God lays sore and heavy afflictions upon us we are bound, under principles of self-preservation, to endeavour what we may to free ourselves from them; otherwise we sin against nature and the God of nature. Therefore if God reduce thee to poverty, by some stroke depriving thee of thy estate, it is not patience but a lax and sinful carelessness to sit still with thy hand in thy bosom, neglecting all honest industry to procure a comfortable subsistence, pretending that thou art willing to submit to the will and dispensation of God. If God bring sore and perhaps mortal disease upon thee, it is not patience but presumption and impiety to refuse the means which are prepared proper to thy recovery, under the pretence that thou art willing to bear whatever God is pleased to lay on thee. Generally, whatever calamity thou liest under, it is not patience, but obstinacy, to refuse deliverance when thou mayest obtain it without violating thy duty or dishonouring God" (Ezek. Hopkins.

Positively, patience consists of a willing submission to the dispensations of Divine providence. When Job said, "Shall we receive good at the hand of God, and shall we not receive evil?" (ii, 10), that was the language of patience. "The cup which My Father hath given Me, shall I not drink it?" (John xviii, 11) was the supreme example of this grace. It is the ready acquiesence of the soul under whatever God sees fit to lay upon it. It is the calm enduring of provocation and persecutions, especially trials which come unexpectedly. It is a steady and thankful bearing of all troubles, how ever grievous and long protracted, mortifying the opposite passions of fear, anger, anxiety, inordinate grief; refusing to be overwhelmed by those troubles, persevering in the discharge of duty unto the end; relieving one's self by faith in what is to be had in God, and from Him by communion with Him: resting in His love, leaning on His arms, and encouraging ourself by expectation of that eternal and blessed glory which awaits us after our appointed race is run.

Patience consists of that due tranquillizing or composing our minds which issues in the quieting of our unruly passions. Those may be very impatient persons, and fret and fume within, who express but little emotion outwardly. That impatience which finds no external vent is the most injurious and dangerous to character: as those latent fevers which lurk within and prey upon the animal spirits, when there appears but little intemperate heat in the limbs, are the most to be feared. Patience calms those storms and tempests which are apt to arise in the heart when a person is under any sore and heavy affliction. It is indeed impossible but that affections will be stirring, but this grace takes off the vigour and violence of them. All those turbulencies and uproars of the passions, all those wilful and wild emotions which distract reason and rend the soul, rendering us unfit for the service of God or the employment of our business, these patience ought to quell, and in measure does suppress. He who can rule his body better than his soul, his actions than his passions, lacks the principal part of patience.

All this must be done upon *right grounds*. This requires us to distinguish sharply between natural and Christian patience. There is a natural patience sometimes found in those devoid of true grace, yea, such a strength of character, a fortitude of mind, a tranquillity of spirit, which often puts, or should put, the people of God to shame. Yet that is only a moral virtue, proceeding only from natural and moral principles. Ah, says the Christian, and how am I, who naturally am so impulsive, so fiery, so fickle, to ascertain whether *my* patience be of a superior order? By the principles from which it proceeds, the motives actuating it, and the ends for which it is put forth. Moral virtue proceeds only from the principles of reason, and is actuated by such arguments as human prudence furnishes, and it is exercised to promote self-esteem or the respect of our fellows. Many an unregenerate person, by a process of self-discipline, has hardened himself to bear the evils which befall him, by persuading himself it is folly to rebel against fate and torment himself over the inevitable, telling himself that what cannot be cured must be endured, that to give way to peevishness is childish and will effect no good, and that to yield to a spirit of fury will but lower him in the eyes of others.

But spiritual patience proceeds from a principle of grace, is actuated by higher motives, and is induced by greatly superior considerations than those which regulate the most refined and self-controlled unregenerate person. Spiritual patience springs from faith (James i, 3), from hope (Rom. viii, 25), from love (II Thess. iii, 5; James i, 12). It is nourished by the Scriptures (Rom. xv, 4), that is, by what is taught us and exemplified therein. Patience eyes the sovereignty of God, to which it is our duty to submit. It eyes His benevolence and is assured that the most painful affliction is among the all things which He is making work together for our good. It looks off from the absolute nature of the affliction, considered as it is in itself, to the relative nature of it, as it is dispensed to us by God, and therefore concludes that though the cup be bitter, yet in our Father's hand it is salutary. Though the chastisement itself be grievous, patience realizes it will, if we be duly exercised, make us partakers of God's holiness here and of His glory hereafter. Patience eyes the example which Christ has left us and seeks grace to be conformed thereto. The Christian strives to exercise patience not out of self-esteem and because he is mortified when his passions get the better of him, but from a desire to please God and glorify Him.

The careful reader will find in the last three paragraphs several hints upon those *means* which are best suited to promote and strengthen patience— such as looking well to his cardinal graces: faith, hope, love. But one or two others we will here mention, among which we place high the complete resigning of ourselves to God. Since most outbursts of impatience are occasioned by a crossing of our wills, then it behoves each Christian to daily ascertain how fully his will is surrendered to God, and to be diligent in cultivating a spirit of submission unto Him. While that yieldedness to God does not include the reducing of ourselves as serfs unto our fellow men, still less the condoning of the wrongs they have done, yet it does require us to be not unduly occupied with the instruments of our afflictions, but rather look beyond them unto Him who has some good reason for using them to stir up our nests.

Meditate frequently upon *the patience of God*. What infinite patience does He exercise toward us! He bears far more from us than we can possibly do from Him. He bears with our sins, whereas we bear only His chastisements, and sin is infinitely more opposite to His nature than suffering is to ours. If He is so longsuffering with our innumerable offences, how ill it becomes us to fret and murmur at the least correction from His hand! Meditating upon the *faithfulness* of God helps us to bear trials with more fortitude. There is no condition which needs more and there is none which has so many promises attending it as a suffering and persecuted one. God has promised support under it (Psa. lv, 22), His presence in it (Isa. xliii, 2), deliverance from it (I Cor. x, 13): He is faithful to His Word. Ponder His wisdom and goodness and you will find in *them* sufficient reason to acquiesce in His providences. If afflictions came by blind chance, we might indeed bemoan a hard fate; but since they are appointed by an omniscient and loving Father, they must be for our gain.

The absence and the opposites of those things which foster patience are hindrances to it. Space only allows us to specify one particular evil which prevents the exercise and growth of this grace, and that is a making too much of the creature. The more we set our hearts and hopes upon creature enjoyments, the more bitter is our disappointment when they fail us, or be taken away. Jonah was "exceeding glad" of the gourd which the Lord prepared to shade and shelter him (iv, 6), but he was "angry, even unto death" when it withered away. That is recorded for our warning! If you immoderately value any earthly comfort you will immoderately chafe at its removal. Pride is another enemy to patience. So is effeminate softness.

LIFE AND TIMES OF JOSHUA

21. The Miracle

As a reward for Joshua's past faithfulness and in order to equip him more thoroughly for the great task before him, the Lord determined to put signal honour upon His servant so that Israel might assuredly know that as the mighty God had been with Moses so He would be with his successor (iii, 7). That at once turns our thoughts back to Exodus xiv, and it is both interesting and instructive to trace out the many points of contrast and comparison between what occurred at the Red Sea and here at Jordan. Let us consider first those respects in which they differed.

First, the one terminated Israel's exodus from the house of bondage, while the other initiated their entrance into the land of promise. Second.

the former miracle was wrought in order that Israel might escape from the Egyptians, the latter to enable them to approach and conquer the Canaanites. Third, in connection with that, the Lord caused the sea to go back by a strong east wind (Ex. xiv, 21); but with reference to this no means whatever were employed—to demonstrate that He is not tied unto such, but employs or dispenses with them as He pleases. Fourth, the earlier miracle was performed at night time (Ex. xiv, 21), the latter in broad daylight. Fifth, at the Red Sea multitudes were slain, for the Lord "made the waters to return upon the Egyptians, so that it covered the chariots and the horsemen: all the host of Pharaoh that came into the sea after them, there remained not so much as one of them" (Ex. xiv, 28); whereas at the Jordan not a single soul perished. Sixth, the one was wrought for a people who just previously had been full of unbelief and murmuring, saying unto Moses: "Because there were no graves in Egypt, hast thou taken us away to die in the wilderness? wherefore hast thou dealt thus with us?" (Ex. xiv, 11); the other for a people who were believing and obedient (ii, 24; iii, 1).

Seventh, with the sole exception of Caleb and Joshua all the adults who benefited by the former miracle perished in the wilderness because of their unbelief, while not a single one of those who were favoured to share in the latter failed to "possess their possessions." Eighth, at the Red Sea the waters were "divided" (Ex. xiv, 21), but here at the Jordan they were not so— rather they were made to "stand upon a heap" (Josh. iii, 13). Ninth, in the former the believer's judicial death unto sin was typed out; in the latter, his legal oneness with Christ in His resurrection, to be followed by a practical entrance into his inheritance. Tenth, consequently, whereas there was no "sanctify yourselves" before the former, such a call was an imperative require-ment for the latter (Josh. iii, 5). Eleventh, the response made by Israel's enemies to the Lord's intervention for Israel at the Red Sea was, "I will pursue, I will overtake, I will divide the spoil, my lust shall be satisfied upon them" (Ex. xv, 9); but in the latter, "It came to pass when all the people of the Amorites, which were on the other side of Jordan westward, and all the kings of the Canaanites . . . heard that the Lord had dried up the waters of Jordan . . . that their heart melted, neither was there spirit in them any more" (Josh. v, 1). Twelfth, after the working of the former "Israel saw the Egyptians dead upon the sea shore" (Ex. xiv, 31); after the latter a cairn of twelve stones memoralized the event (Josh. iv, 20-24).

It is surely remarkable that there are as many analogies between the two miracles as dissimilarities. Yet that illustrates a principle which the attentive observer will find exemplified all through Scripture, and which the young student is advised to make careful note of. "Two" is the number of *witness*— as the Lord sent forth the apostles in pairs to testify of Him. It was the minimum number for such under the Law (John viii, 17), for if the sworn testimony of two different men agreed, this was considered conclusive. Thus two is also the number of comparison and contrast. Hence it will be found that when there are *only two* of a kind, such as the miracles of the Red Sea and the Jordan, there is always a number of marked resemblances and divergencies between them. Some may like to work out for themselves the parallels and oppositions between the Old and New Testaments, Sinai and Sion, the first and second advents of Christ, the respective careers of Moses and Joshua, the ministries of Elijah and Elisha, and so on. The same principle is exemplified where a Greek word occurs but twice: as "*apopnigo*" (Luke viii, 7, 23), "*apokueo*" (James i, 15, 18), "*panoplia*" (Luke xi, 22;

Eph. vi, 11). So too when two parables, miracles, incidents, are placed in juxtaposition.

The following are some of the points of resemblance between these two. (1) In each case the miracle was connected with water. (2) Neither was done in a corner or beheld by only a few, but was witnessed by the whole nation of Israel. (3) Each was preceded by an act required of God's servant—Moses, in the stretching forth of his hand (Ex. xiv, 21); Joshua, in giving command to the people. (4) Each was the removal of a formidable barrier in Israel's path. (5) Each had the design of authenticating Israel's leader (Ex. xiv, 31; Josh. iv, 14). (6) Each presented a severe test unto Israel's faith and obedience (Ex. xiv, 15; Josh. iii, 3). (7) In each case they passed over dry-shod. (8) Both miracles were wrought in silence: neither was accompanied by shouts of triumph, nor was there any sounding of the rams' horns—as, later, in the case of the miraculous fall of Jericho's walls (Josh. vi, 9, 20). (9) Afterward both the Red Sea and the waters of the Jordan returned again to their normal state. (10) Each inaugurated a new period in Israel's history. (11) In both there was a prodigious display of Jehovah's power to the consternation of His enemies. (12) Both miracles were celebrated by songs of praise.

Some of our readers may think that we made a slip in the last point: they will recall the songs of Israel in Exodus xv and ask, But where is there any song of praise celebrating what occurred at the Jordan? Separate celebration there is none, but the two miracles are conjoined and made the special subject of sacred ode, namely in Psalm cxiv, to which we would now direct attention. Many of those who are best qualified to express a considered opinion on the merits of poetry have freely testified that in this psalm the art of sacred minstrelsy has reached its climax: that no human mind has ever been able to equal, much less to excel, the grandeur of its contents. In it we have most vividly depicted the greatest of inanimate things rendering obeisance unto their Maker. As one beautifully summarized it, "The God of Jacob is exalted as having command over river, sea and mountain, and causing all nature to pay homage and tribute before His majesty."

Psalm cxiv is a remarkable one in several respects. First, it is written without any preface. It is as though the soul of its author was so elevated and filled with a sense of the Divine glory that he could not pause to compose an introduction, but rather burst forth at once into the midst of his theme, namely, the wondrous works which were wrought for Israel of old, of which they were the actual eye-witnesses and beneficiaries. Second, in it the rules of grammar are ignored, for in verse two we find the possessive pronoun used without a preceding substantive. The presence of God is concealed in the first verse, for, as Isaac Watts pointed out, "If God had appeared before, there could be no wonder when the mountains should leap and the sea retire— therefore, that these convulsions of nature may be brought in with due surprise, His name is not mentioned till afterwards." Third, this psalm was fittingly made a part of "the Hallelujah" which the Jews of all later generations were wont to sing at their passover supper. Fourth, all that is portrayed in this psalm was typical of the still greater wonders wrought by the redemptive work of Christ.

That psalm celebrates the marvels performed by Jehovah on behalf of His people of old, particularly their exodus from Egypt and His conducting them through the Red Sea and the Jordan. Such glorious acts of God's power and grace must never be forgotten, but owned in gladsome praise. "When Israel went out of Egypt, the house of Jacob from a people of strange language, Judah was His sanctuary, Israel His dominion" (verses 1 and 2). The Lord delivered His people from the house of bondage that they might serve Him and show forth His praises, in the duties of worship and in obedience to His Law.   In order thereto, He set up His "sanctuary" among them—first in the tabernacle, then in the temple, finally in Christ His incarnate Son—in which He gave special tokens of His presence.   Further, He set up His "dominion" or throne among them, being Himself their Lord, King and Judge.   Observe well how that here, as everywhere, privilege and duty, Divine favour and human responsibility, are *united*.   God acted graciously.   God maintained the rights of His righteousness.   As His "sanctuary" Israel was separated unto God as a peculiar people, a nation of priests, holy unto the Lord.   As His "dominion" they were a theocracy, governed directly by Him. So *we* have been redeemed that we should "*serve* Him . . . in holiness and righteousness . . . all the days of our life" (Luke i, 74, 75).   If we enjoy the favours of His "sanctuary" we must also submit to His "dominion."

"The sea saw, and fled; Jordan was driven back.   The mountains skipped like rams, the little hills like lambs" (verses 3, 4).   In those words the inspired poet depicts inanimate creation trembling before its Maker.   It was because Jehovah was Israel's "sanctuary" and "dominion" that the Red Sea fled before them.   Sinai quivered and the waters of Jordan were effectually dammed.   The Almighty was at the head of His people, and nothing could stand before Him, or withstand them.   "The sea saw": it now beheld what it never had previously, namely, "the pillar of cloud" (Ex. xiv, 19)—symbol of Jehovah's presence; and, unable to endure such a sight, fled to the right and to the left, opening a clear passage for the Hebrews.   Jordan, too, as the ark of the covenant entered its brim, was driven back, so that its rapid torrent was stayed, yea, fled uphill.   Graphic figures were those of that invincible operation of Divine grace in the hearts of God's elect, when the mighty power of God is so put forth that turbulent rebels are tamed, fierce lusts subdued, proud imaginations cast down, and self-sufficient wiseacres are brought to enter the kingdom of Christ as "little children"!

"What ailed thee, O thou sea, that thou fleddest? thou Jordan, that thou wast driven back?   Ye mountains that ye skipped like rams, ye little hills like lambs?" (verses 5, 6).   That is the language of holy irony, the Spirit of God pouring contempt upon the unbelieving thoughts of men who foolishly imagine that the Almighty can be withstood, yea, thwarted by the creatures of His own hands.   "What ailed thee, O thou sea?": the poet apostrophizes it in the terms of mockery.   "Wast thou so terribly afraid?   Did thy proud strength then utterly fail thee?   Did thy very heart dry up, so that no resistance wast left in thee?"   Such an interrogation also teaches us that it behoves us to inquire after the reason of things when we behold the marvels of nature, and not merely gaze upon them as senseless spectators.   We have here also a foreshadowing and sure prophecy of the utter impotency of the wicked in the last great day: if the granite cliffs of Sinai were shaken to their base when Jehovah descended upon it, what consternation and trembling will seize the stoutest hearts when they stand before their awful Judge! See verse 7.

Psalm cxiv is by no means the only place where we find celebration made of the miracles witnessed at the Red Sea and Jordan and the other marvels wrought about the same time.   The prophet Habakkuk also links together those two wonders, and in language which serves to cast further light upon the Lord's design therein—teaching us the importance and necessity of carefully comparing Scripture with Scripture, if we would obtain a full view of any event or subject, for each passage makes its own distinct contribution unto the whole. In Joshua we behold the Lord acting more in His sovereign grace and covenant faithfulness on behalf of the seed of Abraham, but Habakkuk informs us He was exercising *righteous indignation* against His enemies, who had devoted themselves unto the most horrible idolatry and unspeakable immorality. It was in holy wrath against both the Egyptians and the Canaanites that God put forth His mighty power, when "the iniquity of the Amorites" had come to the "full" (Gen. xv, 16). The whole of Habakkuk iii is exceedingly graphic and solemn, though we must do no more here than make a bare quotation of portions of it.

The Holy One is vividly pictured as manifesting Himself in the whole of that district which lay to the south of Judah, including Sinai, when "His glory covered the heavens and the earth was full of His praise" (verse 3). "He stood and measured the earth" (verse 6) or "caused the earth to tremble," as the Jewish Targum renders it, and as appears to be required by the parallelism of the next clause: "He beheld [merely "looked upon"!], and drave asunder the nations." That sixth verse may be regarded as the "text" which is illustrated by God's control over the forces of nature. "Was the Lord displeased against the rivers? was Thine anger against the rivers? [when He made the lower waters of the Jordan to flee away, and the higher ones to "stand on a heap"]; was Thy wrath against the sea, that Thou didst ride upon Thine horses and Thy chariots of salvation?" (verse 8), when, as an invincible Conqueror, Thou didst carry all before Thee! "The mountains [of Sinai] saw Thee and trembled: the overflowing of the water [Josh. iii, 15] passed by: the deep uttered his voice and lifted up his hands on high" (verse 10)—see Joshua iii, 16—as though in token of submission to and adoration of their Maker. "The sun and moon stood still in their habitation" (verse 11)—see Joshua x, 12, 13. "Thou didst march through the land in indignation, Thou didst thresh the heathen *in anger*" (verse 12).

Returning to Joshua iii. "Behold the ark of the covenant of the Lord of all the earth passeth over before you into Jordan. . . . And it shall come to pass, as soon as the soles of the feet of the priests that bear the ark of the Lord, the Lord of all the earth, shall rest in the waters of Jordan, that the waters of Jordan shall be cut off from the waters that come down from above; and they shall stand upon a heap" (verses 11, 13). "He who is your covenant God with you, has both the right and power to command, control, use and dispose of all nations and all creatures. He is 'the Lord of all the earth' and therefore He needs not you, nor can He be benefited by you: therefore it is your honour and happiness to have Him in covenant with you; all the creatures are at your service, when He pleases all shall be employed for you. When we are praising and worshipping God as Israel's God, and ours through Christ, we must remember that He is the Lord of the whole earth, and reverence and trust in Him accordingly. . . . While we make God's precepts our rule, His promises our stay, and His providence our guide, we need not dread the greatest difficulties we may meet with in the way of duty" (Matthew Henry).

Here we may see yet another reason—beyond those we have previously pointed out—why the sacred ark was carried so far in advance of the people (verse 4), namely, that the whole congregation might have a better and clearer view of the miracle which God was about to perform for them. The host of Israel standing so far in the rear would have a much plainer opportunity of witnessing and adoring the glorious power of their God.

THE DOCTRINE OF REVELATION

5. The Existence of God

Second, *as revealed in man.* Creation makes manifest the Creator, and having considered some of the mighty products of Omnipotence therein, we turn now to that which comes closer home unto each of us. We are not obliged to go far afield and turn our attention to objects in the heavens or the depths of the ocean in order to find evidences of God's existence—we may discover them in ourselves. Man himself exhibits a Divine Maker, yea, he is the chief of His mundane works. Accordingly we find that Genesis i, after giving a brief but vivid account of how the heavens and earth were called into existence by a Divine fiat and both of them furnished for the benefit of the human race, God made man last—as though to indicate *he* is the climax of His works. In each other instance we are told "God said," "God called," "God created," etc., but in our case there is a marked difference: "And God said, Let *Us* make man in Our image, after Our likeness" (i, 26), as if to signify (speaking after the manner of men) there was a special conference of the Divine Trinity in connection with the formation of that creature who should be made in the Divine image. All the works of God bear the impress of His wisdom, but man alone has stamped upon him the Divine likeness.

The fact that man was made by the Triune God and "in Their image" plainly indicates that he was constituted a tripartite being, consisting of spirit and soul and body—the first being capable of God-consciousness, the second of self-consciousness, and the third of sense-consciousness. The dual expression "in Our image, after Our likeness" imports a twofold resemblance between God and man in his original condition: the former referring to the holiness of his nature, the latter to the character of his soul—which competent theologians have rightly distinguished as "the moral image" and the "natural image" of God in man. That is a real and necessary distinction, and unless it be observed we inevitably fall into error when contemplating the effects of man's defection from God. To the question, Did man *lose* the image of God by the fall? the orthodox rightly answer in the affirmative; yet many of them are quite at a loss to understand such verses as Genesis ix, 6, and James iii, 9, which teach that fallen man *retains* the image of God. It was the moral image which was destroyed when he apostatized, and which is restored to him again at regeneration (Eph. iv, 24; Col. iii, 10). Fallen man is made in the image of his fallen parent, as Genesis v, 3, and Psalm li, 5, solemnly attest. But fallen man still has plainly stamped upon him the natural image of God, evidencing his Divine origin. What that "natural image" consists in we will now consider.

In our last issue we called attention to some of the wonders observable in the human body, and if God bestowed such exquisite workmanship upon the casket, what must be the nature of the gem within it! That "gem" is the spirit and soul of man, which was made in the natural image of God—we shall not here distinguish between them, but treat of them together under the generic term "soul." If the human body bears upon it the impress of the Divine hand, much more so does the soul with its truly remarkable faculties and capabilities. The soul is endowed with understanding, will, moral perception, memory, imagination, affections. Man is comprised and possessed of something more than matter, being essentially a spiritual and rational being, capable of communion with his Maker. There was given unto man a nature nobler than of any other creature's on earth. Man is an intelligent being, capable of thinking and reasoning, which as much excels the instinct of animals as the finished product of the artist's brush does the involuntary raising of his hand to protect his face, or the shutting of his eyes without thought when wind blows dust into them. From whence, then, has man derived his intelligence?

The soul is certainly something distinct from the body. Our very consciousness informs us that we possess an understanding, yea, an intelligent entity which, though we cannot see, yet is known by its operations of thinking, reasoning, remembering. But matter possesses no such properties as those; no, not in any combination of its elements. If matter *could* think, then it would still be able to do so after the soul was absent from the body. Again, if matter had the power of thought, then it would be able to think only of those things which are tangible and material, for no cause can ever produce effects superior to itself. Intelligence can no more issue from non-intelligence than the animate from the non-animate. A stone cannot think, nor a log of wood understand a syllogism. But the human soul is not only capable of thinking, it can also commune with itself, rejoice in itself. Nor are its ratiocinations restricted to itself: it is so constituted that it can apprehend and discourse of things superior to itself. So far from being tied down to the material realm, it can soar into the heavens, cognise the angels, and commune with the Father of spirits.

Consider the vastness of the soul's capacity! What cannot it encompass? It can form a concept of the whole world, and visualize scenes thousands of miles away. As one has pointed out, "it is suited to all objects, as the eye to all colours or the ear to all sounds." How capacious is the memory to retain so much, and such variety! Consider the quickness of the soul's motions: nothing is so swift in the whole course of nature. Thought is far more rapid in its action than the light-waves of ether: in a single moment fancy may visit the Antipodes. With equal facility and agility it can transport itself into the far away past or the distant future. As the desires of the soul are not bounded by material objects, so neither are its motions restrained by them. Consider also its power of volition. The will is the servant of the soul, carrying out its behests, yet it knows not how its commissions are received. Now *matter* has no power of choice, and what it is devoid of it certainly cannot convey. As man's intelligence must have its source in the supreme Mind, so his power of volition must proceed from the supreme Will.

The nature of man also bears witness to the existence of God in the operations and reflections of his *conscience*. If the external marvels of creation exhibit the wisdom and power of the Creator, this mysterious faculty of the soul as clearly exemplifies His holiness and justice. Whatever be its nature or howsoever we define it, its forceful presence within presents us with a unique phenomenon. This moral sense in man challenges investigation and demands an explanation—an investigation which the infidel is most reluctant to seriously make, and for which he is quite unable to furnish a satisfactory explanation. "Conscience is a court always in session and imperative in its summons. No man can evade it or silence its accusations. It is a complete assize. It has a judge on its bench, and that judge will not be bribed into a lax decision. It has its witness-stand, and can bring witnesses from the whole territory of the past life. It has its jury, ready to give a verdict, "guilty" or "not guilty," in strict accordance with the evidence; and it has its sheriff, Remorse, with his whip of scorpions, ready to lash the convicted soul. The nearest thing in the world to the bar of God is the court of conscience. And though it be for a time drugged into a partial apathy or intoxicated with worldly pleasure, the time comes when in all the majesty of its imperial authority this court calls to its bar every transgressor and holds him to a strict account" (A. T. Pierson).

Conscience is that which conveys to the soul a realization of right and wrong. It is that inward faculty which passes judgment upon the lawfulness or unlawfulness of our desires and deeds. It is an ethical instinct, a faculty of moral sensibility, which both informs and impresses its possessor, being that which, basically, constitutes us responsible creatures. It is an inward faculty which is not only of a vastly superior order, but is far keener in perception than any of the bodily senses: it both sees, hears and feels. Its office is twofold: to warn us against sin, to prompt us unto the performance of duty, and this it does according to the light shining into it—from natural reason and Divine revelation. Though the heathen be without the Bible, yet their conscience passes judgment on natural duties and unnatural sins. Hence, the more spiritual light a person has, the greater his responsibility, and it is according to that principle and on that basis he will be dealt with at the grand Assize. "That servant which knew his lord's will and prepared not, neither did according to his will, shall be beaten with many stripes. But he that knew not, and did commit things worthy of stripes, shall be beaten with few. For unto whomsoever much is given, of him shall be much required" (Luke xii, 47, 48). Punishment will be proportioned to light received and privileges enjoyed.

To this moral sensibility of man as the basis of his accountability, the apostle refers in Romans ii. "For when the Gentiles [heathen] which have not the Law, do by nature the things contained in the Law, these, having not the Law, are a law unto themselves" (verse 14). The "nature" of anything is the peculiarity of its being, that in virtue of which it is what it is: it is that which belongs to its original constitution, in contradistinction from all that is taught or acquired. This ethical sense is an original part of our being, and is not the product of education—a power of discrimination by which he distinguishes between right and wrong is created in man. The natural light of reason enables the uncivilized to distinguish between virtue and vice. All, save infants and idiots, recognize the eternal difference between good and evil: they instinctively, or rather intuitively, feel this or that course is commendable or censurable. They have a sense of duty: the natural light of reason conveys the same. Even the most benighted and degraded give evidence that they are not without a sense of obligation: however primitive and savage be their mode of life, yet the very fact that they frame some form of law and order for the community, proves beyond any doubt they have a definite notion of justice and rectitude.

The very nature of the heathen, their sense of right and wrong, leads to the performing of moral actions. In confirmation thereof, the apostle went on to say, "which show the work of the Law written in their heart, their conscience also bearing witness [to the existence of God and their accountability to Him], and their thoughts the meanwhile [or "between themselves," margin] accusing or excusing [the conduct of themselves and of] one another" (Rom. ii, 15). The "work of the Law" is not to be understood as a power of righteousness operating within them, still less as their actual doing of what the Law requires; but rather the function or design of the Law, which is to direct action. The natural light of reason informs them of the distinction between right and wrong.   "Their conscience *also* bearing witness," that is, in addition to the dictates of reason, for they are by no means the same thing.   Knowledge of duty and the actions of conscience are quite distinct: the one reveals what is right, the other approves of it, and condemns the contrary.   They have sufficient light to judge between what is honest and dishonest, and their moral sense makes this distinction before commission of sin, in the commission, and afterward—as clearly appears in their acquitting or condemning one another.

Those who have given Romans ii, 14, any serious thought must have been puzzled if not stumbled by the statement that those in Heathendom "do by nature the things contained in the Law," since they neither love the Lord God with all their hearts nor their neighbours as themselves—the sum of what it requires.   The American Revised Version is much to be preferred: "Do by nature the things of the Law, which describes not the yielding of obedience to the Law, but the performing of its functions.   The proper business of the Law is to say, 'This is right, that is wrong; you will be rewarded for the one, and punished for the other.'   To command, to forbid, to promise, to threaten—these are 'the *things* of the Law,' the 'work' of it (verse 15).   The apostle's assertion is this—an assertion exactly accordant with truth, and directly bearing on his argument:

"The Gentiles who have no written Divine Law, perform by nature from their very constitution, to themselves and each other, the *functions of* such a law.   They make a distinction between right and wrong, just as they do between truth and falsehood.   They cannot help doing so.   They often go wrong by mistaking what is right and what is wrong, as they often go wrong by mistaking what is true and what is false.   But they approve themselves and one another when doing what they think right; they disapprove themselves and one another when they do what they think to be wrong; so that, though they have no written law, they act the part of a law to themselves.   This capacity, this necessity of their nature, distinguishes them from brutes, and makes them the subjects of Divine moral government.   In this way they show 'that the work of the law'—the work which the Law *does*—is 'written in their hearts,' enwoven in their constitution, by the actings of the power we call conscience.   It is just, then, that they should be punished for doing what they know to be wrong, or might have known to be wrong" (Professor Brown).

Man is the only earthly creature endowed with conscience.   The beasts have consciousness and a limited power to acquire knowledge, but that is something very different.   Certain animals can be made to obey their masters. With the aid of a stick, even a cow may be taught to refrain from plucking the green leaves over the garden fence, which her mouth craves—the memory of the beatings she has received for disobedience incline her to forgo her inclinations.   Much more intelligent is a *domesticated* dog: he can be trained to understand that certain actions will meet with reward, while others will receive punishment.   But memory is a very different thing from that ethical monitor within the human breast, which weighs whatever is presented to the mind and passes judgment either for or against all our actions, secretly acquainting the soul with the right and wrong of things.   Wherever we go this sentinel accompanies us: whatever we think or do, it records a verdict. Much of our peace of mind is the fruit of a non-accusing conscience, while not a little of our disquietude is occasioned by the charges of wrong-doing which conscience brings against us.

Conscience is an integral part of that light which "lighteneth every man which cometh into the world." Forceful testimony is borne to its potency by the rites of the heathen and their self-imposed penances, which are so many attempts to appease the ones they feel they have offended. There is in every man that which reproves him for his sins, yea, for those to which none other is privy, and therefore the wicked flee when no man pursueth. At times the stoutest are made to quail. The most hardened have their seasons of alarm. The spectre of past sins haunts them in the night watches. Boast loudly as they may that they fear nothing, yet "there were they in great fear where no fear was" (Psa. liii, 5)—an inward horror where there was no outward occasion for uneasiness. When there is no reason for fright, the wicked are suddenly seized with panic and made to tremble like an aspen leaf, so that they are afraid of their own shadows.

The fearful reality of conscience is plainly manifested by the fact that men who are naturally inclined to evil nevertheless disapprove of that which is evil, and approve of the very good which they practise not. Even though they do not so audibly, the vicious secretly admire the pure, and while some be sunk so low they will scarcely acknowledge it to themselves, nevertheless they wish they could be like the morally upright. The most blameworthy will condemn certain forms of evil in others, thus evincing they distinguish between good and evil. Whence does that arise? By what rule do they measure moral actions, but by an innate principle? But how comes man to possess that principle? It is not an attribute of reason, for at times reason will inform its possessor that a certain course of conduct would result in gain to him, but conscience moves him to act in a way which he knows will issue in temporal loss. Nor is it a product of the will, for conscience often acts in opposition to the will, and no effort of the will can still it. It is a separate faculty which, in various degrees of enlightenment and sensitiveness, is found in civilized and uncivilized.

Now even common sense tells us that someone other than ourselves originated this faculty. No law can be without a lawgiver. From whence then this law? Not from man, for he would fain annihilate it if he could. It must have been imparted by some higher Hand, which Hand alone can maintain it against all the violences of its owner, who, were it not for this restraining monitor, would quickly reduce the world to a charnal house. If then we reason rationally, we are forced to argue thus: I find myself naturally obliged to do this and shun that, therefore there must be a Superior who obliges me. If there were no Superior, I should myself be the sole judge of good and evil, yea, I should be regulated only by expediency and recognize no moral distinctions. Were I the lord of that principle or law which commands me, I should find no conflict within myself between reason and appetite. The indubitable fact is, that conscience has an authority for man that cannot be accounted for except by its being the voice of God within him. If conscience were entirely isolated from God, and were independent of Him, it could not make the solemn, and sometimes the terrible, impressions it does. No man would be afraid of himself if self were not connected with a higher Being than himself.

As God has not left Himself without witness among the lower creatures (Acts xiv, 17), neither has He left Himself without witness within man's own breast. There is not a rational member of the human race who has not at some time more or less smarted under the lashings of conscience. The hearts of princes, in the midst of their pleasures, have been stricken with anguish

while their favourites were flattering them. Those inward torments are not
ignorant frights experienced only by children, which reason throws off later
on, for the stronger reason grows, the sharper the stings of conscience, and not
the least so in maturity and old age. It often operates when wickedness is
most secret. Numerous cases are on record of an overwhelming terror over-
taking wrongdoers when their crimes were known to none, and they have condemned themselves and given themselves up to justice. Could that self-accuser
originate from man's own self? He who loves himself would, were it possible,
destroy that which disturbs him. Certainly conscience has received no
authority from its possessor to lash himself, to spoil the pleasures of sin, to
make him "like the troubled sea, which cannot rest."

The very fact there is that in man which condemns him for sins committed in secret, argues there is a God, and that he is accountable unto Him.
He has an instinctive dread of a Divine Judge who will yet arraign him.
"They *know* the judgment of God" (Rom. i, 32) by an inward witness. It
is a just provision of the Lord that those who will not reverently fear Him,
have a tormenting fear of the future. Why is it that, despite all their efforts
to escape from the conclusion that God is, they dread a retribution beyond
death?—often demonstrated by the most callous wretches in their last hours
by asking for the chaplain or "priest." If there be no God, why do men
strive to silence conscience and dispel its terrors? And why are their efforts
so unavailing? Since they cannot still its accusations, some Higher Power
must maintain it within the soul. That the most enlightened nations recognize
men have no right to *force* the conscience, is a tacit acknowledgment it is
above human jurisdiction, answerable only to its Author. Conscience is the
vicegerent of God in the soul, and will torment the damned for all eternity.

THE GREAT CHANGE

"Search the Scriptures" (John v, 39), "comparing spiritual things with
spiritual" (I Cor. ii, 13). *That* is what we sought to heed in the preceding
articles. Therein twenty-five different passages were collated—all of which
we are persuaded treat of some aspect or other of "the miracle of grace" or
the great change—and in varying measure engaged our attention. It will be
observed that in some of them it is the illumination of the understanding
which is in view (Acts xxvi, 18), in others the searching and convicting of the
conscience (Rom. vii, 9), and in others the renovation of the heart (Ezek.
xxxvi, 26). In some it is the subduing of the will (Psa. cx, 3) which is emphasized, in others casting down reasonings and bringing our thoughts into
subjection (II Cor. x, 5), and in others the writing of God's laws in our minds
and hearts. In some the miracle of grace appears to be a completed thing
(I Cor. vi, 11), in others the great change is seen as a gradual process (II Cor.
iii, 18; Phil. i, 6). In one something is removed from its subject (Deut. xxx, 6),
while in another something is communicated (Rom. v, 5). In different
passages the figures of creation (Eph. ii, 10), of renewing (Titus iii, 5), and
of resurrection (I John iii, 14) are employed.

If it be asked, Why has it pleased the Holy Spirit to describe His work
so diversely and use such a variety of terms and figures? several answers may
be suggested. First, because the work itself, though one, is so many-sided.
Its subject is a complex creature and the process of salvation radically affects

every part of his composite being. Just as sin has marred each part of our constitution and has corrupted every faculty the Creator gave us, so grace renews and transforms every part of our constitution and purifies every faculty we possess. When the apostle prayed, "The very God of peace sanctify you *wholly,* and your whole spirit and soul and body be preserved blameless unto the coming of our Lord Jesus Christ" (I Thess. v, 23), he was asking that God would graciously preserve and perfect that which He had already wrought in His people, and the terms he there used intimated the comprehensiveness and entirety of the grand miracle of grace. This is a gem possessing many facets and our estimate of it is certain to be most faulty if we confine our view to only one of them.

Second, because God would thereby warn us from supposing that He acts according to a stereotyped plan or method in His saving of sinners. Variety rather than uniformity marks all the ways and workings of God, in creation, providence, and grace. No two seasons are alike—no field or tree yields the same crop in any two years. Every book in the Bible is equally the inspired Word of God, yet how different in character and content is Leviticus from the Psalms, Ruth from Ezekiel, Romans from the Revelation! How varied the manner in which the Lord Jesus gave sight to different ones who were blind: different in the means used and the effect produced—one, at first, only seeing men as though they were trees walking (Mark viii, 24)! How differently He dealt with religious Nicodemus in John iii and the adulterous woman of John iv, pressing on the one his imperative need of being born again, convicting the other of her sins and telling her of "the gift of God"! The great God is not confined to any rule and we must not restrict His operations in our thoughts: if we do, we are certain to err.

Third, because God would thereby teach us that, though the work of grace be essentially and substantially the same in all its favoured subjects, yet in no two of them does it appear identical in all its circumstantials—neither in its operations nor manifestations. Not only does endless variety mark all the ways and workings of God, but it does so equally in His *workmanship.* This is generally recognized and acknowledged in connection with the material world, where no two blades of grass or two grains of sand are alike. But in the spiritual realm it is very far from being perceived and owned: rather is it commonly supposed that all truly regenerate persons conform strictly unto one particular pattern, and those who differ from it are at once suspected of being counterfeits. This should not be. The twelve foundations of the new and holy Jerusalem, in which are the names of the twelve apostles of the Lamb, are all composed of "precious" stones, but how diverse is each! The first jasper, the second sapphire, the third a chalcedony, the fourth emerald, etc. (Rev. xxi)—different in colour, size and brilliancy. Each Christian has his own measure of faith and grace "according to the measure of the gift of Christ" (Eph. iv, 7).

Fourth, because God would thereby make it easier for His children to recognize themselves in the mirror of the Word. Possessed of honest hearts and fearful of being deceived, some find it no simple matter to be thoroughly convinced that they have truly experienced the great change. So far from sneering at their trepidation, we admire their caution: where the eternal interests of the soul are concerned only a fool will give himself the benefit of the doubt. But if a miracle of grace has been wrought in the reader, there is no good reason why he should long be in uncertainty about it. As in water face answers to face, so the character of the renewed soul corresponds to the description of such furnished by the Word of Truth. That description, as we have seen, is given with considerable variety, sometimes one feature or aspect being made prominent, sometimes another. It is like a photographer taking a number of different pictures of the same person: one with his countenance in repose, another with him smiling; one a full-face view, another of his profile. One may appear to do him "more justice" than another or be more easily "recognized," yet all are likenesses of himself.

Let then the exercised reader impartially scrutinize himself in the mirror of the Word and see if he can discern in himself some of the marks of the regenerate, as those marks are there delineated. Observe well we say "some of" those marks, and not all of them. Though you may not be sure that Ezekiel xxxvi, 26, has taken place in you, perhaps you know something of what is recorded in Acts xvi, 14, and Romans v, 5. Because your first conscious "experience" was not like that of Romans vii, 9, perhaps it closely resembled that of Zaccheus, who came down from the tree and "received Him joyfully" (Luke xix, 6). Commenting on the quickness of his conversion, Whitefield aptly said to those who queried whether any were genuine Christians who had not undergone some "terrible experience" of conviction or terror of the wrath to come, "You may as well say to your neighbour you have not had a child, for you were not in labour all night. The question is, whether a real child is born, not how long was the preceding pain"!

There is nothing in the sacred record to show that either Lydia or Zaccheus felt anything of the terrors of the Law before their conversion, yet from what is said of them in the sequel we cannot doubt the reality of their conversion. Though you may not be sure whether God has put His laws into your mind and written them on your heart, yet you should have no difficulty in perceiving whether or no you "love the brethren" as such, and if you *do*, then you may be fully assured on the Word of Him that cannot lie, you have "passed from death unto life." The fact that you are afraid to aver that God has renewed you after His image and created you "in righteousness and true holiness" does not of itself warrant you inferring you are still in a state of nature. Test yourself by *other* passages and see if you can discern in your soul some of *their* marks of regeneration, such as a grieving over sin, a hungering after righteousness, a panting for communion with God, a praying for fuller conformity unto Christ. Has the world lost its charm, are you out of love with yourself, is the Lamb of God a desirable Object in your eyes? If so, you possess at least some of the distinctive marks of the regenerate.

Since we are seeking to write these articles for the benefit of young preachers as well as the rank and file of God's people, let us point out that the nature of this great change may also be determined by contemplating it as *the begun reversal of the Fall*: "begun reversal," for what is commenced at regeneration is continued throughout our sanctification and completed only at our glorification. While it be true that those who are renewed by the Holy Spirit gain *more* than Adam lost by the Fall, yet we have clear Scripture warrant for affirming that the workmanship of the new creation is *God's answer* to man's ruination of his original creation. Great care needs to be taken in cleaving closely to the Scriptures in developing this point, particularly in ascertaining exactly what was the moral and spiritual condition of man originally, and precisely what happened to him when he fell. We trust that a patient perusal of what follows will convince the reader of both the importance and value of our discussion of these details at this stage—the more so since the children have sadly departed from the teaching of the fathers thereon.

Even those sections of Christendom which boast the most of their soundness•in the Faith are defective here. Mr. Darby and his followers hold that Adam was merely created innocent (a negative state), and not in (positive) holiness. Mr. Philpot said, "I do not believe that Adam was a spiritual man, that is, that he possessed those spiritual gifts and graces which are bestowed upon the elect of God, for they are new covenant blessings in which he had no share" (*Gospel Standard*, 1861, page 155). One error ever involves another. Those who deny that fallen man possesses any responsibility to perform spiritual acts (love God, savingly believe in Christ) must, to be consistent, deny that unfallen man was a spiritual creature. Different far was the teaching of the Reformers and Puritans. "And where Paul treats of the restoration of this image (II Cor. iii, 18), we may readily infer from his words that man was conformed to God not by an influx of His substance, but by the grace and power of His Spirit." And again, "As the *spiritual life* of Adam consisted in a union to his Maker, so an alienation from Him was the death of his soul" (Calvin, *Institutes*).

"Adam had the Spirit as well as we: the Holy Spirit was at the making of him and wrote the image of God upon his heart, for where holiness was, we may be sure the Spirit of God was too . . . the same Spirit was in Adam's heart to assist *his graces* and cause them to flow and bring forth, and to move him to live according to those principles of life given him" (Goodwin, 6/54). And again, commenting on Adam's being made in the image and likeness of God, and pointing out that such an "image" imports a thing "permanent and inherent," he asked, "what could this be but habitual inclinations and dispositions unto whatsover was holy and good, insomuch as *all holiness* radically *dwelt in him*" (page 202). So too Charnock: "The righteousness of the first man evidenced not only a sovereign power, as the Donor of his being, but a holy power, as the pattern of His work. . . . The law of love to God, with his whole soul, his whole mind, his whole heart and strength, was originally writ upon his nature. All the parts of his nature were framed in a moral conformity with God, to answer His Law and imitate God in His purity" (vol. ii, page 205).

In his *Discourse on the Holy Spirit* (chapter iv, His "Peculiar works in the first creation"), when treating of "the image of God" after which Adam was created (namely, "an ability to discern the mind and will of God," an "unentangled disposition to every duty" and "a readiness of compliance in his affections"), J. Owen said, "For in the *restoration* of these abilities unto our minds in our renovation unto the image of God in the Gospel, it is plainly asserted that the Holy Spirit is the imparter of them, and He doth thereby restore His own work. For in the new creation the Father, in the way of authority, designs it and brings all things unto a head in Christ (Eph. i, 10), which *retrieves* His original work. And thus Adam may be said to have had the Spirit of God in his innocency: he had Him in those peculiar effects of His power and goodness, and he had Him according to the tenor of that covenant whereby it was possible that he should utterly lose Him, as accordingly it came to pass." The superiority of the new covenant lies in its gifts being unforfeitable, because secured in and by Christ.

"God made man *upright*" (Eccl. vii, 29)—the same Hebrew word as in Job i, 8, and Psalm xxv, 8: "This presupposes a law to which he was conformed in his creation, as when anything is made regular or according to rule, of necessity the rule itself is presupposed. Whence we may gather that this law was no other than the eternal indispensable law of righteousness, observed in all points by the second Adam. . . . In a word, this law is the very same which was afterwards summed up in the Ten Commandments . . . called by us the Moral Law, and man's righteousness consisted in conformity to this law or rule" (Thomas Boston, *Human Nature in its Fourfold State*). "When God created man at first, He gave him not an outward law, written in letters or delivered in words, but an inward law put into his heart and concreated with him, and wrought in the frame of his soul . . . *spiritual* dispositions and inclinations, in his will and affections, carrying him on to pray, love God and fear Him, to seek His glory in a spiritual and holy manner" (Goodwin). The external command of Genesis ii, 17, was designed as the *test* of his responsibility, and at the same time it served to make manifest that his "uprightness" was mutable.

When Adam left the Creator's hand the law of God was in his heart, for he was endowed with holy instincts and inclinations, which tended unto his doing that which was pleasing unto God and an antipathy against whatever was displeasing to Him. That "law of God" within him was his original *character* or constitution of his soul and spirit—as it is the "law" or character of beasts to care for their young and of birds to build nests for theirs. Should it be asked, Is there any other Scripture which teaches that God placed His law in the heart of unfallen Adam? we answer, Yes, by clear and necessary implication. Christ declared "Thy Law is within My heart" (Psalm xl, 8), and Romans v, 14, tells us that Adam was "the figure of Him that was to come." Again, just as we may ascertain what grain a certain field bore from the stubble in it, so we may discover what was in unfallen man by the ruins of what is still discernible in fallen humanity: "the Gentiles do *by nature* the things contained in the Law" (Rom. ii, 14)— their consciences informing them that immorality and murder are crimes: there is still a shadow in his descendants of the character originally possessed by Adam.

But Adam did not continue as God created him. He fell, and terrible were the consequences. But it is only by adhering closely to the terms used in the Word that we can rightly apprehend the nature of those consequences; yea, unless we allow Scripture itself to interpret those terms for us, we are certain to err in our understanding of them. Possibly the reader is ready to exclaim, There is no need to make any mystery out of it: the matter is quite simple—those "consequences" may all be summed up in one word—"death." Even so, we must carefully inquire what is meant there by "death." "Spiritual death," you answer. True, and observe well that presupposes spiritual life, and that in turn implies a spiritual person, for surely one endowed with spiritual life must be so designated. However, our inquiry must be pressed back a stage farther, and the question put, Exactly what is connoted by "spiritual death"? It is at this point so many have gone wrong and, departing from the teaching of Holy Writ, have landed in serious error.

It is to be most carefully noted that God did not say to Adam, "In the day that thou eatest thereof thy spirit or thy soul shall surely die," but rather "*thou* shalt surely die" (Gen. ii, 17). It was not some *thing* in or some part of Adam which died, but Adam himself! That is very, very far from being a distinction without any difference: it is a real and radical difference, and if we tamper with Scripture and change what it says, we depart from the Truth. Nor is "death" an extinction or annihilation; instead, it is a *separation*. Physical death is the severance or separation of the soul from the body, and spiritual death is the separation of the soul from God. The prodigal son was "dead" so long as he remained in "the far country" (Luke xv, 24), because away from his Father. I Timothy v, 6, tells us, "she that liveth in pleasure is dead while she liveth"; that is, she is spiritually dead, dead Godwards, while alive and active in sin. For the same reason, "the lake which burneth with fire and brimstone" is called "the Second Death" (Rev. xxi, 8), because those cast into it are "punished with everlasting destruction *from the presence of the Lord*" (II Thess. i, 9).

Man was created a tripartite being, composed of "spirit and soul and body" (I Thess. v, 23). That is unmistakably implied in the Divine account of his creation: "God said, Let *Us* make man in *Our* image, after *Our* likeness" (Gen. i, 26); the Triune God made man a trinity in unity! And when man fell, he *continued to be* a tripartite being: no part of his being was extinguished, no faculty was lost when he apostatized from God. It cannot be insisted upon too strongly that no essential element of man's original constitution was forfeited, no component part of his complex make-up was annihilated at the Fall, for multitudes are seeking to hide behind a misconception at this very point. They would fain believe that man lost some vital part of his nature when Adam ate of the forbidden fruit, and that it is the absence of this part in his descendants which explains (and excuses!) all their failures. They console themselves that they are more to be pitied than blamed: the blame rests on their first parents, and they, forsooth, are to be pitied because he deprived them of the faculty of working righteousness. Much preaching encourages that very delusion.

The truth is that fallen man today possesses identically the same faculties as those with which Adam was originally created, and his accountability lies in his making a good use of those faculties, and his criminality consists in the evil employment of them. Others seek to evade the onus of man by affirming that he *received a nature* which he did not possess before the Fall, and all the blame for his lawless actions is thrown upon that evil nature: equally erroneous and equally vain is such a subterfuge. No material addition was made to man's being at the Fall, any more than some intrinsic part was taken from it. That which man lost at the Fall was his primitive *holiness*, and that which then entered into his being was *sin*, and sin has defiled every part of his person; but for *that* we are to be blamed and not pitied. Nor has fallen man become so helplessly the victim of sin that his accountability is cancelled; rather does God hold him responsible to resist and reject every inclination unto evil, and will justly punish him because he fails to do so. Every attempt to negative human responsibility and undermine the sinner's accountability, no matter by whom made, must be steadfastly resisted by us.

It is by persuading men that the spirit died at the Fall, or that some concrete but evil thing was then communicated to the human constitution, that Satan succeeds in deceiving so many of his victims: and it is the bounden duty of the Christian minister to expose his sophistries, drive the ungodly out of their refuge of lies, and press continually upon them the solemn fact that they are without the vestige of an excuse for their own rebellion against God. In the day of his disobedience Adam himself died, died spiritually, and so did all his posterity in him. But that spiritual death consisted not of the extinction of anything in them, but of their separation from God: no part of Adam's being was annihilated, but every part of him was *vitiated*. It was not the essence but the rectitude of man's soul and spirit which sin destroyed. By the Fall man relinquished his honour and glory, lost his holiness, forfeited the favour of God, and was severed from all communion with Him; but he still retained *his human nature.* All desire Godwards, all love for his Maker, all real knowledge of Him was gone. Sin now possessed him, and to the love and exercise of it he devoted himself. Such too is *our* natural condition.

RESTRICTED FORGIVENESS

Writing upon "A *Persisting* Sinner being an *unpardoned* sinner," the Puritan, Jos. Caryl, said: "There is abundant mercy for returning sinners, but I know of none for those who resolve to go on in sin. There is a promise *of* repentance, and a promise *to* repentance, but there is no promise that doth not either offer or require repentance. 'Repent, and thou shalt be saved' is the tenor of the Gospel, as well as 'believe and thou shalt be saved.' Though many who are going on in their sins are overtaken by grace, yet there is no grace promised to those who go on in their sins. The holiest are threatened with wrath if they do: surely then none are put into an expectation of mercy if they do. The promises either find us repenting, or they cause us to repent. No sinner is pardoned *for* repentance, nor *without* it. Job speaks that language more clearly in the words that follow: 'If I be wicked, woe unto me' (Job x, 15)."

(continued from back page)

to another *in the fear of God"* (Eph. v, 21) is the grand principle which should ever move us. Moreover, it is to be steadily borne in mind that this rule is to regulate the inward man as well as the outward. The whole of God's Law is "spiritual" (Rom. vii, 14), and requires conformity of heart unto its statutes. This golden rule is no exception: it is to regulate our affections as well as our actions. It prohibits secret grudgings and enmity against our fellows, and enjoins good will and benevolence. Vain is our profession that we love God if our actions evince we hate our fellow creatures. It should also be pointed out that this rule includes the right of private judgment. If you maintain you are entitled to have *your own* political views, or, what is far more important, to form your own opinion of what the Bible teaches on any subject of which it treats, then accord unto everyone else the same privilege. Differences of opinion are certain to arise, but they never justify your cherishing a bitter spirit, imputing unworthy motives unto, or acting harshly toward, those who differ from you.

We doubt not that many of our readers have, by Divine grace, sincerely endeavoured to regulate their conduct by this rule, yea, have put the interests and welfare of others *before* their own; and in them Christ is glorified. But we fear there is likely to be quite a number, even of those who receive this magazine, who need to take this message to heart, humbly confess to God their failures thereon, and definitely seek grace to cultivate a more unselfish spirit and a greater concern for the well-being and comfort of those with whom they have to do. This precept is many-sided in its application. If you desire others to sympathize with you while in trouble, then see to it that you "weep with them that weep" (Rom. xii, 15). If you covet the prayers of your brethren, be diligent in interceding for them.

Now God's people are in real danger of being corrupted by the evils to which we have just alluded. Unless they are very much on their guard they will quickly become infected by the same spirit, the more so as the multitude of empty professors all around them are becoming increasingly conformed to the wicked world. When church members are so boorish and overbearing, walking roughshod over others, indifferent to what annoyance and discomfort they cause their neighbours, the young Christian is apt to think, What is the use of *my* making a stand for that which is right and proper? Better swim with the stream than be regarded as a crank. But that is a temptation from the Devil, which must be steadfastly resisted. "Thou shalt not follow a multitude to do evil" (Ex. xxiii, 2); *their* carelessness and callousness is no reason why *you* should be unconcerned as to what inconvenience and distress your selfish conduct may inflict upon others. "Every one of us shall give account of himself to God" (Rom. xiv, 12); meanwhile Christ requires His disciples to conform to the standard He has given them, regulate their lives by this golden precept, and be identifiable by their meekness, modesty, gentleness and righteousness.

This is a rule which is witnessed to in every man's breast. Each normal person has enough regard for himself that he quickly feels an injury and censures the one who has wronged him. He has therefore but to apply this principle to his own actions and the righteousness of it at once appears. Thus none can plead ignorance, nor is thoughtlessness any valid excuse. Are you pleased when hearing from old friends? Then fail not to write unto them. Are you inconvenienced when someone fails to return an article you have loaned? Then make conscience of promptly returning anything—be it but a book—which you have borrowed. Are you displeased when others are dilatory in paying what they owe you? Then see to it you settle all your bills promptly. Are you distressed when your nerves are shocked and your rest disturbed by the selfish inconsideration of other tenants in the same house or by your neighbours? Then cease banging doors yourself, and if you have children or a dog suffer them not to be a nuisance to others. If someone be ill in the next house, or has to get his sleep during the day, disturb him not.

If spirituality be not practical it is worthless. Wherever vital godliness is in a healthy state its possessor will be duly influenced in all his relations, and he will seek faithfully to discharge every duty which he owes, not only unto God, but to his fellow men also. Grace teaches its subjects to "live soberly [selfward], righteously [manward], and godly [Christward] in this present world" (Titus ii, 12). The Christian should be as ready to do good as to receive good. "Whatsoever ye would that men should do to you, do ye even so to them." Here is a comprehensive precept which covers the whole of our obligations unto our fellows. Negatively, refrain from injuring any; positively, seek to do good unto all. Be fair and just, honourable and honest, in all your dealings. Though others be not so, perform *your* duty. We must not be forward in standing up for our own rights and backward in considering those of others. If you are hurt when others slight, speak evil of, or oppress you, see that you are innocent of such sins. Treat others with the same consideration, courtesy and kindness as you wish to receive from them.

Such deportment must be rendered not merely as a "mark of good breeding," but as an act of obedience to God. "Submitting yourselves one

(continued on preceding page)

XXVI JUNE 1947 No. 6

STUDIES IN THE SCRIPTURES

"Search the Scriptures." *John v, 39*

Publisher and Editor—ARTHUR W. PINK,
29 Lewis Street,
Stornoway, Isle of Lewis,
Scotland.

IDENTIFICATION OF THE GODLY

Our design in preparing a short article each year under this title is threefold. First, to test Christian professors, for it is highly probable that some of our readers have been deceived by that ill-balanced preaching which is so rife, wherein the whole emphasis is laid upon "believing," and nothing is said of repentance and reformation, and scarcely anything on the imperative necessity of bringing forth the fruits of righteousness in order to authenticate our claim to being Christians. Second, to help doubting souls, by describing some of the features of the regenerate, so that they may the better recognize whether or no they have been Divinely renewed. Not a few, because of the defective teaching they sit under, are needlessly kept languishing in "Doubting Castle" and we long to be used in delivering them from its dismal dungeons, and bringing them out into the sunshine of the Gospel. Third, to deepen the assurance of the saints, that they may be more firmly rooted and established in the Truth, and *know* they have passed from death unto life, so that their "joy may be full" (I John i, 4).

We turn now to point out another mark which distinguishes the regenerate from the unregenerate, basing our argument on those words, "Not knowing that the goodness of God leadeth thee to repentance" (Rom. ii, 4). It should be pointed out that that verse is not speaking from the viewpoint of God's eternal purpose, nor is its design to teach us (by implication) how repentance is effectually wrought in the elect. Quite otherwise. Since it occurs in a passage which is little understood, we will take this opportunity to offer a few remarks upon its general scope. Romans ii, particularly verses 1-16, is an expansion of the solemn truth made known in i, 18. It sets forth those principles by which God will act in the Day of Judgment—principles which at once commend themselves unto every quickened conscience. The first is, he who condemns in others what he does himself, thereby condemns himself (verse 1). Second, God's judgment will be according to the real state of the case, everything being taken into impartial consideration (verse 2). Third, the special goodness of God, whether exercised toward a particular individual of a nation, forms no ground of exemption from merited punishment, but when unimproved will only serve to aggravate their condemnation (verses 3-5).

(continued on back page)

Important Notices

Please advise promptly of change in address, otherwise copies will be lost in the mails.

We are glad to send a sample copy to any of your friends whom you believe would be interested in this publication.

This magazine is published as " a work of faith and labour of love," the editor and his wife gladly giving their services free. There is no regular subscription price, as we do not wish the poor of the flock to be deprived. This does not mean that those looking for something for nothing may " help themselves." Those getting this magazine who are financially able and who receive spiritual help from its pages, are expected to gladly contribute towards its expenses; otherwise their names are dropped from our list.

Will those forwarding International Money Orders please have them made out to us at Stornoway, Isle of Lewis, Scotland. Checks (Cheques—Eng.) made out on U.S.A. Banks are not negotiable here, so please do not send them.

All unsigned articles are by the Editor.

CONTENTS

THE PRAYERS OF THE APOSTLES

42. Colossians i, 9-12

"Strengthened with all might according to His glorious power, unto all patience and longsuffering with joyfulness" (verse 11). Since we hope to return to the subject of patience, when (D.V.) we reach II Thessalonians iii, 5, we will say nothing further upon it here. Nor is there any need to descant upon "longsuffering," since the term defines itself—signifying a prolongation of patience unto the end of the trial. Yet in view of the *connections* in which those terms are found, we may distinguish between them thus: "patience" looks more to the attitude of the heart Godward while we are being tried, "longsuffering" respects our attitude toward the instruments which He makes use of in the trial. Thus, "longsuffering" includes the ideas of being slow to anger with those who persecute or afflict us, meekly bearing for Christ's sake those injuries which His enemies inflict upon us, refusing to retaliate when we are oppressed, following the example our Master has left us, "Who when He was reviled, reviled not again." "Love suffereth long and is kind" (I Cor. xiii, 4). But "patience and longsuffering with joyfulness" calls for a fuller consideration.

"My brethren, count it all joy when ye fall into divers temptations" or "trials" (James i, 2). Many will be ready to say, That is asking of me an impossibility: I cannot conjure up joy by any effort of will; only the Lord can produce rapture in my heart. But joy, my reader, is not a thing apart, unrelated to the faculties of the soul, unconnected with the state of our minds. I cannot indeed command the sun to appear, but when it *is* shining, I can retire into the shade and there sulk in my chilliness. So too the heart may turn away from the Sun of righteousness, and instead of dwelling upon His love and loveliness, occupy the mind with gloomy objects and subjects. The Christian is just as responsible to be joyous, as he is to be holy. It is his duty to be joyous in adversity as well as prosperity, when the Devil rages against us as when he leaves us in peace for a season; and we *shall* do so if our minds be properly employed and our hearts delight themselves in the Lord.

None of the empty pleasures of this world afford any solid happiness. As the natural man passes from childhood to old age, he does but change his toys, only to discover that no gratification of his senses yields any real satisfaction. Neither sorrow nor joy are caused by environment or circumstances; nor is joy to be found in any creature. "Although the fig tree shall not blossom, neither shall fruit be in the vines . . . the fields shall yield no meat, the flock shall be cut off from the fold, and there shall be no herd in the stalls": what then? I will deplore the situation, and make myself wretched by contemplating a death of starvation? No indeed: rather, "Yet I will *rejoice* in the Lord, I will joy in the God of my salvation" (Hab. iii, 17, 18). Note well that "I will" of personal resolution. As the king may be miserable in his palace (I Kings xxi, 5, 6; Eccl. ii, 1-11), so the manacled and bleeding occupants of the dungeon may sing praises (Acts xvi, 25); yea, while sorrowing over things around us, we may continually rejoice (II Cor. vi, 10).

James i, 2, does not exhort us to rejoice in the trials as such, but by an act of spiritual judgment to regard them as joyous, giving three reasons why Christians should do so. "Knowing this [being fully persuaded of it] that the trying of your faith worketh patience." Two things are there included which should mightily further our joy. First, that all our sufferings and afflictions are for the trial of faith, and that is a great privilege. If we were possessed of more spiritual discernment, we should readily perceive that as the *communication* of saving grace to a soul is the greatest blessing which can be bestowed in this world, so to have that grace *tested*, exercised and drawn forth to the glory of God, is the next greatest mercy. For that grace to approve itself unto God in a manner that is well pleasing to Him, is a matter of vast moment. So for the genuineness of my faith to be made manifest by overcoming the world—esteeming the reproach of Christ greater riches than the treasures of Egypt; by valuing the smile of God more than fearing the frowns of men; by firmly enduring persecution when others fall away (Matt. xiii, 21), should bring much comfort to the soul.

Second, this trying of faith "worketh patience." Trials are not only designed for the approving of faith, but for the improving, i.e. that it may yield its peaceable fruits. The more faith enables us to truly rest in the Lord and stand our ground under afflictions, the more we become inured to and patient under them. As faith draws out the heart unto and stays the mind upon God, the soul is brought into a more sober frame and more cordially acquiesces in the Divine will. Faith brings home to the heart the dominion which God has over a man's person and life, and this quietens evil uprisings against Him. Faith assures the heart of the love of God and its interests in Him, and that strengthens him in the greatest distresses. When Ziklag was burned, David's goods plundered, and his wives carried away by the Philistines, he "encouraged himself in the Lord his God" (I Sam. xxx, 6). The more a Christian bears meekly but perseveringly, the more he is enabled *to bear*—the muscles of his graces become stronger by use. If trials produce such fruits, ought we not to rejoice in them!

Third, "Blessed [or "happy"] is the man that endureth temptation." Why? "For when he hath been tried he shall receive the crown of life" (James i, 12). That is the reward given to the victor in the day to come, in the happy expectation of which the soul may count it all joy that he is now being afflicted and persecuted. The object of his rejoicing is not his sufferings, for they considered in themselves are grievous; but rather the issue thereof. Paul reminded the Hebrews "ye took joyfully the spoiling of your goods"—why so?—"knowing in yourselves that ye have in heaven a better and enduring substance" (Heb. x, 34). Thus it was with the Saviour Himself: "Who for *the joy* that was set before Him, endured the cross" (Heb. xii, 2). And thus has He assured His followers, "Blessed are ye, when men shall revile you, and persecute, and shall say all manner of evil against you, falsely, for My sake; *rejoice,* and be exceeding glad, for great is your reward in heaven" (Matt. v, 11). When we "glory in tribulations" (Rom. v, 3)—because we realize the advantages which will accrue both here and hereafter—we are "more than conquerors."

"Giving thanks unto the Father, which hath made us meet to be partakers of the inheritance of the saints in light" (verse 12). This is the closing section of our prayer, and we may notice that in it the apostle exemplifies his exhortation. "Be anxious for nothing: but in everything by prayer and supplication, *with thanksgiving,* let your requests be made known unto God" (Phil. iv, 6). When we come to the throne of grace, petitions and praise should ever accompany each other. There should be the thanksgiving of grateful love for mercies already received; of confident faith in God's promises, that He will certainly bestow the things for which we now ask—so far as to do so will be for His glory and our highest good; of joyous expectation of the things which He hath prepared and are awaiting us on high. The general relation of this verse to those preceding is apparent: the "being filled with the knowledge of God's will in all wisdom and spiritual understanding" (verse 9), is to find expression in a worthy walk (verse 10), in the exercise of patient endurance (verse 11), in grateful thanksgiving (verse 12).

The *order* of those things is not only according to the Analogy of Faith, but it is verified in the experience of the saints in the several stages of their growth in grace. Conscious of his ignorance, it is a knowledge of God's will (as made known in the Word) which most engages the attention of the babe in Christ. As the Spirit graciously opens the Scriptures to his understanding and applies them to his heart, he becomes more concerned with honouring the Lord in his daily walk and being fruitful in every good work. As he grows still older and meets with more trials and tribulations, he has an increasing realization of his need for being Divinely strengthened, so that he may not faint beneath the burdens of life and the difficulties of the way; that he may not become weary in well doing, but run the race set before him; and meekly submit to all the dispensations of God's providence. Finally, as he approaches the end of his journey, he is more and more occupied with the glorious inheritance awaiting him, wherein he will have done for ever with sin and suffering. The more joyful he is (verse 11) the more will he be filled with the spirit of thanksgiving.

The order of these things here also inculcates, in a most searching manner, an important practical lesson. This giving of thanks unto the Father does not occur at the beginning of the prayer, but at its *close.* Thereby it is intimated that none of us is warranted in concluding that *he* is among the number whom He "hath made meet for the inheritance," unless the things previously mentioned are in some measure really found in him. It would be highly presumptuous for me to complacently assume that I am fit for heaven, *unless* I be sincerely endeavouring to walk worthily of the Lord

unto all pleasing, being fruitful in every good work, and unless I possess
my soul with patience, longsuffering, and rejoice when I am persecuted for
Christ's sake. Not that these things are qualifications for heaven, but rather
the *evidences* that Divine grace has suitably fashioned my soul thereunto. It
is not that these things are the procuring cause by which I shall enter the
glory, but the marks that God has already "wrought me for" it.

On the other hand, it is equally necessary that we note carefully the
tense of the verb here. It is not a promise that God "*will* make us meet for
the inheritance," nor is the reference unto a present process that He is now
"*making* us meet." That is one of the serious errors of Romanists, who
teach that Christians must undergo a refining season of discipline in this
life to fit them for the courts above, which discipline is only completed by
the purifying fires of purgatory ridding them of their remaining corruptions.
Nor has the teaching of many Protestants been much better. Some of them
in their presentation of what is termed "progressive sanctification" have
handled it in a very legal manner and brought many of God's people into
cruel bondage thereby. How widespread is this confusion appears in such
expressions as being "meetened for glory," "ripened for heaven." Few
indeed make use of this prayer in giving thanks unto the Father because He
has already made them meet for the inheritance.

Our present verse, then, brings before us a subject of vital moment and
great practical importance, albeit one of which most of God's children today
are sadly defective in their apprehensions. Many of them who ought to be
rejoicing in the liberty of the Gospel are enthralled in some form of legal
bondage. Comparatively few of them are exulting in the self-abasing and soul-
satisfying consciousness that they are "*complete* in Him" who is their Head
(Col. ii, 10). If the only consequences of this were the disturbing of their
peace and overcasting of their joy, such evils would call for an earnest effort
to correct them. How much more so when, in addition, the absence of such
assurance (which is their legitimate portion) dishonours the Lord, cramps
their energies, obscures their graces and renders their spiritual state uncertain
both to themselves and to others.

One form of this evil is found even in many who have a clear knowledge
of the ground on which God justifies the ungodly: that after a person has
tasted of the blessedness of "the man whose transgression is forgiven, whose
sin is covered," there remains much to be done before the soul is ready to
enter his eternal rest. They hold that after his justification the believer
must undergo a process of sanctification, and for this reason he is left for
a time amid the trials and conflicts of a hostile world. The prevalency of
this notion appears in much preaching, many hymns, and especially in
prayers, for while many Christians may be frequently heard pleading to be
made meet, rarely indeed do we hear one giving thanks to the Father because
He *hath* made us meet for the inheritance of the saints. Those labouring
under such an impression can never know when the process is completed,
nor can they say with any confidence to a dying man "Believe on the Lord
Jesus Christ, and thou shalt be saved" here and now, for it would flatly
contradict their own ideas.

One would suppose that those toiling under this view must be staggered
by their own experience and observation. They see those whom they confidently regard as Christians cut off in apparently very different stages of this
process, and if the completion of it be what is styled "perfect sanctification,"
then in how few cases, so far as we can perceive, is any such preparation for

glory actually attained! On their death-beds the most eminent saints confess themselves thoroughly dissatisfied with their attainments! Yet many who deem themselves the most orthodox insist that while justification is an act completed at once, "sanctification is a progressive work." If by that expression they intend our growth in grace and the manifestation of it in this life, there can be no objection; but if it import a preparation for heaven, and that such preparation is to be the grand object of the believer's life, it is to be rejected as a God-dishonouring and soul-enslaving error—a flat contradiction of the text before us.

These three things (none others or any more) are indispensable to qualify any sinner for heaven. First, he must be predestinated thereto by the Father, which was effected "on the vessels of mercy which He had afore [by His eternal decree] prepared unto glory" (Rom. ix, 23). Second, he must have a valid legal right and title unto the inheritance: this the believing sinner has in the merits of Christ, who by His one offering "hath *perfected forever* them that are sanctified" (Heb. x, 14). Third, he must be experimentally fitted for the kingdom of God, and this he is by the regenerating act of the Holy Spirit. As the natural babe is born complete in parts (though not in their development), so that no new member or faculty can be added—though they are susceptible of expansion, with a fuller expression and clearer manifestation; so it is with the spiritual babe in Christ. "He that *hath wrought us* for the self-same thing [i.e. the glory to come—see context] is God," and proof thereof is, "who also hath given us the earnest of the Spirit" (II Cor. v, 5).

"The work of God the Spirit in regeneration is *eternally complete*. It admits of no increase or decrease. It is one and the same in all believers. There will not be the least addition to it in heaven: not one grace, holy affection, or disposition, *there* which is not in it *now*. The whole of the Spirit's work, therefore, from the moment of regeneration to our glorification, is to draw out those graces into actual exercise, which He hath wrought in us. And though one believer may abound in the fruits of righteousness more than another, yet there is not one of them more regenerate than another. This work of the Spirit, in which our meetness for the eternal fruition of God consists, is alike in all, in each, in every one that is born of the Spirit. The babe in Christ, dying as such, is as capable of high communion with God as Paul in the state of glory. The regenerate soul cannot have any addition to the holiness of that new principle imparted from the Spirit to them. He cannot be a partaker of every grace of the Holy Spirit more completely than he is already" (S. E. Pierce).

Our "meetness" for heaven is evidenced by the very terms here used. First, it is called an "inheritance," and that is not something we purchase by good works, nor procure by self-denial and mortification (as the Papists insist): rather is it that to which we lawfully succeed by our relationship to another. Primarily, it is that to which a child succeeds because of his relation to his father, or as the son of an earthly king inherits the crown. In this case the inheritance is ours by virtue of our being the *sons* of God—which we become actually at the new birth. "If children, then heirs, heirs of God and joint-heirs with Christ" (Rom. viii, 16, 17). If we inquire more distinctly what this "inheritance" is, the next verse (Col. i, 13) tells us: it is "the kingdom of God's dear Son" into which we are already translated. Joint-heirs with Christ must share His kingdom. He has *now* made us "kings and priests unto God" (Rev. i, 5).

Second, it is "the inheritance of *the saints*," and this Christians are from the first moment they savingly believe in Christ, for they are then sanctified or sainted by the very blood which procured their forgiveness (Heb. xiii, 12). Every Christian was sanctified essentially when he was anointed by the Spirit: whether we regard it as separation from those dead in sin, consecration unto God, or made holy by renewal in His image. Third, it is "the inheritance of the saints *in light*," and we were "made meet" for it when by the new birth we became "the children of light" (I Thess. v, 5). It was then we were "delivered from the power of darkness" and called "into God's marvellous light." By nature we were totally unfit for the inheritance, but by the gracious operation of the Spirit we are now meet for it, for He has made us sons, heirs, "light in the Lord."

"They were made meet because brought out from a state of alienation from the knowledge of God, the life of God, the love of God and the glory of God, to know God, to express the life of God, to taste the love of God, and to be willingly and cheerfully devoted to the service and glory of God. Are we come to the enjoyment of all these inestimable privileges: to be fellow citizens of the saints and of the household of God (Eph. ii, 19), brought nigh to God, have free access to Him—with boldness; sprinkled by the blood of Christ? Are these the common privileges which all believers are made the partakers of, and after this can any gainsay that any believer in Christ is *not* made meet to partake of the heavenly inheritance? Surely they who do so can swallow the greatest absurdity. Thou canst thus give thanks" (W. Mason, *The Gospel Magazine*, November 1773).

It is indeed a monstrous absurdity to deny their meetness for the heavenly inheritance of whom God declares, "but ye are washed, but *ye are sanctified*, but ye are justified in the name of the Lord Jesus, and by the Spirit of our God" (I Cor. vi, 11); whom "now hath He reconciled" (Col. i, 21), "made nigh by the blood of Christ" (Eph. ii, 13), indwelt by His Spirit, delighted in as His sons, and to whom He says "all things are yours" (I Cor. iii, 21). Rightly did Spurgeon affirm, "The true believer is fit for heaven now, at this very moment. That does not mean he is sinless, but that he has been accepted in the Beloved, adopted into the Family, and fitted by Divine approbation to dwell with the saints in light." That no refining process of discipline, no preparation on our part, no progressive sanctification or growth in grace is necessary, in order to meeten a babe in Christ for Paradise, is conclusively shown by the case of the dying thief, who in the *first day* of his saving faith was immediately translated from the convict's gibbet to the inheritance of the saints in light.

The question, Why does God leave the Christian in this world for a season if he be already fit for heaven? admits of a simple but sufficient answer —for His own glory. As a monument of His mercy, an example of His distinguishing love, a witness of His sufficient grace, a proof of His faithfulness in bearing with his infirmities and supplying all his need. To give him an opportunity to honour Him in the place where he had so dishonoured Him. To serve as salt in a corrupt community.

"Giving thanks unto the Father who hath made us meet for the inheritance." That is not the language of solicitude, but of gratitude. Let it be duly noted that the apostle was not here himself giving thanks on behalf of these saints, but rather he requests God that *they* might do so! Then let every Christian reader join the writer in fervently thanking the Father for *having* fitted him for eternal glory. The sloughing off of "the flesh" at death is not a qualification for heaven, but the removal of a disqualification.

LIFE AND TIMES OF JOSHUA

22. Its Lessons

Before mentioning some of the different aspects of Truth which are illustrated in Joshua iii, let us look at the miracle there recorded. "And it came to pass, when the people removed from their tents to pass over Jordan, and the priests bearing the ark of the covenant before the people; and as they that bare the ark were come unto Jordan, and the feet of the priests that bare the ark were dipped in the brim of the water, for Jordan overfloweth all his banks all the time of harvest." (verses 14, 15). First, observe well the *time* when this wonder was wrought. It was in the spring of the year, when the river was in spate. At that season the snows on Mount Lebanon (near which Jordan had its rise) melted, when there was an annual inundation of the valley. God selected a month when conditions were such as to form the most suitable background for an illustrious display of His power. He did not defer the crossing of the river until the end of summer, when it had been at its lowest, but chose the month when it was at its broadest and deepest, that His hand might be the more plainly seen. I Chronicles xii, 15, tells us Jordan continued to "overflow" in the days of David.

Next, we would take note of a little detail here which brings out the minute accuracy of Scripture and attests its historical verity, and that in a most artless manner. Joshua iii, 15, tells us it was "the time of harvest." Now the "barley harvest" came first (Ruth i, 22), and after an interval of a month or so the "wheat harvest" (Ruth ii, 21, 23). Now the Jordan was crossed on the tenth day of the fourth month (Josh. iv, 19), or four days before the Passover, which fell in with the barley harvest. From Exodus ix, 31, we learn that the barley ripened at that season, for the plague of hail was only a day or two before the Passover. From that verse we learn that the "flax" crop ripened at the same time, and, since the climate of Palestine differed little from that of Egypt, this, no doubt, was the case in Canaan too. Thus, by a comparison of Joshua iii, 13, and iv, 19, with Exodus ix, 31, we see that Israel crossed the Jordan when both the barley and the *flax* were ripe. What a silent but convincing confirmation does that furnish of the incidental statement that Rahab hid the spies "with the stalks of *flax*" (ii, 6)! This is one out of scores of similar instances adduced by J. J. Blunt in his remarkable book (out of print) *Undesigned Coincidences* to manifest the veracity of the Word.

"That the waters which came down from above stood and rose up upon a heap very far from the city Adam, that is beside Zaretan, and those that came down toward the sea of the plain, the salt sea, failed and were cut off; and the people passed over right against Jericho" (verse 16). First, the waters were cleft asunder so that those which came down from above—i.e. from the mountains—were invincibly dammed, so that the down-flowing torrent was supernaturally stayed. It was as though an enormous but invisible sluice had suddenly shut off the stream at its source. Second, the huge volume which had already descended was made to turn backward and stand on a heap in a congealed mass—which in our judgment was more remarkable than what occurred at the Red Sea. That solid wall of water must have appeared like some mammoth buttress, yet without any apparent support. Third, the waters which were already in the Jordan valley rapidly drained away into the Dead Sea, leaving the whole of the river's bed dry—"as far downward, it is likely, as it swelled upward" (Matthew Henry). Most vividly did R. Gosse depict this prodigy.

"At any time the passage of the river by such a multitude, with their wives and children, their flocks and herds, and all their baggage, would have presented formidable difficulties; but now the channel was filled with a deep and impetuous torrent, which overflowed its banks and spread widely on either side, probably extending nearly a mile in width; while in the very sight of the scene were the Canaanitish hosts, who might be expected to pour out from their fortress and exterminate the invading multitude before they could reach the shore. Yet these difficulties were nothing to Almighty power, and only serve to heighten the effect of the stupendous miracle about to be wrought. No sooner had the feet of the priests touched the brim of the overflowing river than the swollen waters receded from them; and not only the broad lower valley but the deep bed of the stream was presently emptied of water, and its pebbly bottom became dry. The waters which had been in the channel speedily ran off, while those which would naturally have replaced them from above were miraculously suspended, and accumulated in a glassy heap, far above the city Adam . . . nearly the whole channel of the Lower Jordan from a little below the Lake of Tiberias to the Dead Sea was dry."

"And the priests that bare the ark of the covenant of the Lord stood firm on dry ground in the midst of Jordan, and all the Israelites passed over on dry ground until all the people were passed clean over Jordan" (verse 17). What a test of the priests' faith and obedience was that!—a much more severe one than that required of them in verse 8. There they were only bidden to step into the brink of the water, which at most occasioned but a temporary inconvenience, though since they had to do so *before* any miracle was wrought, it called for unquestioning submission to the Divine will. But here they were required to remain stationary in the centre of the river bed, which to sight was a most perilous situation—with the great mass of the higher waters liable to suddenly rush down and engulf them. But there they patiently abode, for it must have taken many hours for such a huge multitude to pass over on foot. God's servants are not only called upon to set His people an example of implicit confidence in and full obedience to Him, but to take the lead when dangers threaten and acquit themselves courageously and perseveringly. The Lord fully vindicated the priests' obedience, holding back the mighty torrent until after they too crossed to the farther side; thereby denoting that the same power which divided the waters kept them suspended.

Consider now some of the lessons taught us here.

(1) We are shown the fundamental things which God requires from His people. First, they must "sanctify themselves" (verse 5), the essential elements of which are separation from sin and the world, entire consecration of ourselves unto God. Thereby we evince that He has won our hearts. Second, they must obediently follow the ark of the covenant, ordering their actions by it. In the ark was the Divine Law—the articles of the covenant. They must, in resolve and earnest endeavour, be regulated by the will of God in all things, doing whatsover He commanded them. Third, they must steadily and thankfully view the propitiatory which formed the lid of the ark. Here we behold the blessed balance. The ark spoke of the righteous demands of God upon us, the mercy-seat of His gracious provisions for us. Humbly confess your sins to God, and thankfully plead the cleansing blood

of Christ. If we conduct ourselves by those three basic rules all will be well.

(2) What a glorious God do we serve! He is possessed of all-mighty power and infinite wisdom. All the powers and elements of nature are subject to Him and make way for His presence. When He so pleases He can alter all the properties of those elements and change the course of nature. Nothing is too hard for that One who has turned liquid floods into solid walls, who has caused the sun to stand still (yea, to go backward: II Kings xx, 11), who has made flinty rocks to pour out fountains of water, ravens to feed Elijah, iron to swim, fire not to burn. "He turneth rivers into a wilderness and the water-springs into dry ground. . . . He turneth the wilderness into a standing water and dry ground into water-springs. And there He maketh the hungry to dwell" (Psa. cvii, 32-35). And if such a God be *for us,* who can be against us?

(3) Man's extremity is God's opportunity. The Lord waits to be gracious. Often He suffers our circumstances to become critical, yea, desperate, before He appears on our behalf. Here was Israel ready to enter Canaan, and there was the Jordan "overflowing his banks"—a season which to carnal reason seemed the most unfavourable of all. Ah, but it afforded the Lord a most fitting occasion to display His sufficiency. "Though that opposition made to the salvation of God's people have all imaginable advantage, yet God can and will conquer it. Let the banks of Jordan be filled to the brim, filled till they rush over it, it is as easy to Omnipotence to divide them and dry them up, as if they were never so narrow, never so shallow: it is all one unto the Lord" (Matthew Henry). Then let not the Christian reader give way to despair because the conditions in which he finds himself are altogether beyond his power to overcome. Your troubles may have already reached the high-water mark, but when they "overflow" and all appears to be lost, then you may expect the Lord to show Himself strong in your behalf.

(4) We have here an illustration of the grand truth expressed in Romans viii, 28, "For we know that *all* things work together for good to them that love God." Alas, there are times when many a Christian has unbelievingly said with Jacob "all these things are against me" (Gen. xlii, 36), and even though some may not have gone that far, yet few could plead guiltless to having feared that *some* things were against them. Did not the flooded valley appear to be directly against Israel, working for their ill? Yet, in reality, the very overflowing of the Jordan was among the all things contributing to their good, for it furnished an occasion for their God to the more manifestly display His power for them, so that instead of hindering, that inundation actually promoted their good—strengthening their faith in the Lord. How that should reassure the hard-pressed saint today! The very thing or things which are inclining you to give way to despair will yet prove a blessing in disguise, and you will have reason to acknowledge with David "it is *good* for me that I have been afflicted" (Psa. cxix, 71). The dark dispensations of Divine providence, the tribulations you experience, are for the trying and development of your graces.

(5) We have here an exemplification of what is stated in Genesis i, 6-9, where we are told that on the second day "God made the firmament, and divided the waters which were under the firmament from the waters which were above the firmament." By the latter "waters" we understand the reference to be unto something other than the ordinary moisture suspended in the atmosphere, namely, to those "floods" of Genesis vii, 11, 12. "By

the dividing of the waters from the waters [at the Jordan] and the making of the dry land [there] to appear, God would remind them of that which Moses by Divine revelation had instructed them in concerning the work of creation. That, by what they now saw, their belief of that which they there read might be assisted, and they might know that the God whom they worshipped was the same God that made the world and that it was the same power which was engaged and employed for them" (Matthew Henry). Thus this miracle of Joshua iii serves to illustrate the verity of Genesis i, 6-9.

(6) We also behold a striking but solemn type of Christ effecting the work of our redemption. The ark adumbrated Him as the Covenant-head of His people: borne by the priests, signifying that His work was wrought in His official character. The Divine appointment that the ark must go so far in advance of the people (Josh. iii, 4) foreshadowed the blessed but awe-inspiring fact that Christ was *alone* in performing the work of redemption: "there is none to help" (Psa. xxii, 11) was His plaintive cry. Peter declared that he was ready to accompany his Master unto death, but He answered, "whither I go, thou canst not follow Me now" (John xiii, 36). And why? Because Christ was about to endure the wrath of God and experience the awful curse of the Law in the stead of His people. The "Jordan" was not only an emblem of death, but of *judgment*—"dan" meaning "judging" (Gen. xxx, 6). Observe well that in Joshua iii, 15, we are most significantly told that the river fled back to the place of Adam, to intimate that Christ bore the judgment of all our sins, even "original sin"—the condemnation which the first man's transgression brought upon us, as well as the additional guilt of all our own iniquities.

(7) How to act when confronted by difficulty or danger. Though we dwelt upon this at some length in a previous article, yet because we deem it the most important practical lesson inculcated, we make further reference to it now. Perplexing problems, baffling situations, being faced with formidable obstacles are, from time to time, the experience of each Christian: how then is he to conduct himself? Without again enlarging upon the necessity of his taking full stock of the obstacle and of his own inability to remove it, of his refusing to lean unto his own understanding or resort to any carnal expediency, of his being regulated only by the Word of God and walking "in newness of life," we will stress but one feature, the central one: his looking trustfully, expectantly, and perseveringly unto the Lord to make a passage for him through his "Jordan." In a word, to keep the eye of faith steadfastly fixed on the Anti-typical Ark, to grasp firmly His promise, "When thou passeth through the waters, I will be with thee; and through the rivers, they shall not overflow thee . . . for I am the Lord *thy* God: the Holy One of Israel, thy Saviour" or "Deliverer" (Isa. xliii, 2).

(8) For the Christian there is nothing whatever to fear in death, is another truth writ large across Joshua iii. Yet the fact remains that, excepting sin, there is nothing so much dreaded by not a few of God's children: with them a horror of sin proceeds from a spiritual principle, of death from their natural constitution. But death can no more harm a saint than the Jordan did any of the children of Israel, and that for the very same reasons. Christ has vanquished death, as in a figure the ark of the covenant vanquished the Jordan. It was as that sacred vessel entered the brim that its waters fled before it, and in consequence all who followed it passed through dry shod. So it was Christ's going before His people into death which has rendered it impotent to hurt them, and therefore they exultantly

cry, "O death, where is thy sting? O grave, where is thy victory? The sting of death is sin, and the strength of sin is the Law, but thanks be to God which giveth us the victory through our Lord Jesus Christ" (I Cor. xv, 55-57), for He endured the Law's penalty upon our behalf and extracted the fatal sting from death. For the believer death is the portal into the heavenly Canaan.

THE DOCTRINE OF REVELATION
6. The Existence of God.

Third, *as seen in human history.* Since God be the Creator of all things, it logically follows that He is their perpetual Preserver and Regulator; and since man be the chief of His earthly creatures, it is unthinkable that God has left him entirely to himself. The same all-mighty Being who created every part of it, directs the vast machinery of the universe and controls equally all the hearts and actions of men. But the same unbelief which seeks to banish God from the realm of creation, denies that He has any real place or part in the moral government of the world. The one, it is said, is regulated by the (impersonal) "laws of Nature," while man, endowed with "free will," must not be interfered with, but left to work out his own destiny, both individually and collectively considered. We have shown how utterly irrational is such a view as it pertains to the material sphere, and it is no more difficult to demonstrate how thoroughly untenable it is as applied to the moral realm. The palpable facts of observation refute it. The affairs of every individual, the history of each nation, the general course of human events, alike bear evidence of a higher Power superintending the same.

In reading history most people are contented with a bare knowledge of its salient facts, without attempting to trace their causes or ascertain the connection of events. For the most part they look no farther than the motives, designs and tendencies of human nature. They perceive not that there is a *philosophy* of history. They rise not to the realization that the living God has absolute sway over this scene, that amid all the confusion of human wills and interests, all the malice and wickedness of Satan and his agents, the Lord God omnipotent reigneth—not only in heaven but over this earth—shaping all its affairs, directing all things to the outworking of His eternal purpose. Because the reading of human history is done so superficially, and few have more than a general acquaintance with its character, our present line of argument may not be so patent or so potent unto some of those who peruse this article. Nevertheless, it should be more or less obvious unto any person of ordinary intelligence that in the course of the centuries there are clear marks of an over-ruling and presiding Power above the human.

Since there can be no effect without a previous cause, no law without a law-giver, neither do events come to pass fortuitously. Any thoughtful student of history is obliged to conclude that its records are something more than a series of disconnected and purposeless incidents: rather do they evince the working out of a plan. True, its wheels often appear to move slowly, and not infrequently at cross-purposes, nevertheless the sequel shows they work surely. It is in the *combination* of events leading up to some grand end that the workings of Divine providence most clearly appear. As we perceive the wisdom of the Creator in so admirably fitting each member of the human body to perform its designed functions, so we may discern the hand of the moral Ruler of this world in the adapting of appropriate means to the accomplishment of His ends, in the suitability of the instruments He has selected thereunto, in making each separate human actor play his part, each individual contribute his quota in producing the desired effect. As in the mechanism of a watch, each pivot is in place, each wheel in motion, so that the main-spring guides its index, so in the complicated machinery of history every single circumstance pays its mite toward the furthering of some grand object.

Proofs of a presiding Providence are to be found in the life of each individual. Where is the man who has not passed through experiences which made him feel in his heart there must be a God who watches over him. In the unexpected and remarkable turns in the course of his affairs, in the sudden thoughts and unaccountable decisions which lead to most important results, in his narrow escapes from grave danger, he has evidence of a higher power at work. Even the most giddy and thoughtless are, at times, forced to take notice of this. That we *are* under a Moral Government which dispenses rewards and punishments in a natural way is also plain to our senses and proved by personal experience. Vicious actions speedily meet with retribution, by involving their perpetrator in disgrace, by often reducing him to poverty, subjecting him to bodily disease and mental suffering, and bringing about an untimely death. On the other hand, we find that virtuous actions not only result in inward peace and satisfaction, but lead to respect, health and happiness.

If there be no living God presiding over this scene, how can we possibly account for the almost exact ratio between the two sexes? Each year there are born into this world millions of males and of females, and yet the balance between them is perfectly preserved. Their parents had no say in the matter, nor did medical science regulate it! The only rational explanation is that the sex of each child is determined by the Creator. Again, if there be no personal Creator fashioning human countenances, how are we to explain their unvarying variation? The features of the human countenance are but few in number, yet so much does their appearance differ, both singly and in their combination, that out of countless millions no two people look exactly alike! Suppose the opposite. If a likeness were common, what incalculable inconvenience and confusion would ensue. If only one hundred men in a single large city had the same build and countenance, impersonation would be practised without fear of detection, and criminals could not be identified. Such endless dissimilarities among those descended from common parents must have the Almighty for their Author.

That the One from above regulates all human affairs is demonstrated on every side of us, look where we may. In the instances alluded to above the individual is entirely passive, for it is by no decision of his that he is born male or female, black or white, a giant or a dwarf. But consider something yet more striking, namely, that even our *voluntary actions* are secretly directed from on high. Each year hundreds of thousands of both young men and women choose their ordinary vocations or careers: what is it which moves them to make a proportionate selection from such a variety of alternatives? Is it nothing but blind chance that each generation is supplied with sufficient physicians and dentists, lawyers and school teachers, mechanics and manual labourers? Many of our youth emigrate: what hinders *all* from so doing? Some prefer a life on the land, others on the sea—why? Take something still more commonplace: today the composer of this article has written and mailed seven letters—suppose every adult in Great Britain did the same! The complicated machinery of modern life would speedily break down and utter chaos would obtain were not an omniscient and omnipresent Being regulating it.

It may be objected that the machinery of our complex social life does not always run smoothly: that there are strikes and lock-outs which result in much inconvenience, that at times the railroads are blocked with traffic, that hotels are overcrowded, and so on. Granted, yet such occurrences are the exception rather than the rule. But we may draw an argument of Divine providence from the very commotions and confusions which *do* obtain in the world. Seeing it does occasionally pass through disturbances, is it not evident that there must be a mighty Power balancing these commotions, yea curbing them, so that they do not speedily issue in the total ruin of the world? The same One who has put the fear of man into wild beasts and a natural instinct for them to avoid human habitations, preferring to resort unto the jungles and deserts, to prowl for their prey in the night, and in the morning return to their caves and dens, sufficiently places His restraining hand upon the baser passions of men as to ensure that degree of law and order which makes life possible amid fallen and depraved creatures. Were that restraining Hand altogether removed, any guarantee of safety and security would be *non est*.

God is no idle Spectator of the affairs of this earth, but is the immediate Regulator of all its events, and that, not only in a general way, but in all particulars, from the least to the greatest. If, on the one hand, not a sparrow falls to the ground without the Divine will (Matt. x, 29), certain it is that on the other no throne can be overturned without His ordering. "For of Him, and through Him, and to Him, are all things: to whom be glory forever. Amen" (Rom. xi, 36). God is not only "King of saints," but He is "King of nations" (Jer. x, 7) as well. God reigns as truly over His foes as He does over His friends, and works through Satan and his demons as truly as by His holy angels. "The king's heart is in the hand of the Lord, and He turneth it whithersoever He will" (Prov. xxi, 1). God presides over the deliberations of parliaments and influences the decisions of cabinets. Human governments act only as they are moved by a secret power from heaven. Jehovah rules in the councils of the ungodly equally as in the prayerful counsels of a church assembly. The designs, decisions and actions of all men are directed by Him unto those ends which He has appointed, yet that in nowise annuls their moral agency or lessens their own guilt in sinning.

The government of this world is as much a work of God as was the creation of it, and while there be some things as inscrutable about the one as the other, yet each alike bears unmistakably upon it the Divine impress. There are riddles in each which the wisest cannot solve, but there are also wonders in each before which all should be awed. Broadly speaking, the moral government of God consists in two things: in directing the creatures' actions, in apportioning rewards and punishments according to the actions of rational creatures. No evil comes to pass without His permission, no good without His concurrence; no good or evil without His over-ruling—ordering it to His own ends. "The eyes of the Lord are in every place, beholding the evil and the good" (Prov. xv, 3), and in His balances everything is weighed. The distributions of Divine mercy and of vengeance are, to some extent, apportioned in this life, but more particularly and fully will they be made manifest in the day to come. God rules in such a way that His hand should be neither too evident nor too secret, and by adopting this middle course room is left for the exercise of faith, while the unbelief of infidels is rendered without excuse.

Nothing happens simply because it must, that is, of inexorable necessity. Fate is blind, but Providence has eyes—all is directed by wisdom and according to design. The history of each nation is the outworking of the Divine plan and purpose concerning it. Yet it is equally true that the history of each nation is determined by its own attitude toward God and His Law. In the experience of each one it is made to appear that " Righteousness exalteth a nation, but sin is a reproach to any people (Prov. xiv, 3). Thus the Word of God and the providence of God are complementary: the former sheds light on the latter, while the latter illustrates and exemplifies the former. Therefore in His government of this world, God displays His manifold perfections: His wisdom and goodness, His mercy and justice, His faithfulness and patience. The rise, progress and triumphs of each nation, as also its decline, fall and ignomiy, are according to both the sovereign will and the perfect righteousness of the Lord. He rules " in the midst of His enemies " (Psa. cx, 2), yet His rule is neither capricious nor arbitrary, but a wise and just one. The prosperity of nations generally tends to the increase of vice through affording fuller opportunity to indulge its lusts; and in such cases sore calamities are necessary for the checking of their wickedness, or, when it has come to the full, to destroy them as the Egyptian and Babylonian empires were.

The history of Israel affords the most striking example of what has been pointed out above. So long as they honoured God and walked in obedience to His law, so long they prospered and flourished—witness their history in the days of Joshua and David; but when they worshipped the idols of the heathen and became unrighteous in their conduct man with man, sore chastisements and heavy judgments were their portion, as in the times of the Judges and of the Babylonian captivity. Observe too the futile attempts made by the most powerful of their enemies to secure their extirpation: the efforts of Pharaoh, of Haman, of Sennacherib to overthrow the purpose of Jehovah concerning His people resulted only in their own destruction. Note how an exact retribution—" poetic justice " worldlings would call it—overtook Jezebel: " In the place where dogs licked the blood of Naboth " (I Kings xxi, 19), who was murdered at the orders of that wicked queen, *there* was her corpse consumed by dogs (II Kings xi, 36). On the other hand, behold how God blessed those who showed kindness to His people: as Rahab and the whole of her family being delivered when Jericho was destroyed because she had sheltered the two Israelitish spies; and the Shunnamite woman supernaturally provided for throughout the sore famine for her befriending of the prophet Elijah. What incredulity regards as " coincidencies " right reason views as wondrous providences.

The book of Esther furnishes a most vivid illustration and demonstration of the invisible yet palpable working of God in human affairs. In it we are shown the Jews brought to the very brink of ruin, and then delivered without any miracle being wrought on their behalf. The very means employed by their enemies for their destruction were, by the secret operations of God, made the means of their deliverance and glory. Writing thereon, Carson rightly said: " The hand of God in His ordinary Providence linked together a course of events as simple and as natural as the mind can conceive, yet as surprising as the boldest fictions of romance." The series of events opens with the king of Persia giving a banquet. Heated with wine, that monarch gave orders for his royal consort to appear before the assembled revellers. Though such a request was indecorous and distasteful to the queen, yet it is remarkable she dared to disobey her despotic husband. Whether a sense of decency or personal pride actuated her we know not, but in voluntarily acting according to her own feelings she ignorantly fulfilled the will of Him whom she knew not. That the king should subject her to a temporary disgrace for her refusal to heed his behest might be expected, but that he should give up for ever one whom he so much admired is surprising.

How extraordinary it was that the deposing of Vashti made way for the elevating of a poor Jewess to the rank of queen of the Persian empire! Was it nothing but a "happy coincidence" that she should be more beautiful than all the virgins of over a hundred provinces? Was it only a piece of "good luck" that the king's chamberlain was pleased with her from the first moment of her arrival, and that he did all in his power to advance her interests? Was it simply "fortunate" for her that she instantly met with favour when the king set eyes upon her? Was it only by blind chance that the conspiracy of two of the king's servants was thwarted and that Mordecai and all his people were saved from disaster? Haman was sure of victory, having obtained the king's decree to execute his bloody designs. Why was it, then, that the king was sleepless one night, and why should he arise and, to pass the time away, scan the court records? Why did his eye happen to alight on the reported discovery of the plot on his own life? Why had Mordecai been the one to uncover the scheme and his name entered into the report? Why was the king now—at this critical juncture in Israel's affairs—so anxious to ascertain whether Mordecai had been suitably rewarded? Cold logic is not sufficiently credulous to regard these things, and the grand sequel to them all, as so many fortuitous events.

The book of Esther plainly evinces that the most trifling affairs are ordered by the Lord to subserve His own glory and effect the good of His own people. Though He works behind the scenes, He works none the less really. He does indeed govern the inanimate world by general laws of His own appointing, yet He *directs* their operations—or suspends them when He pleases—so as to accomplish what He has decreed. He has also established general moral laws in the government of mankind, yet He is not tied by them: sometimes He uses means, at others He uses none. As the sun and rain minister to the nourishment and comfort of the righteous and wicked alike, not from the necessity of general laws but from the immediate providence of Him who has ordained all things, so the free determinations of men are so controlled from on high that they effect the eternal designs of God. So too that book reveals that it is in the *combination* of incidents the working of Providence most plainly appears. There is a wonderful concatenation of events which leads to the accomplishment of God's glorious purpose: the actions of each person are links in the chain to bring about some appointed result—if one link were removed the whole chain would be broken. All lines converge on and meet in one centre: all things concur to bring about the decreed event.

If the record of any Gentile nation were fully chronicled, and had we sufficient discernment and perspecuity, we should perceive as definite a connection between one event—which now appears to us isolated—and another, and the hand of God controlling *them* as in the history of Israel. But even a fragmentary knowledge of general history should be sufficient to reveal to any man the directing hand of God in it and the testimony it bears to the truth of the Bible. It abounds in illustrations that "The race is not to the swift, nor the battle to the strong" (Eccl. ix, 11). The most numerous and powerful armies are no guaranty of success, as has frequently been demonstrated. Providence disposes the event: without any miraculous interference the best trained and equipped forces have been defeated by much weaker ones. The discovery of America by Columbus, in time for that land to afford an asylum for persecuted Protestants, the invention of printing just before the Reformation, the destruction of the "Invincible Armada" of Spain, are more than "coincidences." Why has England always had a man of outstanding proportions—genius, valour, dynamism, dogged determination—at each critical juncture of her history? Cromwell, Drake, Nelson, Wellington, Churchill, were the special gifts of God to a people under His peculiar favour.

A real if mysterious Providence is obviously at work, controlling the gradual growth of each empire and of the combination of nations: as in the federation of the ten kings of Revelation xvii, 16, 17—the Divine plan is brought to fruition by those whose intention it is to accomplish their *own* purpose. "For God hath put it in their hearts to fulfil *His* will," though that in nowise lessens their sin: none but the hand of the Almighty can bring good out of evil and make the wrath of His enemies to praise Him. The more their chronicles be studied, the stronger should be our conviction that only the action and interposition of God can account for many of the outstanding events in human history. The rise and careers of individual tyrants also illustrates the same principle. How often have the workings of Providence verified the Word that "the triumphing of the wicked is *short*" (Job xx, 5). At longest it is but brief because limited by the span of this life, whereas their sufferings will be eternal. But often God blows upon the plans of ambitious oppressors, crosses their imperious wills, and brings them to a speedy ruin in this world: He did so with Napoleon, the Kaiser, Mussolini and Hitler! He raised them on high that He might cast them down by a more terrible fall.

THE GREAT CHANGE

Let none conclude from the last few paragraphs that we do not believe in the "total depravity" of man, or that we do so in such a manner as practically to evacuate that expression of any real meaning. Most probably the writer believes more firmly in the utter ruin of fallen human nature than do some of his readers, and views the plight of the natural man as being more desperate than they do. We hold that the state of every unregenerate soul is such that he *cannot* turn his face Godward or originate a single spiritual thought, and that he has not even so much as the wish or will to do so. Nor let it be inferred from our preceding remarks that we deny the evil principle or "the flesh" as being existent and dominant in the natural man: we most emphatically believe—both on the testimony of the Word of Truth and from personal experience of its awful potency and horrible workings—that it is. But we also hold that great care should be taken when seeking to visualize or define in our minds what "the flesh" consists of. It is a principle of evil and not a concrete or tangible entity. The moment we regard it as something material, we confuse ourselves.

It is because all of us are so accustomed to thinking in the terms of matter that we find it difficult to form a definite concept of something which though immaterial is *real*. Nor is it by any means a simple task for one to express himself thereon so that he will be coherent unto others. Man lost no part of his tripartite nature when he fell, nor was a fourth part then communicated to him. Instead, sin—which is not a material entity—entered into him, and vitiated and corrupted his entire being. He was stricken with a loathsome disease which defiled all his faculties and members, so that his entire spirit and soul became precisely like one whose body is thus described: "From the sole of the foot even unto the head there is no soundness in it; but wounds, and bruises, and putrefying sores" (Isa. i, 5). A potato is still a potato even when frozen, though it is no longer edible. An apple remains an apple when decayed within. And man still retained his human nature when he apostatized from God, died spiritually, and became totally depraved. He remained all that he was previously minus only his *holiness*.

When man fell he died spiritually and, as we have shown, death is not annihilation, but separation. Yet that word "separation" does not express the full meaning of what is signified by "spiritual death." Scripture employs another term—"*alienation*," and that too we must take fully into account. "Alienation" includes the thought of severance, but it also imports an *opposition*. A dear friend may be separated from me physically, but a cruel enemy is bitterly antagonistic to me. Thus it is with fallen man: he is not only cut off from all communion with the Holy One, but he is innately and inveterately hostile to Him—"alienated" in his affections. We are not here striving about mere "words," but calling attention to a most solemn truth and fact. It is thus that the Scripture depicts the condition of fallen mankind: "Having the understanding darkened, being alienated from the life of God, through the ignorance that is in them, because of the hardness of their heart" (Eph. iv, 18); yea, it solemnly declares that "the carnal mind is enmity against God" (Rom. viii, 7), and "enmity" is not a negative and passive thing, but a positive and active one.

"Dead in trespasses and sins" (Eph. ii, 1) is the fearful diagnosis made of fallen man by the Divine Physician. Yet though that language be true to fact and is no exaggeration, still it is a *figure,* and unless we interpret it in strict accord with Scripture, we shall falsify its meaning. It is often said that the spiritual state of the natural man is analogous to that of a corpse buried in the cemetery. From one standpoint that is correct; from another it is utterly erroneous. The natural man is a putrefying creature, a stench in the nostrils of the Holy One, and he can no more perform a spiritual act Godwards than a corpse can perform a physical act manwards. But there the analogy ends! There is a contrast between the two cases as well as a resemblance. A corpse has no responsibility, but the natural man *has*! A corpse can perform *no* actions; different far is the case of the sinner. He *is* active, active against *God*! Though he does not love Him (and he ought!), yet he is filled with enmity and hatred against Him. Thus spiritual death is not a state of passivity and inactivity, but one of aggressive hostility against God.

Here then, as everywhere, there is a balance to be preserved; yet it is rarely maintained. Far too many Calvinists, in their zeal to repudiate the free-willism of Arminians, have at the same time repudiated man's moral agency; anxious to enforce the utter helplessness of fallen men in spiritual matters, they have virtually reduced him to an irresponsible machine. It has not been sufficiently noted that in the very next verse after the statement "who were dead in trespasses and sins," the apostle added, "Wherein [i.e. that state of spiritual death] ye *walked* [which a corpse in the grave could not!] according to the course of this world, according to the spirit of the power of the air, the spirit that now worketh in the children of disobedience. Among whom also we all had our conversation ["conduct"] in times past in the lusts of our flesh, fulfilling the desires of the flesh and of the mind" (Eph. ii, 1-3). So that in one sense they were dead (i.e. Godward) while they lived (i.e. in sin), and in another sense they *lived* (a life of self-seeking and of enmity against God), while *dead* to all spiritual things.

By the fall man both lost something and acquired something. Term that something a "nature" if you will, so long as you do not conceive of it as something material. That which man lost was holiness, and that which he acquired was sin, and neither the one nor the other is a substance, but rather a moral quality. A "nature" is not a concrete entity, but instead that which characterizes and impells an entity or creature. It is the "nature" of gravitation to attract; it is the nature of fire to burn. A "nature" is not a tangible thing, but a power impelling to action, a dominating influence—an "instinct" for want of a better term. Strictly speaking a "nature" is that which we have by our *origin,* as our partaking of *human nature* distinguishes us from the celestial creatures who are partakers of angelic nature. Thus we speak of a lion's "nature" (ferocity), a vulture's nature (to feed on carrion), a lamb's nature (gentleness). A "nature," then, describes more what a creature is by birth and disposition, and therefore we prefer to speak of holiness or imparted grace as a "*principle* of good," and indwelling sin or "the flesh" as a principle of evil—a prevalent disposition which moves its subjects to ever act in accord with its distinguishing quality.

If it be kept in mind that, strictly speaking, a "nature" is that which we have *by our origin,* as partaking of human nature distinguishes us from the celestial creatures on the one hand and from the beasts of the field (with their animal nature) on the other, much confusion of thought will be avoided. Furthermore, if we distinguish carefully between what our nature intrinsically consists of and what it "accidentally" (non-essentially) became and becomes by virtue of the changes passing upon it at the fall and at regeneration, then we should have less difficulty in understanding what is signified by the Lord's assuming *our nature.* When the Son of God became incarnate He took unto Himself human nature. He was, in every respect, true Man, possessed of spirit (Luke xxiii, 46), soul (John xii, 27), and body (John xix, 40): "in *all* things it behoved Him to be made like unto His brethren" (Heb. ii, 17)—otherwise He could not be their Surety and Mediator. This does not explain the miracle and mystery of the Divine incarnation, for that is incomprehensible, but it states the fundamental fact of it. Christ did not inherit our corruption, for *that* was no essential part of manhood! He was born and ever remained immaculately pure and holy; nevertheless, He took upon Him our nature intrinsically considered, but *not* as it had been defiled by sin; and therefore is denominated "the son *of Adam*" (Luke iii, 38).

When, then, we say that by the fall man became possessed of a "sinful nature" it must not be understood that something comparable to his spirit or soul was *added to* his being, but instead that a principle of evil entered into him, which defiled every part of his being, as frost entering into fruit ruins it. Instead of his faculties now being influenced and regulated by holiness, they became defiled and dominated by sin. Instead of spiritual propensities and properties actuating his conduct, a carnal disposition became the law of his being. The objects and things man formerly loved, he now hated; and those which he was fitted to hate, he now desires. Therein lies both his depravity and his criminality. God holds fallen man responsible to mortify every inclination unto evil, to resist and reject every solicitation unto sin, and will justly punish him because he fails to do so. Nay more, God requires him and holds him accountable to love Him with all his heart and to employ each of his faculties in serving and glorifying Him: his failure so to do consists solely in a voluntary refusal, and for that He will righteously judge him.

Now the miracle of grace is *God's answer* to man's ruination of himself, His begun reversal of what happened to him at the Fall. Let us now establish that fact from the Scriptures and show this concept is no invention of ours. The very fact that Christ is denominated "the last Adam" implies that He came to right the wrong wrought by the first Adam—though only so far as God's elect are concerned. Hence we find Him saying by the Spirit of prophecy, "I *restored* that which I took not away" (Psa. lxix, 4). A lengthy article might well be written on those comprehensive words: suffice it now to say that He recovered both unto God and His people what had been lost by Adam's defection—to the One His manifestative honour and glory; to the other, the Holy Spirit and holiness in their hearts. What Christ did for His people is the meritorious ground of what the Spirit works in them, and at regeneration they begin to be restored to their pristine purity or brought back to their original state. Therefore it is that the great change is spoken of as the "*renewing* of the Holy Spirit" (Titus iii, 5), that is, a renovating and restoring of spiritual life to the soul.

"Lie not one to another, seeing that ye have put off the old man with his deeds, and have put on the new man, which is renewed in knowledge after the image of Him that created him" (Col. iii, 9). Those to whom the apostle was writing had, by their profession and practice, "put off" or renounced "the old man," and by lip and life had avowed and exhibited the new. That new man is here said to be "*renewed* in knowledge," which cannot be the obtaining of a knowledge which man never had previously, but rather the recovery and restoration of that spiritual knowledge of God which he had originally. That is confirmed by what follows: "*after* the image of Him that created him," i.e. at the beginning. Man was originally made "in the image of God" (Gen. i, 27), which imported at least three things. First, he was constituted a tripartite being by the Triune God; and this he continued to be after the Fall. Second, he was created in His *natural* image, being made a moral agent, endowed with rationality and freedom of will; this too he retained. Third, God's *moral* image, being "made upright," endued "with righteousness and true holiness"; which was lost when man became a sinner, but is restored to him by the miracle of grace.

That which takes place in the elect at regeneration is the *reversing* of the effects of the Fall. The one born again is, through Christ, and by the Spirit's operations, restored to union and communion with God (I Pet. iii, 18). The one who previously was spiritually dead, alienated from God, is now spiritually alive, reconciled to God. Just as spiritual death was brought about by the entrance into man's being of a principle of evil, which darkened his understanding and hardened his heart (Eph. iv, 18), so spiritual life is the introduction of a principle of holiness into man's soul, which enlightens his understanding and softens his heart. God communicates a *new principle* one which is as real and potent unto good as indwelling sin is unto evil.

Grace is now imparted, a holy disposition is wrought in the soul, a new temper of spirit is bestowed upon the inner man. But no new faculties are communicated unto him: rather are his original faculties (in measure) purified, enriched, elevated, empowered. Just as man did not become less than a threefold being when he fell, neither does he become more than a threefold being when he is renewed. Nor will he in heaven itself: his spirit and soul and body will then be *glorified*—completely purged from every taint of sin, and perfectly conformed unto the image of God's Son.

But is not a "new nature" received by us when we are born again? If that term (in preference to "another principle") be admitted and used, we must be careful lest we carnalize our conception of what is connoted by that expression. Much confusion has been caused at this point through failure to recognize that it is a *person*, and not merely a "nature," who is born of the Spirit: "*he* is born of God" (I John iii, 9). The selfsame person who was spiritually dead Godwards (separated and alienated from Him) is now spiritually alive Godwards—reconciled and brought back into union and communion with Him. The same person whose entire being (and not merely some part of him!) was dead in trespasses and sins, wherein he walked according to the course of this world, according to the evil spirit who worketh in the children of disobedience, fulfilling the lusts of the flesh; his entire being is now alive in holiness and righteousness, and he walks according to the course of God's Word, according to the power and promptings of the Holy Spirit, who worketh in the children of obedience, moving them to fulfil the dispositions and develop the graces of the spirit or "new nature."

This must be so, or otherwise there would be no preservation of the *identity* of the individual: we repeat, it is the individual himself who is born again, and not merely something *in* him. The person of the regenerate is constitutionally the same as the person of the unregenerate, each having a spirit and soul and body. But just as in fallen man there is *also* a principle of evil which has corrupted each part of his threefold being—which principle may be styled his "sinful nature" (if by that be meant his evil disposition and character), as it is the "nature" of swine to be filthy; so when a person is born again another and new principle is introduced into his being, which may be styled a "new nature," if by it be meant a disposition which propels him in a new direction—Godwards. Thus, in both cases, "nature" is a moral principle rather than a tangible entity. "That which is born of the Spirit is spirit"—spiritual and not material, and must not be regarded as something substantial, distinct from the soul of the regenerate, like one part of matter added to another; rather is it that which *spiritualizes* his inward faculties as the "flesh" had carnalized them.

When treating of regeneration under the figure of the new birth some writers (ourself included in earlier days) have introduced analogies from natural birth which Scripture by no means warrants, and which, by its employment of *other* figures it disallows. Physical birth is the bringing forth into this world of a creature, a complete personality which before conception had no existence whatever. But the one regenerated by God *had* a complete personality before he was born again! To that statement it may be objected, Not a *spiritual* personality. True, but keep steadily in mind that spirit and matter are opposites, and we only confuse ourselves if we think or speak of that which is "spiritual" as being something concrete. Regeneration is not the creating of a person who hitherto had no existence, but the spiritualizing of one who had—the renewing and renovating of one whom sin had unfitted for communion with God, and this by the imparting to him of a principle, or "nature," or *life,* which gives a new and different bias to all his faculties. Ever beware of regarding the Christian as made up of two distinct personalities.

A century ago a booklet was published in England purporting to prove that "A child of God cannot backslide," and many in a reputedly orthodox circle were evilly affected by it. Its author argued "a regenerated man possesses two natures: an old man of sin, and a new man of grace; that the old man of sin never made any progress in the Divine life nor ever can, consequently he can never go back from that in which he had never made any advances. The new man of grace never sinned nor ever can sin, so that he likewise can never go back or imbibe the least taint or particle of sin. How then can the child of God backslide?" A reviewer exposed this sophistry by mentioning a Papist in Germany who was a royal bishop that was very fond of hunting, and who was friendly admonished of the inconsistency of the chase with the mitre. His reply was, "I do not hunt as bishop, but as prince," to which it was answered, "If the prince should break his neck while a-hunting and went to hell, what would become of the bishop!" That was answering a fool according to his folly!

The "old man" and the "new man" indwell and belong to the same individual, and can no more be divorced from *his person* than the bishop could be separated from the prince. It is not merely something *in* the Christian but the Christian *himself* who backslides. What we have called attention to above is but the corollary, a carrying out to its logical conclusion of another error, equally mischievous and reprehensible, though not so fully developed, namely, wherein the "two natures" in the believer are made so prominent and dominant that the person possessing them is largely lost sight of and his responsibility repudiated. Thus, it is just as much an idle quibble to reason that neither "the flesh" or old nature, nor "the spirit" or new nature, is capable of backsliding. It is the person possessing those two natures (or principles) who backslides, and for that God holds him accountable and chastens him accordingly. Unless believers are much on their guard, they will eagerly snatch at any line of teaching which undermines their accountability and causes them to slur over the exceeding sinfulness of *their* sins, by finding a pretext for supposing they are more to be pitied than blamed.

The youth differs much from the infant, and the adult from the immature youth; nevertheless, it is *the same individual,* the same human person, who passes through those stages. Human beings we are; moral agents, responsible creatures we shall ever remain, no matter what be the precise nature of the internal change we experienced at regeneration (nor how the character of that experience be defined or expressd), or whatever change awaits the body at resurrection: we shall never lose our essential personality or *identity* as God created us at the first. Let that be clearly understood and firmly grasped: we remain *the same persons* all through our history. Neither the deprivation of spiritual life at the Fall, nor the communication of spiritual life at the new birth, affects the reality of our being in possession of *human nature.* By the Fall we did not become less than men; by regeneration we do not become more than men—though our relation to God is altered. That which essentially constitutes our manhood was not lost, and no matter what be imparted to us at regeneration, our individuality and personal identity as a responsible being remains unchanged.

(continued from back page)

who is his daily Benefactor. He neither discerns the trend of God's kindness nor comprehends his own duty with reference thereto. He is either so filled with self-righteousness as to consider temporal blessings are his due, or so besotted as to draw an entirely false inference from them. The great majority insanely regard God's goodness as a mark of indulgence, or as His indifference to their deplorable conduct. God's very patience hardens their hearts and causes them to continue in sin, supposing that He will ever be tolerant with them, even though they go on defying Him unto the end of their days. "Not knowing" means in a *practical way*, not duly improving the same. Because Divine justice lingers in its execution the wicked assume it has no real existence and consists only of empty threats. Instead, God holds back the hand of His wrath to prolong man's opportunity for repentance: "Let it alone this year . . . if it bear fruit well; and if not, after that thou shalt cut it down" (Luke xiii, 7-9).

God is good and doeth good. It is true that man is born unto trouble as the sparks fly upward, yet he is the recipient of much which relieves his misery, for the mercy of God is over all the works of His hands. He daily loadeth men with His benefits, but those benefits meet with a very varied reception. Many receive them with callous unconcern: the ox knoweth his owner, and the ass his master's crib, but multitudes of men and women refuse to recognize the Hand that ministers so tenderly to them. The patience of God not only affords time and opportunity for repentance, but it furnishes motives and encouragement thereto—revealing our duty unto One so benevolent and affording ground to hope for His acceptance of us if we respond to His gracious overtures in the Gospel; only man's depravity and perversity prevents the improvement of His forbearance. But, instead, the majority harden their hearts, as they did during the terrible air raids, closing their ears to God's voice in them. A few appear thankful for His mercies, and verbally acknowledge God's goodness; but there they stop—there is no repentance, no reformation of life.

But how different is it with the regenerate! God's goodness does lead *them* "to repentance"! Even His temporal blessings affect their hearts, so that they are made to sincerely exclaim: "I am not worthy of the least of all the mercies and of all the truth which Thou has showed unto Thy servant." The Divine blessings they receive, so far from hardening and causing them presumptuously to proceed with high-handed rebellion, melt them, and cause them gratefully to ask: "What shall I render unto the Lord for all His benefits toward me?" (Psa. cxvi, 12). The more tokens of God's goodness they receive, the more are they convicted of their undeservingness. Instead of abusing His forbearance, they are amazed at His patience with them.

It is no proof that you are a child of God because He has borne long with your waywardness, for God endures "with much longsuffering the vessels of wrath fitted to destruction" (Rom. ix, 22). Nor is it any proof that you are a Christian because God has ministered freely unto you in temporal mercies, for "He maketh his sun to rise on the evil and the good, and sendeth rain on the just and on the unjust" (Matt. v, 45). But it *is* an evidence that you are one of God's children if His forbearance has touched your heart and moved you to marvel at His patience toward you. It *is* an evidence you are a quickened soul if the realization of God's goodness has filled you with godly sorrow and led you to amend your life. Here, then, is one of the distinguishing marks between the regenerate and the unregenerate: the *effects* which God's goodness has upon their hearts and the *response* which they make unto the same.

It was the expectation of the Jews that their descent from Abraham (Matt. iii, 9; John viii, 33), and the special favours they enjoyed from Jehovah, would secure them from the doom that would overtake the Gentiles. In that they erred fatally. Nor are they by any means alone in cherishing such a vain delusion. It is a very common assumption on the part of the children of disobedience that the showering of heaven's providential bounties upon them is a sure sign there is nothing for them to fear. "Because sentence against an evil work is not executed speedily, therefore the heart of the sons of men is fully set in them to do evil" (Eccl. vii, 11). They make the very kindness of God a licence to continue in sin and regard His longsuffering as indifference to their wickedness. Because their lives are spared and prolonged when many of their careless companions are cut off, or because they are given a larger portion than others of their fellows of what this world provides, they conclude that God will never deal severely with them. They err greatly, for after their hardness and impenitent heart they are but treasuring up unto themselves wrath "against the day of wrath and revelation of the righteous judgment of God" (Rom. ii, 5).

"Despisest thou the riches of His goodness and forbearance and long-suffering: not knowing that the goodness of God leadeth thee to repentance." The "goodness of God" is a general term for His benignity and munificence. The "riches" thereof import the high value and great abundance of them, and are thus termed to excite our wonderment. The principal reference is to God's providential blessings and bounties unto the children of men, and which are "despised" by them when their hearts are unaffected by the same. The "riches of His forbearance" tells of the restraint which God exercises in not immediately executing His vengeance upon such base ingrates. The "riches of His longsuffering" describes the amazing extent of His forbearance in delaying to punish those who so greatly abuse His mercies—a degree not yet completely exhausted. He still grants them "space to repent" (Rev. ii, 21). Present immunity from punishment by no means signifies that the sinner may continue to defy God with impunity. Far from it. Rather is the prolongation of his day of opportunity and the continuation of God's mercies designed to lead him to repentance.

"Not knowing that the goodness of God leadeth thee to repentance." The apostle, then, is not speaking here of men's ignorance of that gracious influence which in the day of God's power makes His people willing to throw down the weapons of their warfare against Him, but rather of their failure to perceive *the design* of His moral government. It is not the Divine decree which is in view, but the moral tendency of God's providential dispensations. It is what theologians rightly term the "external call," addressed unto the responsibility of all, by the privileges they enjoy and the advantages which are theirs (compare Prov. i, 24; Isa. v, 4!). Though the Divine bounties bestowed upon the unregenerate do not soften their hearts, and though the wondrous patience of God with them does not move them to forsake their sins, yet such is the design or moral tendency of both the one and the other. That they do not so eventuate is solely the fault of their base recipients. They *ought to* produce repentance in all: if they do not, the impenitent are left "without excuse," and their case is aggravated in proportion to the mercies they have abused.

"Not knowing": such is the carnal stupidity and moral insensibility of the natural man. He fails to understand the gracious design of the One

(*continued on preceding page*)

XXVI   JULY 1947   No. 7

STUDIES IN THE SCRIPTURES

"Search the Scriptures." John v, 39

Publisher and Editor—ARTHUR W. PINK,
29 Lewis Street,
Stornoway, Isle of Lewis,
Scotland.

IGNORANCE ENJOINED

No, we have not suddenly turned Papist nor are we about to inflict upon our readers a piece in support of Rome's favourite dictum, namely, that "Ignorance is the mother of devotion"—in accord with which is their idea that it is dangerous to place the Scriptures in the hands of the laity, and therefore they should be withheld from them. We are very, very far from subscribing to anything so puerile and impious. The way of the wicked is as darkness, but the way of the righteous is as light—open and above-board. Truth courts investigation and challenges the closest scrutiny. Spiritists may prefer the darkened room, and the poor dupes of the Pope admire the secret confessional, but "Wisdom crieth without: she uttereth her voice in the streets: she crieth in the chief places of concourse" (Prov. i, 20, 21). Nevertheless, there is an ignorance which is desirable and which serves as a protection to those who maintain it. There is an ignorance of which no Christian needs be ashamed, yea, one which the Holy Spirit has enjoined, and therefore is praiseworthy. "I would have you wise unto that which is good, and simple concerning evil" (Rom. xvi, 19).

In the context the apostle had warned the saints to be on their guard against false teachers, and to "*avoid*" those who propagated that which is "contrary to that doctrine which ye have learned": men who deceive the hearts of the simple (or unwary) "by good words and fair speeches," but who "serve not our Lord." It was not that Paul deemed them unestablished in the Faith or unstable therein, rather did he affirm "for your obedience [faith and practical response to the will of God as it was made known to them by His messengers] is come abroad unto all men," which commendation he supplemented with "I am glad thereof on your behalf." Yet being solicitous of their welfare with a godly jealousy, he added, "But yet I would have you wise unto that which is good and simple concerning evil." Your reception of the Gospel and responsiveness unto the Truth is well known, and evil men are likely to take advantage of this: see to it then that your docility is coupled with prudence and be watchful of those who would corrupt you.

"I would have you wise unto that which is *good*." Let that be your all-absorbing quest: be intelligent—both in knowledge and practice—in the Word and ways of God, so that you are fitted to "Prove all things, hold fast

(continued on back page)

Important Notices

Please advise promptly of change in address, otherwise copies will be lost in the mails.

We are glad to send a sample copy to any of your friends whom you believe would be interested in this publication.

This magazine is published as " a work of faith and labour of love," the editor and his wife gladly giving their services free. There is no regular subscription price, as we do not wish the poor of the flock to be deprived. This does not mean that those looking for something for nothing may " help themselves." Those getting this magazine who are financially able and who receive spiritual help from its pages, are expected to gladly contribute towards its expenses; otherwise their names are dropped from our list.

Will those forwarding International Money Orders please have them made out to us at Stornoway, Isle of Lewis, Scotland. Checks (Cheques—Eng.) made out on U.S.A. Banks are not negotiable here, so please do not send them.

All unsigned articles are by the Editor.

CONTENTS

THE PRAYERS OF THE APOSTLES

43. I Thessalonians iii, 11-13

" Now God Himself and [or " even "] our Father, and our Lord Jesus Christ, direct our way unto you. And the Lord make you to increase and abound in love one toward another, and toward all [saints], even as we toward you: to the end He may stablish your hearts unblameable in holiness before God even our Father, at the coming of our Lord Jesus Christ with all His saints." There are five things in connection with this prayer which call for our consideration. First, its *occasion*: it is necessary to ponder what is said in the foregoing verses in order to appreciate the request in verse eleven. Second, its *intensity,* which is intimated in the " night and day praying exceedingly that we might see your face " (verse 10). Third, its *objects*: God the Father and His Son in His mediatorial character (verse 11). Fourth, its *petitions,* which are two in number (verses 11 and 12). Fifth, its *design:* that their hearts might be established " unblameable in holiness before God " (verse 13). May the Holy Spirit condescend to act as our Guide while we endeavour to fill in that outline.

It was at an early date of his ministerial labours that Paul, accompanied by Silas and the youthful Timothy, visited Thessalonica—now called Salonica. Originally he had purposed to preach the Gospel in Asia, but had been forbidden by the Spirit; then he sought to enter Bithynia, but again God suffered him not (Acts xvi, 6). Arriving at Troas, the Divine will was made known to the apostle by means of a vision in the night (something which no one should now expect), wherein there appeared to him " a man from Macedonia " who besought them " Come over into Macedonia and help us " (Acts xvi, 9). First, Paul and his companion made a very brief stay at Philippi, where, after being made a blessing to Lydia and her household, the Enemy stirred up fierce opposition, which resulted in the beating of Paul and Silas and their being cast into prison; only for God to intervene by a miracle of grace, which eventuated in their release. From Philippi they came to Thessalonica, where was a synagogue of the Jews, which Paul entered and for three Sabbath days reasoned with them out the Scriptures; yet from a comparison of I Thessalonians i, 9, with Acts xvii, 1-10, it seems clear that the majority of those saved during his short sojourn in that city were *Gentiles*.

The enmity of the Serpent was manifested at Thessalonica almost as bitterly as at Philippi, so that after a short stay there the brethren " sent away Paul and Silas by night." Nevertheless, brief as had been their visit, the Seed had been sown, the blessing of God had rested upon the preached Word, and an effectual testimony was there raised up to the glory of His great name. So much so, that His servant declared of that infant church, " ye are ensamples to all that believe in Macedonia, and Achaia. From you sounded out the Word of the Lord not only in Macedonia and Achaia but also in every place your faith to Godward is spread abroad" (I Thess. i, 7, 8). What a sore grief it must have been to leave these young and unestablished converts, and how deeply Paul yearned to be with them again, appears in his statement, " But we, brethren, being taken from you for a short time in presence, not in heart, endeavoured the more abundantly to see your face with great desire. Wherefore we would have come unto you, even I, Paul, once and again, but Satan hindered us" (ii, 17, 18).

Paul was no stoical fatalist who reasoned that there was not any need for him to be concerned about the spiritual welfare of those babes in Christ, that since God had begun a good work in them, He would assuredly carry it forward to completion. No, very far from it. He was *fearful* that they might be stumbled at the opposition which had been evoked, puzzled why God did not put forth His power and subdue that opposition, and be dismayed by the flight of His ambassador. Paul was uneasy whether their young faith could withstand such rude shocks. Therefore he sent one of his companions to inquire of their condition and to help them. " For this cause, when I could no longer forbear, I sent to know your faith, *lest* by some means the Tempter have tempted you, and our labour be *in vain*" (verse 5). Let those of our readers who may have imbibed some hyper-Calvinist poison carefully ponder those words of the apostle, and honestly ask themselves the question what place such a statement could possibly have in their *own* theology.

It is blessed to behold how God sets a balance to the trials and comforts of His people. The apostle was sorely exercised over the situation of those young believers, when God graciously afforded his heart relief. " But now when Timotheus came from you unto us, and brought us good tidings of your faith and love, and that ye have good remembrance of us always, desiring greatly to see us, as we also you. Therefore, brethren, we were comforted over you in all our affliction and distress by your faith" (verses 6, 7). How graciously God times His mercies! The good news brought by Timothy was just the cordial which the burdened soul of Paul now needed. But note the order in which he mentions the two things of verse six. He does not place first their kindly remembrance of himself and their longing to see *him* again. No, rather does he give precedence to the favourable report supplied of their "faith and love"—*that* was for him the grand and principal item in the "glad tidings" of his messenger! How characteristic was that of this self-effacing herald of Christ! Those words, "your faith and love," were a brief but comprehensive expression of their spiritual case: if *those* graces were in healthy exercise, Paul knew there could be nothing seriously wrong with them.

"For now we live, if ye stand fast in the Lord. For what thanks can we render to God again for you, for all the joy wherewith we joy for your sakes before our God" (verses 8, 9). How those words reveal again the spirit of the apostle! No mother's heart beats with more tender affection unto her offspring than does that of the genuine evangelist or pastor unto his own children in the Faith.   His delight lies in their spiritual progress: "my brethren dearly beloved and longed for, my joy and *crown*" (Phil. iv, 1) was how Paul regarded his converts.   Said another of the apostles, "I have no greater joy than to hear that my children walk in the Truth" (II John iv). Contrariwise, no mother suffers severer pangs of grief over the illness of her babes or their waywardness when they be grown up, than does a true servant of God as he witnesses the backsliding or apostasy of those who made a credible profession of faith under his ministry.   So much then for the setting of our present passage, or the occasion of this prayer.

"Night and day praying exceedingly that we might see your face and might perfect that which is lacking in your faith" (verse 10).   Their "greatly desiring to see us" (verse 6) found an answering response in the hearts of Paul and his companions.   The language which he here used indicates the vehemence of his desire and the earnestness of his supplication.   No cold and mechanical praying was his, but earnest and persistent.   The word here rendered "praying" means "beseeching," being the one employed in connection with the leper, who, in his dire need and deep longing, "besought" the Lord to heal him (Luke v, 12).   It is not the perfunctory, nor the flowery petition which brings down answers from above; but "the effectual *fervent* prayer of a righteous man" which "availeth much."   Some are more occupied with their eloquence and the correctness of their grammar than they are with the frame of their spirit and the state of their heart—at which God ever looks. When the soul truly longs for a certain favour from God, the sincerity and intensity of that longing will be evinced not only by earnest crying to Him, but by importunity—asking, seeking, knocking, "night and day" until the request is granted.

It may be inquired, Why is so much exertion and pains called for, seeing that God is fully acquainted with all our need and has promised to supply the same?   First and foremost, for the exercise of our graces.   God is pleased to try our faith and patience, for nothing more honours and pleases Him than to behold His people continuing to supplicate for that which he appears to deny them—as in the case of the Syrophenician woman (Matt. xv, 28).   Real praying is no child's play.   Ponder that exhortation of the apostle's to the Roman saints: "*strive* together in prayer" (xv, 30).   It is a word taken from the gymnastic contests, in which the combatants put forth their utmost strength.   If we are to prevail with God, then we have to put forth all that is within us; we must "stir up ourselves" (Isa. lxiv, 7) to "lay hold" on God. So again, it is recorded of Epaphras on behalf of the Colossians, "always labouring fervently for you in prayers, that ye may stand perfect and complete in all the will of God" (iv, 12).   Such praying cost him something!   Yes, and such praying resulted in something!

Is it not at this very point that *our praying* is so sadly defective?   It is too mechanical and formal.   There is the absence of an ardent spirit, of soul-exertion, of reality.   Does someone rejoin, But it lies not within *my* prerogative to exercise faith or supplicate acceptably and effectually when I will?   I have no spiritual power of my own.   We sometimes wonder exactly what is meant by such language, and fear that in most cases it proceeds from a serious error, or else it is an idle excuse behind which dilatory souls seek to shelter. It is quite wrong for the Christian to suppose that he has *less spiritual* ability and strength than he has natural.   The fact is that man, be he regenerate or unregenerate, is a dependent creature, wholly dependent upon his Maker for every breath he draws, every thought he thinks, every act he performs, spiritual *or* natural, for " in Him we live, and move, and have our being." Man may pride himself in his self-sufficiency, boast of his free will, and imagine he is lord of himself, but he only deceives himself, and denies his creaturehood in so doing.

When Pilate vaunted himself to Christ, " Knowest Thou not that I have power to crucify Thee, and have power to release Thee? " He answered: " Thou couldest have no power against Me, except it were given thee from above" (John xix, 11). Roman official though thou art, and invested with Caesar's authority, yet thou art utterly impotent, with no more inherent and self-sufficient power to perform a natural act than has a lump of inanimate clay, *until* God vouchsafes it unto thee. The clear teaching of Holy Writ is, that man has not a particle more of natural power in and of himself than he has spiritual power. " But thou shalt remember the Lord thy God [thy relation to Him, and thy complete dependency upon Him], for *He* it is that *giveth thee power* to get wealth" (Deut. viii, 18), i.e. who supplies thee with health, strength and wisdom to perform natural acts, and who alone determines the measure of thy success therein. " For she did not know [nevertheless it was a fact!] that *I gave her* corn and wine and oil, and multiplied her silver and gold [yes, even when] they prepared [the same] for Baal" (Hos. ii, 8). Ah, says the hyper-Calvinist, *that* is exactly what I believe, that man is utterly helpless in himself.

May we ask you, What effect does such a belief have upon you? What fruit in your daily life does it issue in? Does it merely result in Mahommedan apathy or fatalistic inertia, or does it cast you back upon God, so that you *seek His enabling* for everything? Scripture not only reveals the dependency of the creature upon its Maker, his inherent helplessness, but it also teaches that man is a responsible creature, a rational and moral agent, accountable unto God for all his thoughts, words and deeds. Do you " believe" *that* too? If not, your creed is radically defective. You are *responsible to* glorify your Maker, to be subject unto His authority, to do those things which are pleasing in His sight. But, you reply, I am *unable* to do so. True, and you are equally unable to dig your garden unless God grant you strength, or to attend unto your financial matters, unless He gives you wisdom. Do you therefore lie in bed and do nothing? The only difference between our power and powerlessness to perform natural and spiritual acts is this, that our hearts are *averse* from the latter. The natural man hates God, and the things of the Spirit are foolishness unto him. Material things he loves, and therefore he pursues them eagerly.

Let us bring this matter down to a very simple and homely level. Here is a housewife who desires to make a cake. Suppose for the sake of our illustration, that God has, in His grace, already supplied her with all the necessary ingredients. In such a case, if she does not ask God for wisdom to perform her task successfully, if she does not concentrate her mind on what she is engaged in, if she becomes careless while the pan is in the oven, and the cake is a complete failure, whose fault is it? If then God has endowed you with reason, given you His Word to instruct, promised His Spirit to all who ask for Him (Luke xi, 13), and bidden you call upon Him for the supply of every temporal and spiritual need, who is to blame if you receive not? While without Christ we can do nothing (John xv, 5), yet strengthened by Him we " *can* do all things" (Phil. iv, 13). It is therefore an idle excuse, a piece of wicked hypocrisy, if we plead our helplessness as an extenuation of our coldness and formality in prayer, and are not earnest and fervent in supplicating the throne of grace.

Having enlarged upon the *intensity* of the apostle's prayer rather more than we intended, let us return unto the desire which prompted the same, namely, " that we might perfect that which is lacking in your faith " (verse 10). First, those words reveal the exalted standard which this servant of the Lord kept before him and the high ministerial level at which he aimed. Notwithstanding the fact that Timothy had just brought to him " good tidings " of their " faith and love " (verse 6), still that did not content him, for he knew " there remaineth yet very much land to be possessed " (Josh. xiii, 1). Let the pastor be thankful when he beholds his sheep in a healthy condition, but let him also labour for their *further* growth. Second, we behold here the faithfulness of Paul. He did not feed their vanity by complimenting them upon their attainments, but gives them to understand that, so far from having cause to be complacent, there was still room for much improvement, and that they needed to continue pressing forward unto those things which are yet before. Let the minister give credit to whom credit is due, but sedulously avoid fulsome praise, knowing that " a flattering mouth worketh ruin " (Prov. xxvi, 28).

" That we may perfect that which is lacking [" the things lacking," for it is the plural number in the Greek] in your faith." How many professing Christians would resent such a statement as that! Yea, in such a sickly condition are some of God's own people in this hyper-sensitive age, that their poor feelings would be hurt if such an imputation was made against them— little wonder that politicians are so quick to resent lawful criticism when those who are supposed to love *the truth* are so effeminate and touchy: the one is but the reflection of the other! Yet it is a fact that the most spiritual and mature Christian *has* various things " lacking in his faith." First, in its scope: how many portions of the Word he has not yet apprehended, how many of its precepts and promises are still unappropriated. Second, in its operations: there is not the fruit from it which there should be in our daily lives. Third, take " faith " here as a *grace* also, and how much darkness and doubting still mars the best of us. So it was with these Thessalonians, and just as Paul longed to visit the saints at Rome so that he might " impart unto them some spiritual gift " (i, 10), in like manner he desired to see again these young converts of his that he might be of further help to them.

" That we might perfect the things which are lacking in your faith." It is egotism which lies behind that touchiness which resents an imputation of our ignorance. O when shall we learn that *pride*—even more so than unbelief—is the chief adversary to our making progress in the things of God. The more truly wise any man is, the more conscious is he of his ignorance, of the paucity of his knowledge. It is only the conceited tyro, the one who has a mere smattering of his subject, who vainly imagines he is master of it, and refuses to receive further instruction from his fellows. " If any man think that he *knoweth* anything, he knoweth nothing yet as he ought to know " (I Cor. viii, 2). As we have said so often in these pages, the grand secret of success in the Christian life is *to continue* as we began. And, among other things, that means to be emptied of our self-sufficiency, to maintain before God the attitude of a little child, to preserve a teachable spirit, and that to the very *end* of our lives. If that be ours, then we shall daily be aware of how much there is still " lacking " in *our* faith, and shall welcome every available help, no matter how weak may be the instrument.

Since he was providentially detained from immediately carrying out his desire, Paul prayed for and wrote to them. "Now God Himself even our Father, and our Lord Jesus Christ, direct our way unto you" (verse 11). Thus this prayer, like the "grace and peace be unto you from God our Father and the Lord Jesus Christ" found at the beginning of most of his epistles, was addressed conjointly to the Father and the Son in His mediatorial character. Therein we behold the Saviour's absolute Deity, for it was an act of worship which was here being rendered to Him, and the Divine Law is explicit: "thou shalt worship the Lord thy God, and *Him only* shalt thou serve" (Matt. iv, 10). We are expressly forbidden to accord Divine homage to any creature. When the awestruck John fell down to worship an angel, he promptly said, "See thou do it not" (Rev. xxii, 10). Instead of the angels being fit objects of worship, as Rome blasphemously teaches, the Divine edict is "Let all the angels of God worship *Him*" (Heb. i, 6), which, as the context shows, is the incarnate Son. Being co-essential and co-eternal with the Father, the command is "that all should honour the Son even as they honour the Father. He that honoureth not the Son, honoureth not the Father which hath sent Him" (John v, 23).

Prayer is not only to be offered unto God in the name of Christ, but it is also to be offered directly *unto Him* as our Lord and Saviour. When a successor unto Judas was to be chosen for the apostolate, prayer was made unto the "Lord" (Acts i, 2-4); apart from the fact that "the Lord" always has reference to *Christ* (unless there be something in the passage which clearly distinguishes the Father from Him), John vi, 70, and xv, 16, oblige us to regard that allusion as being unto the Son. The dying Stephen specifically addressed his petitions unto the Lord Jesus (Acts vii, 59, 60). From Acts ix, 14, 21, it is clear that it was customary for the early Christians to "call upon His name," i.e. supplicate Him. Upon his conversion Saul of Tarsus was bidden to "call on the name of the Lord" (Acts xxii, 16). So prominent a feature was this in the lives of the primitive saints, that they received their characteristic designation from the same: "all that in every place call upon the name of Jesus Christ our Lord" (I Cor. i, 2). While Timothy was directly bidden to "call on the Lord out of a pure heart" (II Tim. ii, 22).

THE LIFE AND TIMES OF JOSHUA

23. The Priesthood

Before we turn to consider the contents of Joshua iv and contemplate the *memorials* that God ordered to mark the Jordan miracle, we should look more definitely at a prominent detail in chapter three which did not receive due attention in the preceding articles, and which supplies an important link between the two chapters, namely, the prominent part played by *the priests* in bearing the ark of the covenant, the "ark of the Lord, the Lord of all the earth," before which the lower waters of the Jordan fled and the upper water "stood upon a heap." Therein we behold the nation of Israel in its primary relations to God. In the books of Exodus, Leviticus and Numbers we are shown the establishment of God's way with them and the declaration of His will and purpose through Moses, who was both their Divinely appointed commander and mediator, while Aaron was their great high priest. That relationship was reaffirmed in the opening verses of Joshua: "As I was with Moses, so I will be with thee. I will not fail thee, nor forsake thee" (i, 4). Besides that assurance to Joshua personally, as the successor of Moses, there was the necessary continuation of the high priest and the Levitical priesthood in Israel's midst.

The priesthood in their service had charge of the ark and the order of the tabernacle which was erected at Shiloh (xviii, 1), neither of which Joshua nor his armed men were suffered to touch. Each of those great functionaries held their respective appointments directly from the Lord, and the two in their *combined action*—whether in the sanctuary of God or in the camp of Israel—executed the will of Jehovah concerning both His majesty and holiness, which was thus the glory of His people. The priesthood and the tabernacle were indispensable as their way of approach unto God as worshippers, while outwardly the relations of God with Israel, by the ark of the covenant, were manifested in the sight of all their enemies. That was equally true during the ministration of Aaron in the wilderness, or the Levites with Joshua when the waters of Jordan fled, or while marching around the city of Jericho and its walls fell down flat. Just as Moses and Aaron were inseparable in their varied ministrations from the exodus of Egypt and onward, so were the priest and the captain of Israel's hosts at the door of the tabernacle in Shiloh when the land was divided among Israel's tribes (xviii, 10).

Not only were those two distinctive orders and services established by God at the beginning (adumbrated as early as Ex. iv, 14, 15!), but when Aaron died on mount Hor, we are told that "Moses stripped Aaron of his garments and put them on Eleazar his son," and this he did "as the Lord commanded in the sight of all the congregation" (Num. xx, 27, 28). In like manner, when the death of Moses drew nigh on mount Abarim (the "mountain" is ever the symbol of *government*), he besought the Lord "to set a man over the congregation" (Num. xxvii, 16), and the Lord bade him, "Take thee Joshua the son of Nun, a man in whom is the Spirit, and lay thine hand upon him [the figure of *identification*] and set him before Eleazar the priest and before all the congregation, and give him a charge in their sight" (verses 18, 19). The connection, and yet the contrast between them, was intimated thus: "And he shall stand before Eleazar the priest, who shall ask counsel for him, at the judgment of Urim before the Lord: at his [Joshua's] word shall they go out and at his word shall they come in; both he and all the children of Israel with him" (Num. xxvii, 21).

What has just been pointed out serves to explain the fact that in the book which bears his name, Joshua (though the commander-in-chief of Israel) is seen to be subservient unto Eleazar the priest—four times the two are mentioned together, and in each instance Eleazar is given the precedence. This order and those Divine appointments were the basis of the history of Israel under Joshua and the anointed priesthood, with "the ark of the covenant of the Lord your God" which they bore along, for that ark (as was pointed out in an earlier article) was not only the witness of Joshua's *presence* in the midst of His people, but also the symbol of His *relations* with them. God ever takes care of His own glory and yet at the same time promotes the full blessing of His people according to His eternal purpose. He never allows those two things to be separated, or to pass from His own immediate control but works them out together, for He has made their felicity an integral part of His glory. How fitting then that the ark of the covenant should be in advance of the twelve tribes as they went forward into their inheritance and unto the mount (Zion) of God's holiness.

But let us pause for a moment and point out the practical bearing of this upon ourselves. It is indeed a most wonderful and blessed thing that the great God has inseparably connected His own manifestative glory and the good of His own people, yet it is one which should have a moving and melting effect upon our hearts, and cause us to see diligently to it that our lives are duly ordered and made suitable thereto. Without entering into details, let us summarize in two brief statements the obligations which that grand truth devolve upon us. First, we should ever be on our guard against separating our present communion with God from the revealed pathway of His glory. Communion with God can only be had and maintained while we tread "the way of holiness" (Isa. xxxv, 10), for we cannot glorify Him unless we walk in obedience to Him. Second, Christ Himself must be the Object of our eye (Heb. xii, 2) and heart (Song of S. viii, 6): upon Him our affections are to be set (Col. iii, 1, 2), to Him we are to live (Phil. i, 21), for it is *in Him* the glory of God and the present and eternal blessedness of His people meet.

In Psalm lxxviii, 61, the ark is designated "His glory," and when (in token of His displeasure with Israel and of the severance of their communion with Him) God suffered the ark to be captured by the Philistines, the daughter-in-law of the high priest cried, "The glory is departed from Israel" (I Sam. iv, 22). But here in Joshua iii that "glory" advanced at the head of Israel and opened a way for them into Canaan. But every eye was to be upon "the ark of the covenant of the Lord *your* God," who went before them to find a "resting place" worthy of Himself, in which to keep His appointed service and share His delights with His people. Accordingly we find, in the heyday of Israel's prosperity, that Solomon prayed at the dedication of the temple on Mount Zion, "Now therefore arise, O Lord God, into Thy resting place, Thou, and the ark of Thy strength: let Thy priests, O Lord God, be clothed with salvation, and let Thy saints rejoice in Thy goodness" (II Chron. vi, 41, 42)—which will receive its final and complete fulfilment when the prayer of Christ in John xvii, 24, receives its answer.

Now it was "the priests, the Levites" who were appointed to bear the ark, which, when Israel saw in motion, was their signal for advance—"then ye shall remove from your place and go after it" (iii, 3). As the congregation did so, the first thing which they beheld was the manner in which God gets glory to Himself, namely, by driving back that which intercepted their way, putting forth His mighty power on their behalf as "the Lord your God." That which we are particularly concerned with now is the fact that it was when "the feet of the priests that bare the ark were dipped in the brim of the water . . . that the waters which came down from above stood and rose up upon a heap very far from the city of Adam, that is beside Zaretan; and those that came down toward the sea of the plain, the salt sea, failed, and were cut off; and the people passed over right against Jericho" (Josh. iii, 15, 16). Thereby the priesthood are given a distinguished position on this occasion, and are placed in the forefront in this book because of their conse-cration and appointment to the service of the sanctuary. Yet their prominence did not derogate from the honour of Joshua as the leader of the people, for *he* is the one who gave direction unto the priests (iii, 6)!

That is very remarkable, and should be duly pondered. When the Lord said unto Joshua, "This day will I begin to magnify thee in the sight of all Israel, that they may know that, as I was with Moses, so I will be with thee," the very next thing was, "And thou shalt *command* the priests that bear the ark of the covenant" (iii, 8). Even when Eleazar, the high priest, comes more distinctively into the forefront in connection with the assigning of the inheritance of the tribes, he does not interfere with the place which God had given Joshua. One of the principal values of these inspired records is the *conjoint action* of Eleazar and Joshua when they could act together. The same feature of the honourable and prominent place accorded the priesthood, and yet Joshua's authority over them, is seen again in chapter six, in connection with the taking of Jericho, for not only did the ark of the covenant go before all the men of war, but that in turn was preceded by "seven priests bearing the seven trumpets of rams' horns," before whose blast the walls fell down; yet it was Joshua who issued orders to these priests (vi, 6).

We have dwelt the longer upon this prominent feature of the book of Joshua (about which we shall have more to say, D.V., as we pass on to the later chapters) not only because it has been largely ignored by those who have written thereon, but also and chiefly, because of the deep importance of the same when considered, first, in connection with the Lord Jesus Christ; and, second, in connection with His people. It has indeed been widely recognized that Joshua is one of the outstanding characters of the Old Testament, who foreshadowed our Saviour, and if we are spared to complete this series we hope to show that he did so in no less than fifty details. But it has been perceived by very few indeed that *Eleazar* was equally a type of Christ, and that the two must be viewed in conjunction in order to behold the completeness of their joint adumbrations. That should be apparent at once from their immediate predecessors, for we need to join together Moses *and* Aaron in order to obtain the Divinely designed prefiguration of the One who was both "The Apostle *and* High Priest of our profession, Christ Jesus" (Heb. iii, 1). Thus it was also with Joshua and Eleazar.

That the history of the children of Israel was a typical one and that it adumbrated the experiences, the provisions made for, and the salvation of the whole election of grace, is too plain for any anointed eye to miss. Their oppression by Pharaoh and their groaning amid the brick kilns of Egypt present an unmistakable picture of our servitude to Satan and bondage under sin, our condition by nature as the consequence of our fall in Adam. Their utter inability to free themselves from the cruel yoke of the Egyptians forcibly portrayed our own native impotency to better our condition. The sovereign grace of God in raising up a deliverer in the person of Moses, was a prophecy in action of the future coming forth of the Divine Deliverer to emancipate His people. The provision of the lamb and the efficacy of its blood to provide shelter from the angel of death on the night of the passover, yet more clearly revealed what is now fully proclaimed by the Gospel. While the overthrow of Pharaoh and his hosts at the Red Sea and Israel's sight of the "Egyptians dead upon the seashore" (Ex. xiv, 30) told of the completeness of our redemption and the putting away of our sins from before the face of God.

The subsequent history of Israel in the wilderness, their testings and trials there, their failures and successes, the gracious and full provision which the Lord made for them, have rightly been contemplated as shadowing forth the varied experiences of the saints as they journey unto their eternal Inheritance. But the typical value of the second half of Exodus and much of the book of Leviticus has been far less generally discerned. The delivering of His people from their enemies was but a means to a far grander end, namely, that they should be brought into a place of favour and nearness unto God; and Exodus xxv-xl and most of Leviticus make known the provisions which God has made for the maintenance of their communion with Him, and this in such a way that the requirements of His ineffable holiness were duly maintained and the obligations of their moral agency and their duties as a redeemed people should be fitly discharged. Their relations with Jehovah were maintained on the one hand, through the Divinely appointed priesthood; and on the other, by their obedience to the Divine commandments. Only thereby could they draw nigh unto the Holy One as acceptable worshippers, and only thereby could they receive from Him the necessary instructions for their guidance.

The typical significance of the book of Joshua, while maintaining and enforcing the truth made known in the foregoing books, supplements and complements the earlier history. Here it is Israel, under God, possessing their possessions, brought into that rest which had been promised their fathers. In regard to this, we prefer to speak in the language of one whom we consider was better qualified to treat upon this subject. "The earthly Canaan was neither designed by God, nor from the first was it understood by His people to be, the ultimate and proper inheritance which they were to occupy; things having been spoken and hoped for concerning it which plainly could not be realized within the bounds of Canaan. The inheritance was one which could be enjoyed only by those who had become the children of the resurrection, themselves fully redeemed in soul and body from all the effects and consequences of sin—made more glorious and blessed, indeed, than if they had never sinned, because constituted after the image of the heavenly Adam. And as the inheritance must correspond with the inheritor, it can only be man's original possession restored—the earth redeemed from the curse which sin brought on it, and, like man himself, be the fit abode of a Church made like, in all its members, to the Son of God.

"The occupation of the earthly Canaan by the natural seed of Abraham was a type, and no more than a type, of this occupation by a redeemed Church of her destined inheritance of glory; and consequently everything concerning the entrance of the former on their temporary possession was ordered so as to represent and foreshadow the things which belong to the Church's establishment in her permanent possession. Hence, between the giving of the promise, which, though it did not terminate in the land of Canaan, yet included that, and through it prospectively exhibited the better inheritance, a series of important events intervened, which are capable of being fully and properly examined in no other way than by means of their typical bearing of the things hereafter to be disclosed respecting that better inheritance.

"If we ask, why did the heirs of promise wander about so long as pilgrims, and withdraw to a foreign region before they were allowed to possess the land, and not rather, like a modern colony, quietly spread, without strife or bloodshed, over its surface, till the whole was possessed? Or, why were they suffered to fall under the dominion of a foreign power from whose cruel oppression they needed to be redeemed, with terrible executions of judgment on the oppressor, before the possession could be theirs? Or why, before that event, also, should they have been put under the discipline of law, having the covenant of Sinai, with its strict requirements and manifold obligations of service, superadded to the covenant of grace and promise? Or why, again, should their right to the inheritance itself have to be vindicated from a race of occupants who had been allowed for a time to keep possession of it, and whose multiplied abominations had so polluted it that nothing short of their extermination could render it a fitting abode for the heirs of promise? The full and satisfactory answer to all such questions can only be given by viewing the whole in connection with the better things of a higher dispensation—as the first part of a plan which was to have its counterpart and issue in the glories of a redeemed creation, and for the final results of which the Church needed to be prepared, by standing in similar relations and passing through like experiences in regard to an earthly inheritance.

"The whole series of transactions which took place between the confirmation of the covenant of promise with Jacob, and the actual possession of the land promised, and especially of course the things which concerned that greatest of all the transactions, the revelation of the Law from Sinai, is to be regarded as a delineation in the type, of the way and manner in which the heirs of God are to obtain the inheritance of the purchased possession. Meanwhile, there are two important lessons which the Church may clearly gather and which she ought never to lose sight of: First, that the inheritance, come when and how it may, is the free gift of God, bestowed by Him as sovereign Lord and Proprietor on those whom He calls to the fellowship of His grace. Second, that the hope of the inheritance must exist as an animating principle in their hearts, influencing all their procedure. Their spirit and character must be such as become those who are the expectants as well as heirs of that better country, which is an heavenly; nor can Christ ever be truly formed in the heart, until He be formed as 'the hope of glory'" (P. Fairbairn, Vol. I of his *The Typology of Scripture,* 1865).

THE DOCTRINE OF REVELATION

7. The Existence of God

In our last we called attention to the revelation which God has made of Himself in *human history,* that is, to the cumulative evidence which the affairs of individuals and of nations furnish that a Divine Person has full control over those affairs, and orders and directs them all unto the accomplishment of His own eternal purpose. The Ruler of this world makes use of the opinions and motives, the resolves and actions of men, yea, overruling their very crimes to further His design and promote His own glory. Every occurrence upon the stage of human events is not only to be traced back to the Divine counsels, but should be viewed as the outworking of a part of His vast plan. We should behold *God* in all the intrigues of courts and governments, in all the caprices of monarchs, in all the changes of kingdoms and empires; yea, in all the persecutions of the righteous, as really and as truly as in the progress of the Gospel: though in the former it is more the secret workings of His justice, as it is the more open manifestations of His grace in the latter. "The lot is cast into the lap, but the whole disposing thereof is of the Lord" (Prov. xvi, 33) whether or no we perceive it.

The One who rules the planets is equally master of every human despot. In our last we supplied proof of that in connection with Ahasueras. Consider now another example. As a judgment upon their long-continued sinfulness, God delivered the Jews into the hands of an invading power, and suffered the flower of their nation to be carried captive into Babylon. Yet His judgment was tempered with mercy, for He assured His covenant though wayward people that after seventy years they should return to Palestine. That promise was definite and sure: but how was it to receive its fulfilment? They were utterly incapable of delivering themselves from the midst of the mightiest empire on earth, and there was no friendly and powerful nation demanding their emancipation. How then was the word of the Lord to be made good? God had indeed delivered their forefathers from Egypt by a series of great marvels, but from. Babylon He freed them without a single miracle. The manner in which He did so supplies a striking example of His providential workings and an illustrious illustration of *how* He shapes the history of nations.

"Now in the first year of Cyrus, king of Persia, that the word of the Lord by the mouth of Jeremiah might be fulfilled, the Lord stirred up the spirit of Cyrus, king of Persia, that he made a proclamation throughout all his kingdom, and put it also in writing, saying, Thus saith Cyrus, king of Persia, The Lord God of heaven hath given me all the kingdoms of the earth; and He hath charged me to build Him a house at Jerusalem, which is in Judah. Who is there among you of all His people? his God be with him, and let him go up to Jerusalem which is in Judah, and build the house of the Lord God of Israel (He is the God), which is in Jerusalem. And whosoever remaineth in any place where he sojourneth let the men of his place help him with silver, and with gold, and with goods, and with beasts, beside the freewill offering for the house of God that is in Jerusalem." (Ezra i, 1-4).

This is the famous Cyrus whose name occupies a prominent place upon the scroll of secular history. He was the ordained conqueror of Babylon, and when the empire of Nebuchadnezzar and Darius fell before his sword, instead of keeping the Jews in bondage, he decreed their liberation. But why should he do so? Was he a worshipper of Jehovah and a lover of His people? Far from it: he was a heathen idolater! The prophecy of Jeremiah had evidently been read by him, though it effected not his conversion, for he continued a devotee of his own gods. But God so impressed his mind by that prophecy and secretly wrought in him a desire and determination to free the Jews, that he made an authoritative proclamation to that effect. God gave His people favour in the eyes of the Persian king, and wrought in him both to will and to do of His good pleasure; yet in the forming and carrying out of his decision, Cyrus acted quite freely. Thus with the greatest of ease God can effect His own purpose, and without the use of force remove any obstacle standing in the way.

If (as so many students of prophecy believe) God has predestined that the Jews shall, after centuries of weary wandering among the Gentiles, once more occupy the land of Palestine, and if His time be now ripe for the fulfilment of that decree, then neither the Arabs nor anyone else can prevent their doing so. Whatever method or means God uses will in no wise alter the fact that there will be spread before the eyes of the world a demonstration that One immeasurably superior to man is ordering its affairs. Time will show: but up to now it looks as though God is repeating what He did in and through Cyrus. First, He moved the British Government to take over the mandatory control of Palestine, which has been administered for a quarter of a century at great inconvenience and at heavy cost of life and money, without a "thank you" from any one. Now He has "stirred up the spirit" of the U.S. Government to insist on the entry of more and more Jews into that land. God has "His way in the whirlwind" (Nah. i, 3).

Let us now carefully consider the objection of the sceptic. If an infinitely wise and benevolent Being be in full control of all the affairs of earth, then why is there so much evil, so much suffering and sorrow? Justice is a rare commodity between individuals or nations—the ruthless and powerful seize the prey, while the conscientious and honest are bespoiled. Mercy appears to be mainly a consideration of prudence, for who acts generously or leniently when another is thwarting his own interests?—witness, for example, the toll of the road. If a God of love presides over the scene, then why has He permitted the horrible holocaust of the past few years, with such widespread havoc and misery? The first answer is, Because the earth is inhabited by *a rebellious race,* which has revolted from its Maker, and is now being made to feel that "the way of transgressors is hard" (Prov. xiii, 15). When man himself was the one who deliberately dashed into pieces the cup of felicity which was originally placed in his hands, he has no legitimate ground for complaint if he now finds that the potion which he has brewed for himself is as bitter as gall and wormwood.

The infidel may reject with scorn the contents of the first three chapters of Genesis, but in so doing he casts away the only key which unlocks to us the *meaning* of human history, the only explanation which *rationally* accounts for the course of human affairs. If it be true that man was made by a holy and gracious God and was under moral obligations to serve and glorify Him, and if instead of so doing he cast off allegiance to Him and apostatized, what would we expect the consequences to be? Why, that man should be made to feel His displeasure and reap what he had sown. If this world lies under the righteous curse of its Creator because of man's sin and its Ruler be displaying His justice in punishing offenders and vindicating His broken Law, in what other ink than that of blood and tears may we expect human history to be written? Does the alternative hypothesis of evolution offer a more satisfactory solution? Very far from it. If man started at the bottom of the ladder and during the course of the ages has gradually ascended, if the human race be slowly but surely improving, how comes it that this twentieth century has witnessed such an unprecedented display of savagery and degradation!

If an omniscient and beneficent God be governing this world why is there so much wickedness and wretchedness in it? We answer, in the second place, to demonstrate *the truth of His own Word.* The accounts which that Word gives of the corruptions of human nature have been widely refused, as being too gloomy a diagnosis of the same. The descriptions furnished by Scripture of man's depravity have been haughtily despised by the wise of this world. Nevertheless, the annals of human history furnish abundant verification of the same. It may not be palatable to read, "Behold, I was shapen in iniquity, and in sin did my mother conceive me" (Psa. li, 5), that "man is born like a wild ass's colt" (Job xi, 12), that "The wicked are estranged from the womb, they go astray as soon as they be born, speaking lies" (Psa. lviii, 3), yet universal observation discovers clear proof of the verity of the same. Children do not have to be taught to be intractable, to lie and steal. Remove restraints, leave them to themselves, and it quickly appears what is born and bred in them. The widespread juvenile delinquency of our own day is very far from exemplifying any *progress* of the human race!

It certainly is not flattering to proud human nature to be told in the unerring Word of Truth that, as the result of the Fall, man's heart is "deceitful above all things and desperately wicked" (Jer. xvii, 9), yet every newspaper we open contains illustrations of the teaching of Christ that, "out of the heart proceed evil thoughts, adulteries, fornications, murders, thefts, covetousness, wickedness, deceit, lasciviousness, an evil eye, blasphemy, pride, foolishness: all these evil things come *from within,* and defile the man" (Mark vii, 21-23). Thousands of years ago God described mankind thus: "Their throat is an open sepulchre: with their tongues they have used deceit, the poison of asps is under their lips, whose mouth is full of cursing and bitterness. Their feet are swift to shed blood. Destruction and misery are in their ways, and the way of peace have they not known." And why is this? The closing words of the same passage tell us: "There is no fear of God before their eyes" (Rom. iii, 13-18). Who that has any acquaintance with the chronicles of history can deny that indictment? Who with the present state of society before his eyes can gainsay it? The very Word of God which men will not receive by faith is being verified to their very sight!

Why does God permit so much human misery? We answer, in the third place, to manifest the glory of *His own perfections*. The frightful calamity *of war* causes many to deny or seriously doubt the reality of Divine providence, for when that fearful scourge falls upon the nations, it appears to them that Satan rather than the Lord has charge of things and is the author of their troubles. At such a time God's own people may find it difficult to stay their minds on Him and rest implicitly in His wisdom and goodness. Yet the Word reveals that God is no mere distant Spectator of the bloody conflicts of men, but that His righteous and retributive agency is immediately involved therein, though that neither mitigates the guilt of the human instigators nor destroys their free agency. Their consuming egotism, insatiable greed, horrible barbarities, proceed entirely from themselves and are of their own volition; nevertheless, the Most High *directs* their lusts to the execution of His own designs and renders them subservient to His own honour.

The affairs of nations are ordered by a Divine hand. Their rise, development and progress are "of the Lord," so also are their decline, adversities and destruction. God's dealing with Israel of old was not exceptional, but illustrative of His ways with the Gentiles throughout the last nineteen centuries. While Israel's ways pleased the Lord, He made their enemies to be at peace with them; but when they gave themselves up to idolatry and lasciviousness, war was one of His sore scourges upon them. Whenever Divine judgment falls upon either an individual or a nation, it is because *sin* has called loudly for Him to vindicate His honour and enforce the penalty of His Law. Yet warning is always given before He strikes: "space to repent" is provided, the call to forsake that which displeases Him, opportunity to avert His wrath; and if this warning be disregarded and the opportunity to escape His vengeance be not improved, then is His judgment doubly righteous. Ordinarily God makes use of *men*—a Nebuchadnezzar, a Caesar, a Hitler—as the instruments by which His judgment is inflicted, thereby demonstrating His sovereignty over all, who can do nothing without Him, yet who must play the part which He has ordained.

In various ways does the Ruler of this world manifest the glory of His attributes. By the display of His infinite patience in bearing with so much longsuffering those who defy Him to His face and continue in their obduracy. By exhibiting the exceeding riches of His mercy in sometimes calling the most outrageous rebels out of darkness into His marvellous light, bringing them to repentance and granting them pardon: thus it was with King Manasseh and Saul of Tarsus. By manifesting the strictness of His untempered justice in hardening others in sin to their own destruction. "Behold therefore the goodness and the severity of God: on them which fell, severity; but toward thee goodness, if thou continue in His goodness: otherwise thou shalt also be cut off" (Rom. xi, 22). By showing forth His wondrous power, both in directing and curbing human passions. "Surely the wrath of man shall praise Thee [as that of Pharaoh's was made to do]: the remainder of wrath shalt Thou restrain" (Psa. lxxvi, 10), for He holds in check the fiercest as much as He sets bounds to the turbulent seas.

The depravity of human nature, the potency and prevalency of evil, and the power and malice of the Wicked one in whom the whole world lieth, only makes more evident and wonderful the providence of God. Since holiness be so universally hated and the saints of the Lord so detested and persecuted by the great majority of their fellow men, had not God so signally interposed for their preservation, the last of His people had long since perished amid the enmity and fury of their implacable enemies. Were there no other evidence that the living God governs this world, this one should suffice: that though His servants and sons have been so strenuously opposed in this scene, yet they have never been totally rooted out of it; that though the most powerful governments have sought their complete destruction, and though they were weak and possessed of no material weapons, yet a remnant always survived!—as real a marvel that as the preservation of the three Hebrew youths in the fiery furnace of Babylon.

What has just been pointed out has not received the attention which it justly claims, for it is a conspicuous feature of history and one that has been frequently repeated. The saints of God in Old Testament times, in the early centuries of this Christian era, and throughout the Dark Ages, when both pagan and papal Rome made the most determined efforts to completely annihilate them, had good reason to confess, " If it had not been *the Lord* who was on our side, when men rose up against us, then they had swallowed us up quick, when their wrath was kindled against us. Then the waters had overwhelmed us, the stream had gone over our soul; then the proud waters had gone over our soul. Blessed be the Lord who hath not given us as a prey to their teeth" (Psa. cxxiv, 2-6). It is quite possible, perhaps likely, that before this present century has run its course, the restraining hand of God will again be wholly removed from their foes and His people subjected to martyrdom. Should such prove the case, He will, unto the end, maintain to Himself a witness in the earth.

Why is there so much suffering and sorrow in this world? Fourth, for *the good and gain* of God's own people. As there is not a little in the realm of creation which sorely puzzles both the naturalist and the scientist, as there is much in God's written Word that is opposed to proud reason, so many of His governmental works often appear profoundly mysterious. That the wicked should prosper so much and flourish as the green bay tree, while the righteous are often in sore straits and at their wit's end to make ends meet; that the most unscrupulous attain unto positions of prestige and power, while the most virtuous and pious have been counted as "the offscouring of all things," and ended their days in a dungeon or by suffering a cruel martyrdom; that when God's judgments fall upon a nation they are no respecter of persons, the relatively innocent suffering from them as severely as the most guilty: these and similar cases which might be instanced present real problems to those who reflect upon the same.

True, but the more thoughtfully they be examined, especially in view of *the hereafter,* the less difficulty they present. The thoughts of the materialist and sceptic extend no farther than the narrow bounds of this life, and consequently he sees these things in a false perspective. Because of their misuse of them, the temporal mercies enjoyed by the wicked become a curse, hardening them in their sins and fattening them for the slaughter. On the other hand, afflictions often prove a blessing in disguise unto believers, weaning their affections from the things of earth and causing them to seek their joy in things above. God often thwarts their carnal plans because He would have their hearts occupied with better objects. The more they are dissatisfied in the creature and discover that everything under the sun yields only vanity and vexation of spirit, the more inducement have they to cultivate a closer communion with the One who can fully satisfy their souls.

It is not meet that the righteous should always be in a prosperous and happy case in their temporal estate, for then they would be most apt to seek their rest therein. On the other hand, if their portion were that of unrelieved affliction and misery, while the lot of the wicked was uniformly one of plenty and ease, that would be too severe a trial of faith. Therefore God wisely *mixes* His dispensations with each class respectively. God so orders His providences that His people shall live by faith and not by sight or sense. That is not only for their weal, but for God's honour. He frequently regulates things so that it may appear that the saints trust Him in the dark as well as in the light. An outstanding example of that is seen in the case of Job, who was afflicted as few have ever been, yet in his blackest hour he averred "though He slay me, yet will I trust in Him" (xiii, 15). How greatly is He glorified by such conduct! Tribulations are needful for the testing of profession, that the difference between the wheat and the chaff may appear. Heresies are necessary that lovers of Truth may be made manifest (I Cor. xi, 19). Trials are indispensable, that patience may have her perfect work.

If in every instance the righteous were rewarded and the wicked punished in this life, the Day of Judgment would be fully anticipated: but by furnishing some present instances of both the one and the other, the great Assize is presaged and the government of God vindicated. If temporal mercies and spiritual blessings were now evenly distributed, no demonstration would be made of the absolute sovereignty of Him who dispenses His favours as He pleases, and bestows upon or withholds from each individual that which seems good unto Himself. There are not more inequalities in the dispensations of Providence than in the realm of creation. In its widest aspect there is a noticeable and striking *balance* observable in the apportionment of mercies. As in Old Testament times Divine favours were largely confined to the seed of Abraham, so in the New Testament era unto the Gentiles. Something analogous thereto is seen in God's conduct toward the eastern and western parts of the earth. For two thousand years after the Flood, learning, government and piety were largely confined to the east, while our forefathers in the west were a horde of savages. For the last two thousand years the Gospel, with all its beneficent by-products, has travelled westward. Perhaps in the next two thousand years it will again move eastward.

That the living God controls all circumstances, commands all events, rules every creature, makes all their energies and actions fulfil His will, provides a sure and comfortable resting place for the heart. The present outlook may be dismal, but God reigns and is making all things work together for the glory of His name and the good of His people. If the human race is to occupy this earth for several more generations, or perhaps many centuries, then certain it is that out of the throes through which it is now passing shall issue the furtherance of the Gospel and the promotion of Christ's kingdom. The annals of human affairs can only be read intelligently and interpreted aright as we perceive that history is *His-story*. In the final Day of Manifestation it will be plain to all that "He hath done all things well"; meanwhile, faith now knows that it is so. ———————

THE GREAT CHANGE

We will now endeavour to summarize all that has been set before the reader concerning the great change which takes place in one who is born again, renewed spiritually, resurrected, by the operations of the Spirit of God. Perhaps this can best be accomplished by making some epitomized statements and then offering some further remarks on those against which certain of our readers may be most inclined to take issue. *Negatively,* that great change does not consist of any constitutional alteration in the make-up of our being, no essential addition being made to our persons. We regard it as a serious mistake to consider the natural man as possessed of but soul and body, and as only having a "spirit" communicated to him when he is regenerated. Again, it is a still worse error to suppose that indwelling sin is eradicated from the being of a born-again person: not only does Scripture contain no warrant to countenance such an idea, but the uniform experience of God's children repudiates it. Nor does the great change effect any improvement in the evil principle. The "flesh," with its vile properties and lusts, its deceiving and debasing inclinations, its power to promote hypocrisy, pride, unbelief, opposition unto God, remains unchanged unto the end of our earthly course.

Yet it would be utterly wrong for us to conclude from those negatives that regeneration is not entitled to be designated a "miracle of grace" or that the change effected in its subject is far from being a *great* one. A real, a radical, a stupendous, a glorious change *is* wrought, yet the precise nature of it can only be discovered in the light of Holy Writ. While it is indeed an experimental change, yet the subject of it must interpret the same by the teaching of Scripture, and not by either his own reason or feelings. Nor should that statement be either surprising or disappointing. The miracle of grace effects a great change Godwards in the one who experiences it, and God is not an Object of sense nor can He be known by any process of reasoning. We may then summarize by saying the great change, positively considered, consists first of a radical *change of heart Godwards.* God discovers Himself unto the soul, makes Himself a living reality unto it, reveals Himself both as holy and gracious, clothed with authority and yet full of mercy. That personal and powerful revelation of God unto the soul produces an altered disposition and attitude toward Him: the one alienated is reconciled. the one who shrank from and was filled with enmity against Him, now desires His presence and longs for communion with Him.

Such a vital and radical change in the disposition and attitude of a soul Godwards is indeed a miracle of grace, and cannot be described as anything less than a great change. It is as real and great as was the change when man apostatized from his Maker; as vivid and blessed a change spiritually as the resurrection will effect physically: when that which was sown in corruption, in dishonour, in weakness, shall be raised in incorruption, glory and power; when our vile body shall be changed, "that it may be fashioned like unto His glorious body" (Phil. iii, 21). For one who was a total stranger to the ineffably glorious God to now become experimentally and savingly acquainted with Him, for one who sought to banish Him from his thoughts to now find his greatest delight in meditating upon His perfections, for one who lived in total disregard of His righteous claims upon him to be made a loyal and loving subject, is a transformation which human language—with all its adjectives and superlatives—cannot possibly do justice unto. In the words of Divine inspiration, it is a "passing from death unto life," a being "called out of darkness into God's marvellous light," a being "created in Christ Jesus unto good works."

Second, that great change consists in a *moral purification of the inner man.* Though this be the most difficult aspect of it for us to understand, yet the teaching of the Word thereon is too clear and full to leave us in any uncertainty as to the same. Such expressions as "Then will I sprinkle clean water upon you, and ye shall be clean: from all your filthiness and from all your idols will I cleanse you" (Ezek. xxxvi, 25), "but ye are washed, but ye are sanctified" (I Cor. vi, 11), "Ye have purified your souls in obeying the Truth" (I Pet. i, 22) would be meaningless if there had been no internal transformation. Our characters are formed by the Truth we receive: our thoughts are more or less moulded, our affections directed, and our wills regulated by what we heartily believe. Truth has a vital, effectual, elevating influence. Any man who professes to take the Word of God for his Guide and Rule and is not altered by it, both internally and externally, is deceiving himself. "The Truth will make you free" (John viii, 32): from the dominion of sin, from the snares of Satan, from the deceits of the world. The tastes, the aims, the ways of a Christian are assimilated to and fashioned by the Word.

A radical change Godwards which is accompanied by a moral purification within, necessarily consists, in the third place, of a thoroughly altered attitude toward the *Divine Law*. It cannot be otherwise. "The carnal mind is enmity against God": it is completely dominated by ill will unto Him. The evidence adduced by the Spirit in demonstration of that fearful indictment is this, "and is not subject unto the law of God, neither indeed can be" (Rom. viii, 7): the one is the certain outcome of the other—hatred for the Lawgiver expresses itself in contempt for and defiance of His Law. Before there can be any genuine respect for and subjection to the Divine Law the heart's attitude towards its Governor and Administrator must be completely changed. Conversely, when the heart of any one has been won unto God, His authority will be owned, His government honoured, and his sincere language will be, "I delight in the Law of God after the inward man"—i.e. the soul as renewed by the Spirit (Rom. vii, 22). Thus, while the unregenerate are denominated "the children of disobedience" (Eph. ii, 2) the regenerate are called "obedient children" (I Pet. i, 14), for obedience is one of their characteristic marks, evidencing as it does the general tenor and course of their lives.

After all that has been said in previous articles, it ought not to be necessary for us to interrupt our train of thought at this point and consider a question which can only prove wearisome unto the well-taught reader; but others who have drunk so deeply from the foul pools of error need a word thereon. Are there not two "minds" in a born-again person: the one carnal and the other spiritual? Certainly not, or he would have a dual personality, and a divided responsibility. By nature his mind was, spiritually speaking, *deranged*—how else can a mind which is "enmity against God" be described? But by grace his mind has been restored to sanity: illustrated by the demoniac healed by Christ, "sitting, and clothed, and in his right mind" (Mark v, 15); or as II Timothy i, 7, expresses it, "For God hath not given us the spirit of fear, but of power, and of love, and of *a sound mind.*" It is true his original carnality ("the flesh") still remains, ever seeking to regain complete control of his mind; but Divine grace suffers it not to *so* succeed that his mind ever becomes "enmity against God." There will be risings of rebellion against His providences, but a renewed person will nevermore hate God.

A real and radical change of heart Godwards will, in the fourth place, be marked by a thoroughly altered attitude *towards sin*. And again we say, it cannot be otherwise. Sin is that "abominable thing" which God "hates"

(Jer. xliv, 4), and therefore that heart in which the love of God is shed abroad will hate it too. Sin is "the transgression of the Law" (I John iii, 4), and therefore each one who has been brought to "delight in the Law" will detest sin and earnestly seek to resist its solicitations. That which formerly was his native element has become repugnant to his spiritual inclinations. Sin is now his heaviest burden and acutest grief. Whereas the giddy worldling craves after its pleasures and the covetous seek after its riches, the deepest longing of the renewed soul is to be completely rid of the horrible activities of indwelling sin. He has already been delivered from its reigning power, for God has dethroned it from its former dominion over the heart, but it still rages within him, frequently gets the better of him, causes him many a groan, and makes him look forward with eager longing to the time when he shall be delivered from its polluting presence.

Another important and integral part of the great change consists in the soul's deliverance from the toils of *Satan*. Where the heart has really undergone a radical change of disposition and attitude toward God, toward His Law, and toward sin, the great Enemy has lost his hold on that person. The Devil's power over mankind lies in his keeping them in ignorance of the true God, in the scorning of His Law, in holding them in love with sin; and hence it is that he "hath blinded the minds of them that believe not, lest the light of the glorious Gospel of Christ . . . should shine unto them" (II Cor. iv, 4). While God permits him to succeed therein, men are his captives, his slaves, his prisoners, held fast by the cords of their lusts. But it, was announced of the coming Saviour that He would "proclaim liberty to the captives and the opening of the prison to them that are bound" (Isa. lxi, 1). Accordingly when He appeared we are told that He not only healed the sick, but also "all that were oppressed of the Devil" (Acts x, 38). The regenerate have been delivered "from the power of Satan" (Acts xxvi, 18; Col. i, 13) and made "the Lord's free men." True, he is still suffered to harass and tempt them from without, but cannot succeed without their consent; and if they steadfastly resist him, he flees from them.

In those five aspects of the great change we may perceive the *begun reversal* of what took place at man's apostasy from God. What were the leading elements in the Fall? No doubt they can be expressed in a variety of ways, but do they not consist, essentially, of these? First, in giving ear unto Satan and heed to the senses of the body, instead of to the Word of God. It was in parleying with the Serpent that Eve came under his power. Second, in preferring the pleasures of sin (the forbidden fruit which now made such a powerful appeal to her affection—Gen. iii, 6) rather than communion with her holy Maker. Third, in transgressing God's Law by an act of deliberate disobedience (Rom. v, 19). Fourth, in the loss of their primitive purity: "and the eyes of them both were opened, and they knew that they were naked, and they sewed figleaves together and made them aprons" (Gen. iii, 7). Their physical eyes were open previously (!) but now they had a discovery of the consequences of their sin: a guilty sense of shame crept over their souls, their innocence was gone, they perceived what a miserable plight they were now in—stripped of their original righteousness, condemned by their own conscience.

Fifth, in becoming alienated from God: "And they heard the voice of the Lord God walking in the garden in the cool of the day" (Gen. iii, 8). And what was their response? Did they rejoice at His gracious condescension in thus paying them a visit? Did they welcome their opportunity to cast themselves upon His mercy? Or did they even fall down before Him in brokenhearted confession of their excuseless offence? Far otherwise. When the Serpent spoke, Eve promptly gave ear to and conferred with him; but now that the voice of the Lord God was audible, she and her guilty partner fled from Him. "Adam and his wife hid themselves from the presence of the Lord among the trees of the garden." A guilty conscience warned them that it was the approach of that Judge whose Law they had broken, and they were terror-stricken at the prospect of having a face-to-face meeting with the One against whom they had rebelled. They dared not look upon Holiness incarnate, and therefore sought to escape from His presence. Thereby they evidenced they had *died spiritually*—their hearts being separated and alienated from Him! Their understanding was "darkened" and their hearts in a condition of "blindness" (Eph. iv, 18); a spirit of madness now possessed them, as appears in their vain attempt to hide among the trees from the eyes of Omniscience.

Those then were the essential elements in the Fall, or the several steps in man's departure from God. A parleying with and coming under the power of the Devil, sin's being made attractive in their sight, inclining unto the act of disobedience, resulting in the loss of their primitive purity and their consequent alienation from God. The attentive reader will observe those things are in the inverse order of those mentioned above as constituting the five leading characteristics of the great change wrought in those who are the favoured subjects of the miracle of grace. Nor is the reason for that far to seek: *conversion* is a turning round, a right-about face, a being restored to a proper relation and attitude toward God. Let us employ a simple illustration. If I journey five miles from a place and then determine to return to it, must I not re-traverse the fifth mile before coming to the fourth, and tread again the fourth before I arrive at the third, and so on until I reach the original point from which I departed? Was it not thus with the ragged and famished prodigal, who had journeyed into the far country: he must return unto the Father's House if he would obtain food and clothing.

If the great change be the *reversing* of what occurred at the Fall, then the order of its constituents should necessarily be viewed *inversely*. First, being restored to our original relation unto God, which was one of spiritual union and communion with Him. That is made possible and actual by the renewing us after His image, which consists of "righteousness and true holiness," a saving and experimental knowledge of His ineffable perfections; or in other words, by the renovation and moral purification of our souls, for it is only the "pure in heart" (Matt. v, 8) who see God as He actually is—our rightful Lord, our everlasting Portion. Only then does the Divine Law have its due and true place in our hearts: its authority being owned, its spirituality esteemed, the fulfilling of its holy and just requirements being our sincere and resolute aim. Obviously it cannot be until we have a right attitude toward God, until our hearts truly love Him, until after His Law becomes the rule and director of our lives, that we can perceive the exceeding sinfulness of sin, and consequently loathe, resist, and mourn over it. And just so far as *that* be the case with us, are we morally delivered from the power of Satan: while the heart beats true to God the solicitations of His enemy will be repellent to us rather than attractive.

But let us point out once more that this great change is not completed by a single act of the Spirit upon or within the soul, but occurs in distinct *stages*: it is commenced at regeneration, continues throughout the whole process of our experimental sanctification, and is only consummated at our glorification. Thus, regeneration is only the *begun* reversing of what occurred at the Fall. The very fact that regeneration is spoken of as a Divine begetting and birth at once intimates there is then only the beginning of the spiritual life in the soul, and that there is need for the growth and development of the same. "He which hath begun a good work in you will finish it" (Phil. i, 6) is the plain declaration and blessed assurance of what is implied by the "birth," and such statements as "the inward man is renewed day by day" (II Cor. iv, 16) and our being "changed into the same image *from* glory *to* glory as by the Spirit of the Lord" (II Cor. iii, 18) tell us something of the Divine operations within the souls of the regenerate while the great change is continued and brought, little by little, unto completion. That miracle of grace which was begun at regeneration is gradually carried forward in us by the process of sanctification, which appears in our growth in grace or the development of our graces.

If the reader desires a more detailed analysis and description of what that process consists of, how the great change is carried forward in us by sanctification, we may delineate it thus. First, by the illumination of the understanding which enables the believer to grow "in the knowledge of the Lord" and gives him a clearer and fuller perception of His will. Second, by the elevation and refining of the affections, the Spirit drawing them forth unto things above, fixing them on holy objects, assimilating the heart thereto. Third, by the emancipation of the will, God working in the soul "both to will and to do of His good pleasure," giving us both the desire and the power to concur with Him, for He deals with us not as mere automatons but ever as moral agents. Thus it is our responsibility to *seek* illumination, to prayerfully study His Word for the same, to occupy our minds (by constant meditation) and exercise our hearts with spiritual objects, and to diligently seek His enablement to avoid everything which would hinder and use all the means appointed for the promotion of our spiritual growth. As we do so, that process will issue and appear, fourth, in the rectification of our life.

From what has just been pointed out it plainly appears that they err greatly who suppose that regeneration consists of nothing more than the communication of a new nature or principle to an individual, leaving everything else in him just as it was before. It is the person himself who is regenerated, his whole soul which is renewed, so that all its faculties and powers are renovated and enriched thereby. How can everything else in him be unchanged, how otherwise can we designate the blessed transformation which the miracle of grace has wrought in him, than by styling it "a great change"—a real, radical and thorough one; since his understanding (which was previously darkened by ignorance, error and prejudice) is now spiritually enlightened, since his affections (which formerly were fixed only on the things of time and sense) are now set upon heavenly and eternal objects, and since his will (which hitherto was enslaved by sin, being "free *from* righteousness"—Rom. vi, 20) is now emancipated from its bondage, being "free *from* sin" (Rom. vi, 18). That glorious transformation, that supernatural change, is what we chiefly have in mind when we speak of "the moral purification" of the soul.

Just as the Fall introduced the principle of sin into man's being, which resulted in the death of his soul Godwards—for death is ever the wages of sin—so in the reversing of the Fall, a principle of holiness is conveyed to man's soul, which results in his again being spiritually alive unto God. Just as the introduction of sin vitiated and corrupted all the faculties of the soul, so the planting of a principle of holiness within vitalizes and purifies all its faculties. We say again that man lost no portion of his original tri-partite nature by the Fall, nor was he deprived of any of his faculties, but he did lose all *power* to use them Godwards and for His glory, because they came completely under the dominion of sin and were defiled by it. And again we say that man receives no addition to his original constitution by regeneration, nor is any new faculty then bestowed upon him, but he *is* now empowered (to a considerable degree) to use his faculties Godwards and employ them in His service; because so long as he maintains communion with God they are under the dominion of grace and are ennobled, elevated, and empowered by the renewing of the Spirit.

(continued from back page)

very prone to give ear unto an "evil report," and unless they steadfastly resist him, the Devil will see to it they are kept fully supplied. Since "speaking evil of another" is forbidden (James iv, 11), giving ear unto such is equally so. The next time some gossiper wants to acquaint you with the latest falls of So-and-so, recall this injunction, "simple concerning evil," and say, Excuse me, I do not wish to hear about it! Unless you do so, "evil communications [will] corrupt good manners" (I Cor. xv, 33).

Third, *worldly evil.* If Satan fails to absorb us with the treasures and pleasures of the world, then he will seek to occupy and weigh us down with its affairs. In the parable of the Sower Christ showed that the seed which fell on the third kind of ground was rendered useless by the thorns which "grew up and choked it." Among other things, those "thorns" symbolized "the *cares* of this world" (Mark iv, 19). In different individuals those "cares" assume a variety of forms: in some it is anxiety to obtain the necessities of life; in others, concern over wayward children. But there are many of God's children whose temporal needs are provided for and who have no relatives to occasion them distress, and yet who are heavily burdened with "the cares of this world." Many a foolish soul is allowing himself or herself to become an "Atlas"—carrying the weight of the world on their shoulders. If *they* were individually responsible for the *governing* of the world they could scarcely take matters more seriously or lose more peace on its account.

Posing as an "angel of light," Satan is occupying many with the affairs of earth under the pretext of their being so many heralds of the nearness of Christ's return. The alarming international situation, distressing conditions in the political and social realms, the decadence of "Protestantism," and the advances of Romanism are appealed to (just as they were a century ago!) as "proofs" that the Lord is at the very door. There is nothing in such teaching that edifies the soul or promotes a closer walking with God. On the contrary, an absorption with such matters instead of drawing the affections unto things above and purifying the mind, drags down the one and defiles the other. If such speakers and writers would give "the Antichrist" a long rest and preach *Christ,* it would be far better. All this emotional and sensational claptrap on "the signs of the times" will neither hasten nor retard Christ's return by a single moment! But for the believer to read secular literature and listen-in to the radio in order to be better informed on current events, turns his attention away from what is profitable, defiles his mind, and disturbs his peace. "Let the potsherd strive with the potsherds of the earth," but be thou "*wise* unto that which is GOOD and *simple* concerning [all forms of] EVIL."

that which is good" (I Thess. v, 21). "And simple concerning evil": "simple" is here opposed to "wise" and so must signify unknowing and unpractised in the ways of sin. In the light of the preceding verses the primary reference is to the evil doctrine of false teachers—be content to remain uninformed, unacquainted with anything that would pollute your faith; but in view of what immediately follows—"and the God of peace shall bruise *Satan* under your feet shortly"—it obviously has a wider meaning: remain ignorant of *everything* which would defile your pure minds. Moule renders it "uncontaminated [by defiling knowledge] as to what is evil." To appeal to your curiosity, to occupy your minds with what is foul, to get your hearts absorbed with evil rather than good, is one of the principal stratagems of the great Enemy. This Divine warning is much needed today. Let us point out a threefold application of "I would have you . . . simple concerning evil."

First, of *doctrinal evil*. There is a great deal of false teaching, often in a novel and attractive dress, now being disseminated both orally and by the printed page. Some of its leading promulgators have acquired a considerable reputation for their learning, originality, oratory, and pleasing personality. They draw big crowds, and some of God's people—though they have been warned against their errors—determine to give these men a hearing, and often the consequences are most injurious—in no case are they harmless. It is to that spirit of inquisitiveness the Devil applies his temptation, as it is against the exercise thereof we are expressly commanded "from such *turn away*." Not to do so is to parley with what is deadly for the soul. If you have begun to yield, then the Divine Word is "*Cease, my son, to hear the instruction that causeth thee to err from the words of knowledge*" (Prov. xix, 27); if you do not, disastrous will be the outcome. If unfallen Eve could be beguiled by lies, how much easier for *you* to be deceived if you deliberately expose yourself unto error.

"*Cease, my son, to hear the words that causeth thee to err from the words of knowledge*": by parity of reason that also signifies *read them not*. There are those who would be ashamed to be seen attending meetings where known error was taught, who nevertheless do not hesitate to peruse a book written by an errorist. Priding themselves that they are too well grounded in the Faith to be shaken, yet curious and desirous of ascertaining just what this man or this sect teaches, not a few purchase their pernicious literature, and to make it easier for them to do so Satan often sends the purveyors of such to their door. We have personally met more than one who was reared in orthodoxy, who bought or borrowed a "Christadelphian," "Russellite" or "Seventh-day Adventist" book, and later became an ardent supporter of their lies. The Devil ensnares many in this way. Parents need to be most careful what literature enters their home! Stifle your inquisitiveness and be content to remain ignorant of what is being taught in "the synagogues of Satan."

Second, "I would have you . . . simple concerning" *carnal* "*evil*." We want the reader to bear in mind that this simple dehortation from an acquaintance with anything which would defile the soul is followed immediately with "*And* the God of peace shall bruise *Satan* under your feet shortly," which plainly intimates it is against *his* efforts to corrupt we must ever be on the alert. The Devil is most persevering, and if he cannot poison our minds with one sort of evil, he will seek to befoul them with another. Now there is a class of people—by no means confined to the female sex—who are ultra-curious about the affairs of others, "busybodies" (I Tim. v, 13), and such are

(continued on preceding page)

XXVI   AUGUST 1947   No. 8

STUDIES IN THE SCRIPTURES

"Search the Scriptures." John v, 39

Publisher and Editor—ARTHUR W. PINK,
29 Lewis Street,
Stornoway, Isle of Lewis,
Scotland.

CHRISTIAN SERVICE

Christian service is obviously the service of a Christian, and if words have any meaning it is the work he does or the duty he discharges unto another in the character of a *servant*. That raises four questions. What *is* a "servant"? What are the distinctive *marks* of one? *Whose* servant is he, or who is his master?—for master and servant are just as truly correlative terms as are husband and wife, parent and children. What is the *nature* of the "service" unto which Christians, all Christians, are called by God? If all ambiguity of thought and confusion of terms is to be avoided, then we need to obtain answers to those questions from the Word of Truth, and then "hold fast the form of sound words" (II Tim. i, 13) and not perplex ourselves and mislead other people by using them in a way quite foreign from their Scriptural import. God's Word is made up of words, and as soon as we wrest its language and invest its terms with a signification different from the way in which the Spirit has used them, we land into error.

What is "Christian service"? Many of our readers, especially American ones, will deem it unnecessary to ask such a question. One of the favourite slogans over there is, "We are saved to serve." When special meetings are held for Christians, for "the deepening of the spiritual life," for "a baptism of the Spirit," or for entering upon "the victorious life," one of the pleas used is, Such an experience is necessary to fit you for Christian service. On the lips of many religious people "Christian service" signifies Christian *usefulness:* to be a regular attender at church and a liberal contributor to its finances; to become teacher of a class or leader of a young people's society; to engage in evangelistic activities and do personal work; to "witness for Christ" by verbally announcing His power to save and satisfy, telling others of "what He means to me." Yet, as the term is used in Scripture, one may do all those things and not be engaged in any Christian *service*.

When Christ said "ye cannot *serve* God and *mammon*" (Matt. vi, 24) it is clear He did not mean, Be useful unto mammon or bear witness for mammon, but rather be a lover of and subject unto it. The word is quite plainly defined in "Know ye not, that to whom ye yield yourselves servants to obey, his servants ye are to whom ye obey" (Rom. vi, 16). Thus, such expressions as "the servants of sin" (Rom. vi, 20), "serving divers lusts and

(*continued on back page*)

Important Notices

Please advise promptly of change in address, otherwise copies will be lost in the mails.

We are glad to send a sample copy to any of your friends whom you believe would be interested in this publication.

This magazine is published as " a work of faith and labour of love," the editor and his wife gladly giving their services free. There is no regular subscription price, as we do not wish the poor of the flock to be deprived. This does not mean that those looking for something for nothing may " help themselves." Those getting this magazine who are financially able and who receive spiritual help from its pages, are expected to gladly contribute towards its expenses; otherwise their names are dropped from our list.

Will those forwarding International Money Orders please have them made out to us at Stornoway, Isle of Lewis, Scotland. Checks (Cheques—Eng.) made out on U.S.A. Banks are not negotiable here, so please do not send them.

All unsigned articles are by the Editor.

CONTENTS

THE PRAYERS OF THE APOSTLES

44. I Thessalonians iii, 11-13

We turn now to consider the *petitions* of this prayer. They were two in number: the one more immediately concerning Paul himself; the other, the Thessalonian saints. The former is recorded in verse 11: "Now God Himself, even our Father, and our Lord Jesus Christ, direct our way unto you." First, that request concerned the taking of a journey. Second, it concerned a ministerial journey. Third, the one who desired to take it was exercised over it and wanted his steps to be ordered of the Lord. Expressed in those terms (and they are a legitimate and simple analysis of the petition), it should at once be apparent that there is something here of interest and moment to each of *us*: in other words, that this petition has been placed on permanent record for our benefit—for our instruction and guidance. It is thus that we should ponder each verse of Scripture, seeking to ascertain what there is in it which provides help for the details of our daily lives. God's Word is given us as "a lamp unto our feet and a light unto our path" —for us to walk by, an unerring Guide to direct our way through the maze of this world. To put it in another way, the apostle has here left us an example which it is our wisdom to follow.

The strongest willed and most resolute person on this earth cannot take a journey of so much as a hundred yards unless God wills it and enables him. "Go to now [a word of rebuke], ye that say, Today or tomorrow we will go into such a city . . . whereas ye know not what shall be on the morrow. . . . For that, ye ought to say, If the Lord will, we shall live, and do this or that" (James iv, 13-15). Even though God grant us permission to carry out our plan, that is very far from saying that He will prosper the same. How that serves to illustrate what we said in our last upon the entire dependency of man upon his Maker! In the verse now before us we are shown *what effect* that fact, that truth, should have upon us. It should counteract our spirit of self-sufficiency.   It should cast us upon the Lord, seeking His enablement for all things.   That was exactly what the apostle was here doing: acknowledging his dependency upon God and supplicating Him concerning his journey to Thessalonica.

"O Lord, I know that the way of man is not in himself: it is not in man that walketh to direct his steps" (Jer. x, 23).   How very few professing Christians believe that!   Nevertheless, that is the truth, and therefore are we bidden, "Trust in the Lord with all thine heart, and lean not unto thine own understanding.   In all thy ways acknowledge Him, and He shall direct thy paths" (Prov. iii, 5, 6), yet not without our concurrence.   God treats with us as rational creatures, as moral agents, and therefore are we required to trust Him fully, to repudiate the competency of our own reason, and to own Him in all our conduct.   "The steps of a good man are ordered by the Lord" (Psa. xxxvii, 23)—not so those of a wicked man, though *his* steps are "ordained" or appointed.   Sometimes God lets us have our own way, as He did Israel of old, and then we miss His best and He sends "leanness into our souls" (Psa. cvi, 15).

During the recent national emergency, when the first claim on all forms of transport was the carrying of munitions and the conveying of troops, Government posters were displayed everywhere requesting the public to ask themselves the question, "Is this journey really necessary?"   That should have a message for *us* concerning our present subject: the first question for each of us to determine is simply this: is it my plain duty (as required by my calling, or my obligations to others) to take this journey?   If there be any uncertainty, then spread the matter before God and seek wisdom from Him.   Observe how frequently it is recorded of the man after God's own heart (i.e. who in his official life was so completely subject to the Divine will) that when contemplating a journey "David enquired of the Lord" (I Sam. xxiii, 2, 4; xxx, 8; II Sam. ii, 1; v, 19, 23), seeking His guidance each time and waiting upon Him.   When your path *is* plain, then definitely beg God to give you "good speed" (Gen. xxiv, 12) and grant you journeying mercies. Act on Psalm xxxvii, 5, and count upon the fulfilment of its promise.   While on your journey, so far as conditions permit, endeavour to redeem the time by profitable reading (Acts viii, 28).

Turning now to *ministerial journeys*: first, we would observe that in Paul's case God's will respecting them was not made known to him uniformly, nor did he have any "unmistakable leading" as some today boast of.   He and his companions had "assayed to go into Bithynia" and we are told "but the Spirit suffered them not" (Acts xvi, 7): if it be asked, Was he then acting in the energy of the flesh? we answer, Certainly not, no more than David did when he purposed to build the temple.   His trip to Macedonia was the result of a vision, but that was exceptional.   Often persecution forced him to flee elsewhere.   Sometimes Paul's movements were regulated by direct command from God; at others by providential circumstances; at others by his own spiritual instincts and desires.   When he bade farewell to those at Ephesus he said, "I will return again to you, if God will" (Acts xviii, 21)—permits and enables.   Our "times" are in *His* hand (Psa. xxxi, 15), and though we propose this or that, it is God who disposes (Prov. xix, 21).   Later, he did return unto Ephesus (Acts xix, 1).

"I will come to you shortly, if the Lord will" (I Cor. iv, 19).   Speaking generally, the apostles knew no more about the common events of life than did other men, nor were they (usually) directed by a supernatural impulse for their journeys. "Making request, if by any means now at length, I might have a prosperous journey by the will of God to come unto you" (Rom. i, 10). Those words should teach us that while the will of God concerning any event is not yet ascertained we have the right and liberty to desire and pray for what we desire, providing that our desires be conformed to God's holiness and our requests subject to His will—our desires must at once be renounced as soon as it be clear that they are not agreeable to the Divine will. Rightly did Moule point out that "The indifference of mystic pietism, which at least discouraged articulate contingent petitions, is unknown to the apostles." And again, "His inward harmony with the Divine will never excluded the formation and expression of such requests, with the reverence of submissive reserve." Only One has ever had the right or necessary qualification to say "Father, I will."

"For which cause also I have been much hindered from coming to you. But now having no more place in these parts, and having a great desire these many years to come unto you; whensoever I take my journey into Spain, I will come to you: for I trust to see you in my journey" (Rom. xv, 22-24). The opening, "For which cause" is explained in the preceding verses: it was the pressure of continuous evangelistic labours which had been the principal thing that had made him defer his visit: from which we learn that the call of *duty* deterred him from carrying out his earlier inclination. "God's dearest servants are not always gratified in everything they have a mind to. Yet all who delight in God have 'the desire of their heart' fulfilled (Psa. xxxvii, 4), though *all* the desires in their heart be not humoured" (Matthew Henry). It is to be noted that Paul said "I trust to see you," not "I *shall* do so," for he knew not what a day might bring forth. We ought to be very slow in making any promise, and those we do should ever be qualified with "If God permit."

"For I will not see you now by the way: but I trust to tarry with you, if the Lord permit" (I Cor. xvi, 7). Here again we see the beloved apostle making personal acknowledgment of both the providential and spiritual government of Christ and his subserviency thereto. The two things must concur: his purpose and conviction of duty be formed by the Spirit indwelling him, and his external circumstances be so ordered as to confirm and make possible the execution of his purpose. Paul was several times crossed in his intentions. Sometimes he was forbidden by the Spirit (Acts xvi, 7), sometimes hindered by Satan (I Thess. ii, 18), at others prevented or long delayed by the pressure of work or by the persecution of his enemies. It is very doubtful if he ever took his journey into Spain (Rom. xv, 24). But at Matthew Henry said, "However, Paul, forasmuch as it was in thine heart to bring the Gospel into Spain, thou didst well in that it was in thine heart: as God said to David (II Chron. vi, 8). The grace of God often with favour accepts the sincere intention, when the providence of God in wisdom prohibits the execution. Do we not serve a good Master, then! (II Cor. viii, 12)."

It is our desire and aim to furnish something in these pages suited to the needs of all classes of its readers. Since this magazine goes to several scores of those who are engaged in the ministry, we feel that a word or two should now be offered for their particular benefit ere we turn from the present subject. One of the matters which, at some time or other in his career, deeply exercises the conscientious servant of God is that of his particular field of labour, and more especially when he is justified in leaving one field for another. Great care and caution need to be used and prayer for patience as well as wisdom. Ours is markedly an age of discontent and restlessness, and not only are most of God's people more or less infected by its evil spirit, but many of His servants are influenced by the same and suffer from a wander lust. Some who make a change of pastorate every two or three years, suppose they find a warrant in so doing from the experience of the apostle Paul; but that is a mistake. *He* was never settled in a *pastorate,* but instead was engaged in missionary or evangelistic activities, and therefore he furnishes no example to be followed by those who have the care of local churches.

The first thing is to spare no pains in endeavouring to make sure that a particular portion of the Lord's vineyard is the one where He would have you labour. If it be a "church" (?) where you would be required to employ worldly and carnal methods in order to "attract the young people" or to "maintain its finances," that is no place for a servant of Christ. Take time and trouble to find out what the local conditions are, and you will probably be spared from entering a position where the *Holy* Spirit would not use you. Far better minister to a small company of saints than to a large one of unregenerate church-members. No plan should be formed without reference to God's will, and His glory and the good of His people must ever be that at which you aim. If assured that God led you into your present field, be very slow in entertaining any thought of removal: an invitation to a more "attractive" field is far more likely to be a Divine *testing* of your heart than an intimation God would have you make a move. Consult not your own inclinations, but the welfare of those to whom you are ministering. Seek grace to "endure hardness as a good soldier of Jesus Christ" (II Tim. ii, 3) and let *faithfulness* rather than "success" be your earnest endeavour.

"Now God Himself even our Father, and our Lord Jesus Christ, direct our way unto you." That prayer demonstrates that Paul was no fatalist who argued that since God has predestinated every thing that comes to pass, there was no need for him to be uneasy about his plans for the near future— that had been a wrong conclusion to draw. No, he was deeply exercised that his steps might be ordered of God, and therefore did he trustfully commit his way unto Him (Psa. xxxvii, 5). In spite of his intense desire to visit these saints (verses 6, 10), he refused to rush matters and act in the energy of the flesh. Nor did he assume that *their* yearning to see him again was a "clear intimation" of God's will in the matter: he waited to be definitely guided from on high. It is not for any minister of the Gospel to effect his own design without the Divine leave: rather must it be by God's permission and providence, by His directing and ordering, that each journey is to be taken. Until His will is clear, remain where you are (Rom. xiv, 23). If you be at the parting of the ways, entreat the Lord to *block* the one He would not have you take. Never force matters, nor act hastily.

The "God Himself" is emphatic: literally, "But Himself, God even our Father, and our Lord Jesus Christ, may direct our way to you." The "Himself" is in contrast with "we would have come unto you, even I Paul, once and again; but *Satan* hindered us" (ii, 18). If God Himself direct us, then none can hinder! In what way Satan had "hindered" Scripture does not inform us, and therefore it is useless and impious for us to speculate about it. It was not that Satan had in anywise hindered the execution of God's purpose, but only the fulfilling of the apostle's "desire." God blessedly over-ruled and outwitted Satan, for in consequence of Paul's being hindered in the first century, *we* in this twentieth now have the benefit of this epistle! In the all-too-brief comments of Ellicott's commentary a valuable point is here brought out: "the verb 'direct' is in the singular (which of course the English cannot express), showing the *unity* of Father and Son, and the *equality* of the two Persons." There was a blessed propriety in Paul's conjoining the Son with the Father in *this* petition, for it acknowledged Him as the One who holds the stars in His hand (Rev. i, 16) and who opens and shuts all doors (Rev. iii, 7).

"And the Lord make you to increase and abound in love one toward another, and toward all, even as we toward you" (verse 12). This is the second petition, but we shall not dwell upon it at the same length as the former: not because it is of less importance, but because it calls for less explication. What is needed here is not so much exposition as the turning of these words into earnest supplication. If ever there was a time in the history of Christendom when God's people needed to entreat the throne of grace for an increase and abounding again of love, it is surely now. The exercise and manifestation of this cardinal grace is at an exceedingly low ebb. Sectarian bigotry, carnal strife, roots of bitterness, thrive on every hand. Yea, things are in such a deplorable state today that many of God's own people hold quite a wrong idea as to its nature and fruits. Most of them confound natural affability and temperamental geniality for love. A hearty handshake, a warm welcome, may be had at the *world's* clubs and social centres, where Christ is not even professed! The love for which the apostle here prayed was a holy, spiritual, and supernatural one.

Spiritual love proceeds from a spiritual nature and is attracted by a sight of the Divine image in the saints. "Every one that loveth Him that begat, loveth him also that is begotten of Him" (I John v, 1). No one can love holiness in another but he who has holiness in his own soul. Many love particular Christians because they find them to be sweet-tempered or generous-hearted, but that is merely *natural* and not spiritual love. If we would love the saints spiritually we must disregard what they are temperamentally by nature, and contemplate them as the objects and subjects of God's love and for what we see of Him in them. Only thus shall we be able to rise above individual peculiarities and personal infirmities, and value them with a true spiritual affection. This does not mean that we shall ignore their offences, or condone their sins (Lev. xix, 17), yet often what we regard as "slights" from them is due to our own pride—hurt because we do not receive the notice which we consider is our due. It is not good for the people of God to know too much of each other (Prov. xxv, 17). Familiarity breeds contempt.

Neither the reality nor the depth of Christian love is to be measured by honeyed words or endearing expressions. We have found from experience that those who have addressed us as "Dear Mr. Pink" and signed themselves "Yours truly" have worn far better than others who greeted us as "Beloved brother" and closed with "Yours affectionately in Christ." Actions speak louder than words. Gushy people are proverbially superficial and fickle. Those less demonstrative are more stable. Still waters run deep. Spiritual love always aims at the good of its object. It is exercised in edifying conversation, seeks to strengthen and confirm faith, exalt God's Word, and to promote piety. The more another magnifies Christ, the more should he be endeared to me. We do not mean mere glib talk about Christ, but that overflowing of heart toward Him which compels the mouth to speak of Him. Love the saints for the Truth's sake, for being unashamed to avow their faith in such a day as this. Those who reflect most of the image of Christ and carry about with them most of His fragrance, should be the ones we love the most.

Love for the brethren is ever proportioned unto our love for the Lord Himself, which at once explains why the former is now at such a low ebb. The sectarian bigotry and the roots of bitterness growing all around us are not hard to explain. Love *to God* has waned! "Thou shalt love the Lord thy God with all thy heart, mind and strength" comes before "thou shalt love thy neighbour as thyself." But the love of material things and the cares of this world have chilled the souls of many Godwards. Our affections must be set steadfastly upon the Head of the Church before they will wax warm unto its members. Where the Lord be given His rightful place in our hearts, His redeemed will also be given theirs. Then love will not be confined to that narrow ecclesiastical circle in which our lot is cast, but will embrace the entire household of faith. Then will there be "love unto *all* the saints" (Eph. i, 15), and that will be evidenced by "supplication for all saints" (Eph. vi, 18)—those in the four corners of the earth, whom you have never seen. "Salute *every* saint" (Phil. iv, 21): poor as well as rich, weak as well as strong.

A word now on the *connection* of this petition with the former one. At first glance there appears to be none, for what relation is there between one being guided in a journey, and others loving one another? Yet from the fact that this one opens with the word "And" we are given plain intimation there *is* a coherence between them, and *what* that is a little meditation should discover. What would be the use of the apostle visiting the Thessalonian assembly if strife and division prevailed in their midst? Under such circumstances the Lord would not clothe his words with power, and instead of Paul's ministry building them up, at best he would have to reprove and rebuke them for their carnality, for most certainly *he* was not one of those who would ignore what was wrong and act as though things were all right. Nothing more quickly grieves and quenches the Spirit than dissension and a spirit of ill-will in the assembly. A servant of God is heavily handicapped when he has to labour under such conditions. If then this company of saints was to enjoy a profitable season under the further teaching of the apostle, it was essential that their love unto each other be in a flourishing condition.

"And the Lord make you to increase and abound in love one toward another." This petition was addressed more specifically unto the Head of the Church, from whom all "nourishment" and "increase" of its members flow (Col. ii, 19). It is "of His fulness" we receive (John i, 16) and from Him "the supply of the Spirit" (Phil. 1, 19) is given; yet for the same we are required to seek. This request supplies a striking illustration of what we pointed out in earlier articles, namely, that we are not to infer from the apostle asking for some particular thing that those for whom he supplicated were deficient therein, but rather the reverse. It was because he perceived that a certain grace was in healthy exercise he felt encouraged to ask God for *an increase* of the same. Such was unmistakably the case here. He had opened his epistle by referring to their "labour of love" (i, 3), and later declared "But as touching brotherly love ye need not that I write unto you, for ye yourselves are taught of God to love one another. And indeed ye do it toward all the brethren" (iv, 9, 10). Why then this petition? "That ye increase more and more" (iv, 10)! The answer to this "large petition" is recorded in II Thessalonians i, 3.

"To the end He may stablish your hearts unblameable in holiness before God, even our Father, at the coming of our Lord Jesus Christ with all His saints" (verse 13). Limits of space oblige us to be very brief. 1. This expresses his design in his petitions. Our hearts are sadly fickle and inconstant in their frames, and need Divine establishing against the fear of man, the frowns of the world, and the temptations of Satan. 2. Holiness before God was the grand *object* in view, and the abounding of love the *means* for promoting the same (Col. iii, 14). 3. The establishing of our hearts (which God ever eyes) is our great need, yet how little concern is there about *their* state! Much head and hand religion, but the heart neglected! So far as we recall, never once have we heard this petition used in public prayer! 4. At the return of Christ these desires will be fully realized—see next article, D.V.

THE LIFE AND TIMES OF JOSHUA
24. The Memorials

That which is recorded in the book of Joshua fully maintains the Truth presented in the Pentateuch, yet its typical teaching carries us considerably beyond what is there set forth. This is to be expected, especially when we bear in mind (as we must do continually while pondering its contents) that it was the *new* generation of Israel which is here in view. The lesson taught at the supernatural crossing of the Jordan conducts us farther in the unfolding of the Gospel than what was signified at the Red Sea. There, it was the might of God put forth on behalf of His covenant people in the total destruction of that antagonistic power which had held them captive so long and had refused to let them go. Here, it was His vanquishing of that obstacle which barred the way into their inheritance. When Satan's captives are freed at the miracle of regeneration, he does not henceforth ignore them and leave them in peace: though he cannot prevent their entrance into the "purchased possession," yet he is ever assailing them in one form or other as he seeks to keep them from a *present* enjoyment of the same. What is required from us in order to thwart those designs of our Enemy, we are seeking to show in the course of this series of articles.

But it was the Divine side of things, the provisions God made for Israel's entrance into and occupation of the land of Canaan with which we were more concerned in our last. Those provisions were, first, the appointing and qualifying of Joshua to be the leader of Israel, the typical "captain of their salvation." Second, the ark of the covenant, which (we repeat) was both the witness of Jehovah's presence in Israel's midst and the symbol of His relations to them. And third, the priesthood, culminating in their service in "the tabernacle which was pitched in Shiloh." Thus, as we hope to yet show, not only are we required to turn unto the epistles of Paul to the Romans, the Ephesians and the Colossians, in order to find the antitypical truths of what was spiritually adumbrated *of us* by Israel in the book of Joshua, but also to his epistle to the Hebrews. We know of only one other writer who has called attention to that fact, in an article written before we were born, and which appeared in a magazine (*The Bible Treasury*) under the title of "The Book of Joshua and the Epistle to the Hebrews," unto which we gladly acknowledge our indebtedness and of which we made free use.

We are now to take notice of the Divine command which Joshua received, to take twelve stones from the bed of the Jordan, "out of the place where the priests' feet stood firm" (iv, 3), which were made a "memorial" unto future generations, and in addition, the setting up of "twelve stones in the midst of Jordan" (v, 9). At the Red Sea Israel neither left twelve stones in its bed, nor took twelve with them unto the other side. Instead, Pharaoh and his chosen captains, his chariots and his host, God drowned therein, so that Israel sang "The depths have covered them: *they* sank into the bottom as a *stone*" (Ex. xv, 4, 5). "But the children of Israel walked upon dry land in the midst of the sea, and the waters were a wall unto them on their right hand and on their left. Thus the Lord saved Israel that day out of the hand of the Egyptians" (Ex .xiv, 29, 30), and put the song of redemption into their mouths, saying, "The Lord hath triumphed gloriously" (Ex. xv, 1, 13). At the Red Sea Jehovah showed Himself strong on the behalf of that people who had previously found shelter under "the blood of the lamb," and whom He now brought nigh unto Himself—"unto Thy holy habitation" (Ex. xv, 13, 17).

But at the Jordan a further and grander lesson was taught Israel, something which went beyond the truth of redemption by blood and by power, even that of *resurrection*. Fundamental and blessed as is the truth taught us by the cross of Christ, there is something further which is even more vital and glorious, and that is our Lord's victory over the grave. When the apostle throws out that irrefutable challenge, "Who shall lay anything to the charge of God's elect?" his triumphant answer is, "It is God that justifieth, who is he that condemneth? It is Christ that died, *yea rather*, that is risen again" (Rom. viii, 33, 34). It is abundantly clear in I Corinthians xv (see especially verses 3 and 4, 14, 17) that the resurrection of Christ is not only an integral part of the Gospel but its distinctive and outstanding feature; and those evangelists who go no farther than the cross are preaching only half of the Gospel. But more, the saints themselves are greatly the losers if their faith and spiritual apprehensions stop short at the atoning death of Christ, for unspeakably precious as it is to recognize *our* death unto sin in the death of the Surety, still more blessed is it to perceive our federal union with Him and our title to the inheritance in His triumph over death.

At the Jordan the redeemed of God were shown their own passage through death and resurrection by the figure of the twelve stones placed in the Jordan and the twelve stones taken out of it. It was at this point that Israel entered upon a new stage in their history, yet perpetuating all the essential features which had previously marked them as the peculiar people of the Lord—as will be seen when we examine (D.V.) into the new circumcising at Gilgal, the celebration of the passover, and the appearing of the Captain of the Lord's host with drawn sword (chap. 5). Nevertheless, as said above, that which characterized the crossing of the Jordan is in sharp contrast with what took place at the Red Sea. There, instead of the priests bearing the ark of the covenant being seen, it was Israel's enemies which lay there, consumed as stubble by the wrath of the Lord. On the other hand, no Canaanites were in Jordan, not a single foe was overthrown there; yet it was sanctified to the Lord and to Israel by the priests and the ark of the covenant for glory and victory as truly as were the waters of the Red Sea when they returned and engulfed the host of Pharaoh in terrible judgment—that glory and victory quickly appears in the sequel.

As previously pointed out, the river Jordan was not only the emblem of death, but of judgment also, as the word itself signifies—"jor," literally, "spread," and "dan" which means "judging" (Gen. xxx, 6). The use made of this river in New Testament times supplies clear confirmation, for the Jordan was where the Lord's forerunner exercised his ministry, of whom it was foretold "prepare ye the way of the Lord." And *how* did he do so? By preparing a people to receive Him. In what manner? By preaching "Repent ye," i.e. *judge yourselves;* and those who did so were (most appropriately) baptized of him in the Jordan "confessing their sins" (Matt. iii, 8); and by that "baptism of repentance unto the remission of sins" (Mark i, 4) they acknowledged that death was their due, and therefore were they (symbolically) placed in a watery grave. There too, the Lord Jesus as the Surety and Sinbearer of His people identified Himself with them by being placed beneath its waters, thereby pledging Himself unto that "baptism" of death (Luke xii, 50) wherein He met the needs of all who truly repent or adjudge themselves worthy of death, when all "the waves and billows" of God's wrath (Psa. xlii, 6) passed over Him.

The good Shepherd entered the river of judgment on behalf of His sheep, making for them a new covenant by His atoning death, delivering thereby from judgment all who follow Him: "this is My blood of the new covenant, which is shed for many for the remission of sins" (Matt. xxvi, 28) He declared only a few hours before the crucifixion, when He instituted the memorial of His death. That was typified by the entrance into Jordan of the ark of the covenant "borne by the priests" and at once the flow of its waters was stayed, so that the people who followed it passed over dryshod, though the ark itself did not come out of the Jordan until it had secured a passage for all the people (iii, 17). Profoundly suggestive and significant are those words "For the priests which bare the ark stood in the midst of Jordan until *every thing was finished* that the Lord commanded Joshua to speak unto the people, according to all that Moses commanded Joshua" (iv, 10). How that reminds us of "Jesus, knowing that *all things were now accomplished,* that the Scripture might be fulfilled, saith, I thirst . . . when Jesus therefore had received the vinegar He said, It is finished, and He bowed His head and gave up the spirit" (John xix, 28, 30). All that the justice of God demanded, all that the Law required ("Moses commanded") had been rendered by the antitypical Joshua.

"And it came to pass, when all the people were clean passed over Jordan, that the Lord spake unto Joshua, saying, Take ye twelve men out of the people, out of every tribe a man, and command ye them, saying, Take you hence out of the midst of Jordan, out of the place where the priests' feet stood firm, twelve stones, and ye shall carry them over with you, and leave them there in the lodging place where ye shall lodge this night" (iv, 1-3), i.e. in Gilgal (verse 19). That those stones were large ones is evident from the fact that they were to be carried upon the "shoulder." The men who carried them had been selected beforehand (iii, 13), ready for this task, that there might be no delay in connection with what lay immediately before the nation —the encamping of that vast multitude for the night in a suitable place, namely, at one which was afterwards called Gilgal, and which some inform us was about mid-way between the river Jordan and the city of Jericho. In the light of Joshua iv, 4, "then Joshua called the twelve men whom he had prepared of the children of Israel," we personally regard that as a foreshadowing of the antitypical Joshua, who at an early stage of His ministry "called unto Him the twelve" (Mark vi, 7):

"And Joshua said unto them, Pass over before the ark of the Lord your God into the midst of Jordan, and take you up every man of you a stone upon his shoulder, according unto the number of the tribes of Israel: That they may be *a sign* among you, that when your children ask their fathers in time to come, saying, What mean ye by these stones? Then ye shall answer them, That the waters of Jordan were cut off before the ark of the covenant of the Lord: when it passed over Jordan, the waters of Jordan were cut off; and these stones shall be for a *memorial* unto the children of Israel for ever " (verses 5-7). The two words we have italicized call attention to the double design which those stones were intended to serve, which will be more intelligible to the reader when he bears in mind that those twelve stones "did Joshua pitch in Gilgal" (verse 20). They were not left flat on the ground but orderly formed into a cairn or monument. The Hebrew word for "pitch" there, Young's Concordance defines as "To cause to stand, raise." Twenty times this verb is rendered "set up" in the Authorized Version. It is the same word which is used in connection with the erection of the Tabernacle when it was complete (Ex. xl, 2, etc.). Thus, those large stones were arranged in such a manner, possibly placed one on top of another monolith-like, so as to attract the attention and invoke the inquiry of those who should afterwards behold them.

That monument of stones was designed first as a "sign" unto Israel. It was a message for their hearts via their eyes rather than ears. It was an enduring sermon in stone. It spoke of the goodness and power of God exercised on their behalf at the Jordan. That word "sign" is a very full one—our Lord's miracles are termed "signs" (John xx, 30; Acts ii, 22). The two wonders which Moses was empowered to work before his brethren were called "signs" (Ex. iv, 1-9), they authenticated him as their Divinely-appointed leader and signified that the power of the Almighty was with him. In Deuteronomy xi, 18, and Judges vi, 17, "sign" has the force of token or representation—of Israel's being regulated by God's Word, and of the Lord's granting success to the commission He had committed to Gideon. In other passages a "sign" was a portent or pledge of something concerning the future —I Samuel x, 1-9; II Kings xix, 29. In each of those senses may "sign" be understood in Joshua iv, 6. That cairn of stones was to signify that Israel had not crossed the Jordan by their own ability, but because of the miracle-working power of God. It was a representation unto them that they had passed through the river's bed dryshod. More especially, it was an earnest and *pledge* of what God would yet do for them.

Second, that monument was designed as a "memorial" that Israel had passed through the river of death, that they were now (typically) on resurrection ground, that *judgment lay behind them*. Israel upon the Canaan side of Jordan adumbrated that blessed truth expressed by our Redeemer in John v, 24, where He so definitely assures His people that each soul who hears His word and believes on the One who sent Him "hath everlasting life, and shall not come into condemnation, but is passed from death unto life." The reason why he shall *not* "come into condemnation" is because in the person of his Surety he has already been condemned and suffered the full judgment of God upon all his sins, and therefore, judicially, as federally united to Christ, he "is passed from death [that death which is the wages of sin] unto life"—that "life" which is the award of the Law, as it was "magnified" by the Saviour and "made honourable" (Isa. xlii, 21). As the ark of the covenant entered the river of death and judgment the flow of its waters was stopped until the ark had secured a safe passage for all who followed it; so Christ endured the unsparing wrath of God that by His atoning death those who were legally one with Him, and who are made voluntary followers of Him, shall be delivered from all future judgment.

In addition to the monument erected on the Canaan side of the river we are told that " Joshua set up twelve stones in the midst of Jordan, in the place where the priests which bare the ark of the covenant stood; and they are there unto this day" (iv, 9). Thus there was a *double* monument to perpetually commemorate Israel's passing through the place of judgment: the one in the midst of the Jordan, the other in their new camping-ground at Gilgal. What anointed eye can fail to see in them the *two signs* and memorials which Christ has instituted to symbolize that, as the result of their faith in His atoning death, His people have not only passed through death and judgment, but are now united to a risen Christ and are "alive unto God"! The meaning of the two ordinances appointed by Christ clearly confirms this, for each of them speaks of both death and resurrection. " Know ye not, that so many of us as were baptized into Jesus Christ were baptized into His *death*? Therefore we were buried with Him by baptism into death, that like as Christ was *raised* from the dead by the glory of the Father, even so we also should walk in newness of life" (Rom. vi, 4, 5; and cf. Col. ii, 12). Christian baptism is designed to symbolize the believer's union with Christ in His death, burial, and resurrection, as well as being his personal profession that he is dead to the world and has resolved to walk in newness of life.

The Lord's Supper also, while it celebrates our passage with Christ through death, yet it is with the added blessedness and triumph of being now on the resurrection side of judgment. Just as the *twelve* stones which had been in Jordan were formed into a *single* cairn in the camp at Gilgal—type of " the Israel of God" (Gal. vi, 16) in its entirety, made into " one body"— was a testimony that the twelve tribes had passed through the unfordable river; so the Lord's supper, partaken of by those who were once lost sinners under condemnation, is a testimony that they have passed over, and being on resurrection ground can look forward not to judgment but to the consummation of their hope and bliss. This is clear from I Corinthians xi, 26, "For as often as ye eat this bread and drink this cup, ye do show the Lord's death *till He come.*" The Lord's supper not only looks back to the cross but forward to Christ's return in glory, and therefore is it designated a "feast" (I Cor. v, 8) and not a fast, and instead of " bitter herbs" (Ex. xii, 8) being eaten, the "wine" of gladness is drunk.

THE DOCTRINE OF REVELATION
8. The Existence of God

Fourth, *as unveiled in the Lord Jesus.* In the dispensations of His providence, the revelation which God has made of Himself unto mankind has been a progressive one. First, He is manifested in the realm of creation, and that with sufficient clearness as to leave all without excuse if they perceive not that He is. Second, God is revealed in man himself, so that his very constitution evinces his Divine origin and his conscience bears witness of his accountability to his Maker. Third, God is plainly to be seen in human history: most patently in His dealings with the Jews during the past thirty-five centuries; yet with sufficient clearness everywhere as to attest that He is the moral

Governor of this world, the Regulator of human affairs. But over and above these—O wonder of wonders—God has become *incarnate*. In the person of His blessed and co-equal Son, God deigned to clothe Himself in our flesh and blood and manifest Himself unto the sons of men. For the space of thirty-three years He appeared among men and displayed His glory before their eyes; yea, gave proof of His matchless mercy by performing a work, at infinite cost to Himself, which has made it possible for Him to righteously save the very chief of sinners.

"In the beginning was the Word, and the Word was with God, and the Word was God . . . and the Word became flesh and dwelt among us" (John i, 1, 14). It is by means of *words* that we make known our wills, reveal the calibre of our minds and the character of our hearts, and communicate information unto others. Appropriately, then, is Christ designated "The Word of God," for He has made the Transcendent immanent, the incomprehensible God intelligible to us. Thus too is He denominated "the image of the invisible God" (Col. i, 15) and the "Alpha and the Omega" (Rev. i, 8)— the One who spells out the Deity unto us. "The only begotten Son, which is in the bosom of the Father, He hath declared" or "told Him forth" (John i, 18). In Christ's life of impeccable purity, we behold God's holiness; in His utter selflessness, God's benevolence; in His peerless teaching, God's wisdom; in His unrivalled miracles, God's power; in His gentleness and long-suffering, God's patience; in His love and grace, the outshining of God's glory.

The record of Christ's unprecedented life is found in the four Gospels. Those Gospels were written by men who were constantly in Christ's company during the days of His ministry, being an ungarnished record of what they personally saw with their own eyes and heard with their own ears. Numerous copies of those Gospels have been in known existence since the first century of this Christian era. Only three explanations of them are feasible. First, that they were written by deluded fanatics. But the character of their contents, the calmness of their tenor, the absence of anything savouring of enthusiasm, cause anyone capable of weighing evidence to promptly reject such an hypothesis. The dreams of visionaries had never received such widespread credence. Second, that they were the inventions of deceitful men. But that could not be, otherwise their contemporaries had exposed them as impostors. Wicked men could not have devised the Sermon on the Mount! Third, that they were written by honest men, who chronicled actual facts.

The person of the Lord Jesus presents a baffling problem, yea, an insoluble enigma unto infidelity. Scepticism is quite unable to supply any rational explanation of the phenomenon which He presents. Yet "what think ye of Christ?" is a question which cannot be avoided or evaded by anyone who professes to use his reasoning powers or lays any claim to being an educated person. The obvious fact confronts believer and unbeliever alike that the appearing of Jesus Christ on the stage of this world has exerted a more powerful, lasting, and extensive influence than has any other person, factor, or event that can be named. To say that Christ has revolutionized human history is only to affirm what His bitterest foes are compelled to acknowledge. He dwelt in no palace, led no army, overthrew no mundane empire, yet His fame has spread to the ends of the earth. He wrote no book, framed no philosophy, erected no temple, yet He occupies a place in literature and religion which none else has ever achieved. How is this to be explained? Unbelief can furnish no answer! Nor can it refute, for the historicity of Christ is established far more conclusively than that of Socrates and Plato.

Viewed simply from the human plane the Lord Jesus presents a phenomenon which admits of no human explanation. The law of heredity cannot account for Him, for He transcends all merely racial characteristics. Though according to the flesh He was the Son of Abraham, yet He is bounded by no Jewish limitations. Instead, He is the Man of men, the Pattern Man. The Englishman and the Dutchman, with their vastly different racial temperaments, the stolid German and the warm Italian, behold their Ideal in Christ: He rises above all national restrictions. The law of environment cannot explain Him, for He was born in poverty, lived in a small town, received no collegiate training, toiled at the carpenter's bench. Such an environment was not conducive to the development of thought and teaching which was to enlighten the whole world. Christ transcends all laws. There is nothing provincial about Him. "The Son of man" is His fitting title, for He is the Representative Man.

Christ was not tinctured or affected by the age in which He lived. And that can be said of no one else. Study the characters and teaching of any of the outstanding figures of history, and we are at once aware that they were coloured by their own generation. By common consent we make certain allowances for those who lived in former times, and agree that it would not be just to measure them by present-day ideals. Men of the most sterling worth were, in measure, marred by the crudities, coarseness, or superstitions of their contemporaries. But the Lord Jesus is the grand Exception. You may test Him by the light of this twentieth century—if light it be—or you may judge Him by any century, and no lack or blemish is to be found in Him. His teaching was pure Truth without any admixture of error, and therefore it stands the test of all time. His teaching was neither affected by the prevailing traditions of Judaism, by that of Grecian philosophy, nor by any other influence then abroad. The timeless value of Christ's teaching is without parallel. That of Socrates and Plato has long since become obsolete, but Christ's is as pertinent and potent now as the day He uttered it.

There is no part of Christ's teaching which the subsequent growth of human knowledge has had to discredit. Therein it is in marked contrast with that of all other men, whose dicta have to be constantly revised and brought up to date. There is a universal quality to His teaching which is found in none other's: an originality, a loftiness, an adaptability. There is nothing petty, local, or transient about it. It is of general application, suited to all generations and to all peoples. It possesses a vital and vitalizing freshness without a parallel. It is profound enough for the mightiest intellect, practical enough for the artizan, simple enough for the little child. It is profitable for youth, for maturity, and old age alike. It furnishes that which is needed by those in prosperity, brings comfort to those in adversity, and has imparted a peace which passeth all understanding to thousands who lay upon beds of suffering, and while they passed through the valley of the shadow of death. Those are *facts* attested by a multitude of witnesses whose testimony cannot be fairly impeached.

Unto Christ the master minds of the ages have paid homage. Such mighty intellects as Lord Bacon and Isaac Newton, Michael Faraday and Lord Kelvin, Milton and Handel, Calvin and John Locke, and a host of others who towered above their fellows in mental acumen and genius, bowed before Him in adoring worship. Not that Christianity is in any need of human patronage to authenticate it, but that it may be evinced to the thoughtful ones of this rising generation that Christians are far from being a company of credulous simpletons. Christianity is not something suited only to little children or old ladies in their dotage. When the young men of this age behold such hard-headed men as General Dobbie, the valiant defender of Malta, and Field-Marshal Montgomery, the Commander-in-chief of the British Army, unashamedly acknowledging Christ as *their* personal Lord and Saviour, they have before them that which clearly challenges them to seriously consider the claims of Christ and carefully examine His teachings—instead of contemptuously ignoring the same as something unworthy of their best attention.

Napoleon Bonaparte, the military genius of a century ago, declared, "Alexander, Caesar, Charlemagne and myself have founded empires, but upon *what* did those creations of our genius depend? Upon *force*. Jesus Christ alone established His empire upon love, and to this very day millions would die for Him. I think I understand something of human nature, and I tell you, those were men and I am a man; Jesus Christ is more than a man. I have inspired multitudes with such an enthusiastic devotion that they would have died for me . . . but to do this it was necessary that I should be *visibly* present, with the electric influence of my looks, of my words, of my voice. When I saw men and spoke to them, I lighted up the flame of self-devotion in their hearts. Christ alone has succeeded in raising the mind of men toward the Unseen, that it becomes insensible to the barriers of time and space. Across a chasm of eighteen hundred years Jesus Christ makes a demand which is, beyond all others, difficult to satisfy.

"He asks for the human *heart*. He will have it entirely for and to Himself. He demands it unconditionally, and forthwith His demand is granted. Wonderful! In defiance of time and space, the soul of man, with all its powers and faculties, is annexed to the empire of Christ. All who simply believe in Him experience that remarkable, supernatural love towards Him. This phenomenon is unaccountable: it is altogether beyond the scope of man's creative powers. Time, the great destroyer, is powerless to extinguish this sacred flame; time cannot exhaust its strength, nor put a limit to its reign. This it is which strikes me most. I have often thought of it. This it is which proves to me quite convincingly the Divinity of Jesus Christ." Paul Richter said of Christ: "The holiest among the mighty, the mightiest among the holy, who with His pierced hands has lifted empires off their hinges, turned the stream of centuries out of its channel, and still governs the ages."

Alexander, Napoleon, Lincoln, are dead, and we refer to them in the *past* tense. But not so with Christ. We do not think or speak of Him as One who *was*, but as One who is. The Lord Jesus is far more than a memory. He is the great "I am": the same yesterday and today and for ever. He is more real to mankind, His influence is still more prevalent, His followers are more numerous in this twentieth century than they were in the first. On what principle, scientifically, can we rationally account for the dynamical influence of the Lord Jesus today? That One now at a distance of almost two millenniums is still moulding human thought, attracting human hearts, transforming human lives, with such mighty sway that He stands forth from all other teachers as the sun makes the stars recede into dimness and pale before the lustre of His refulgence. As a strictly scientific question, the mystery of Christ's influence demands an adequate solution. It requires neither science nor philosophy to *deny*, but it does to *explain*. The only satisfactory explanation is that Christ is God, omnipotent and omnipresent.

We call attention now to what has well been termed "The Logic of the Changed Calendar": what follows is an enlargement of some notes we made nearly forty years ago from a book entitled *The Unrealized Logic of Religion.* Few people stop to inquire for an explanation of one of the most amazing facts which is presented to the notice of everybody, namely, the fact that all civilized time is dated from the birth of Jesus Christ! This is the twentieth century, and from what event are those centuries dated? From the birth of a Jew, who, according to the view of infidels, if He ever existed, was a peasant in an obscure province, who was the author of no wonderful invention, who occupied no throne, who died when, as men count years, He had scarcely reached his prime, and who died the death of a criminal. Now if the Lord Jesus Christ were nothing more than what sceptics will allow, then is it not utterly unthinkable that the chronology of the civilized world should be reckoned from *His* birth? The effect must correspond to the cause, and there is no agreement between such a phenomenon and such an inadequate producer.

To have some common measure of time is, of course, a necessity of organized society, but where shall we find an adequate starting point for the calendar?—i.e. one which will be acceptable to all civilized nations! A world-shattering victory, the founding of some many-centuried city, the birth of a dynasty, the beginning of a revolution: some such event, it might reasonably be expected, would give time a new starting point. But no conqueror's sword has ever cut deep enough on Time to leave an enduring mark. The Julian era, the Alexandrian era, the era of the Sileucidae, all had their brief day and have vanished. There is for civilized men but one suitable, enduring and universally recognized starting point for civilized time, and that is *the manger at Bethlehem!* And how is that strange yet startling fact to be explained? It was imposed neither by the authority of a conqueror, the device of priests, the enactment of a despot, nor even by Constantine; but by slow and gradual consent.

The name of Jesus Christ did not emerge in the calendar till five centuries after His death—a space of time long enough for Him to be forgotten had He been an impostor. It took another five hundred years to become universally accepted; and the process is linked to no human name. Here then is a phenomenon that scepticism cannot explain: that without any conspiracy of Christian fanatics Jesus Christ has altered the almanacs of the world. The one event which towers above the horizon of history serves as a landmark to measure time for all civilized races. The Lord of time has indelibly written His signature across time itself; the years of the modern world being labelled by common consent the years *of our Lord!* Every letter you receive (though penned by an atheist), every newspaper carrying date of its issue (though published by Communists), bears testimony to the historicity of Christ! The One who entered this world to shape its history to a new pattern changed its calendar from A.M. to A.D.

All that had transpired previously in human history counted for nothing. The name of the most famous of the world's generals or of its most powerful monarchs was not deemed worthy to be imprinted upon all succeeding centuries. By a deep, unanimous, inarticulated and yet irresistible instinct, each nation has recognized and recorded on its almanacs the true starting point of its life. Several attempts have been made to establish another point of departure for recorded time. Islam has made a faint but broken mark upon the centuries, relating time to the sword; but the Moslem almanac is confined to but a cluster of half-civilized races. La Place, the astronomer, proposed to give stability and dignity to human chronology by linking it to the stars, but the world approved not.   France sought to popularize its Revolution, and count 1793 as year one, but her calendar lasted but thirteen years.   The centuries belong to Christ and pay homage to Him by bearing *His* name!

Young men, young women, who are at present being tossed to and fro upon a sea of doubt, there is no reason why you should remain there. It will be your own fault if you fail to secure firm ground to stand upon.   You may imagine Christians make an idle boast when they affirm " we *know,*" and declare " That is exactly what you do not: you suppose, you hope, you believe.   The dream may be alluring, the hope pleasing, but you cannot be sure."   If so, you err.   The children of God have infallible proof, and if you follow the right course, assurance will be yours too.   The value and Divinity of Christ's teaching may be personally *verified* by yourself.   How? " If any man will do His will," said Christ, " he shall *know* of the doctrine " (John vii, 17).   If you will read the record of it in the Gospels, submit to Christ's authority, conform to His requirements, regulate your life by His precepts, then *you* shall obtain a settled conviction that He " spake as never man spake," that His are the words of Truth.

Nay, further.   If you be an honest inquirer, prepared to follow the truth wherever it leads—and it will be out of the mists of scepticism and away from the fogs of uncertainty—you may obtain definite and conclusive proof that Christ *is* and that He is the Rewarder of those who diligently seek Him. His invitation is, " If any man thirst, let him come unto Me and drink " (John vii, 37), and upon compliance, He promises to satisfy that thirst. *Test Him for yourself.*   If the empty cisterns of this world—its poor pleasures or its intellectual speculations—have failed to satisfy your soul, Christ can.   He declares, " Come unto Me all ye that labour and are heavy laden, and I will give you rest " (Matt. xi, 28).   If you have toiled in vain for peace and your conscience be burdened with a sense of guilt, then cast yourself on the mercy of Christ right now, and you shall find " rest unto your soul "—such as this world can neither give nor take away.   Then *you too* will know the reality and certainty of His so great salvation.   Put Him to the proof!

THE GREAT CHANGE

That which occasions the honest Christian the most difficulty and distress as he seeks to ascertain whether a miracle of grace has been wrought within him is the discovery that so much remains what it always was, yea, often his case appears to be much *worse* than formerly—more risings of opposition to God, more surgings of pride, more hardness of heart, more foul imaginations. Yet that very consciousness of and grief over indwelling corruptions is, itself, both an effect and an evidence of the great change.   It is proof that such a person *has* his eyes open to see and a heart to feel evils which previously he was blind unto and insensible of.   An unregenerate person is not troubled about the weakness of his faith, the coldness of his affections, the stirrings of self within.   *You* were not yourself so while you were dead Godwards!   But if such things now exercise you deeply, if your eyes be open to and you mourn over that within to which no fellow creature is privy, must you not be very different now from what you once were?

But, asks the exercised reader, if I have been favoured with a super-natural change of heart, how can such horrible experiences consist therewith? Surely if my heart had been made pure there would not still be a filthy and foul sea of iniquity within me! Dear friend, that filth has been in you from birth, but it is only since you were born again that you have become increasingly *aware* of its presence. A pure heart is not one from which all sin has been removed, as is clear from the histories of Abraham, Moses, David. The heart is not made wholly pure in this life: as the understanding is only enlightened in part (much ignorance and error still remaining), so at regeneration the heart is cleansed but in part. Observe that Acts xv, 9, does not say "purified their hearts by faith," but "purifying"—a continued process. A pure heart is one which is attracted by "the beauty of holiness" and longs to be fully conformed thereunto, and therefore one of the surest proofs I possess a pure heart is my abhorring and grieving over impurity—as Lot dwelling in Sodom "*vexed* his righteous soul" by what he saw and heard there.

Then are we not obliged to conclude that the Christian has *two* "hearts" —the one pure and the other impure? Perhaps the best way for us to answer that question is to point out what is imported by the "heart" as that term is used in Scripture. In a few passages, where it is distinguished from the "mind" (I Sam. ii, xxxv; Heb. viii, 10) and from the "soul" (Deut. vi, 5), the heart is restricted to the affections; but generally it has reference to *the whole inner man,* for in other places it is the seat of the intellectual faculties too, as in "I gave my heart to know wisdom," etc. (Eccl. i, 17)—I applied my *mind* unto its investigation. In its usual and wider signification the "heart" connotes the one indwelling the body. "The heart in the Scriptures is variously used: sometimes for the mind and understanding, sometimes for the will, sometimes for the affection, sometimes for the conscience. *Generally* it denotes the whole soul of man and all the faculties of it" (J. Owen). We have carefully tested that statement by the Word and confirmed it. The following passages make it clear that the "heart" has reference to the man himself as distinguished from his body.

Its first occurrence is, "God saw that the wickedness of man was great in the earth and every imagination of the *thoughts of* his heart was only evil continually" (Gen. vi, 5). "Before I had spoken in my heart" (Gen. xxiv, 45) plainly means "within myself." It does so in "Esau said in his heart"— determined in himself (Gen. xxvii, 41). "Now Hannah, she spake in her heart" (I Sam. i, 13). "Examine *me,* O Lord, prove me: try my reins [motives] and my *heart*" (Psa. xxvi, 2)—my inner man. "With my whole heart [my entire inner being] have I sought Thee" (Psa. xxvi, 2). In the New Testament the "mind" often has the same force. On Romans xii, 2, C. Hodge pointed out, "The word *nous* ["mind"] is used, as it is here, frequently in the New Testament (Rom. i, 28; Eph. iv, 17, 23; Col. ii, 18, etc.). In all these and similar cases it does not differ from the heart, i.e. in its wider sense, for *the whole soul.*" Ordinarily, then, the "heart" signifies the whole soul, the "inner man," the "hidden man of the heart" (I Pet. iii, 4) at which God ever looks (I Sam. xvi, 7).

Now "the heart" of the natural man (that is, his entire soul—understanding, affections, will, conscience) is "deceitful above all things, and desperately wicked" (Jer. xvii, 9), which is but another way of saying he is "totally depraved"—the whole of his inner being is corrupt. And therefore God bids us "Circumcise yourselves to the Lord and take away the foreskins of your hearts . . . *wash thine heart* from wickedness [in true repentance from the love and pollution of sin] that thou mayest be saved" (Jer. iv, 4, 14). Yea, He bids men "Cast away from you all your transgressions . . . and make you a new heart" (Ezek. xviii, 31), and holds them responsible so to do. That man cannot effect this change in himself by any power of his own is solely because he is bound by the cords of his sins: the very essence of his depravity consists in being of the contrary spirit. So far from excusing him, that only aggravates his case, and compliance with those precepts is as much man's duty and as proper a subject for exhortation as is faith, repentance, love to God. So in the New Testament, "purify your hearts ye double minded" (James iv, 8).

"Make you a new heart." But, says the awakened and convicted sinner, that is the very thing which I am unable to produce: alas, what shall I do? Why, cast yourself upon the mercy and power of the Lord, and say to Him as the leper did, "If Thou wilt, Thou canst make me clean." Beg Him to work *in* you what He requires *of* you. Nay, more, lay hold of His Word and plead with Him: Thou hast made promise "A new heart also will I give you" (Ezek. xxxvi, 26), so "do as Thou hast said" (II Sam. vii, 25). It is a most blessed fact that God's promises are as large as His exhortations, and for each of the latter there is one of the former exactly meeting it. Does the Lord bid us circumcise our hearts (Deut. x, 16)? Then He assures His people "I will circumcise thine heart" (Deut. xxx, 6). Does He bid us purify our heart (James iv, 8)? He also declares "From all your filthiness and from all your idols will I cleanse you" (Ezek. xxxvi, 25). Are Christians told to cleanse themselves "from all filthiness of the flesh and spirit, perfecting holiness in the fear of God" (II Cor. vii, 1)? Then they are promised "He which hath begun a good work in you will finish it."

God, then, does not leave the hearts of His people as they were when born into this world, and as they are described in Jeremiah xvii, 9. No, blessed be His name, He works a miracle of grace within them, which changes the whole of their inner man. Spiritual life is communicated to them, Divine light illumines them, a principle of holiness is planted within them. That principle of holiness is a fountain of purity, from which issue streams of godly desires, motives, endeavours, acts. It is a supernatural habit residing in every faculty of the soul, giving a new direction to them, inclining them Godwards. Divine grace is imparted to the soul subjectively, so that it has entirely new propensities unto God and holiness and newly created antipathies to sin and Satan, making us willing to endure suffering for Christ's sake rather than to retain the friendship of the world. To make us partakers of His *holiness* is the substance and sum of God's purpose of grace for us, both in election (Eph. i, 4), regeneration (Eph. iv, 24), and all His dealings with us afterwards (Heb. xii, 10). Not that finite creatures can ever be participants of the essential holiness of God, either by imputation or transubstantiation, but only by fashioning us in the *image* thereof.

It is the communication of Divine grace, or the planting within us of the principle and habit of holiness, which both purifies the heart or soul, and which gives the death-wound unto indwelling sin. Grace is not only a Divine attribute of benignity and free favour that is exercised *unto* the elect, but it is also a powerful influence that works *within* them. It is in this latter sense the term is used when God says "My grace is sufficient for thee," and when the apostle declared "by the grace of God, I am what I am." That communicated grace makes the heart "honest" (Luke viii, 15), "tender" (II Kings xxii, 10), "pure" (Matt. v, 8). An *honest* heart is one that abhors hypocrisy and pretence, that is fearful of being deceived, that desires to know the truth about itself at all costs, that is sincere and open, that bares itself to the Sword of the Spirit. A "tender" heart is one that is *pliant* Godwards: that of the unregenerate is likened unto "the nether millstone" (Job xli, 24), but that which is wrought upon by the Spirit resembles wax—receptive to His impressions upon it (II Cor. iii, 3). It is *sensitive*—like a tender plant—shrinking from sin and making conscience of the same. It is compassionate, gentle, considerate.

In addition to our previous remarks thereon, we would add that a heart (or "soul") which has been made inchoately yet radically pure, and which is being continually purified, is one in which the love of God has been shed abroad, and therefore it loathes what He loathes; one wherein the fear of the Lord dwells, so that evil is hated and departed from. It is one from which the corrupting love of the world has been cast out. A pure heart is one wherein faith is operative (Acts xv, 9), attracting and conforming it unto a Holy Object, drawing the affections unto things above. It is one from which self has been deposed and Christ enthroned, so that it sincerely desires and earnestly endeavours to please and honour Him in all things. It is one that is purged, progressively, from ignorance and error by apprehending and obeying the Truth (I Peter i, 22). A pure heart is one that makes conscience of evil thoughts, unholy desires, foul imaginations, which grieves over their prevalency and weeps in secret for indulging them. The purer the heart becomes, the more is it aware of and distressed by inward corruptions.

The Puritans were wont to say that at regeneration sin receives its "death-wound." We are not at all sure what exactly they meant by that expression, nor do we know of any Scripture which expressly warrants it—certainly such passages as Romans vi, 6, 7, and Galatians v, 24, do not; yet we have no objection to it providing it be understood something like this. When faith truly lays hold of the atoning sacrifice of Christ the soul is for ever delivered from the condemnation and guilt of sin, and it can never again obtain legal "dominion" over him. By the moral purification of the soul it is cleansed from the prevailing love and power of sin, so that the lusts of the flesh are detested and resisted. Sin is divested of its reigning power over the faculties of the soul, so that full and willing subjection is no longer rendered to it. Its dying struggles are hard and long, powerfully felt within us, and though God grants brief respites from its ragings, it breaks forth with renewed force and causes us many a groan.

In our earlier days we rejected the expression "a change of heart" because we confounded it with "the flesh." The heart *is* changed at regeneration, but "the flesh" is *not* purified or spiritualized, though it ceases to have uncontrolled and undisputed dominion over the soul. Indwelling sin is not eradicated, but its reign is broken and can no longer produce hatred of God. The appetites and tendencies of "the flesh" in a Christian are precisely the same after he is born again as they were before. They are indeed "subdued" by grace, and conversion is often followed by such inward peace and joy it appears as though they were dead, but they soon seek to reassert themselves, as Satan left Christ "for a season" (Luke iv, 13), but later renewed his assaults. Nevertheless, grace opposes sin, the "spirit" or principle of holiness strives against the flesh, preventing it from having full sway over the soul. As life is opposed to death, purity to impurity, spirituality to carnality, so there is henceforth experienced within the soul a continual and sore conflict between sin and grace, each striving for the mastery.

While then it be true that there are two distinct and diverse springs of action in the Christian, the one prompting to evil and the other unto good, it is better to speak of them as two "principles" than "natures." To conceive of there being two minds, two wills, or two hearts in him, is no more warrantable than to affirm he has two souls, which would mean two moral agents, two centres of responsibility, which would destroy the identity of the individual and involve us in hopeless confusion of thought. "Take heed, brethren, lest there be in any of you an evil heart of unbelief, in departing from the living God" (Heb. iii, 12) would be meaningless if the saint possessed *two* "hearts"—the one incapable of anything *but* unbelief, the other incapable *of* unbelief. The Christian is a unit, a person with one heart or soul, and he is responsible to watch and be sober, to be constantly on his guard against the workings of his corruptions, to prevent sin hardening his heart so that he comes under the power of unbelief and turns away from God.

"Incline my heart [my whole soul] unto Thy testimonies and not to covetousness" (Psa. cxix, 36). This is another one of many verses which expose the error of a Christian's having two "hearts," the one carnal and the other spiritual, and making them synonymous with "the flesh" and "the spirit." It would be useless my asking God to incline "the flesh" (indwelling sin) unto His testimonies, for it is radically opposed unto them. Equally unnecessary is it for me to ask God *not* to incline "the spirit" (indwelling grace) unto covetousness, for it is entirely holy. But no difficulty remains if we regard the "heart" as the inner man: "incline *me* unto Thy testimonies," etc. The saint longs after complete conformity unto God's will, but is conscious of much within him that is prone to disobedience, and therefore he prays that the habitual bent of his thoughts and affections may be unto heavenliness rather than worldliness: let the reasons and motives unto godliness Thou hast set before me in Thy Word be made effectual by the powerful operations of Thy Spirit.

The heart of man must have an object unto which it is inclined or whereto it cleaves. The thoughts and affections of the soul cannot be idle or be without some object on which to place them. Man was made for God, to be happy in the enjoyment of Him, to find in Him a satisfying portion, and when he apostatized from God he sought satisfaction in the creature. While the heart of fallen man be devoid of grace it is wholly carried out to the things of time and sense. As soon as he is born, he follows his carnal appetites and for the first few years is governed entirely by his senses. Sin occupies the throne of his heart, and though conscience may interpose some check, it has no power to incline the soul Godwards, and sin cannot be dethroned by anything but a miracle of grace. That miracle consists in giving the soul a prevailing and habitual bent Godwards. The heart is taken off from the *love of* base objects and set upon Christ, yet *we* are required to keep our hearts with all diligence, mortify our lusts, and seek the daily strengthening of our graces.

Great as is the change effected in the soul by the miracle of grace, yet, as said before, it is neither total nor complete, but is carried forward during the whole subsequent process of sanctification, a process that involves a daily and lifelong conflict within the believer, so that his "experience" is like that described in Romans vii, 13-25. The Christian is not the helpless slave of sin, for he resists it—to speak of a "helpless victim" *fighting* is a contradiction in terms. So far from being helpless, the saint can do all things through Christ strengthening him (Phil. iv, 13). As a new object has won his heart, his duty is to serve his new Master: "yield yourselves unto God as those that are alive from the dead, and your members as instruments of righteousness unto God" (Rom. vi, 13)—use to His glory the same faculties of soul as you formerly did in the pleasing of self. The Christian's responsibility consists in resisting his evil propensities and acting according to his inclinations and desires after holiness.

The great change in and upon the Christian will be completed when dawns that "morning without clouds," when the Day breaks "and the shadows flee away." For then shall he not only see the King in His beauty, see Him face to face, but he shall be made "like Him," fashioned unto the body of His glory, fully and eternally conformed unto the image of God's Son.

WELCOME TIDINGS

God moves in a mysterious way His wonders to perform, yet is it not infinitely superior to any which our short-sighted policy would devise? For many years past we have prayed that God would "enlarge our coast" (I Chron. iv, 10), that a greater number of hungry souls might share with us some of the wondrous riches of His grace. Yet instead of our circulation increasing, it has decreased considerably from what it was twenty years ago. This has puzzled and exercised us, for all other requests concerning the magazine have been so manifestly granted. Only of late have we clearly perceived that the above has been no exception, though it has been realized mediately rather than directly. To illustrate: a reader asks, "What is your thought on a minister using your sermons almost *in toto?* We feel that perhaps it is a case of God's overruling for His own glory, and we rejoice to know that He has given you a sort of vicarious oral ministry when we least expect it. Your articles on —— are forcibly preached, and attended with great blessing. An acknowledgment of their source was given, albeit a bit belated." Thus, in supplying seed to other sowers our labours are being multiplied, and through the mouths of many ministers the substance of our articles is reaching thousands of people who do not read them. Our prayer-helpers will rejoice to know that this magazine is now being taken by over one hundred preachers! Each of the following is an excerpt from a different pastor's letter recently received by us.

"The members of the church of which I am pastor, and my wife, can testify to the fact that your efforts to help me have not been in vain. They know that since I began studying your writings and receiving your letters my ministry has been more spiritual and heart-searching" (Alabama). "For some time past I have been receiving your magazine. There are no words capable of expressing what they have meant to me" (Kentucky). "God has seen fit to richly bless my life and ministry through your writings" (Pennsylvania). "Your Studies have been read with real profit; your —— was very helpful in the preparation of a series of sermons" (Connecticut). "Your Studies have been a big help in showing me how to make my ministry one of the Holy Spirit, and not one of the flesh" (Tennessee). "I have never read any expositions that have brought such blessing, for which I thank God and you" (West Virginia). "I thank the Lord for your faithfulness, and your understanding of the needs of the times" (New Jersey). "Your works have been of unlimited value to my life and ministry" (Texas). "It is a wonderful strengthener to my faith to know there are still some teaching the same truth, only in a much better way than I by God's grace am striving to do" (Iowa). "I have again had much blessing and joy from your Studies" (Australia).

"I have received much blessing, and find your writings the richest and deepest so far in my Christian journey" (Canada).   "I can assure you that I am helped and encouraged, if rebuked betimes by your writings" (England).   "I am much impressed by the faithful level-headed exposition which you evince in your articles" (Glasgow).

One or two brief observations on the above.   (1) When God does not answer our prayers in the way *we* expect or in the direction in which we are looking to, that is no proof He has not already done so.   (2) Praise the Lord and take courage from those welcome tidings, and see in them an evidence that the earth is far from being given over to the Devil!—God will maintain a witness (in more places than one!) unto the end.   (3) We earnestly request the Lord's people to pray daily for those pastors: to our knowledge, some of them are already encountering opposition.   (4) Beg God to give us all needed grace and wisdom, for while ours is a glorious privilege, yet it entails unspeakably solemn responsibilities.

(continued from back page)

"Christian service," then, is the response made by a regenerate soul unto the Lordship of Christ, the voluntary and hearty subjecting of himself to His dominion, the carrying out of His revealed will.   In a word, it consists of *obedience unto God:* not merely in one particular or direction only, but in a full and entire obedience.   Christian service is a "running in the way of His commandments" (Psa. cxix, 35), an acknowledging Him "in *all* our ways" (Prov. iii, 6); and that calls for a diligent searching of the Scriptures, that we may ascertain the details of His will and discover those things which are pleasing or displeasing unto Him.   But am I not to "witness for Christ"? Certainly, but how? By your lips or your life? By your words or your works? "Let your *light* so shine" and light shines *silently,* though none the less effectively. We are to "*show forth* His praises" (I Pet. ii, 9) in the home, in the office, factory, shop, in the world, and unless we do so *there,* God will not accept what we do in the church. Only so far as our daily walk is regulated by Christ's precepts are we *serving* Him.

Most of the so-called "Christian service" which now obtains in the religious world is seen and heard of men, but much of the service which God has appointed His people is beheld by none but Himself. Most that passes for "Christian service" has a tendency to puff up with a sense of self-importance, but that which God assigns humbles, by a realization of how far short we come of measuring up to His standard. Much of the humanly invented "service" is wrought in the energy of the flesh, whereas that which God requires from us can only be performed by the enabling of His grace. Those activities now so prevalent in the religious realm occupy with the creature, but that service which God has enjoined fixes the eye on His glory.

N.B. It would be a real help to us when (D.V.) ordering our January and February copies from the printers if all new readers renewed for 1948 before this year is out!

pleasures" (Titus iii, 3), "the servants of corruption" (II Peter ii, 9) mean being the willing and *obedient subjects of* sin, lusts, corruption. A "servant" is one who is not at his own disposal, but is at the beck and call of another, having voluntarily yielded and agreed to do his bidding. It is thus we find him described in the Scriptures: "As the eyes of servants look unto the hand of their masters [for an intimation of their will], and as the eyes of a maiden unto the hand of her mistress, so our eyes wait on the Lord our God" (Psa. cxxiii, 2).

Such too is the New Testament description. Said the centurion, "I also am a man set under authority, having under me soldiers: and I say unto one, Go, and he goeth; and to another, Come, and he cometh; and to my *servant*, Do this, and he doeth it" (Luke vii, 8). Servants, then, are not in their own power to please themselves, but are under the control of another, to be employed entirely at his discretion. Now the Christian is *God's* "servant." He is so by purchase (I Cor. vi, 19, 20). He is so by covenant, having solemnly entered into a compact with God, to perform the duties of a servant that he may enjoy the privileges of one. He has recognized and yielded to God's claims upon him. Previously he was his own servant, fulfilling the desires of the flesh, gratifying himself. But upon his conversion he surrendered to the Lordship of Christ, took His yoke upon him, to henceforth submit to His rule over him and be subject unto His will in all things.

Thus to "serve the Lord" is not to do something *for* Him, as though we showed Him a favour, but it is to render something *unto* Him. It is to perceive His just requirement of me, to own His absolute authority, to dedicate myself wholly unto Him. It signifies that I take the place and honestly endeavour to discharge the obligations of a servant, and a "servant" is one who does as his Master bids him, who seeks to please Him and promote His interests. Above, we pointed out what "serving" mammon does not signify, let us now define it positively. To "serve" mammon is to love riches and make them my dominant quest, to devote all my faculties and energies unto the acquiring of the same. So to "serve" Christ is to love Him, to give Him the supreme place in my heart and life, to devote all my powers and strength unto the doing of what He requires and abstain from all He prohibits. Love to Christ is to be expressed in obedience unto Him: "If ye love Me, keep My commandments."

God glories in His people in this particular character: "My servant Moses" (Num. xii, 7), "My servant David" (II Sam. ii, 8), "My servant Job" (i, 8). As the saints glory in being able to say "my God," "my Lord," "my Saviour," so God glories in them as *His* "servants," because He has honour and pleasure by such. It is our honour to be God's servants, and He is pleased to consider Himself honoured by our *obedience*, yea more so than by our worship: "Hath the Lord as great delight in burnt offerings and sacrifices as in obeying the voice of the Lord? Behold [attend to this!], TO OBEY is better than sacrifice and to hearken than the fat of rams" (I Sam. xv, 22). He was supremely honoured when His own beloved Son took upon Him "the form of a servant." Said the Father, "Behold My Servant, whom I uphold; Mine elect, in whom My soul delighteth" (Isa. xlii, 1). And of what consisted the *service* of Christ? In ministering unto others, in dying for sinners? Incidentally, yes; but fundamentally and essentially in that He came not to do His own will "but the will of Him that sent Him" (John vi, 38), in that He "became *obedient* unto death" (Phil. ii, 8)!

(Continued on preceding page)

XXVI   SEPTEMBER 1947   No. 9

STUDIES IN THE SCRIPTURES

"Search the Scriptures." John v, 39

Publisher and Editor—ARTHUR W. PINK,
29 Lewis Street,
Stornoway, Isle of Lewis,
Scotland.

PRAYER SINS

We hope that this unusual title will startle some of our readers and shake them out of their complacency. The fact that it *is* unusual is a sad commentary upon the religious conditions of this age. Much has been written during our lifetime on the privileges and potency of prayer, considerably less on prayer as a duty and the conditions which must be met in order to be ensured of an answer; but scarcely anything on the sacredness and solemnity of prayer, particularly along the line of warning God's children against the sins they commit when "asking amiss" (James iv, 3). And yet a little reflection should convince the young Christian that here too the flesh needs to be mortified, the heart quickened, the understanding enlightened, if he is to pray *acceptably* unto God. The very fact that it is the Holy One he is to approach calls for the exercise of the utmost circumspection, lest he insult and offend Him.

In Psalm cxli, 3, we find David praying, "Set a watch, O Lord, before my mouth; keep the door of my lips." We wonder how many of our readers could—without looking it up—describe the context. Probably many of them suppose it is a petition asking God to curb our unruly tongues when in the presence of our fellows: that we may be restrained from the angry retort when provoked, kept from the evil of idle gossip, and tale-bearing, etc. Instead, the preceding verses are in no wise treating of our converse with men and women: something far more weighty and solemn is there in view, namely, the use of our tongues when engaged *in prayer*: see verses 1 and 2, and then connect verse 3. It is indeed permissible to make a wider application and use of verse 3, but its first and immediate reference is to our praying.

Who had thought it necessary to make *this* request in *such* a connection: that after asking "Let my prayer be set forth before Thee as incense" David should at once add, "Set a watch, O Lord, before my mouth"? Ah, dear reader, if the setting of that request comes as a surprise to us, does it not indicate what urgent need there is for us to *test* OUR ideas of "prayer" by the Scriptures? to re-examine the subject and have our thoughts thereon formed by the Word? If our tongues be so unruly when in the presence of our equals, is there no danger of them trespassing when we open our lips before the Most High? If our hearts need to be warmed, our faith strengthened, our minds

(continued on back page)

Important Notices

Please advise promptly of change in address, otherwise copies will be lost in the mails.

We are glad to send a sample copy to any of your friends whom you believe would be interested in this publication.

This magazine is published as "a work of faith and labour of love," the editor and his wife gladly giving their services free. There is no regular subscription price, as we do not wish the poor of the flock to be deprived. This does not mean that those looking for something for nothing may "help themselves." Those getting this magazine who are financially able and who receive spiritual help from its pages, are expected to gladly contribute towards its expenses; otherwise their names are dropped from our list.

Will those forwarding International Money Orders please have them made out to us at Stornoway, Isle of Lewis, Scotland. Checks (Cheques—Eng.) made out on U.S.A. Banks are not negotiable here, so please do not send them.

All unsigned articles are by the Editor.

CONTENTS

THE PRAYERS OF THE APOSTLES

45. I Thess. v, 23, 24

Five things claim our consideration when pondering this prayer. First, its *connection*: the opening "And" of verse 23 links it to that which precedes, and that, in turn, supplies help to an understanding of the petition here. Second, its *Addressee,* namely ,"The God of peace," the precise force of which requires to be ascertained and then appropriated by faith. Third, its *request*: that these saints might be "sanctified wholly," concerning the meaning of which there has been much needless difference of opinion. Fourth, its *design*: that the saints should be so sanctified that they might "be preserved *blameless* unto the coming of the Lord Jesus Christ," an expression which, admittedly, calls for particularly careful and prayerful examination. Fifth, its *assurance*: "Faithful is He that calleth you, who also will do it" (verse 24), which imports the apostle had no doubt but that God would grant his request and accomplish his design—a proof he had not asked for something which is unrealizable in this life by any of God's children. May the spirit of prayer be granted unto our readers as they seek to weigh what we have written in the balances of the Sanctuary.

First, *its connection.* One of the ablest of the Puritans said, verse 23 "Has no coherence or dependence with the foregoing, for the conclusion of the epistle doth begin here." With all due respect for that renowned expositor, we think his judgment was faulty on this occasion, failing to give sufficient consideration unto its opening "And." In this instance we much prefer the remark of another of the Puritans: "All the duties and graces enjoined in the foregoing verses belonged unto their sanctification, which though their duty, was not absolutely in their own power, but was a work of God in them and upon them. Therefore that they might be able thereto and might comply with his commands, the apostle prayed that God would thus sanctify them throughout" (J. Owen). The order followed by the apostle is significant: exhortation unto saints, supplication unto God—calling upon them to the performance of their several duties and then entreating God to further quicken them thereunto. Prayer was never designed to be a substitute for diligence in keeping God's precepts, but is a means whereby we obtain grace for obedient conduct. Diligent endeavour and fervent prayer are never to be separated.

As the apostle approached the end of this epistle he issued a series of short but weighty exhortations, the last of which was "Abstain from all appearance of evil" (v, 22). In the light of the verse immediately preceding that signifies, first, shun whatever savours of error. False doctrine is most dishonouring unto God and highly injurious to the souls of His people, and therefore is to be feared and avoided as the plague. God has warned us concerning those men who teach anything contrary to His eternal Truth, "their word will eat as doth a canker" (II Tim. ii, 17). But, second, evil practice as well as evil doctrine is to be refrained from and that, in the least degree, yea, the very semblance of it. He who would avoid great sins must make conscience of little ones, and he who would avoid both great and little ones must consequently shun also the very appearance of sin. Such things as vanity of apparel and a display of jewellery, bobbed hair and painted lips, still more immodest attire, betray an absence of that spirit which hates even "the garment spotted by the flesh" (Jude 23).

There is a real and close moral connection between "Abstain from all appearance of evil" and the exhortation immediately preceding: "Prove all things, hold fast that which is good" (verse 21). The word for "prove" signifies "examine, weigh, try" all things. Whatever you hear and read, whatever counsel you receive even from Christians, whatever course of conduct others follow and which you may be doubtful about, bring to the test of God's Word, and whatever survives that test "hold fast," and let not the sneers or frowns of men cause you to relinquish it. The more you make it a practice of measuring "all things" by that standard, the keener will be your discernment to detect whatever is opposed thereto: "through Thy precepts I get understanding: therefore I hate every false way" (Psa. cxix, 104). The latter cannot be said without the former: "I esteem all Thy precepts concerning all things to be right, and I hate every false way" (Psa. cxix, 128). Thus, it is only as we form the habit of "proving all things" and then "holding fast that which is good," that we are morally enabled to "Abstain from all appearance of evil."

On the other hand, our obedience unto "Prove all things, hold fast that which is good" does not render superfluous or needless our also heeding "Abstain from all appearance of evil," for no matter how well informed we may be from the Word, nor how strong may be our hatred of evil, there is still an enemy within ready to betray us. Therefore we need to spurn even the borders of evil and turn away our eyes from the very sight of it. If we do not, our souls will soon become receptive to the Devil's lies. "Corrupt affections indulged in the heart and evil practices allowed in the life will greatly tend to promote fatal errors in the mind; whereas purity of heart and integrity of life will dispose men to receive the Truth in the love of it. We should therefore abstain from all appearance of evil, from that which looks like sin or leads to it. He who is not shy of the appearances of sin, who shuns not the occasions of sin, who avoids not the approaches of sin, will not long abstain from the actual commission of sin" (Matt. Henry). So much then for the connection or immediate context of this prayer.

Second, *its Addressee.* "And the very God of peace sanctify you wholly," or more literally, "And Himself the God of peace may sanctify you wholly." This appellation of God was expounded by us in considerable detail when treating of Romans xv, 33 (in the June 1944 issue), so that there is the less occasion for us now to write upon it at length. Yet since few of our new readers have access to that article, we will repeat in substance what is most relevant to our present passage. There it was pointed out that the names accorded to God in the Scriptures make known to us His glorious being and character, and that it is by meditating upon each of them singly, by mixing faith with them, and by giving *all* of them due place in our minds, that we are enabled to form a better and fuller conception of what He is in Himself, and of the varied relations which He sustains unto us. We not only do Him a great injustice, but we are largely the losers ourselves if we habitually think and speak of God according to *only one* of His names. We need to ponder and make use of all the Divine titles if we are to form a well-rounded and duly balanced apprehension of His perfections and realize what a God is ours.

This particular title, "the God of peace," has at least a fivefold reference. First, it tells us what God is essentially, namely, the Fountain of peace. Second, it announces what He is economically or dispensationally, namely, the Ordainer or Covenantor of peace. Third, it reveals what He is judicially, the Provider of peace—a reconciled God. Fourth, it declares what He is paternally, the Giver of peace unto His children. Fifth, it proclaims what He is governmentally, namely, the Orderer of peace in the churches and in the world. It is with the last three our present passage has most to do. First, it respects God in His judicial relationship with His people. When they sinned in Adam a breach was made, so that God was legally alienated from them and they were morally alienated from Him. Though there was no change in His everlasting *love* for them, yet because of their apostacy from Him in the Adam fall, and because of their own multiplied transgressions against Him, God, as the moral Governor of the universe, could not ignore that awful breach, and as the Judge of all the earth His condemnation and curse rested upon them. The elect equally with the non-elect are "by nature the children of wrath" (Eph. ii, 3). and as long as they remain in unbelief they are under the wrath of God (John iii, 36), the objects of His penal hatred (Psa. v, 5), repulsive to the Holy One. But His wisdom devised a way whereby He could be reconciled to His alienated people.

That "way" consists of what Christ did for them, what His Spirit works in them, and what they are themselves made willing to do. Christ obeyed the precept of the Law on their behalf and suffered its penalty in their stead. Thereby the great Surety of the Church made complete satisfaction to God's justice, placated His wrath and established an equitable and stable peace. When Christ endured the curse of the broken Law, He "made peace [between God and His people] through the blood of His cross" (Col. i, 20), healing the fearful breach, reconciling the Divine Judge to them, establishing perfect and abiding amity and concord. In that way were *the Divine* interests secured. But more: He procured for His people the Holy Spirit (Gal. iii, 13, 14) and thereby adequate provision was made to meet *their* dire needs. Desperate indeed is their case by nature and by practice: dead spiritually, rebels against God, their minds enmity against Him, wedded to idols, in love with sin. But by the quickening and illuminating power of the Holy Spirit they are convicted of their wickedness, made willing to throw down the weapons of their revolt, flee to Christ for refuge and take His yoke upon them. Thereby do they respond to the Divine call " be ye reconciled to God " (II Cor. v, 20) and thus do they have " peace with Him " (Rom. v, 1).

Thus we see the appropriateness of this Divine title when the apostle was making request for the further sanctifying of the saints: the " God of peace " is the One who was pacified by the blood of Christ and reconciled to them when they turned from being lawless rebels and became loyal subjects of His government: the sanctifying Spirit being the surest evidence of their reconciliation to God. Proof of being brought into His favour objectively is our enjoyment of His peace subjectively. The intolerable burden of guilt is removed from the conscience, and we find rest unto our souls." But if that rest is to be *preserved* in our souls, we have to take the most diligent heed to our ways. If we are to enjoy communion with " the God of peace," then all details of our lives must be regulated by His Word. That calls for diligent watchfulness over our hearts, for sin—the arch-enemy of God—still indwells us. Sin it was which first turned the creature into a rebel against the Creator, and unless we daily mortify it in our affections, it will soon be said of us " your iniquities have separated between you and your God, and your sins have hid His face from you, that He will not hear " your prayers (Isa. lix, 2).

Our enjoyment of the *paternal* peace of God is conditioned upon our obedience to Him: " O that thou hadst hearkened to My commandments, then had thy peace been as a river " (Isa. xlviii, 18)—full and unbroken. Our enjoyment of God's paternal peace is conditioned upon our thoughts being filled with and our faith being exercised upon Him: " Thou wilt keep him in perfect peace whose mind is stayed upon Thee, because he trusteth in Thee " (Isa. xxvi, 3). Our enjoyment of God's paternal peace is conditioned upon our making it a practice to cast all our care upon Him: " Be anxious for nothing: but in everything by prayer and supplication with thanksgiving let your requests be made known unto God, and the peace of God which passeth all understanding shall keep your hearts and minds through Christ Jesus " (Phil. iv, 6, 7). The enjoyment of God's *governmental* peace in the local church is the fruit of an unquenched Spirit in its midst, by the exercise of love among its members, and by the maintaining a Scriptural discipline over it corporately. It is sin which produces strife and dissension among saints: " From whence come wars and fightings among you? come they not hence even of your lusts that war in your members? " (James iv, 1), and then communion with the God of peace is at an end.

Third, *its petition*. " And Himself the God of peace sanctify you wholly." For what did the apostle make request? Were not the Thessalonians already sanctified? Certainly they were, both as to their standing before God in Christ, and as to their state in themselves as indwelt by the Holy Spirit. Then precisely what was it that Paul sought on their behalf? Sanctification is many-sided, and unless we distinguish between its several aspects not only shall we have but a vague and blurred concept of the whole, but we shall entertain erroneous ideas of the same and bring our hearts into bondage. As it is more than ten years since we devoted any articles to this most blessed, deeply important, and yet little-understood subject, we will now indicate its chief branches. First, believers were sanctified by *the Father* from all eternity. " To them that are sanctified by God the Father, and preserved in Jesus Christ, called " (Jude i). Note well the order: they were " sanctified " before their preservation (i.e. from death in their unregeneracy) and effectual call. The reference there is to their eternal election, when in His decree the Father set apart His elect from the non-elect for His delight and glory, choosing them in Christ and blessing them with all spiritual blessings in Him before the foundation of the world. On that initial aspect of sanctification we will not dwell.

Second, all believers have been sanctified by *God the Son*. As that is little apprehended we will enter into more detail. Our sanctification by the Son, like that of the Father's, is not subjective but objective, not something we experience within, but something entirely outside of ourselves. By the redemptive sacrifice of Christ the entire Church has been set apart, consecrated unto, and accepted by God in all the excellency of the infinitely meritorious work of His incarnate Son. "We are sanctified through the offering of the body of Jesus Christ once for all . . . For by one offering He hath perfected forever them that *are sanctified*" (Heb. x, 10, 14). Those blessed statements have no reference whatever to anything which the Spirit does in the Christian, but relate exclusively to what Christ has secured for him. They speak of that which results from our federal oneness with Christ. They tell us that by virtue of the Sacrifice of Calvary every believer is not only accounted righteous in the courts of God's justice, but is perfectly hallowed for the courts of His holiness. The blood of the Lamb not only delivers from Hell, but it fits us for Heaven. It is the believer's relation to Christ, and that alone, which entitles him to enter the Father's House; and it is his relation to Christ, and that alone, which now gives him the right to draw nigh to God within the veil (Heb. x, 19).

The grand fact is that the feeblest and least-instructed believer was as completely sanctified before God the first moment he trusted in Christ as he will be in heaven in his glorified state. Said the Saviour on the eve of His death, "For their sakes, I sanctify Myself, that they might be truly sanctified" (John xvii, 19 margin), that is, that they might be really and actually sanctified, in contrast from the merely typical and ceremonial sanctification which obtained under the Mosaic dispensation. Christ was on the point of dedicating Himself to the final execution of the work of making Himself a sacrifice for sin; as the Surety of His people He was about to present Himself to the Father and place Himself on the altar as a vicarious propitiation for His Church. As the consequence of Christ's devoting Himself as a whole burnt-offering unto God, His people are perfectly sanctified. Their sins are forever put away, their persons are cleansed from all defilement; but not only so, the excellency of His work is imputed to them so that they are rendered perfectly acceptable unto God, suited to His presence, fitted for His worship. Priestly nearness to God is their blessed portion as the consequence of Christ's priestly offering of Himself for them. They have the right of access to God as purged worshippers.

"But of Him are ye in Christ Jesus, who of God is made unto us wisdom, even righteousness, and sanctification, and redemption" (I Cor. i, 30). Observe well that this verse is not stating what we are made by Christ, but what God hath made Christ to be unto His believing people: the distinction is real and fundamental, and to ignore it is to deprive ourselves of the most precious half of the Gospel. Christ is here said to be made four things unto us, or as the Greek more nicely discriminates, one thing [Wisdom], which is defined under three heads: the whole speaking of the Church's completeness in her Head (Col. ii, 10). It is what God has made Christ to be unto us objectively and imputatively. Christ is not only our righteousness but our sanctification, by the purity of His person and the excellency of His sacrifice being reckoned to our account. If Israel became a holy people [ceremonially] when sprinkled with the blood of bulls and goats, so that they were admitted and re-admitted to Jehovah's worship; how much more shall the meritorious blood of Christ sanctify us actually, so that we may draw nigh unto God with confidence as acceptable worshippers?   My ignorance does not alter the fact, neither does the weakness of my faith to firmly grasp the same impair it. My feelings and experience have nothing to do with it.   God has done it, and nothing can alter it.

"And thou shalt make a plate of pure gold and grave upon it, like the engravings of a signet, *Holiness to the Lord*. . . . And it shall be upon Aaron's forehead, that Aaron may bear the iniquity of the holy things which the children of Israel shall hallow in all their holy gifts; and it shall be always upon *his* forehead, that *they* may be accepted before the Lord" (Ex. xxviii, 36-39).   That presents to us one of the most precious typical pictures to be found in all the Old Testament.   Aaron, the high priest, was dedicated and devoted exclusively to the Lord.   He served in that office on behalf of others, as their mediator.   He stood before God as the representative of the nation, bearing the names of the twelve tribes on his shoulder and on his heart (Ex. xxviii, 12, 29).   Israel, the people of God, were both represented by and *accepted in* Aaron.   That was not a type of "the way of salvation," but respected the approach to God of a failing and sinning people, whose very prayers and praises were defiled; but whose service and worship were rendered acceptable unto the Holy One through their high priest.   That inscription "holiness to the Lord" on Aaron's forehead was a solemn appointment by which Israel were impressively taught that holiness became the House of God, and that none who are unholy can possibly draw nigh to Him.

Now Aaron foreshadowed Christ as the great High Priest who is "over the House of God" (Heb. x, 21).   Believers are both represented by and accepted in Him.   The "holiness to the Lord" which was "*always*" upon Aaron's forehead, pointed to the mediatorial holiness of the One who "*ever* liveth to make intercession for us."   Because of our federal and vital union with Christ, *His* holiness is *ours:* the perfection of the great High Priest is the measure of our acceptance with God.   Christ has also "borne the iniquity of our holy things": that is, He not only atoned for our sins, but made satisfaction for the defects of our worship.   Not only can nothing be laid to our charge, but the sweet incense of His merits (Rev. viii, 3) renders our worship "an odour of a sweet smell, a sacrifice acceptable, well pleasing to God" (Phil. iv, 17).   Thus are Christians enabled to "offer up sacrifices to God by Jesus Christ" (I Pet. ii, 5).   Christ is the One who meets our every need both as sinners and as saints.   In, through, and by Christ every believer has a flawless sanctification.   The Holy One could not look upon us with the least favour, nor could we draw near unto Him at all, unless He viewed us as perfectly holy, and this He *does* in the person of our Mediator.

A perfect holiness is as indispensable as a perfect righteousness in order for us to have access to, and communion with, the thrice holy God, and in Christ we have the one as truly as we have the other.   The glorious Gospel reveals to us a *perfect* Saviour, One who has completely met every need of His people; yet it is absolutely necessary that we mix faith with that good news if we are to live in the power and comfort of the same.   "Wherefore Jesus also, that He might sanctify the people with His own blood, suffered without the gate" (Heb. xiii, 12).   The precious blood of Christ has not only made expiation for the sins of His people, but it has hallowed and consecrated them unto God, so that He views them not only as guiltless and unreprovable, but also as spotless and holy. The blood of Christ not only covers every stain of sin's defilement, but in the very place of what it covers and cleanses, it leaves its own excellency and virtue. God sees us in the face of His Anointed, as perfect as Christ Himself, and therefore as both justified and sanctified. His oblation has restored us to the full favour and fellowship of God.

THE LIFE AND TIMES OF JOSHUA

25. The Memorials

The spiritual application unto Christians in New Testament times of what is narrated in Joshua iii and iv is of great importance and value, both doctrinally and practically; yet to derive the good of the same, faith has to be exercised and the conscience searched. The entrance of the ark of the covenant into the Jordan was a type of the believer's Surety submitting Himself to judgment and death. The stoppage of its waters as the feet of the priests stepped therein, was a figure of the wrath of God against the sins of His people having spent itself upon the person of their Substitute and great High Priest. Israel's passing over dryshod shadowed forth the wondrous fact that all who put their trust in Christ *and follow Him* are exempted from future judgment: that "There is therefore now no condemnation to them which are in Christ Jesus, who walk not after the flesh but after the spirit" (Rom. viii, 1)—it is by our changed walk that we evidence ourselves to be "in Christ" (i.e. that we are federally and vitally one with Him), as it is our "following" the Shepherd (John x, 4, 27) which proves ourselves to be His "sheep." Israel's emergence from the Jordan spoke of the Church's legal and spiritual resurrection. There is no reason to believe that the nation as such understood the typical import of these things, though probably the regenerate ones in it did so.

It is in the Epistles that we find the clearest and fullest explanations of the redemptive work of Christ and of the Church's interest therein. It is there we are told God ordained Him to be "a propitiation [appeasing sacrifice] through faith in His blood, to declare His righteousness . . . that He might be just and the Justifier of him which believeth" (Rom. iii, 25, 26). It is there we read that He was "delivered for our [believers'] offences and raised again for our justification" (Rom. iv, 25). Those are statements of fact and are addressed to faith. They have nothing whatever to do with our feelings, though, when the renewed soul receives them on the authority of God, his mind is filled with wonderment and awe, his conscience is quietened, and his heart rejoices. That Christ died in the room and stead of all who shall believe on Him is a truth apprehended more or less distinctly by all who have fled to Him for refuge, but that *they died* in and with Him is grasped by few of them. Yet that must be so: in the sight of the law the surety and those he answers for *are one*—when the substitute dies, the one in whose place he suffered is legally dead. One had supposed this was so obvious as to need no labouring.

When Paul declared "I am crucified with Christ" (Gal. ii, 20) he was not referring to an experience of soul or to indwelling sin having received its death-wound, but was stating the inseparable corollary of Christ's vicarious crucifixion. This is abundantly clear from the verse immediately preceding. "For I through the Law am dead to the Law [literally, "died to the Law"] that I might live unto God"—the Law can no longer condemn me and clamour for my death, for its claims have already been met, its curse been executed upon me, in the person of my Substitute. In Christ I suffered *penal* death—which is what *crucifixion* is. As the same epistle states, "Christ hath redeemed us from the curse of the Law, being made a curse for us" (iii, 13). Thus, "I am crucified with Christ" is a declaration which *every* Christian is entitled to make, for it is just as true of the feeblest believer in the family of God as it is of the strongest. All real babes in Christ, whatever be the amount of their knowledge, the degree of their faith, the measure of their attainments, are equally crucified with Christ so far as their standing before God is concerned. There is no truth revealed in the Word more important, more comforting, more assuring for us than that.

"He that is dead is freed from sin" (Rom. vi, 7), or as the Greek reads, "he who has died is justified from sin." The word rendered "freed" ("*dikaioo*") occurs forty times in the New Testament, and is translated "justify" or "justified" 37 times, "justifier" once, "be righteous" (passive) once, and "freed" once. Justification is a forensic term, the sentence pronounced by God (as the Judge of all) upon the believer in Christ: negatively, it signifies absolution from the guilt of every breach of the Law; positively, declaring of him righteous or entitled to the award of the Law. Justification admits of no degrees, and is the irreversible sentence of God. It pertains equally to every one who has faith in the Lord Jesus Christ: "by Him *all* that believe *are* justified [not will yet be] from all things" (Acts xiii, 39). Oh, what peace fills the soul when that Divine word is received with childlike simplicity! It is because the believer has died legally, died in the death of his Substitute, that he is acquitted from all guilt and condemnation, for death cancels everything. It is not that the believer ought to die to sin which is here in view, but that his death is an accomplished fact in the death of his Surety (see Rom. vi, 2). In the crucifixion of Christ he is, by faith, to see himself crucified too.

Not only did the Christian die legally in the death of Christ but he was legally resurrected when his Saviour emerged triumphant from the tomb. It was as the covenant Head of His people that Christ transacted throughout. It was as the Representative of His Church Christ both died and rose again, and therefore its members have a federal interest in the one as much as in the other. But if only a few of the saints have scarcely any apprehension of their judicial crucifixion with Christ, a far less number of them have any realization of their legal identification with the risen Christ. That His life is imparted to them at regeneration they understand, but that all the worth and worthiness of the Magnifier of the law and the Vanquisher of sin and Satan is even now imputed unto them, so that they are as acceptable unto the Judge of all as is Christ Himself, seems too good to be true; yet it is plainly revealed and announced in the Gospel. "Now if we died with Christ, we believe that we shall also live with Him" (Rom. vi, 8): that is, in a law-sense, i.e. a life of *justification*, joint-partakers of the Victor's reward —the consequence of which will be our future glorification.

What has just been stated above is the grandest part of the Gospel, but since it is so little grasped today, we must dwell upon it a while longer. The first half of Romans vi is to be regarded as a continuation and amplification of the second half of chapter five, where the apostle had set forth the basic truth of the *federal headships* of the first and the last Adam's: the one representing the many; the many participating in and sharing the consequences of the act of the one—true alike of what was done by both the first and "the second Man." As Adam's sin and guilt is justly reckoned ours, so Christ's death for sin and unto sin is also legally regarded as that of His people's. But more: the perfect obedience of Christ and His meritorious righteousness is also imputed to us, and in consequence, Christ's reward is also ours. Of those who receive "the gift of righteousness" it is averred they "shall reign by one, Jesus Christ" and "by the righteousness of One the free gift came *upon* [not "unto"!] all men [represented by Him] unto justification of life" (Rom. v, 17, 18). Those are the verses which explain "we shall also *live with Him*" of vi, 8—it is neither a subjective experience nor a future blessing, but an objective reality which obtains now for all believers, that is there in view.

"Now if we died with Christ, we believe that we shall also live with Him." The opening "Now" is not an adverb of time, nor is the "if" one of uncertainty, but the two conjoined (as in the Greek) are the drawing of an inference from the preceding statement, and have the force of "since" or "seeing that." Because we "died with Christ" and are therefore "justified from sin" (verse 8), "we believe"—not "we hope" for something yet future, but by faith in the previous fact conclude—that "justification of life" necessarily follows. The ground of faith's confidence is further amplified in the next verse: "knowing that Christ being raised from the dead, dieth no more." Christ's resurrection not only attested the validity of His atonement, but *our title* to the inheritance. His resurrection to die no more demonstrated the sufficiency of His obedience, for those who died in His death receive "abundance of favour and the gift of righteousness," which entitles them to "reign in life by Jesus Christ" (v, 17, 19). Christ's resurrection in the full complacency of God, crowned with immortal life, was the merited reward of His atoning death, and His people are "joint-heirs" with Him!

Alas, fundamentally important and incalculably precious as is the truth we have just presented, it is likely to be quite "above the heads" of many of God's little ones. For their own sakes, we entreat them to pause for a moment and cry unto God for enlightenment, and then make a special effort to gird up the loins of their minds as we endeavour to pursue the subject further. What did God mean when He said unto Adam "In the day thou eatest thereof, thou shalt surely *die*" and "the wages of sin is *death*"? If we are to give anything like a complete answer, must we not say, first, Adam died *legally*: that is, he fell under the condemnation and curse of that law which he had broken? Second, that he died *spiritually*: that is, his soul was alienated from God, and holiness was displaced by corruption. And third, that he exposed himself unto *eternal* death: that is, he would suffer for ever and ever in the lake of fire and brimstone unless a miracle of grace intervened and plucked him as a brand from the burning. Surely the simplest Christian is able to grasp that definition and see the need for that threefold differentiation.

That is precisely the threefold status and condition of every one of Adam's descendants: the second and third is uniformly acknowledged by all orthodox Christians, but the first has little or no place in their thoughts. That each of us enters this world a fallen and depraved creature, "shapen in iniquity and conceived in sin," and that each of us will spend eternity in Hell unless he be made the subject of a miracle of grace, is generally acknowledged; but upon the *why* this is so and upon the *how* a just God can thus order it, most Christians have a very hazy and inadequate idea. That we have all inherited our defiled and depraved natures from our first parents they know, but as to the Divine justice in their so doing they know not. To be born with a sinful nature is not only a terrible handicap. but it is also a penal infliction. It is not innocent creatures who are thus handicapped, but guilty ones who are so penalized. It is because we legally shared in Adam's offence—he being our federal head and representative—that we share his punishment. *We* sinned in Adam, and we legally died in Adam, and there-fore we enter this world under the curse of God, and thus with a depraved nature.

"The wages of sin is death, but the gift of God is eternal life in Christ Jesus our Lord" (Rom. vi, 23). As that "death" is threefold, so also is that "life." As death there first imports a death of guilt and condemnation, so the life we receive in Christ is a life of *justification from* guilt and condemna-tion—a life-in-Law, our sins put away, righteousness placed to our account. Second, as the former or legal death issues in a spiritual and experimental one, that is, the soul is polluted by sin and its faculties enslaved; so our life of justification is accompanied by a life of *regeneration* and sanctification, whereby the soul is (in measure) renovated, cleansed, and its faculties freed. Third, as sin exposes its subject unto eternal death, one of indescribable woe and suffering, so the life we receive in, through and from Christ will be consummated in everlasting glory and bliss. And again we say, surely the least-instructed saint with spiritual discernment is able to perceive the mean-ing of that threefold definition of "life" and recognize the needs-be for distinguishing between the life of justification (legal) the life of regeneration (experimental), and the life of glorification (eternal) which will be life indeed.

The all-important thing to recognize is that the life we have *in* Christ and then *from* Him is the counterpart of that death we have in and from Adam by virtue of the federal relations which Christ and Adam sustained to those they represented; and that since death came by *sin,* life came by *righteousness.* Unless we connect the life received from Christ at the new birth with His meritorious obedience, we not only rob Him of part of the glory and thanks which are His due, but we fail to recognize that the gift and operations of the Holy Spirit are the direct consequence of the Atonement—merited and obtained by Christ for His people. *Life* was explicitly announced in the Law as the promised reward held out to those who complied with its terms (Lev. xviii, 5), and such was proclaimed by Christ (Luke x, 28), and was twice appealed to by Paul (Rom. x, 5, Gal. iii, 11). So too, life—the very "life" promised by the Law to those who kept it—is offered in the Gospel to those who believe in Christ. Under the Law life was unattainable by fallen men; in the Gospel it is proffered as a free gift, yet the Gospel reveals that "life" is the product of "righteousness"—*see* Romans i, 16, 17; Gal. iii, 21; Rom. v, 21.

As that "death" which is the penalty of the broken Law consists of *its curse*—the enmity and wrath of a sin-hating God; so that "life," which is the reward of the fulfilled Law consists of *blessedness*—the favour and approbation of a righteous-loving God. Now that "life" of the Law's award, that blessing, was promised and pledged to Immanuel in the covenant as the reward for His perfect obedience (Psa. cx, 4; Isa. ix, 6, 7), and it was in anticipation of the same that He "endured the cross, despising the shame" (Psa. xvi, 8-11; Heb. xii, 2). Upon the completion of His work, Christ put in His claim for the reward, and God bestowed the same upon Him (Psa. ii, 8; xxi, 4-6!). And that "life" of the Law, that reward, belongs equally to Christ and those on whose behalf He transacted. It was not as a private person, but as the covenant Head of His people, as the "last Adam," as the Head of His Church, that Christ rose again, ascended on high, and was "crowned with glory and honour." It was as the Representative of His redeemed that Christ entered heaven: "whither the Forerunner is for us entered" (Heb. vi, 20).

The same wondrous truth is set forth again in Ephesians ii. "God . . . even when we were dead in sins, hath quickened us together with Christ" (verse 5). "Dead in sins" refers to a judicial state and not an experimental: it is not the absence of spiritual life, but our law-condition, dead *in guilt,* under sentence of death—condemned and cursed. Neither does the "quickening" refer to anything subjective or internal. It is *not* "quickened *by* Christ," for it is not our individual regeneration which is in view; but "together with Christ"—the corporate vivification of the whole Church when Christ was "quickened" (I Pet. iii, 18). It is our legal or justifying "quickening"—cf. Colossians ii, 13, where "quickened together with Him" is immediately defined as "having forgiven you all trespasses." But more: "And hath raised us up *together* and made us sit *together* in the heavenlies in Christ Jesus" (Eph. ii, 6)—the Church was resurrected and exalted in Christ as the Head of His people. Observe well the repeated "together"—the Head and His members. This was all true in the sight of God *before* our conversion, though, of course, we knew it not and derived no comfort from the same. The whole of Ephesians ii, 5, 6, relates to our standing before God, and not anything within ourselves.

What we have been setting forth is something more than a theological tenet, or even an exposition of little-understood passages. It is the fundamental, most blessed, yet most neglected part of the Gospel. The response which is to be made unto the same is stated in Romans vi, 10, 11, "For in that He died, He died unto sin once for all; but in that He liveth, He liveth unto God (in His acceptance and favour). Likewise reckon ye also yourselves *to be* dead indeed unto sin, but alive unto God in Christ Jesus our Lord." Christ's death removed the entire guilt and exhausted the full penalty of sin, when God "made Him to be sin for us (II Cor. v, 21). *Now* " He liveth unto God" as the Conqueror of sin, death and Satan, as being "justified from sin," as enjoying the unclouded approbation of God. He lives to make good all God's pleasure concerning His people, to secure the fulfilment of the whole of His purpose of grace regarding them. His death and resurrection has obtained a present title to and the future possession of eternal glory for all His redeemed. And believers are so related to Christ, are so federally and legally one with Him, that His death was their death, His life is their life.

Believers are not here bidden *to die* unto sin (by mortification), nor *to live* unto God (by sanctification)—*that* is found in verses 12 and 13; but are first called upon to "reckon themselves" *to be* dead indeed unto sin and alive unto God in Christ their Head. "Reckon" does not mean "suppose" or fancy, for God would occupy us with realities and not fictions; nor does "reckon" signify work yourselves up into a frenzied persuasion of the same. No, it means, regard yourselves as God describes you. Let your thoughts of yourselves concerning your standing before God's throne be according to the Truth testified of you. Since the Gospel declares that every Christian has, in Christ, died unto the guilt and penalty of sin, and has in Christ received the reward of the Law, let him "set to his seal that God is true" (John iii, 33). "Reckon ye also yourselves" to be so. The same Greek word for "reckon" is rendered "to account" in Romans ii. 26: "conclude" in iii. 28: "impute" in iv, 8. The same word is found again in Luke xxii, 37, "He [Christ] was reckoned [legally accounted] among the transgressors."

It is an unspeakable mercy that in the reckoning of God every believer is "dead unto sin" and it is of incalculable comfort when the Christian so regards himself. It is ineffably blessed that in the reckoning of God every believer is "accepted in the Beloved" and is received into His everlasting favour which is "life" indeed (Psa. xxx, 5), and it is to his indescribable joy when the Christian so regards himself. This "reckoning" is not to be based on any feelings or experience, but on the bare Word of God, for we are to walk by faith and not by sense. Romans vi, 11, means: maintain in your consciousness a firm conviction of your union with Christ, yea, your participation in all that He did and is now enjoying. Realize by faith your *identification with* the crucified and glorified Saviour. Do so at all times, and under all circumstances. God so regards you, and it is no presumption for you to do the same; yea, it is highly presumptuous, infidelity, not to do so. Unless you *do*, you cannot serve Him as you should—with freedom, confidence, joy and gratitude. Unless you so "reckon" or regard yourself, there can be no solid peace of conscience and abiding joy of heart. Credit God's Word and He will honour your faith.

In our last we sought to point out the typical significance of the two "memorials" which Jehovah erected to mark Israel's supernatural and triumphant passage through the river of death and judgment. In this we have endeavoured to indicate the spiritual application of those types unto the Christian, or rather have considered some of those passages in the Epistles where the antitypical truth of them is presented in doctrinal form. It is because that wondrous and glorious doctrine is so little apprehended today by the rank and file of God's people that we have devoted a whole article to the same. In our next, we purpose considering the practical teaching contained in Joshua iv.

N.B.—Those possessing the previous volumes of this magazine will find in the September, October and November 1942 issues three articles (entitled "Christian Resurrection") which treat of the same blessed subject dealt with in this one.

DIVORCE

One of the most unmistakable and tragic evidences of the moral decadence of our generation is the enormous increase in the number of divorces. During the last few decades they have literally multiplied. They are common to every strata of society, rich and poor, educated and illiterate alike. They are not confined to the young and immature, the more-experienced and middle-aged, or the elderly; nor is this pernicious phenomenon peculiar to the British Isles, but obtains just as extensively—and in the U.S.A. even more alarmingly—throughout the whole of Christendom. Such a widespread epidemic is proof of the ethical laxity and emotional instability which is now so rife, and it augurs ill for the near future. It is nothing less than a dishonest evasion, a refusal to face facts, which attributes this social scourge unto the last two *wars*, for any one who examines statistics knows that this malady was eating away at the roots of the nation long before 1914, though like many other diseases it has continued to spread through the body politic and is now "coming to a head."

Like many another social and physical evil which the world is now plagued with, this one is but the shadowing forth of what first obtained in the *religious* sphere. It is not sufficiently recognized that conditions in the ecclesiastical realm are quickly reflected in the secular and social, that what marks the latter, first characterized the former. Those bearing the name of Christ are the salt of the earth, but when the salt has lost its savour, it is thenceforth not only good for nothing, but there is no longer anything left to stay the unregenerate carcass from complete putrefaction. When the churches keep to the Divine Rule and its members walk in the path of God's precepts, a powerful influence for good—for morality and respectability, for law and order—is engendered by them; but when the Divine Law is flouted, then lawlessness prevails in the community. When the churches degenerate into social clubs and their members are naught but empty professors—preferring the movies, the dance and the card-party above the prayer-meeting—then they are "germ carriers" which spread disease.

Genuine conversion is an entering into a marriage covenant with God in Christ. It is the soul expressing its love for Him, giving up itself to Him (II Cor. viii, 5), and solemnly vowing to be henceforth ruled only by Him (Isa. xxvi, 13). It is a deliberate and hearty choice of the Lord to be his supreme Delight, his alone Lord, his grand End, his everlasting Portion, and a promising to be faithful unto Him and His interests. That is why the Gospel proclamation and offer is likened unto an invitation to a marriage-feast (Matt. xxii, 1-3, 11, 12). Hence the saints are said to be "married to Another" (Rom. vii, 4). The apostle used the same figure when expressing his tender solicitude and holy jealousy for the Corinthian believers: "I have [ministerially] espoused you to one Husband, that I may present you as a chaste virgin to Christ" (II Cor. xi, 13): he laboured to keep them faithful to their vows, with the unchilled first-love of their betrothal unto the Bridegroom. For the same reason, the grand consummation of redemption, when the Church enters corporately upon its glory-union with the Lord, is designated "the marriage of the Lamb," and She is spoken of as "His wife hath made herself ready" (Rev. xix, 7).

When those who profess to have "turned unto the Lord" forsake Him and go back again into the world and give their hearts unto idols, God charges them with having "transgressed His covenant" (II Kings xviii, 12), to have "dealt falsely in His covenant" (Psa. xliv, 17), and to have "broken His covenant" (Jer. xi, 10). Consequently, we find that the Lord frequently brought against Israel the charge of marital infidelity. "How is the faithful city [Jerusalem] become an harlot!" (Isa. i, 21). "O Ephraim, thou committest whoredom, Israel is defiled" (Hos. v, 3). "Because thou hast forsaken Me and cast Me behind thy back, therefore bear thou also thy lewdness and thy whoredoms" (Ezek. xxiii, 25). The same solemn indictment is brought against a New Testament company which bore the name of the Lord: "Ye adulterers and adulteresses, know ye not that the friendship of the world is enmity against God: whosoever therefore will [is determined to] be the friend of the world, is the enemy of God" (James iv, 4), which shows it is a *spiritual* adultery which is in view—a giving unto the world that love and devotion, time and strength, which the Lord alone is entitled unto.

As natural marriage is a solemn and sacred engagement which is not to be entered into lightly, constituting as it does a lifelong compact, much more should there be the most serious and self-searching deliberation before any one openly professes to be united to the Lord: hence we are bidden to first "sit down and count the cost" (Luke xiv, 28). Christ is most grievously dishonoured and "put to an open shame" by those who may have taken upon them His holy name and avowed themselves "Christians," and later cast off

His yoke, repudiate His sceptre, and return unto their wallowing in the mire. Yet for generations past Christendom has swarmed with such cases individually, while corporately the majority of the "churches" have walked arm-in-arm with the world; but Christ no longer owned them, regarding them as harlots. And the rot spread swiftly from the "religious" to the non-religious elements of society. The "churches" sowed the wind, and now the nations are reaping the whirlwind in an orgy of marital infidelity and immorality—a recent letter in *The Times* states, "the number of illegitimate births today exceeds a thousand a *week*"!

We do not propose to generalize or moralize any further upon the subject, but rather turn to the Holy Scriptures for information and illumination thereon, for many of the Lord's own people today are far from being clear as to exactly what are its real teachings upon the matter, nor are their ministers and instructors by any means agreed—some teaching one thing, others something quite different. Our design will be to supply answers unto the following questions. First, does the teaching of the New Testament differ from that of the Old Testament on this subject? Second, what are the Scriptural grounds for a divorce? or is there but a single one? Third, when the marriage bond is broken by the infidelity of one party, is the innocent one free—in the sight of God, we mean—to marry again? or is he or she henceforth shut up to a life of celibacy?

"And Adam said, This is now bone of my bone and flesh of my flesh: she shall be called Woman because she was taken out of man. Therefore shall a man leave his father and his mother, and shall cleave unto his wife, and they shall be one flesh" (Gen. ii, 23, 24). Here we have the ordination of the marriage institution in Eden before the fall, and the law concerning it Divinely fixed. "*Divinely* fixed," we say, for the Lord Jesus plainly averred that God Himself was the Author of that statement "Therefore shall a man leave his father and his mother and shall cleave unto his wife," for when replying to the Pharisees He said, "Have ye not read, that *He* which made them at the beginning, made them male and female, *and said,* For this cause shall a man leave father and mother, and shall cleave unto his wife" (Matt. xix, 4, 5). The Speaker in Genesis ii, 24, was the Creator, whether the instrument was Adam himself, or Moses at the time he wrote the book of Genesis: if the former, Adam spake by Divine inspiration, and prophetically, for at that time there were no "fathers and mothers."

It is clear then that Genesis ii, 24, was a Divine statute, and, being founded upon nature, an unalterable one. Originally Adam and Eve were one, for Eve was taken out of Adam and therefore it is said at their first creation "in the image of God created He *him,* male and female created He *them*" (Gen. i, 27). Later, by the formation of the woman (Gen. ii, 21, 22), the original one became two. But by marriage the twain became "one flesh," the nearest and dearest union there is in all nature—a Divinely ordained, a legally constituted, and an affectionately formed one. Marriage is a permanent and exclusive union between one man and one woman, and therefore can only be innocently dissolved by death. If ever there was any pretence for the necessity of a man's having more than one wife, it must have been in the days of Adam, when the earth was unpeopled, but the revealed will of God expressly forbade that. First, by His making only a single woman for Adam—creation itself teaches monogamy! Second, by this authoritative statement: "he shall *cleave unto* his wife."

The expression "cleave unto" is a very emphatic and decisive one, as appears from the fact of its being used of the duty involved in our covenant relationship to God: "But cleave unto the Lord your God, as ye have done unto this day" (Josh. xxiii, 8): they were to love Him with all their hearts, to be devoted exclusively unto Him (having no other "gods"), to seek His honour and promote His interests. In like manner is a man to cleave unto his wife. The Hebrew verb is "*debaq*" and is rendered "be joined together" in Job xli, 23, "abide fast" in Ruth ii, 8, "stick" in Ezekiel xxix, 4, "keep fast" in Ruth ii, 23. "Therefore shall a man leave his father and his mother, and shall cleave unto his wife" shows that the bonds of this Divine institution are stronger than those of nature, and intimates not only the nearness of the marital relationship, but its perpetuity. "They are one flesh" definitely prohibts polygamy. Thus was the Divine will concerning the regulation of the sexes and the manner in which the human race was to be propagated clearly made known at the dawn of human history.

In His comment upon that Divine statute in Genesis ii, 24, the Lord Jesus solemnly and authoritatively declared, "Wherefore they are no more twain, but one flesh. What therefore God hath joined together, let not man put asunder" (Matt. xix, 6), which proves that a valid marriage is not only of Divine institution but of God's own making: *He* joining the two together, to ever after have the same interests, and to share each other's comforts or sorrows, even as the members of the same body do. God Himself having yoked them together, each is to have the most conscientious regard to *His* act. In view of the Divine nature of this institution and act, no man, be he whom he may, has any warrant from God to separate man and wife, save only for the one reason specified by Christ, namely, adultery. "No man, or set of men, have any authority from God to dissolve this union, except in the case of fornication. Neither crowned heads, bishops, judges, peers, nor commons, jointly or separately, have any right to violate the laws of God. Jehovah has said the man and his wife are one, and whoever separates them insults God" (Wm. Gadsby, 1851).

"Marriage is not a temporary contract, like that between master and servant, but a union of a man and a woman for life. They cannot separate at their pleasure, or at the expiration of a definite period. They are bound to adhere to each other during the term of their natural lives, and neither of them is at liberty to enter into a new engagement without an offence against the law both of God and man. There is one cause, however, which may terminate the relation during their lifetime, namely, the sin forbidden in the seventh commandment. Adultery, whether committed by the husband or the wife, is a just ground for divorce. It is a direct violation of the marriage vow, giving the aggrieved party a right to demand the dissolution of an engagement which the other has broken, by retracting the pledge solemnly given at its commencement. You will observe, however, that adultery does not *ipso facto* dissolve the conjugal relation: it only invests the sufferer with a right to demand the dissolution of it from the competent authority; if the wife or the husband does not choose to exercise the right, things remain as they were" (Prof. John Dick).

Polygamy was Divinely reprobated from the beginning: by God's creation of but one woman for Adam and by His command for the husband to "cleave unto his wife"—therein He intimated His will for the regulation of the sexes and under what Divine sanction the human family should be propagated. But it was not long after sin had entered this world that men began to defy God's prohibition, for as early as Genesis iv, 19, we read "And Lamech took unto him *two* wives." It should be carefully noted that Lamech was one of the degenerate offspring of *Cain*, and that he was the *sixth* (not the seventh) generation from Adam! That evil example of his ensnared good men at a later date. Some have sought to excuse their sin, arguing that polygamy was virtually a necessity in the early generations of the race, when the earth was so thinly populated. But that is carnal reasoning and a presumptuous and impious inference, for the fact remains that God never authorized either Lamech or any of the patriarchs to take unto him a second wife. Moreover, it is to be carefully noted that whereas God gave orders for "sevens" of the clean beasts to be taken into the ark, He restricted Noah and his sons to their own sole wives!

Going back a little, a word needs to be said upon the matter of the propagation of the human race before the fall, and whether the sons of Adam procured their wives (their own sisters) without the sin of incest. The only writer we are acquainted with who has boldly and honestly faced this problem, and who has, in our humble judgment, dealt with it faithfully and truly, is the late Professor Dabney, of the Union Theological Seminary, Virginia. He rightly pointed out that, "The command to replenish the earth was given to Adam and Eve in their pure estate: which, had it continued, incest, like every other sin, would have been impossible. Who can deny, but that the marriages contracted between the sons and daughters of our first parents, after the fall, were sinful in God's eyes? It is not unreasonable to suppose that, thus, the very propagation of the human race, to which its present earthly existence under the mercy of God is due, began in sin and shame; that its very perpetuation is the tolerated consequence of a flagrant crime!" To which we will add only one remark: in view of *this,* how could the course of human history be different from what it has been? From such a foul spring, nothing but polluted and bitter waters *could* issue.

It is ever a delicate matter, and should be a painful one, for any of God's children to make reference to the failings of their brethren, the more so when they be far more eminent than ourselves in piety and fruitfulness. Though the Holy Spirit has recorded both the virtues and the vices of the patriarchs, yet the latter are to be regarded by us as a warning and not for our imitation. We should remember, too, that the best of men are but men at the best. Only One has walked this earth who remained "without blemish and without spot." That such men as Abraham and Jacob took unto themselves a plurality of wives or concubines may be accounted for perhaps—though certainly not excused—by their heredity and environment. Abraham, we know, was reared amid idolatry and in all probability spent the first half of his life among those who practised polygamy, and thus he "learned the way of the heathen" (Jer. x, 2). Nor were moral conditions in Canaan any better than in Chaldea, and Jacob and others were no doubt guilty of "following a multitude to do evil" (Ex. xxiii, 2). But the cases of Gideon, Elkanah, David and Solomon after the giving of the Decalogue, are harder to account for.

It has been pointed out by some writers who sought to extenuate this sin of the patriarchs that Scripture contains no record of God's reproving them for the same, and therefore it is very reprehensible for us to do so. But that is nothing to the point, for the argument from *silence* is much too precarious to build anything upon it: what *is* recorded in Holy Writ, and not drawing inferences from what is omitted, is our sole rule. Yet, while we do not read that God expressly admonished them for this offence, nevertheless His Word makes it clear that His providential frowns fell upon them for the same. Two things should be duly noted. First, that in the earlier instances some sin or other is specifically mentioned as being the occasion thereof. Thus, Abraham's taking Hagar was because of Sarah's unbelief

(Gen. xvi, 1, 2). And Jacob's taking Rachel to wife after Leah, and his own discontent arising from it, was occasioned by Laban's unjust dealings with him. His cohabiting with Bilhah was due to Rachel's inordinate desire for children; and his taking of Zilpah by Leah's ambitious desire of having the pre-eminence over Rachel and the number of her children (Gen. xxix and xxx).

Second, the displeasure of God upon this sin was almost always intimated by a breach of that peace which is so desirable a blessing in the family. Accordingly we read of an irreconcilable quarrel between Sarah and Hagar, and of Ishmael's hatred of Isaac, which the apostle calls "persecution" (Gal. iv, 29). The repeated contentions that existed in Jacob's family, the envy expressed by the children of one of his wives against those of another, are well known. We must therefore conclude that Isaac's example is rather to be followed in this matter, who had but one wife and who loved her better than the other patriarchs did theirs, whose love was divided among several. The opposition which one wife expressed to another appears in the case of Peninnah against Hannah—the wives of Elkanah (I Sam. i). In our articles upon the life of David we showed how heavily the chastening rod of the Lord came upon him and his household each time he took unto him an additional wife. The sorrows which Solomon brought down upon himself by his folly need no particularizing. Thus, the sad disorder in the households of those who kept a plurality of wives is obviously a beacon to those whose eyes are not blinded by prejudice.

Polygamy was clearly contrary to the Divine institution of marriage, and the jealousies and dissensions which it introduced into those families where we have mention of it, imports that such cases are recorded for our caution and not for our approval. In Leviticus xviii, 18 (see marginal rendering), Moses, in the code which regulated marriage, expressly prohibited the marriage of a second wife in the lifetime of the first, thus enjoining monogamy in terms as clear as those of Christ's. Throughout their ministrations the Prophets frequently gave instructions how a man was to treat his wife, but never his "wives"! But it is objected that polygamy was practised by men too spiritual and too much blessed and owned by God to be capable of continuing to disobey an express precept. But was not even "the sweet Psalmist of Israel" guilty of murder? and clearly the Decalogue forbid *that*! As one has truly said, "The history of good men, alas, shows us too plainly the power of general evil example, custom, temptation, and self-love, blinding the honest conscience" (Dabney).

Finally, attention must be called to Malachi ii, 14, 15. There the prophet was rebuking the sins of the Jews, and particularly those among them who were guilty of "dealing treacherously against the wife of his youth." There he points out, first, that marriage is a "covenant" (verse 14). Second, that the Lord had been "witness between" the guilty husband and the innocent wife. Third, he takes him back to Genesis ii, reminding him that God made but "one" man for "one" woman at the beginning (verse 15). Fourth, he points out that "God had the residue of the spirit" (verse 15), and therefore could have made Adam a dozen wives had He so pleased; but instead He has appointed man but "one" wife in order that "he might seek a *godly seed*" (verse 15), i.e., that his children might be maritally pure and not of different bloods, which polygamy prevents. Rightly did Thos. Ridgley (the best of all the commentators on the Westminster Confession) point out that the "godly seed" has reference to the "practice of their fathers, and *not* that the character of *godly* refers to the children, for they could not be said to be either godly or ungodly as the consequence of their parents having one or more wives."

THE DOCTRINE OF REVELATION
9. The Holy Bible

In the preceding articles we have called attention to some of the evidences which demonstrate the existence of God: as seen in the revelation which He has made of Himself in creation, in man himself, in His shaping of human history, and in the person of His incarnate Son. We turn now to that written communication which He has vouchsafed us, namely, the Scriptures, commonly designated "the Bible," which means "The Book," or more reverently "The Holy Bible"—the Book which is separated from and exalted above all others, the Sacred Book. Concerning it the Psalmist averred, "Thou hast magnified Thy Word above all Thy name" (Psalm cxxxviii, 2): that is, beyond all previous manifestations of the Divine Being. In the Holy Scriptures God has made a full discovery of Himself and a complete disclosure of His will. There His glories are set forth in their meridian clarity and splendour. The Word is a glass in which the character and perfections of God may be seen, and in order to become better acquainted with Him we need to more diligently peruse the same. Alas that so very few of this generation do so. Alas that so many preachers discourage such a duty.

Nearly forty years ago, in one of our earliest publications, we wrote: "To all who are acquainted with the spiritual conditions of our day it is apparent that there is being made at this time a determined attempt to set aside the authority of the Bible. In the press, the pulpit and the pew, its Divine Authorship is being questioned and denied. The Serpent's words to Eve, "Yea, hath God said?" are being heard in every quarter of Christendom. The ancient "landmarks" of our fathers are being abandoned, the foundations of our religion undermined, and for the most part the Bible is no longer regarded as the Word of God.

"In every age the Bible has been the object of attack and assault: every available weapon in the Devil's arsenal has been used in the effort to destroy the Temple of God's Truth. In the first days of the Christian era the attack of the enemy was made openly—the bonfire being the chief instrument of destruction. But in these 'last days' the assault is made in a more subtle manner, and comes from a more unexpected quarter. The Divine origin of the Scriptures is now disputed in the name of 'Scholarship' and 'Science,' and that too by those who profess to be the friends and champions of the Bible. Much of the learning and theological activities of the hour are concentrated in the attempt to discredit and destroy the accuracy and authority of God's Word, the result being that thousands of nominal Christians are plunged into a sea of doubt and tossed about by every wind of the destructive 'Higher Criticism.' Many of those who are paid to stand in our pulpits and defend the Truth of God are now the very ones engaged in sowing the seeds of unbelief and destroying the faith of those to whom they minister."

Today we behold some of the fearful crops which have resulted from that evil sowing: "some of," we say, for it is greatly to be feared that the *full* harvest does not yet appear. Shocking and appalling is the situation which is already spread before us. It has become increasingly evident, even to many who make no pretensions unto spirituality, that the restraining hand of God has been more and more removed from the world, till a spirit of utter law-lessness and recklessness now possesses a large proportion of mankind. But only those with an anointed eye can perceive *why* this is so, namely because the influence formerly exerted by God's Word was suppressed. The majority of church-goers of the preceding generations had instilled into them doubts upon the authenticity of Holy Writ: theological professors and "up-to-date" preachers openly denied its supernatural character. Once the awe-inspiring authority of God's Word was removed, the most potent bridle upon the lusts and passions of the masses was gone. Where there is no longer any fear of Divine judgment after death, what is left to curb the activities of sin?

The present state of society is due to the infidelity of "the churches" during the past century, and the apostasy of Christendom began by losing its grip upon the basic truth of the Divine inspiration of the Scriptures; and there is no hope whatever of Christendom being recovered from its present corrupt condition and woeful plight until it regains that grip, until it recognizes and avows that the Bible is a messenger from Heaven, a direct communication from God, imperiously demanding complete subjection of conscience to its authority and total subjugation of the mind and will to its requirements. It has there-fore become the imperative duty of God's servants to put first things first: to affirm with clarion voice the Divine inspiration and authority of the Holy Bible, to present to their hearers some of the many "infallible proofs" by which it is authenticated, that they may "know the certainty of those things" (Luke i, 4) wherein they are instructed. Thereby God Himself will be honoured, a sure foundation laid for faith to rest upon, the only specific provided for the disease of materialism and infidelity, and the alone barrier against the inroads of Romanism.

There is not a shadow of doubt in our mind that Rome was behind the "Higher Criticism" movement of last century, just as she was of the introduc-tion and spread of Arminianism in England (through Laud) shortly after the Reformation. The Papacy was shrewd enough to recognize that the authority of God's Word must be undermined and its influence upon the nation weakened, before she had any hope of bringing it within her deadly toils. There is nothing she hates and dreads so much as the Bible, especially when it is circulated among the common people in their own tongue, as was clearly shown in the days of queen Mary, of infamous memory. The organization of the Bible Societies, with their enormous output, was a rude shock to Rome, but she promptly countered it through "Modernism," by discrediting the inerrancy of the Scriptures. The promulgation of the so-called "Higher Criticism" has done far more for the spread of infidelity among the masses than did the coarse blasphemies of Tom Paine; and it is among those who have no settled convictions that Rome wins most of her converts!

Now the most effective way to oppose error is to preach the Truth, as the way to dispel darkness from a room is to let in or turn on the light. Satan is well pleased if he can induce those whom God has called to expound His Law and proclaim His Gospel to turn aside and seek to expose the fallacies of the various cults and isms. When the disciples of Christ informed Him that the Pharisees were offended at His teaching, He bade them, "Let them alone: they be blind leaders of the blind" (Matt. xv, 14)—waste no time upon them. When the servants of the Householder asked permission to remove the tares which His enemy had sown in His field, He *forbade* them (Matt. xiii, 29). The business of Christ's ministers is to sow, and continue sowing, the good Seed, and not to root up tares! Their work is to be a positive and constructive one, and not merely a negative and destructive thing. Their task is to "preach the Word" (II Tim. iv, 2), faithfully and diligently, in dependency upon the Spirit, looking to God for His blessing upon the same. And what is so urgently needed today is, that they proclaim with earnest conviction "All Scripture is given by inspiration of God" (II Tim. iii, 16).

That claim is no empty one, but rather one that is attested by unimpeachable witnesses and verified by incontrovertible evidence. It bears in it and upon it the infallible tokens of its Divine origin, and it is the bounden duty and holy privilege of God's servants to present, simply and convincingly, some of the various and conclusive evidence which demonstrates the uniqueness of the Bible. They cannot possibly engage in a more important and needed task than in seeking to establish their hearers in the Divine inspiration of the Scriptures, for it is of the greatest possible moment they should be thoroughly settled in that truth. The human mind cannot engage itself with any inquiry more momentous than this: "Has the Bible come from God? Is it a Divine revelation and communication addressed unto us personally from our Maker?" If it is, then it has claims upon us such as are possessed by no other writings. If it is not, then it is a wicked imposture, utterly unworthy of our serious consideration. Those are the sole alternatives. Hence, this is "the doctrine of doctrines: the doctrine that teaches us all others, and in virtue of which alone they are doctrines" (Gaussen).

Before we call attention to some of the abundant and varied evidence which makes manifest the Divine inspiration of the Scriptures, perhaps we should meet an objection which a few may be inclined to raise: Is it not largely a waste of time for you to furnish demonstration of a truth which no genuine Christian doubts? We do not think so. All of God's people are not equally well established. and in any case faith cannot have too firm a foothold, especially in a day when the tide of infidelity is seeking to sweep everything away into the sea of scepticism. It is good for Christians themselves to be more fully assured that they have not followed "cunningly devised fables," but have an unmistakable "Thus saith the Lord" as the foundation of all their hopes. Moreover, as another has pointed out, "Faith needs food as well as foothold, and it is upon these Divine verities, so plainly revealed and so clearly established in the Word of Truth, that faith finds its choicest provision."

Further, these evidences are of value to the Christian in that they enable him to give an intelligent and rational answer to those who inquire after knowledge. God requires His people to "be ready always to give an answer to every man that asketh you a reason of the hope that is in you, with meekness and reverence" (I Pet. iii, 15). Thus we must be able to reply to any who seriously ask us, Wherefore do you believe the Bible to be the Word of God? But our chief desire and design will be to furnish young preachers with material to use in sermons, aimed at resolving the perplexities and removing the doubts which perturb not a few of their hearers, and so counter and nullify the infidelities of modern "education." Yet here again we must anticipate an objection: Since the regenerate alone are capable of discerning spiritual things, why attempt to convince the unregenerate that the Bible is a Divine book? If faith be the sole ear competent to hear the voice of God, why try to reason with unbelievers?

While it be true that no arguments, however convincing in themselves, can remove the veil of prejudice from the understanding of the unregenerate or convert the heart unto God, yet that is far from allowing that such means possess no value .It has often been said by good men that the Scriptures are addressed to *faith*. That is true, yet only a part of the truth, for if it were taken absolutely, it must follow they are not addressed to any devoid of faith, which is a palpable error. Our Lord bade the sceptical Jews "search the Scriptures," and declared " He that rejecteth Me and receiveth not My words hath one that judgeth him: the Word that I have spoken the same shall judge him in the last day" (John xii, 48), thereby showing plainly the natural man is under binding obligations to heed and be subject unto the Word! The fact is that the Word is addressed to man as a rational creature, as a moral agent, as a responsible being, and it carries its own evidence—evidence which is addressed both to the reason and conscience.

"These arguments are such as are able of themselves to beget in the minds of men—sober, humble, intelligent and unprejudiced—a firm opinion, judgment and persuasion that the Scripture doth proceed from God" (J. Owen). They are evidences which show the irrationality of infidelity, and render those faced with them without excuse for rejecting the same. They are such as nothing but perverse prejudice can restrain men from assenting thereto. It is a fact that of those who have written against the Bible not one has soberly and seriously undertaken to refute the evidence which they knew had been adduced for the veracity of its history, the fulfilment of its prophecies, the reality of its miracles, and the purity and consistency of its doctrine. They close the mouths of gainsayers. Such arguments afford relief to the mind from the objections of sceptics, for if weighed impartially they must produce a moral assurance of the truth of Scripture. Thus they dispose the mind to approach the Bible with confidence and pave the way for receiving it as God's Word.

Such arguments go to show that Christians are not a company of credulous simpletons, but have good reason for their faith. They are a means of strengthening and stablishing those who have accepted the Bible on less satisfactory grounds. Few look farther than human authority and public countenance. The majority believe the Scriptures in the same way as Mohammedans do the Koran: because it is the tradition of their fathers. But wisdom is to be justified of her children, so that they walk in her ways by a rational choice. When the Spouse is asked "What is thy Beloved more than another beloved?" (Song of Sol. v, 9), she is not backward in making reply; and when the worldling asks "What is your Bible above what the heathen appeal to in support of their superstitions," we should be able to give an intelligent answer.

Nevertheless some are still apt to conclude it is useless to enter into such a discussion, insisting that the Bible is to be believed and not argued about, that arguments at best will only produce a human faith. But it is not a thing to be despised if we can prepare the young to *respect* God's Word, and then seek the Spirit's confirmation. Sometimes a human faith makes way for a Divine. The testimony borne by the woman from the well issued in that very sequel: "Now we believe, not because of thy saying, but we have heard Him ourselves and know that this is indeed the Christ, the Saviour of the world" (John iv, 39, 42). It is much to be thankful for when we can persuade people upon good grounds that the Bible is the Word of God, so that they are induced to make trial of it for themselves, for often that leads to their obtaining an experimental verification from the Holy Spirit. The revelation which God has made of Himself unto mankind through His wondrous works, both in creation and in providence, are addressed unto their reasoning faculty, and render them without excuse for their unbelief of His existence. Equally so is the more complete discovery of Himself which God has given to the world in His written Word addressed to the intelligence and conscience of those favoured with it, and therefore will it in the Day to come condemn all who refused to conform unto the Divine will as it is there made known to them. Hence it behoves preachers to press the inerrancy and Divine authority of the Holy Bible.

(Continued from back page)

the first things which enter our minds. If the seraphim veil their faces when standing before the Lord of hosts, what reason have we fallen creatures to exercise humility, godly fear, and spiritual propriety when supplicating Him!

5. *The preferring of carnal requests.* Some affirm that the promise of Christ in John xiv, 13, 14, is a " blank cheque " which He has placed in the hands of believers, that " they may fill it in for what they please, and that God stands pledged to honour the same." But that is a horrible perversion of a sacred ordinance. God has not appointed prayer as a means by which we may satisfy our corrupt affections. " Ye ask, and receive not, because ye ask amiss, that ye may consume it upon your lusts " (James iv, 3). To pray for long life that we may enjoy the world, for prosperity in business that we may improve our social status, for wealth that we may gratify our vanity, is " to ask amiss." We may pray for spiritual things from carnal motives and with fleshly ends: as to request more light from the Word that our personal reputation may be advanced, or for more grace that we may cut a better figure before fellow Christians. Unless we have the glory of God in view, our motives and designs are carnal.

6. *The exercise of self-will.* The chief design of prayer is to bring our hearts into conformity to God. " If we ask anything according to His will, He heareth us " (I John v, 14). The bending of the knee before God imports the attitude of soul which He requires from us, namely, that of humble dependence and acknowledged subserviency. The Throne of Grace is available to suppliants and not dictators. To ask God for something which His Word nowhere warrants, or to insist that He regulate His providences according to my behests, is rank self-will. Much of the so-called praying of this degenerate age is nothing but blatant impudence and presumption. It is not only impious but dangerous to insist that God should grant our selfish requests. Remember the case of Israel: " He gave them their request, *but* sent leanness into their soul " (Psa. cvi, 15).

7. *The utterances of unbelief.* There is little need for us to say much upon this point. " But let him ask in faith, nothing wavering: for he that wavereth is like a wave of the sea driven with the wind and tossed. For let not that man think that he shall receive anything of the Lord " (James i, 6, 7). To " ask in faith " is to exercise confidence in God, to be assured of the lawfulness of the thing requested, to plead and rely upon the merits of Christ, to believe that God will assuredly give that which will be most for His glory and our real good. To " waver " is to give way to doubting, to question God's goodness and faithfulness; and certainly He will not place a premium on that. What need has both writer and reader to beg God " keep the door of my lips " that I commit not any of the prayer-sins mentioned above!

informed, in order to pray aright, does not our speech also need to be directed and *curbed*? Let us now point out some of the more common sins. "Keep the door of my lips" from:

1. *The surgings of pride.* The case of the Pharisee in Luke xviii is a lasting warning against self-gratulation in prayer. But there are other forms of phariseeism besides prating of our good works. One is, "for a show make long prayers" (Luke xx, 47). That, of course, has reference to praying in public, and it is *there* we most need to be on our guard against the workings of pride. To be called upon to pray in the assembly presents a very real test of character and a powerful temptation to sin. Unless such an one is exceedingly careful, he will find himself praying to the congregation rather than to the Lord. It is natural he should wish to make a good impression and convince his fellows of his piety, but nature must be bridled when we are engaged in holy exercises. It is a horrible mocking of God when under the guise of pouring out our hearts before Him we are really seeking to further our reputation before men; as it is also to weary the brethren when he makes "long prayers." It takes grace and courage to pray briefly when called upon to pray in public.

2. *The making of ill-considered pledges unto God.* How many a one upon a bed of sickness or in severe straits has promised God certain things if He would deliver him, only to fail in the actual performance. Even in our dealings with men, we should think well before we speak, and be very slow in engaging ourselves for the future; much more should we be cautious in making commitments with God. "Better is it that thou shouldest not vow, than that thou shouldest vow and not pay" (Eccl. v, 5). "Holy resolutions to do the will and work of God should be taken up in the strength of Divine grace; but to vow this or that or the other thing, had best be left alone" (John Gill). Scripture supplies a number of warnings, especially so the New Testament, against making rash promises and vows to God. Jephthah (Judges xi, 30, 31), Herod (Matt. xiv, 7, 8), Ananias and Sapphira (Acts v), the band of Jews (Acts xxiii, 12). Make no hasty promises or pledges unto God.

3. *The language of insincerity.* Not only should we think before we speak, but make sure that our words express the real desires of our souls. The great Searcher of hearts cannot be imposed upon by pretences of piety. Of old He complained, "This people draweth nigh unto Me with their mouth, and honoureth Me with their lips, but their heart is far from Me" (Matt. xv, 8). To ask God for something we do not feel the lack of, to simulate fervour by raising our voices, to multiply words in order to fill in the time, is to mock Him. To mechanically repeat some form of prayer, or to coldly utter stated petitions, is a species of hypocrisy and a grave affront unto the Omniscient One. Against such sins we need to earnestly beg God to "keep the door of our lips."

4. *The spirit of irreverence.* There is indeed a very real difference between holy intimacy with God and freedom of utterance before Him, and unholy familiarity, nevertheless it is sadly easy for the former quickly to degenerate into the latter. God is clothed with infinite majesty and is ineffably holy, and it ill becomes a worm of the earth to approach and address Him as though it was His equal. "Serve the Lord with fear and rejoice with trembling" (Psa. ii, 11) is the injunction He has laid upon us. It is not only indecorous but impious to rush unto the Throne of Grace without due realization of the August One occupying it, and there gabble off

(Continued on preceding page)

XXVI   OCTOBER 1947   No. 10

STUDIES IN THE SCRIPTURES

"Search the Scriptures." *John v, 39*

Publisher and Editor—ARTHUR W. PINK,
29 Lewis Street,
Stornoway, Isle of Lewis,
Scotland.

PRAYER SIGHS

Those who are unconscious of and unconcerned about the sins which they commit when at their devotions will not be able to enter into the meaning of this piece, for it treats of that which is quite foreign to their experiences. But they who make conscience of the surgings of pride, the promptings of carnality, the workings of unbelief, and the exercise of self-will when supplicating the Lord, will, if He deigns to bless it unto them, find here something to help and comfort them. "The heart knoweth its own bitterness, and a stranger doth not intermeddle with his joy" (Prov. xiv, 10). Each regenerate person has deep exercises of soul and painful pangs of heart which those dead in trespasses and sins have no acquaintance with; yet have they their own peculiar hopes, comforts and delights, which strangers to Christ know nothing of. Those exercises of soul and pangs of heart find expression in sighs and sobs, in moans and groans, yet such as mere nature never produced.

The word "sigh" has a much stronger force in its Scriptural usage than in our ordinary conversation or, we should say, in more modern speech, for three hundred years ago it signified a lament rather than a mark of peevishness. Though not quite so intense as a "groan," yet it approximates very closely thereto, as appears from the fact that the Hebrew *anach* is translated both "sigh" and "groan," as also is the Greek word *stenazo*. Its first occurrence at once intimates its force: "and the children of Israel sighed by reason of the bondage" (Ex. ii, 23), the meaning of which is explained in the next verse: "And God heard their groaning." Their "sighing" expressed their suffering and sorrow under the oppression of their Egyptian taskmasters. So again, we read that the sorely afflicted Job declared "For my sighing cometh before my meat, and my roarings are poured out like the waters" (iii, 24). So by prayer sighs we intend those agitations and breathings of soul which are virtually synonymous with groans.

A "sigh" is an inarticulate declaration, an indistinct cry for deliverance. The saints are sometimes so opposed and troubled that they cannot find language suited to their emotions: where words fail them, the thoughts and feelings of their hearts find expression in sighs and cries. The workings of a Christian's heart under the pressure of indwelling sin, the temptations of Satan, the opposition of the ungodly, the burden of uncongenial society,

(continued on back page)

Important Notices

Please advise promptly of change in address, otherwise copies will be lost in the mails.

We are glad to send a sample copy to any of your friends whom you believe would be interested in this publication.

This magazine is published as "a work of faith and labour of love," the editor and his wife gladly giving their services free. There is no regular subscription price, as we do not wish the poor of the flock to be deprived. This does not mean that those looking for something for nothing may "help themselves." Those getting this magazine who are financially able and who receive spiritual help from its pages, are expected to gladly contribute towards its expenses; otherwise their names are dropped from our list.

Will those forwarding International Money Orders please have them made out to us at Stornoway, Isle of Lewis, Scotland. Checks (Cheques—Eng.) made out on U.S.A. Banks are not negotiable here, so please do not send them.

All unsigned articles are by the Editor.

CONTENTS

THE PRAYERS OF THE APOSTLES

46. I Thessalonians v, 22-24

The word "sanctify" has a twofold meaning: primarily, it signifies the bare setting apart of a thing. In Scripture it usually, though not always, has reference to setting apart unto a sacred use, as the seventh day to be the Sabbath. Exceptions are found in such passages as Isaiah lxvi, 17, where we read of men setting themselves apart to do evil, and Isaiah xiii, 3, where the Lord terms the Medes "My sanctified ones" when about to employ them in the destruction of Babylon. In the majority of cases in the Old Testament to "sanctify" means to separate some object from a common use to a sacred one, consecrating the same unto God, yet without any change being effected in the object itself, as with all the materials and vessels used in the tabernacle. But in its secondary meaning (not "secondary" in importance, but as a derivative) "sanctify" is used in a moral sense, signifying *to make holy,* rendering what was set apart *meet* for the end designed: first by a cleansing (Ex. xix, 10), second by an anointing or equipping (Ex. xxix, 36). In the case of God's elect, to sanctify is to change or purify their dispositions, which brings us to the third main branch of our subject.

The Father's sanctification of His people in His eternal decree and the Church's sanctification in and by the Son federally and meritoriously is made good to and in them personally by God the Spirit: "being sanctified by the Holy Spirit" (Rom. xv, 16). It is not until the Comforter takes up His abode in their heart that the Father's "will" (Heb. x, 10) begins to be actualized and the Son's "blood" (Heb. xiii, 12) evidences its efficacy towards us. It is not to be supposed for a moment that the perfect standing before God which the work of Christ secured for His people leaves their *state* unaffected; that their position should be so gloriously changed and their condition remain unaltered; that holiness should be imputed to them but not also imparted. The redemptive work of Christ was a means to an end, namely, to procure for His people the Holy Spirit, who should make good in them what He had done for them. It is by the Spirit's quickening operation that we obtain vital union with Christ—by means of which the benefits of our federal and legal union with Him actually becomes ours. The "sanctification of the Spirit" (II Thess. ii, 13) is an integral part of that "salvation" unto which the Father chose us and which the incarnate Son purchased for us. Thus the Christian is sanctified by the triune Jehovah.

Our *union with Christ* is the grand hinge on which everything turns. Divorced from Him we have nothing. During our unregeneracy we were "without Christ" and therefore "strangers from the covenants of promise" (Eph. ii, 12). But the moment the Spirit makes us livingly one with Christ, all that He has becomes ours, we are henceforth "joint heirs with Him"— as a woman obtains the right to share all that a man has once she is wedded to him. By virtue of our union with the first Adam we not only had imputed to us the guilt of his disobedience, but we also received from him a sinful nature which vitiated all the faculties of our souls; and by virtue of our federal union with the last Adam we not only have imputed to us the merits of His obedience, but we receive from Him a holy nature which renews all the faculties of our souls. Once we become united to the Vine the life and virtue which is in Him flows into us, and brings forth spiritual fruit. Thus, as soon as the Spirit unites us to Him we are "sanctified *in* Christ Jesus" (I Cor. i, 2). "By one Spirit are we all baptized [spiritually] into one body [of which Christ is the vital and influential Head] and are all made to drink into one spirit" (I Cor. xii, 13).

"But of Him [by no act of ours] are ye in Christ Jesus" (I Cor. i, 30). It is by the quickening operation of the Spirit that the elect are supernaturally and vitally incorporated with Christ, and it is then God makes Him to be unto us "wisdom, even righteousness and sanctification and redemption." "For we are His workmanship *created in* Christ Jesus" (Eph. ii, 10): that new creation is effected by the Spirit and issues in our union with Christ's person. Just as both our standing and state were radically affected by our union with the first Adam, so are they completely changed by virtue of our union with the last Adam. As the believer has a perfect standing in holiness before God because of his federal union with Christ, so his state is perfect before God because he is now vitally one with Christ: he is in Christ, and Christ is in him: "he that is joined to the Lord is one spirit" (I Cor. vi, 17). The moment they were born of the Spirit all Christians were sanctified in Christ with a sanctification to which no growth in grace, no attainments in holiness, can add one iota. He is then a "saint in Christ Jesus" (Rom. i, 2), one of the "holy brethren" (Heb. iii, 1), and it is just because he is such he is called upon to live a holy life.

Our relationship to God is changed when the Spirit sanctifies us by His quickening power, for we are then consecrated to God by the Spirit's indwelling us and making our body His temple. As He came upon the Head ("without measure"), so in due time He is given to each of His members: "ye have an Unction [the Spirit] from the Holy One"—Christ; "the Anointing [the Spirit] which we have received of Him [Christ] abideth in you" (I John ii, 20, 27). It is from that very blessing we derive our name, for "Christian" means "an *anointed* one," the term being taken from the type in Psalm cxxxii, 2. It is the indwelling Spirit which constitutes a believer a holy person. Our relationship to Christ is changed when the Spirit quickens us, for instead of being "without" Him in the world, we are now "joined to" Him. Our actual state is radically changed, for a principle of holiness is planted in the soul, which powerfully affects all its faculties. God now occupies the throne of the heart, the affections are purged from their love of sin, the Law is delighted in so that the will chooses its precepts as its regulator. Nevertheless, the "flesh," or evil principle, remains unchanged.

In one sense the believer's sanctification by the Spirit is complete at the new birth, so that he will never be made any holier than he was at that moment; in another sense his sanctification was incomplete and admits of progress. It was complete in that by virtue of the great change effected in him by the miracle of regeneration he was *then* "made meet to be a partaker of the inheritance of the saints in light" (Col. i, 12), vitally and personally united to Christ, and by the Spirit's taking up His abode in his heart consecrated unto God. It was incomplete in that indwelling sin was not then removed, in that the babe in Christ needs to grow in grace, and in that he is henceforth required to "put off the old man" and "put on the new man" in a practical way, "cleansing himself from all filthiness of the flesh and spirit, perfecting holiness in the fear of God" (II Cor. vii, 1). To enable him thereto the Spirit renews him daily (II Cor. iv, 16), subdues his iniquities in part (Micah vii, 19), stirs him up to the use of means, quickens his graces, draws forth his spiritual life unto spiritual acts upon Christ; and thereby He continues and completes that "good work" (Phil i, 6) which He wrought in the soul at regeneration.

To sum up. Sanctification is first a *blessing* unto which the Father predestinated His people (Eph. i, 3, 4). Second, it is a *gift*, an inalienable and eternal one, which they have in and through Christ. Third, it is a *moral quality*, a holy principle or "nature" communicated by the Spirit. Fourth, it is a *duty* which God requires from us (I Pet. i, 15, 16). Or again we may say, sanctification is a *relationship* into which we are brought with the thrice holy God. Second, it is a *status* we have by virtue of our union with Christ. Third, it is an *enduement* which we experience by the Spirit's operation within us. Fourth, it is a lifelong *work* unto which *we* are called, but for which we are in constant need of "more grace." "Perfecting holiness in the fear of God" (II Cor. vii, 1) by no means intimates that the holiness the Christian now possesses is defective and needs supplementing by his own efforts, but signifies that he is to carry out to its proper use and end that perfect holiness which *is his* in Christ—compare I John ii, 5, which means that by keeping God's commands the design of His love in us is reached; and "by works was [Abraham's] faith made perfect," i.e. achieved its design or intended result. He is to be "in behaviour as becometh holiness" (Titus ii, 3).

"Abstain from all appearance of evil. And the God of peace Himself sanctify you wholly." Both the immediate context and the particular character in which God is here addressed serve to show *which aspect* of our sanctification is in view, namely, our practical holiness or purity of heart and conduct. It is a prayer for Divine enablement to keep the foregoing commands: full sanctification for full obedience. To the preceding exhortations the apostle subjoined earnest supplication, knowing well that only the efficacious grace of God could supply either the will or the power to comply. The standard in verse 22 is an exceedingly high and exacting one: to abhor everything which carries even the appearance of uncleanness, to abstain from everything tending thereto. The more we eye that standard, the more we make conscience of its purity, the more shall we realize the need of much grace to measure up to it, and the more shall we perceive the suitability of this prayer to our case. We are still the subjects of sin—the arch-enemy of God—and the indulging of it not only separates us from God (Isa. lix, 2) and causes dissensions among the saints, but it also produces disorder and confusion among all the faculties of our being. To prevent such warfare the "God of *peace*" is invoked.

The indulgence of our lusts and the allowance of sin derange all the faculties of our being, so that the soul usurps the throne of the spirit (emotions and impulses directing us instead of our understanding or judgment), and the body seeks to dominate both spirit and soul—carnal affections opposing reason. But experimental and practical sanctification puts all into a right order again, and causes peace and harmony. But only the "God of peace" can *so* sanctify us. This is emphasized in our text: "the God of peace Himself," which points a contrast between the feeble efforts after holiness which we are capable of in our own spiritual strength and the all-mighty power which He can exert, and because of the peace and order which His sanctification brings to our whole being. The Christian is indeed sanctified, yet the work of grace begun in him at regeneration is not then completed: there is "first the blade, then the ear, after that the full corn in the ear" (Mark iv, 28). The heart needs to be increasingly cleansed from the pollution of sin, the soul more fully conformed to the Divine image, the daily walk to be more "worthy of the Lord." Yet all the advances we make in the Christian life are but the effects, fruits and evidences of the Spirit's sanctifying us at the new birth. Growth in grace is a *manifestation* of our holiness.

"And the God of peace Himself sanctify you wholly" is to be taken in its widest latitude. First, as a request that all the members of the Thessalonian church, the entire assembly, might be thus sanctified. Second, that each individual member might be unreservedly devoted to God in the whole of his complex being. Third, that each and all of them might be energized and purified more perfectly, strengthened and stirred up to press forward unto complete holiness. Thus I Thessalonians v, 23, is almost parallel with Hebrews xiii, 20, 21. The apostle prayed that all the parts and faculties of the Christian might be kept under the influence of efficacious grace, in true and real conformity to God; that they might be so influenced by the Truth as to be fitted and furnished for the performance of every good work. Though this be our bounden duty, yet it is the work of our reconciled God, by His Spirit in and through us; and this is to be the burden of our daily prayers. The exhortation of verse 22 makes known our duty: the prayer of verse 23 how to be enabled thereto. By nature our hearts were antagonistic to God's holy requirements, and only His power produces an abiding change.

It is the *practical* aspect of sanctification which this prayer is concerned with: that the saint should be Divinely enabled to make manifest in his daily life that sanctification which he has in Christ and bring forth the fruits of the Spirit's indwelling him and the principle of holiness imparted at regeneration; that he should be constantly "denying ungodliness and worldly lusts" and live "soberly, righteously, and godly in this present world; looking for that blessed hope" (Titus ii, 12, 13). As to our standing and state before God, sanctification extends to the whole man—every part of our human nature being the subject of it—and so must it in our devotedness unto God; our body, as well as spirit and soul, is to be dedicated to Him (Rom. xii, 1), and its members employed in the works of righteousness (Rom. vi, 13). "In your whole nature or persons, in all that ye are and do, that ye may—not in this or that part, but—be every whit clean and holy throughout" (J. Owen).

Fourth, *its design*. "And your whole spirit and soul and body be preserved blameless." It is difficult (and perhaps not necessary) for us to determine the precise relation of this clause to the previous one—whether it be an additional request, an explanatory amplification of the word "wholly," or whether it expresses the apostle's design in making that request; personally, we consider it includes the last two. The American R.V. gives "And the God of peace Himself sanctify you wholly: and may your spirit and soul and body be preserved blameless at the coming of our Lord Jesus Christ." Bagster's Interlinear reads, "Now Himself the God of peace sanctify you wholly; and entire your spirit and soul and body blameless at the coming of our Lord Jesus Christ may be preserved." Whatever rendition be preferred, it is clear the verse as a whole teaches that sanctification extends to our entire persons. Equally clear is it that man is a tri-partite being, consisting of an intelligent spirit, a sensual or sensitive soul, and a material body. Man, with his customary perversity, *reverses* this order (witness the motto of the Y.M.C.A.) and speaks of "body, soul and spirit": putting the body first because *it* occupies most of his care!

Since the tri-partite nature of man has been so widely denied we will make some brief observations thereon. That man is a threefold (and not merely twofold) entity is definitely established by the fact that he was created in the image of the Triune God (Gen. i, 26). It is intimated in the account given of the Fall: "The woman saw that the tree was good for food"—it appealed to her bodily appetites; "and that it was pleasant [margin, "a desire"] to the eyes"—it appealed to her sensitive soul; "and a tree to be desired to make one *wise*"—it appealed to her intelligent spirit (Gen. iii, 6). It is a serious error to say that when man fell his spirit ceased to be, and only at regeneration is a "spirit" communicated. The leader of an English denomination in his *Manual* quotes with approval one who said, "The soul of a regenerate man remains unaltered. Its guilt, unbelief, and enmity are the same as before. Its desires, affections, feelings are what they were." Had he said "the flesh" or indwelling corruption, he had been correct; but to affirm that of the *soul* of a regenerate man, denies the miracle of grace. Equally erroneous was his statement "that God has implanted a new essence, which is spirit." No "new essence" is added.

Fallen man is possessed equally of "spirit *and* soul" (Heb. iv, 12). God "formeth the spirit of man within him" (Zech. xii, 1), and at death "the spirit returneth to God" (Eccl. xii, 7). We agree with Zanchius the Reformer that "the spirit includes the superior faculties of the mind, such as reason, and understanding; the soul, the inferior faculties—will, affections, desires." By means of the "soul" we *feel*; by the "spirit" we *know* (Dan. ii. 3, etc.). "Thou shalt love the Lord thy God with [1] all thine heart [spirit], and [2] with all thy soul, and [3] with all thy might" or physical energy (Deut. vi, 5) corresponds with Paul's threefold distinction in our text. The constitution of man *as man* was once for all demonstrated when the Son of God became incarnate, and assumed both "spirit" (Luke xxiii, 46) and "soul" (Matt. xxvi, 38). Yet in saying that unregenerate man possesses a spirit, we do not affirm he has a *spiritual nature*, for his spirit has been defiled by the Fall, though it was not annihilated, and therefore is capable of being "washed and renewed" (Titus iii, 5).

The whole nature of man is the subject of the Spirit's work in regeneration and sanctification, and this is to be manifested by the Christian in a practical way: by every disposition and power of his spirit, each faculty and affection of his soul, all the members of his body. His body has been made a member of Christ (I Cor. vi, 15) and is the temple of the Holy Spirit (I Cor. vi, 19). Since his body be an integral part of his person, and since its inclinations and appetites seek to usurp the functions of his spirit and soul and dominate his actions, the believer is required to bring his body under the control of the higher parts of his being, so that it is regulated by a Scripturally enlightened reason and not by its carnal passions, and thereby that "every one of us should know how to possess his vessel [body] in sanctification and honour" (I Thess. iv, 4). As in unregeneracy we yielded our members to sin, now we are to yield them as servants to righteousness unto holiness (Rom. vi, 19). As one has said, "perfect holiness is to be the *aim* of saints on earth, as it will be the *reward* of the saints in heaven."

Christians *are* "sanctified wholly" in their desires and intentions, and that brings us to the meaning of "preserved *blameless.*" It is not that blamelessness which the covenant of works required, but that of the covenant of grace, wherein God accepts the will for the deed (Neh. i, 11; II Cor. viii, 12). "God expresseth the deed by the will. He interpreteth him to be a perfect man who would be perfect, and calls that person perfect who desires to have all his imperfections cured" (Caryl). Alas that in this day of darkness so few have been taught to distinguish between legal and evangelical blamelessness. When it is said that the parents of John walked "in all the commandments and ordinances of the Lord blameless" (Luke i, 5) it does not mean they lived sinlessly, as verse 20 shows; but that such was their sincere desire and earnest endeavour, and that they habitually walked in a course of conscientious obedience and behaved in such a manner in the general tenor of their conduct that none could charge them with any open sin.

The word "blameless" in such passages as I Corinthians i, 8, Philippians ii, 15, I Thessalonians iii, 13, should be compared with "Blessed are the *undefiled* in the way" (Psa. cxix, 1), which is to be understood according to the tenor of the new covenant, which does not exclude (as the covenant of works did) God's exercise of mercy and the pardon of sin—see Psalm cxxx, 3, 4! The prayer which Christ has given us to use bids us ask not only for deliverance from temptation, but daily pardon. If God dealt with us according to the strict rigour of His Law and required an absolute undefiledness, none would escape His condemnation. It must be understood of evangelical undefiledness, the *sincerity* of our obedience, and refraining from that which would give occasion for others to justly charge us with wrongdoing. While the Christian honestly and earnestly endeavours to show himself approved unto God, while he is truly humbled for his failures and penitently confesses them, while he diligently seeks to walk in the law of the Lord, he is *accounted* "blameless" or "undefiled" in the Gospel sense of those words.

Fifth, *its assurance.* "Faithful is He that calleth you who also will do it" (verse 24). Regeneration guarantees sanctification: our effectual call by God is the earnest of our preservation. Divine grace will complete our experimental and practical holiness. "The Lord will perfect that which concerneth me: Thy mercy, O Lord, endureth for ever" (Psa. cxxxviii, 8). Whether we translate "be preserved blameless *unto* [or "at"] the coming of the Lord Jesus Christ" matters not, for as the "till" in Philippians i, 10, and the "in" of I Corinthians i, 8, show, both are equally the case. Thus, the confidence of verse 24 is parallel with "He which hath begun a good work in you, will perform it until the day of Jesus Christ" (Phil. i, 6).

THE LIFE AND TIMES OF JOSHUA

26. The Memorials

The very fact that God saw fit to devote two whole chapters of His Word unto a description of Israel's crossing of the Jordan is more than a hint that the narration of that memorable incident embodies teaching of much importance and value for His people in succeeding generations. Christians are greatly the losers if they concentrate their attention chiefly upon the New Testament and regard the Old Testament as containing little of vital moment for their souls. If on the one hand the New Testament often illuminates and explains the Old, yet on the other hand there is not a little in the New Testament which cannot be properly understood apart from the Old. In the last two or three articles we sought to indicate the typical and spiritual significance of Israel's passage through the river of death and judgment; on this occasion we propose to point out some of the practical lessons to be learned from the things there recorded. We shall not give a complete exposition of chapter iv, but single out various details for comment, and intimate the many useful truths inculcated by the memorial erected in Gilgal.

"For the priests which bare the ark stood in the midst of Jordan, until everything was finished that the Lord commanded Joshua to speak unto the people, according to all that Moses commanded Joshua: and the people hasted and passed over" (verse 10). There are three things here which are worthy of our observation and admiration. First, the implicit obedience and patient fortitude of the priests. They were the ones who occupied the place both of honour and of danger. They were the ones who bore the ark, before whose presence the waters had "rose up like a heap," held by an invisible Hand. Advancing to "the midst of Jordan," they remained stationary for many hours, until all the vast host of Israel had crossed to the far shore. It was a severe test both of their courage and patience. Therein an example is left the ministers of the Gospel to continue steadfast in their duty, to be a model unto their people of uncompromising fidelity, of undaunted courage, of patient endurance. Second, we see again how that Joshua closely followed the orders he had received from Moses, doing nothing without a Divine command; while the priests, in turn, were required to be regulated by Joshua's orders—the ministers of the Gospel are to be governed solely by Christ.

Third, the deportment of "the people" on this occasion exemplified that which should ever characterize the rank and file of the saints in connection with those who minister unto them in spiritual things. We are told that they "*hasted* and passed over." That denoted their thoughtful consideration of the priests, so that they would not be put to unnecessary delay and strain through their dilatoriness—the slower their movement, the longer the priests would have to stand bearing the ark! The practical lesson is that God's people should do everything in their power to make the spiritual lot of God's servants easier. That can be done by promptly responding to their instructions, by supporting them through earnest prayer, and by being thoughtful of their comfort. That is something which particularly needs to be laid to heart in this day of selfishness and lack of concern for the comfort of others. It is both solemn and blessed to note how *God* took note of this detail, that the Holy Spirit has specifically recorded this thoughtful "haste" of the people. The Lord not only marks *what* we do, but *how* we do it: as in "his princes gave *willingly*" (II Chron. xxxv, 8), "their nobles put their necks to the work of the Lord . . . Zabbi *earnestly* repaired the other piece" (Neh. iii. 5, 20).

"And the children of Reuben and the children of Gad, and half the tribe of Manasseh, passed over armed before the children of Israel, as Moses spake unto them: About forty thousand prepared for war passed over before the Lord unto battle, to the plains of Jericho" (verses 12, 13). Here is a case in point how that one part of Scripture is dependent upon another for its explanation and interpretation. We have to go back to Numbers to discover why *these* particular ones constituted the fighting force of the nation. Those two and a half tribes, who were rich in cattle, desired to have for their portion the fertile lands of Jazer and Gilead, rather than any part of Canaan (verses 1-5). When Moses demurred, they agreed to build sheepfolds for their cattle and fenced cities for their little ones, and then they would go armed before the children of Israel until the remaining tribes had secured their inheritance (verses 16, 17). Moses agreed to their proposal, and they ratified that arrangement; and Moses then gave command to Eleazar and Joshua to see that their promise was made good. Here in Joshua iv we are shown the fulfilment of the same. Those two and a half tribes were the only ones unencumbered with their families and flocks, and thus we see *how suited* they were to be the fighting force, and how graciously God made all things work together for good unto His people.

"On that day the Lord magnified Joshua in the sight of all Israel; and they feared him, as they feared Moses, all the days of his life" (verse 14). Therein we may see how the Lord made good unto Joshua the word He gave him in iii, 7. "Faithful is He that calleth you, who also will do it" (I Thess. v, 24). That detail has been placed upon imperishable record for the encouragement of every servant of the Lord. Ministers of the Gospel may prosecute their labours with absolute confidence in the promises of their Master: not one of them shall fail. He has said of His Word, "it shall not return unto Me void, but it shall accomplish that which I please, and it shall prosper in the thing whereto I sent it" (Isa. lv, 11); then he need not entertain the slightest doubt about the same. He has declared "all that the Father giveth Me shall come to Me," that they "*shall* believe on Me through their [His ministers'] word" (John vi, 37; xvii, 20); then neither the perversity of human nature nor the opposition of Satan can prevent it. He has promised His servants, "Lo, I am with you alway, even unto the end of the world" (Matt. xxviii, 20), then let them conduct themselves accordingly. Let them also learn from Joshua iv, 14, and its context that the surest way for them to gain the respect and observation of their people is to be diligent in personally honouring and obeying God, and caring for their welfare.

"And the Lord spake unto Joshua, saying, Command the priests that bear the ark of the testimony, that they come up out of Jordan. Joshua therefore commanded the priests, saying, Come ye up out of Jordan" (verses 15-17). That is indeed striking: the priests did not take a step until they were Divinely authorized. There they stood hour after hour, and there they still remained after the vast concourse had passed through and reached the other side in safety! Patiently they waited until leave was given them to move. They did not act on their own impulse or initiative, but meekly waited God's time. "The priests did not quit their station till Joshua, who had commanded them hitherto, ordered them from thence: nor did he thus order them till the Lord commanded him: so obedient were all parties to the Word of God, and so entirely confident of His protection" (Matthew Henry). It is ours to render unquestioning obedience to God, and leave the consequences with Him; nor need we have the least fear or hesitation in so doing—we shall not be the losers, but the gainers. "Them that honour Me, I will honour"

(I Sam. ii, 30) is more certain than that night shall follow day, as the writer has often proved.

"And it came to pass, when the priests that bare the ark of the covenant of the Lord were come up out of the midst of Jordan, and the soles of the priests' feet were lifted up unto the dry land, that the waters of Jordan returned unto their place, and flowed over all his banks, as they did before" (verse 18). No sooner did the priests with the ark step upon the shore of Canaan than the Jordan resumed its normal flow, or rather its abnormal condition, for it was then in flood. That at once accentuated the miracle which had just been wrought, making it the more apparent that the stopping of its flow was not from any abnormal natural cause, but that it was the will of their Creator which had temporarily suspended the laws of nature, for the display of His glory and the fulfilment of His promise unto His people. As Israel beheld the upper waters which had been invisibly dammed and the lower ones that had stood up in a heap now suddenly acting as formerly, how apparent it would be unto them that it was the presence and power of their covenant God which had wrought so gloriously for them!

Bearing in mind the meaning of "Jordan," the spiritual application of verse 18 is apparent. It was the presence in its midst of the priests who bore the ark which stayed its course: and it is the godly example and faithful ministry of God's servants which, under the Divine blessing to His people, and through their moral influence upon others, which hold back His judgments upon the world. They are the salt of the earth, which prevents the carcass of the unregenerate mass turning into complete putrefaction. But that "salt" has steadily *diminished* during the last two centuries. As the population of the world has increased, the proportion of the righteous— despite a widespread "profession"—has decreased, and therefore sin has abounded more and more; and so too have the judgments of God. As the entrance of righteous Noah and his family into the ark was the signal for the flood to commence, as the removal of just Lot from Sodom was at once followed by the fire and brimstone from heaven, so the removal of God's eminent servants and saints from the earth (the places of few being filled) has been followed by the Divine judgments which we have witnessed and are still witnessing. Dispensationally, Joshua iv, 18, foreshadowed the awful fact that when the Day of grace is concluded, the world will be completely inundated by the storm of God's wrath.

"And the people came up out of Jordan on the tenth day of the first month, and encamped in Gilgal, in the east border of Jericho" (verse 19). There is nothing meaningless or valueless in the Scriptures. and we are the losers if we ignore or pass hurriedly over its *time marks*. The carnal critic would say, what interest is it unto me which particular day of the month this event occurred; but different far should be the spirit of the believer. But *how* is he to ascertain the significance of this detail? By looking up the marginal references, and if they do not furnish what he needs. by consulting his concordance, where he will find that the first reference to "the tenth day" of the first month (Ex. xii, 2, 3) supplies the key. It was the day when the paschal lamb was selected!—to be slain on the fourteenth (Ex. xii, 6, and see Josh. v, 10). How wonderfully God times everything for His people! "He so ordered things here that Israel entered Canaan four days before the annual solemnity of the passover, and on the very day when the preparation for it was begun, for He would have them enter into Canaan graced and sanctified with that religious feast, and would have them to be reminded of their deliverance from Egypt that, combining the two together, God might be glorified as the Alpha and Omega of their blessing" (Matthew Henry).

"And those twelve stones, which they took out of Jordan, did Joshua pitch [i.e. "erect"] in Gilgal" (verse 20). Probably those large stones were placed on some eminence where there was none other, for they were to be a monument unto the children of Israel for ever" (verse 7). Some surmise, and we think with considerable probability, that when the Pharisees and Sadducees came to John's baptism and he said unto them "Think not to say within yourselves we have Abraham to our father: for I say unto you, that God is able of *these stones* to raise up children unto Abraham" (Matt. iii, 9) he pointed to the very cairn erected by Joshua. Confirmation of this appears to be furnished by John i, 28, which informs us that he baptized in "Bethabara beyond Jordan," for "Bethabara" means "the house of passage," i.e. the place where Israel passed over the river.

"And he spake unto the children of Israel, saying, When your children shall ask their fathers, in time to come, saying, What meaneth these stones? Then ye shall let your children know, saying, Israel came over this Jordan on dry land. For the Lord your God dried up the waters of Jordan from before you, until ye were passed over, as the Lord your God did to the Red Sea, which He dried up from before us, until we were gone over" (verses 21-23). Normal children have inquiring minds and ought not to be snubbed or even discouraged when they ask their parents questions. Rather should parents seek to improve their curiosity as an opening for instruction, *directing* the same into profitable channels. The very inquisitiveness of little ones affords their elders an opportunity to make known unto them the wonderful works of God, that their minds may be informed and their hearts awed by His perfections. But note well, it is *the father* (the "head" of the home) upon whom the main responsibility devolves, to see to it that his children are taught by him the things of God (Eph. vi, 4). Let him not pass on this task to his wife, still less to "Sunday-school teachers."

"That all the people of the earth might know the hand of the Lord that it is mighty: that ye might fear the Lord your God for ever" (verse 24). God's miraculous deliverances of His own people have a message for all the world, and when He is pleased to sanctify the same unto the unregenerate, they are deeply impressed thereby (Dan. iii, 29; vi, 25-27). The effects produced by the Jordan miracle are recorded in v, 1, which properly ends chapter iv: "And it came to pass, when all the kings of the Amorites which were on the side of Jordan westward, and all the kings of the Canaanites which were by the sea, heard that the Lord had dried up the waters of Jordan from before the children of Israel until we were passed over, that their heart melted, neither was there spirit in them any more, because of the children of Israel." The Canaanites were completely dispirited and cowed. realizing their utter incompetency to successfully oppose a people who had the Almighty for their Friend and Benefactor. But we must now seek to formulate the various lessons which we should learn from the memorial erected at Gilgal to mark the miraculous passage of the Jordan.

First, the wonderful works of God are worthy of treasuring in our memories, and He requires that pains be taken by us to see that they are so. It should be carefully noted that Joshua, even in the midst of a most exacting business, was not permitted to neglect the promotion of the Lord's honour. While superintending the passage through the river's bed of that vast concourse of people, with all their baggage (tents, etc.) and cattle, God bade him see to it that he took a man from each tribe and bid them select the twelve stones which were to be carried to Gilgal (iv, 2, 3). Nor did he demur or ask for a more convenient season.

Second, God's ordering of this memorial is a solemn reminder of how prone our hearts are *to forget* His past interpositions on our behalf. Of Israel we are told they "forgat His works and His wonders that He showed them"; and again, that "they soon forgat His works" (Psa. lxxviii, 11; cvi, 13). Alas, is not the same true of us? Even of the apostles Christ asked, "Do ye not yet understand, neither *remember* the five loaves ye took up?" (Matt. xvi. 9).

Third, because of our proneness to forget, suitable means are to be used in assisting us. We are to make conscience of the fact that God has bidden us to "remember all the way which the Lord thy God led thee" (Deut. viii, 2), and that precept should be turned into earnest *prayer* that we may not be negligent therein. We should frequently call to mind our previous experiences of God's faithfulness and tender care of us. This will strengthen the spirit of thanksgiving and cause us to praise God anew. It will deepen our confidence in Him to count upon Him in present emergencies and trust Him for future deliverances. The more we do so, the less shall we fear the experience of death, assured that God will undertake for us as we are called upon to pass through the valley of the shadows, as certainly as He conducted Israel safely through the Jordan (see II Cor. i, 10)!

Fourth, not only God's past deliverances of us are to be treasured up in our memories, but also His mercies unto His people in times gone by. Faith is to look back to what the arm of the Lord hath done "in the ancient days, in the generations of old," and say, "Art not Thou He which hath dried the sea . . . that made the depths of the sea, a way for the ransomed to pass over." And what will be the consequence of such exercise of believing memories? This: "Therefore the redeemed of the Lord shall return, and come with singing unto Zion" (Isa. li, 9-11). Why has God recorded the deliverance of Noah from the flood and of Lot from Sodom but to assure us that "the Lord knoweth how to deliver the godly out of temptation" (II Pet. ii, 5-9). Not only is "what was written aforetime written for our learning and comfort" (Rom. xv, 4), but what God did aforetime is to teach us what He can and will now do for His own. "I remembered Thy judgments of old, O Lord, and have comforted myself" (Psa. cxix, 52).

Fifth, the monument erected at Gilgal teaches us that we should take thought of and seek to make provision for the rising generation. That cairn of stones was erected with the express desire of evoking inquiry from those who should later behold it. God would have the wonders of His power and mercy preserved for posterity. There was to be a permanent witness of what God had wrought for His people; that no impotency or weakness of theirs prevented them reaching the shores of Canaan. It was meant as a sure pledge that God would continue to show Himself strong in Israel's behalf and would overthrow those then in occupation of the land. Thus, we rejoice when readers of this magazine purchase the bound volumes with this design before them. At least one is now thankfully reading those volumes which his mother (now in heaven) purchased from us twenty years ago, when he was unconverted. We cherish the hope that the bound volumes will be read by many long after we are called Home.

Sixth, in the *nature* or character of the two monuments which Joshua was instructed to set up, we see how different are the thoughts and ways of the Lord from those of men. No costly shrine, with useless ornamentations and affected splendour, was to mark the event, but only that which, though impressive, was simple and plain. "Never did triumphant column or arch, with all the magnificence of architecture, form so proper a monument of some celebrated victory as the twelve rude stones from Jordan's channel recorded the miraculous passage of Israel into Canaan under the conduct of the ark of the Lord." Equally true is this of the two signs and memorials which God has appointed for this dispensation. When divested of all priestly and parsonic trappings, how plain and simple, yet how significant and impressive, are the ordinances of baptism and the Lord's supper. The same principle was exemplified by Christ in the choice of His ambassadors—for the most part unlettered fishermen.

Seventh, that monument teaches us that we should recognize and own the corporate *unity* of God's people. It was comprised of twelve stones, taken up by one man from out of each tribe (iv, 2) and erected in Gilgal. That is the more noticeable since two and a half of the tribes had received their inheritance on the eastward side of the Jordan. Yet this cairn on the western shore must have in it not nine or ten, but twelve stones, to signify the oneness of Israel. We behold the same thing again in I Kings xviii, when, centuries later, the division between the northern and southern kingdoms of Israel obtained, and Elijah "took *twelve* stones according to the number of the sons of Jacob, unto whom the word of the Lord came, saying, Israel shall be thy name, and built with them an altar on Mount Carmel" (verses 31, 32), resting by faith on God's Word when what was visible to sight clashed with the same. They were all the elect of God and brethren. So *we* should view God's children, separated as they now are by party partitions and denominational walls, as members of the same Family, and sharing a common interest. Let our hearts embrace and our prayers include the entire household of faith.

DIVORCE

There is but one passage in all the Old Testament which requires us to qualify anything we have said in the earlier paragraphs, only one which taught that a man might divorce his wife for something less than adultery. namely Deuteronomy xxiv, 1-4, and to it we now turn. "When a man hath taken a wife and married her, and it come to pass that she find no favour in his eyes because he hath found some uncleanness in her, then let him write her a bill of divorcement and give it in her hand, and send her out of his house. And when she is departed out of his house, she may go and be another man's wife. And if the latter husband hate her, and write her a bill of divorcement and giveth it in her hand, and sendeth her out of his house; or if the latter husband die, which took her to be his wife, her former husband, which sent her away, may not take her again to be his wife, after that she is defiled; for that is abomination before the Lord."

In pondering the contents of those verses it should be obvious to all impartial minds that they must be interpreted in strict harmony with the Analogy of Faith, that we undoubtedly *err* if our understanding of them clashes with other passages in the Pentateuch. That single but necessary consideration at once obliges us to regard the words "some uncleanness in her" as something other than *moral* uncleanness. "Obliges us," we say, for the Mosaic law had passed sentence of death upon both the adulterer and the adulteress (Lev. xx, 10; Deut. xxii, 22; John viii, 4, 5). Nor could it refer to a serious suspicion of unfaithfulness to the marriage bed, for that would require that the husband should make trial of his wife according to the statute of Numbers v, 12-31, which was expressly given to meet the case of "jealousy" or suspicion. Nor does it seem at all likely that this "uncleanness" was merely of a ceremonial nature, for it was liable to persist so that her second husband "hated" her. Thus, by a process of elimination, it would appear that the allusion was unto some physical defect or disease which caused her to "find no favour" in her husband's eyes.

Furthermore, if we are to be preserved from drawing wrong inferences from Deuteronomy xxiv, 1-4, we must cast upon it the light supplied by our Lord in Matthew xix. There we read that the Pharisees came to Him, "tempting Him" by asking the question, "Is it lawful for a man to put away his wife for *every* cause?" (verse 3). Their design was to discredit Christ in the eyes of a section of the Jewish nation, for there were two conflicting "schools" of teaching among them on the subject, and His enemies imagined that by His answer they would force Him to antagonize one of them—the one holding that nought but marital infidelity constituted a legitimate ground for divorce, the other affirming that the husband has the right, according to his own pleasure or caprice, to put away his wife for the most trivial offence. In His reply, Christ took His interrogators back to the original institution of marriage by God in Eden, and added, "What God therefore hath joined together, let not man put asunder" (verse 6): no human authority has any right to change or tamper with a Divine ordinance.

"They say unto Him, Why did Moses then command to give a writing of divorcement, and to put here away?" To which our Lord replied, "Moses because of the hardness of your hearts suffered you to put away your wives; but from the beginning it was not so" (verses 7, 8). Observe, first, that the Pharisees erred in styling Deuteronomy xxiv, 1, a "command," for it was no part of the Moral Law, but instead pertained to the judicial instructions for Israel's magistrates. So far from God *ordering* the Hebrews to put away their wives for something less than adultery, He merely "suffered" them to do so; it was a concession made only under special circumstances. What those "circumstances" were, our Lord broadly hints at in His "because of the hardness of your hearts." It was a providential permission, allowing the magistrate to authorize the putting away of wives in order to spare them from brutal treatment, and perhaps murder, at the hands of their callous husbands. Thus Deuteronomy xxiv, 1, enunciated no general rule for all times and every occasion, much less did it supply warrant for husbands to put away their wives "for every cause."

It is to be duly noted that in such a case where a Jewish husband "found some uncleanness" in his wife, he was not permitted, in a fit of temper, to act hurriedly and immediately turn her out of the home, but must wait while a legal instrument (which would require a minimum of two witnesses) was drawn up for "a bill of divorcement." In permitting this arrangement God did not "wink at" or connive at a husband's harshness, but mercifully arranged that the wife should be "divorced" rather than be slain because he wished to be free of her. God's attitude unto the matter is plainly revealed in Malachi ii, 16, where He emphatically declares, "For the Lord, the God of Israel, saith, that He *hateth* putting away." That same verse ("for one covereth *violence* with his garment: therefore take heed to your spirit"—passions—"that ye deal not treacherously") also supplies confirmation of what we have said above, and explains what Christ had in mind when He attributed the arrangement of Deuteronomy xxiv, 1, unto Israel's "hardness of heart," namely, the husband's brutality.

Return now to Matthew xix, 3-9. In this fundamental passage we find that our Lord, first, affirmed the inviolability of the marriage covenant (verses 4-6). Second, that He showed Deuteronomy xxiv, 1-4, was not an actual "command," as the Pharisees supposed (verse 7), but only a merciful concession to meet a particular case, a "sufferance" (verse 8). Third, He revealed why that special permission had been given, namely, "because of the hardness of heart" of certain Jewish husbands (verse 8). It was to prevent cruelty and bloodshed. That was also clearly imported by the fact that no such license was accorded the wife, for she being "the weaker vessel," the life of her husband (speaking generally) would not be endangered by a wife who despised him. Fourth, from His emphatic words, "Whosoever shall put away his wife, except it be for fornication [adultery], and shall marry another, committeth adultery" (verse 9), Christ taught that Deuteronomy xxiv, 1-4, is for ever set aside, that no man may now put away his wife merely "because she find no favour in his eyes."

Here, then, is the answer to our first question: a higher and holier standard obtains under Christianity than was tolerated under Judaism. In view of which the disciples said unto Christ, "If the case of the man be so with his wife [that he cannot divorce her for "incompatibility of temperament," or anything else, short of adultery], it is not good to marry" (verse 10—better remain single. To which our Lord answered, "All cannot receive this saying, save [only] them to whom it is given" (verse 11), i.e. those upon whom God bestows the gift of continency. The single state is the ideal one for a Christian (I Cor. vii, 7, 32-34), though in most cases it is fraught with great moral danger, and therefore "it is better to marry than to burn" (I Cor. vii, 9) with consuming lust. Moreover, "marriage is honourable in all" (Heb. xiii, 4), being a Divine institution. It is a gracious provision of the Creator's for the avoidance of fornication (I Cor. vii, 2) and for the lawful producing of children (Rom. vii, 4). N.B.—It is our studied *opinion* that in view of "the present distress" (I Cor. vii, 26) it is the part of wisdom and mercy for married couples to conduct themselves as per I Corinthians vii, 29, for the time may be near when they shall again say, "Blessed are the barren" (Luke xxiii, 29).

"But I say unto you, That whosoever shall put away his wife, save for the cause of fornication [adultery] causeth her to commit adultery; and whosoever shall marry her that is divorced committeth adultery" (Matt. v, 32). Here we have the Divinely authoritative and unambiguous answer to our second question. In the Scriptural meaning of the words, "to put away" one's wife is to legally divorce her, the two expressions being used interchangeably in this very verse. But to put away one's wife is expressly forbidden by the Divine Law, marriage being for life. One exception, and one only to the general rule is authorized by Christ, as is plain from His "saving for [except only] the case of fornication," for since *that* sin be itself the breaking of the marriage contract, it constitutes a valid ground for divorce. In modern terminology "fornication" is a sin committed by an unmarried person ("adultery" only by one joined in wedlock), but in Scripture "fornication" is sometimes used as a generic term for *any* moral uncleanness. In Ezekiel xvi, 29-32, the Lord charges His "Wife" with *both* crimes, and in Revelation ii, 20, 22, it is clear that "fornication" and "adultery" are used interchangeably.

It is to be duly noted that in Matthew xix, 9, our Lord *repeated* what He had laid down so specifically in v, 23, "Whosoever shall put away his wife, except it be for fornication, and shall marry another, and whosoever marrieth her which is put away, doth commit adultery"! Those words are too plain to be misunderstood: nothing but death or unchastity severs the marriage bond. The courts of men may pretend to legalize other grounds for divorce, but they cannot sanctify them, or take away the brand of infamy which the Son of God has placed upon the one who marries another that has not a Scripturally warranted divorce. Something infinitely superior to human legislation must govern and regulate those who fear the Lord. The Word of God, and not our feelings, is to be our sole Rule and Guide in this matter, as in everything else pertaining to our conduct. Neither separation by mutual consent nor desertion dissolves the marriage tie between husband and wife. One thing alone, short of death, does or can do that, namely, *proven* adultery and not merely suspected.

Any man who declares that because a wife has been abandoned by her husband she has a legal ground to sue for a divorce, is guilty of the heinous sin of adding to the Word of God, and constitutes himself a liar. Any man who lives with a woman previously married to another and whose husband is not dead or who has not obtained a legal divorce because adultery was committed, is himself guilty of adultery in the sight of God. Consequently, it follows of necessity that any preacher who recognizes and countenances any pretended or unscriptural divorce is guilty of contravening the Law of Christ. In his earlier days the writer was put to the test. One evening a young man, accompanied by a girl, called at the house where we lodged and asked us to marry them. Seeing a marriage licence in his hand we foolishly assumed that all was in order, and went and called two people to witness the ceremony. But before beginning it we asked to examine the "certificate," and then discovered the man was divorced, and merely on the ground of "incompatibility of temperament." The situation was an embarrassing one, but we told the couple they were not eligible for marriage, and would be sinning before God if they lived together; and refused to "marry" them.

One of the many proofs that the "Apocrypha" is not inspired of God is its teaching on this subject, for so far from agreeing with Holy Writ, it embodies the loose ethics of the carnal mind. Among the vaporizings of the son of Sirach concerning married women is the following: "If she go not as thou wouldest, have her cut off from thy flesh" (Ecclus. xxv, 26): that is, if she displeases thee in any respect, thou art free to put her away. But what better might be looked for when that same book avers "Almsgiving will make atonement for sins" (iii, 20)? Nor need we be surprised that such a system as Romanism, which exalts "human tradition" to the same level of authority as the Word of God (and follows the former when the latter clashes with them!), allows divorce for other causes than the one specified by Christ, even authorizing them for *religious* reasons. But to the Law and the Testimony: "For the woman which hath a husband is bound by the Law to her husband as long as he liveth" (Rom. vii, 2), even though he mistreats her, refuses to provide for her, or completely deserts her.

It is to be greatly regretted that not a few good men, leaders among the Lord's people, have taught otherwise; yet highly as we may esteem them, they are not to be regarded as "rabbins" or "fathers." We are under Divine bonds to "*prove* all things," to weigh every utterance of the most eminent of God's servants in the balances of the Sanctuary, and to hold fast only "that which is good" (I Thess. v, 21). Many have concluded that another cause, in addition to adultery, is sufficient to procure the dissolution of the conjugal tie, namely, the wilful *desertion* of one of the parties. Cruel and ungodly as is such a course, and most pitiable the woman's case when left in ignorance for years whether her husband and protector be dead, yet the marriage is not annulled thereby. As Mr. Philpot pertinently asked, "How long must that absence or desertion be to have this effect? Shall it be a week's, a month's, or a year's absence, that shall do it? And if those terms be too short, where are we to put the limit? If one year's desertion cannot break the marriage tie, can it be broken by ten or twenty years' absence? . . .

"The number of years that he has deserted her, her ignorance where he is, the belief she entertains that he is dead, her desolate condition, her poverty and necessity, her unprotected condition—all these pitiable circumstances do not, cannot, alter the Law of God. He is her husband and she is his wife till death or divorce dissolve the tie. . . . And though this may occasion individual hardship, yet what a general benefit to married women accrues from it! If desertion could dissolve marriage, thousands of unprincipled husbands would avail themselves of it, and no wife could be sure, as now, that she should continue such till her own or her husband's decease" (*The Gospel Standard,* 1853). The very evil which the editor of that magazine pointed out now obtains widely in our midst. But our appeal must be to a higher authority, to the Divine. The Lord Jesus took no notice of desertion as a just cause when speaking on divorce, nor did any of His apostles refer to it as a valid ground. *That* must be for us the Final Court of Appeal, and nothing must be allowed to counter its decision.

But some have supposed that I Corinthians vii, 15, authorizes a divorce for something short of adultery. It ought to be sufficient to point out that such a supposition is utterly untenable, for the Scriptures do not contradict themselves. It is an exceedingly grave matter to say that the apostle taught something quite different from his Master. But he did not. It is his interpreters who failed to understand the scope and meaning of I Corinthians vii, 10-17, and have read into the apostle's language what is not there, yea, have made him to contradict himself, for he could not intend by verse 15 ("But if the unbelieving depart"—desert the Christian partner—"let him depart: a brother or sister is not under bonds in such cases") that the believer is then free to sue out a divorce and upon obtaining it marry again, and then expressly affirm "The wife is *bound* by the law as long as her husband liveth, but if her husband be dead, she is at liberty to be married to whom she will; only in the Lord" (verse 39)! A careful and critical examination of the apostle's drift in that passage seems to be called for.

From the opening words of I Corinthians vii—"Now concerning the things whereof *ye wrote unto me*"—it is evident that not a little in this epistle was written in answer to various questions which had exercised the Corinthian saints during the apostle's absence, concerning which they asked his elucidation, and which he here resolved for them. Though Paul does not quote their particular inquiries in so many words, yet the topics he took up in this epistle indicate the nature of those matters whereon they had sought his counsel, namely, those problems that were raised by their conversion from heathenism to Christianity. Confining ourselves now to the seventh chapter, it is clear that the Lord's people at Corinth had desired light from the apostle on three points. First, should young Christians marry? Second, what was the duty of a Christian whose husband or wife remained an idolater? Third, what was the duty of a Christian slave? The first question is dealt with in verses 1-9, and resumed in verses 25-40; the second, in verses

10-17; the third, in verses 18-24, which is outside the range of our present subject.

We should not be in the least surprised at the Corinthians seeking help on such matters, for be it remembered that scarcely anything more of the New Testament than the first three Gospels had then been written. Let the reader try and imagine himself to be a young Christian in the Corinthian church with none of the Epistles to hand! During the brief stay of Paul in your city you had been converted under his preaching, separated from the world, and given as your blessed hope the coming of Christ to receive His people to Himself. Your whole outlook upon life had been radically changed. But the apostle had left for labours in other parts. You began to wonder how the great blessings and privileges of which you have recently been made the recipient are to affect and regulate the details of your conduct. Such questions as these now deeply exercise you: would my falling in love with a woman and marrying her cast a serious reflection upon my love for Christ? Does devotion to Him require me to remain in the single state, so that *He* may completely fill my heart? If you, my reader, had no written guidance from God thereon, and had been left to yourself, had you decided rightly or wrongly upon the point?

Continuing the same flight of imagination, suppose a rather different case in Corinth. God has recently brought you out of darkness into His marvellous light, but so far from being a single person, you are already married, united to an idolater! Will not the question now be seriously raised in your heart, What is my duty? Can it be pleasing and honouring to Christ that I should continue to co-habit with one who despises and rejects Him? I have sought to present the Gospel to her (or him), but instead of duly weighing the claims of the Lord Jesus, she ridicules and opposes me, and persists in attending the idol's temple. True, I still love her dearly, yet in view of the Saviour's words ("If any man *hate not* his father and mother, and wife and children, and brethren and sisters, yea, and his own life also, he cannot be My disciple"—Luke xiv, 26), must I not separate from her? Had *you* been left to your own understanding, yea, had you followed your "spiritual instincts," had you not determined wrongly? How thankful we should be for the completed Word of God in our hands, by which we are "thoroughly furnished unto all good works" and not left in uncertainty of the Divine will upon such important matters as these!

Not only had it been "natural" for those young Gentile converts to conclude that it was their duty to separate from their heathen partners, not only would their "spiritual inclinations" prompt them thereto, but if they had conferred with the *Hebrew* Christians in their assembly they had assuredly counselled them to do so, for they would at once have appealed unto Ezra x, 3, where those Jews who, during the captivity, had married wives in Babylon were required to "put them away," and their children also. Even though they wavered on the ground that Judaism was obsolete, and consulted the Gospels to see if Christ had uttered any definite word on the subject, they would discover He had said nothing about *mixed* marriages wherein believers and unbelievers were unequally yoked together. Thus, in their perplexity, they sought help from the apostle. In view of Ezra x, 3, there was a real need for him to authoritatively resolve the matter once for all, so that others (such as the newly converted in India or China) might know whether God required them to leave their unconverted partners in marriage, or whether He allowed them to continue living with the same.

THE DOCTRINE OF REVELATION
10. The Holy Bible.

That the Living Oracles of Truth are addressed to the *reason* of men as well as their conscience is definitely established by the fact that God Himself appeals to *prophecy* in proof of the unrivalled character of the communications He made through His servants. Their messages were retrospective as well as prospective, treating of things of the remotest antiquity as well as of those which lay centuries ahead, and thus commanded the entire horizon of history past and future. Their Divine Author places such peculiar value and attaches such importance to those supernatural disclosures as an evidence of inspiration that not less than seven times in the prophecy of Isaiah alone He challenges any false faith or idolatrous cult the world over to produce any revelations like unto His. "Produce your cause, saith the Lord; bring forth your strong reasons, saith the King of Jacob. Let *them* bring forth and show us what shall happen: let them show the former things, what they be, that we may consider them and know the latter end of them, or declare us things for to come" (xli, 21, 22).

"Behold, the former things are come to pass, and new things do *I* declare: before they spring forth I tell you of them" (xlii, 9). "Let all the nations be gathered together and let the people be assembled: who among them can declare this, and show us former things? [such as the creation of the earth, and everything else recorded in the book of Genesis]: let them bring forth their witnesses, that they may be justified [in their claims]; or let them hear, and say, it is truth" (xliii, 9). "I have declared the former things from the beginning; and they went forth out of My mouth, and I showed them; I did them suddenly, and they came to pass" (xlviii, 3). None of the seers of false religion can show either "the former things" or the "latter things": their outlook is restricted to the *present*. Only the Omniscient One can endow His messengers with a vision which reaches back before history began and which looks forward to ages not yet historic.

Again: that the Word of God is addressed to the reason of men is proven from the fact that appeal is made to *the miracles* recorded therein. "And many other signs [i.e. miracles—Acts ii, 22] truly did Jesus in the presence of His disciples [who have recorded many of them] which are not written in this book. But these are written *that ye might believe* that Jesus is the Christ, the Son of God: and that believing, ye might have life through His name" (John xx, 30, 31). The record of the various wonders wrought by God are given in Scripture not merely to furnish information, but to convince us that He is the Author of the Book which chronicles the same, and to bring our hearts and lives in full submission to His authority; and that we receive as our personal Lord and Saviour the One who is Himself God manifest in flesh, and therefore the final Spokesman from heaven. Those whom God employed as His penmen gave to the world a Divine revelation, and He accredited the same with due evidences, so that any receiving them are left without excuse if they despise and reject them.

Now it should be quite evident that if God is to give a personal communication unto fallen man, who is full of unbelief and scepticism, it will be supported with something more than the ordinary evidence of human testimony, that it will be supplemented by extraordinary evidence. A Divine revelation will be confirmed by Divine insignia. If God is to speak audibly to those who forsook Him, it can only be in a way out of the common course. If He commissions messengers to declare His will, they must possess such credentials as demonstrate that they come from Him. Each prophet sent from Him must be authenticated by Him. Those bearing supernatural messages will reasonably be expected to possess supernatural seals and be accompanied with supernatural phenomena. If God directly intervenes to instruct and legislate for the children of men, then clearly revelations and miracles must co-operate and combine. But here the infidel will at once demur, and deny that miracles are either possible or credible.

Nothing is easier than for an atheist to affirm that since the universe exists by eternal necessity and is subject to no change, that miracles cannot take place; but it is impossible for him to make anything approaching a satisfactory demonstration of that assertion. We do not propose to enter upon a lengthy discussion of the subject, deeming it sufficient to appeal to what has been presented in the previous articles in proof that God is, that He created the universe, and is now presiding over it. And then to point out, first, that what men term "the course of nature" is nothing but the agency of God. To declare that either a suspension or an alteration of the laws of nature is impossible, is to endow those laws with the attributes of Deity, and to be guilty of the absurdity of saying that the Lawgiver is subordinate to His own laws. The workman is ever superior to his works, and if God be the Creator and Governor of heaven and earth then He must be free to interfere in His own works whenever He pleases, and to make such interference manifest, by suspending or altering those laws by which He is pleased normally to regulate them.

"What is called the usual course of nature, then, is nothing else than the will of God, producing certain effects in a continual, regular, constant and uniform manner; which course or manner of acting being in every moment arbitrary, is as easy to be altered at any time as to be preserved. . . . To assert the impossibility of a miracle is absurd, for no man can prove, nor is there any reason to believe, that to work a miracle is a greater exercise of power than those usual operations which we daily witness. To restore life to a dead body and to bring it forth from the grave is not attended with any more difficulty than to communicate life to a foetus and to bring it forth from the womb. Both are equally beyond the power of man; both are equally possible with God. In respect of the power of God, all things are alike easy to be done by Him. The power of God extends equally to great things as to small, and to many as to few; and the one makes no more difficulty or resistance to His will than the other" (Robert Haldane).

To proceed one step farther. In a world which is upheld and governed by the living God, miracles are not only possible but *credible*, because probable. If the arrangement of nature be designed for the glory of its Maker and the good of His creatures, then it becomes in the highest degree likely that when any end of extraordinary importance is to be attained, that the laws of nature in their uniform course should be altered and made subservient to that event, that it should be heralded and evinced by extraordinary manifestations. Not only will the laws of the natural world become subservient to any great moral end, but they will be made to promote it. Since the laws of nature be under the direct management of their own Legislator, then not only may He moderate those laws at His own pleasure, but it is reasonable to conclude that He will make those modifications palpable and visible to His creatures when He purposes to effect some unusual influence upon them. Miracles could only be incredible if they were contrary to God's known perfections or contradicted some prior revelation of His will.

"Every thing we see is, in one sense, a miracle: it is beyond our comprehension. We put a twig into the ground, and find in a few years' time that it becomes a tree; but how it draws its nourishment from the earth, and how it increases, we know not. We look around us, and see the forests sometimes shaken by storms, at other times yielding to the breeze; in one part of the year in full leaf, in another naked and desolate. We all know that the seasons have an effect on these things, and philosophers will conjecture at a few immediate causes; but in what manner these causes act, and how they put nature in motion, the wisest of them know not. When the storm is up, why doth it not continue to rage? When the air is calm, what rouses the storm? We know not, but must, after our deepest researches into first causes, rest satisfied with resolving all into the power of God. Yet, notwithstanding we cannot comprehend the most common of these appearances, they make no impression on us, because they *are* common, because they happen according to a stated course, and are seen every day. If they were out of the common course of nature, though in themselves not more difficult to comprehend, they would still appear more wonderful to us, and more immediately the work of God.

"Thus, when we see a child grow into a man, and, when the breath has left the body, turn to corruption, we are not in the least surprised, because we see it every day; but were we to see a man restored from sickness to health by a word, or raised to life from the dead by a mere command, though these things are not really more unaccountable, yet we call the uncommon event a miracle, because it *is* uncommon. We acknowledge, however, that both are produced by God, because it is evident that no other power can produce them. Such, then, is the nature of the evidence which arises from miracles; and we have no more reason to disbelieve them, when well attested and not repugnant to the goodness or justice of God, only because they were performed several ages ago, than we have to disbelieve the more ordinary occurrences of Providence which passed before our own time, because the same occurrences may never happen again during our lives. The ordinary course of nature proves the being and providence of God; these extraordinary acts of power prove the Divine commission of that person who performs them" (T. H. Horne).

Finally, miracles are not only possible and credible but, as indicated in an earlier paragraph, in certain circumstances they are *necessary*. If there was to be a restoration of that intercourse with God which men had severed and forfeited by their defection, it must obviously be by supernatural means. Divine revelation, being of an extraordinary nature, requires extraordinary proofs to certify it. Since it was not to be a revelation made separately to every individual, conveyed to his mind in such a way as should remove all doubting, but rather a revelation communicated to a few and then published to the world, it follows that miracles were called for to confirm the testimony of the messengers of God, to convince others that they spoke by higher authority than their own, and therefore the necessity of miracles was in proportion to the necessity of a revelation being made. By the miracles performed through His servants God gave proof to those who heard them that they were not being imposed upon by fraud when they claimed to utter a "Thus saith the Lord."

A miracle is a supernatural work. It is something which could not be produced by the laws of nature, and it is therefore a deviation from their normal operations. A miracle is an extraordinary Divine work, where an effect is produced contrary to the common course of nature. God was pleased to perform such prodigies to testify His approbation of those who acted as

His mouthpieces, to avouch their messages—the miracles they performed were their letters patent. Whatever God has confirmed by miracles is solemnly and authoritatively ratified. The miracles wrought by Moses and Elijah, and by the apostles of the New Testament were such as were manifestly beyond the powers of any creature to produce and therefore they attested the Divine origin of their messages. Obviously, God would not work such wonders through imposters or in order to confirm lies, but only to witness unto the truth of a Divine revelation—see Mark xvi, 20; Hebrews ii, 3, 4.

Though miracles were both probable and necessary to authenticate unto men a revelation from God, yet it could not reasonably be expected that such sensible tokens or marks of Divine interposition should be renewed in every age or to each individual in the world, for that would completely subvert the regular order of things which the Creator has established. Nor was there any needs be for such a continual repetition of miracles. Once Christianity was established in the world, those extraordinary interventions of God ceased. It was fitting that they should, for God doth nothing unnecessarily. The Jews, every time they heard the Law read to them, did not expect a recurrence of the supernatural happenings of Sinai: those were one solemn confirmation of the Ten Commandments, which were to serve for all generations. Likewise, the Christian doctrine is the same now as it was in the first century, and will remain unchanged to the end of the world: we have a sure and authentic record of it in the Bible. Miracles, like any other facts, may be certified by reliable testimony.

It is by means of testimony that we obtain by far the greater part of our knowledge, and the trustworthiness of such testimony may be as conclusive as sense or mathematical demonstration. Evidence is necessary to establish the fact of revelation, though revelation existed before a line of Scripture came to be written. Those to whom the revelation was not personally made are required to believe it on the testimony of those who received it from the mouth of God. And it is just as unreasonable and illogical not to credit those witnesses as it would be to decline the trustworthiness of the atlas. I might as well refuse to believe there is any such country as New Zealand because I have never seen it for myself or personally spoken to those who have lived there, as reject the Bible as a Divine revelation because I did not personally witness the miracles God wrought to attest its original penmen nor have had personal converse with them. It is only by the evidence of testimony of their contemporaries and then through historians that we know such men as Alexander and Napoleon ever existed.

"On the same grounds of historical testimony, but furnished to us in a measure far more extensive, and connected moreover with a variety of other kinds of evidence, we are assured of the fact that Jesus Christ appeared in the world and that He was born, and lived, and died, in the country of Judea. This is attested by contemporary historians, and no man acquainted with history can be so absurd as to admit the reality of the existence of Julius Caesar and at the same time deny that of Jesus Christ. This is admitted by the greatest enemies of Christianity; and it is also acknowledged on all hands that the Christian religion which is professed at this day took its rise from Jesus Christ, and in the age in which He lived. Till then it is never mentioned; but from that period it begins to be noticed by historians, and shortly after becomes the subject of public edicts, and later produces revolutions in government, both more important and more permanent than that which Julius Caesar effected " (Robert Haldane).

(continued from back page)

do we long and groan for the removal of all obstructions and hinderances. Groaning is a vehement desire, mixed with sorrow, for the present want of what is desired" (John Owen).

Now the spiritual sighs and groanings of the Christian are interpreted by God as *prayers!* Those sacrifices which are acceptable to Him are "a broken and a contrite heart" (Psa. li, 7). Sobbings of soul are of great price in His sight (Psa. lvi, 8). The believer's moans are intelligible language to heaven: "the Lord hath heard the *voice* of my weeping" (Psa. vi., 8): that "weeping" possesses an appeal unto Him which the flowery eloquence of professional praying does not. "Lord, all my desire is before Thee, and my groaning is not hid from Thee" (Psa. xxxviii, 9). Those who wish to be reputed as very humble and holy by professing Christians may go about talking of their corruptions and proclaiming their vileness, but the truly broken-hearted will mourn in secret before God. Romans viii, 23, says we "groan *within* ourselves": our groans may be inaudible not only to other men's ears, but to our own; yet not so to God's. "He knoweth the secrets of the heart" (Psa. xliv, 21) and among those "secrets" are those aspirations of the soul which are expressed in sighs and groans.

Yes, God interprets the unexpressed exercises of a renewed heart. An illustration of that occurs in Exodus xiv, 15. When Moses was confronted with the Red Sea, his soul was deeply stirred before God. Nothing is recorded of his praying or audible groaning, yet the Lord asks "Wherefore criest thou [inwardly] unto Me?" Poor Eli supposed that Hannah was drunken because he observed the moving of her lips but heard not her voice; but the Lord heard, for "she spake in her heart" (I Sam. i, 13). What comfort is *there* for deeply tried saints? You may be one who feels utterly incapable of pray-ing in public (as was the case with the godly father of the writer), and may lament the fact that at times you cannot find words to express yourself before God in private; nevertheless, if you sigh and groan within yourself, He under-stands the longings of your heart, and in due time will satisfy them. Those sighs are as acceptable unto Him as the songs of "the spirits of just men made perfect."

Very remarkable are those words in Romans viii, 26: "The Spirit Himself maketh intercession for us with groanings which cannot be uttered." The deep longings and agitations of heart experienced by the saint for relief are the work of the blessed Comforter, and therefore does God give ear to them. The Holy Spirit excites longings in our souls for deliverance from the power of sin within and the world without. He it is who inspires yearnings after holiness and heavenly mindedness such as are greater than words can express, and, as verse 27 tells us, they are "according to God."

Blessed be His name, God reads every longing caused by His grace within us. He recognizes the symptoms and diagnoses the case of our soul with infinitely more accuracy than the best physician does that of the body. Our tears speak to Him of godly sorrow, our moans as the breathings of a contrite spirit. "From heaven did the Lord behold the earth: to hear the groaning of the prisoner" (Psa. cii, 20)—such "groaning" as that of Romans vii, 14, 19, 23. They are "*His*" prisoners" (Psa. lxix, 33), and therefore "prisoners of hope" (Zech. ix, 12). Here then is consolation: God is privy to our secret sighs, Christ is touched with them (Heb. iv, 15), they ascend as petitions to heaven, and are the sure pledges of deliverance.

the wickedness of the world, the low state of the Cause of Christ on earth, are variously described in Scripture. Sometimes he is said to be "in heaviness" (I Pet. i, 6), to "cry out of the depths" (Psa. cxxx, 1), to "roar" (Psa. xxxviii, 8), to be "overwhelmed" (Psa. lxi, 2), to be "distracted" (Psa. lxxxviii, 13). The tossings and anguish of his soul are depicted as "groanings" (Rom. viii, 23). The groanings of the believer are not only expressive of sorrow, but also of hope, of the intensity of his spiritual desires, of his panting after God, and his yearning for the bliss which awaits him on high (II Cor. v, 2, 4).

Such exercises of soul are peculiar to the regenerate, and by them the Christian may identify himself. If the reader now be the subject of sorrows and sighs to which he was a total stranger while in a state of nature, then he may be assured he is no longer dead in sins. If he finds himself groaning over the infection of his heart and those workings of inward corruption which prevent his perfectly loving and uninterruptedly serving God as he longs to do, that is proof that a principle of holiness has been communicated to his soul. If he mourns over the lustings of his flesh against that principle of holiness, then he must be alive unto God. The worldling will groan over the common troubles of life, such as financial loss, pain of body, the death of a loved one, but that is only the voice of nature. The Christian too will groan over such sorrows, for grace does not destroy the feelings of nature, though it both regulates and sublimates them. But the worldling never weeps in secret over the coldness of his heart or the workings of unbelief.

Where one groans over the workings of indwelling sin, over manifold temptations, over his comparative barrenness, over his being so little like what he longs to be (fully conformed to the image of Christ), those "groans" or "sighs" are the evidences of spiritual life, the pantings of holiness, hungering and thirsting after righteousness. They are, as Mr. Winslow expressed it, "The muffled chimings of Heaven." They are the sure pledges of deliverance (II Cor. v, 4). They are the marks of the Christian's union with Him who was "The Man of sorrows." Before Christ healed the deaf man, we read that "He sighed" (Mark vii, 34), which expressed His deep sympathy with the sufferer, as one "touched with the feeling of our infirmities." And again, when the Pharisees came to Him, "tempting Him" by asking a sign from heaven, we are told that Christ "sighed deeply in His spirit" (Mark viii, 11, 12), which denoted His holy indignation at their sin, godly sorrow for their persons, and grief within His own soul, for He *suffered* when He was "tempted" (Heb. ii, 18)—His holiness *felt* contact with evil.

The more the Christian's light and love increase, the heavier does the burden of indwelling sin become, and the more ardently does he long for deliverance from his body of death. There are sighs and groans which issue not only from sorrows, but from obstructed desires and delayed hopes. The groaning of II Corinthians v, 4—for the glorified state—breathes the fervency and intensity of our longing for the same, in contrast with a stolid indifference or cold formality. The stronger be that longing, the more groaning until it be realized. "The more we grow in faith and spiritual light, the more sensible are we of our present burdens, and the more vehemently do we groan for deliverance into the perfect liberty of the sons of God. . . . The nearer anyone is to heaven, the more he desires to be there. because Christ is there. For the more frequent and steady are our views of Him by faith, the more

(continued on preceding page)

XXVI NOVEMBER 1947 No. 11

STUDIES IN THE SCRIPTURES

"Search the Scriptures." *John v, 39*

Publisher and Editor—ARTHUR W. PINK,
29 Lewis Street,
Stornoway, Isle of Lewis,
Scotland.

ONE THING

"One thing thou lackest" (Mark x, 21). Those words were addressed by our Lord to the rich young ruler who had approached Him with such apparent eagerness and earnestness, and in whom there were some admirable qualities which are rarely found in young men, especially those of affluence. He occupied an honourable position, for Luke xviii, 18, informs us he was a "ruler." He had a clean moral record, for when Christ quoted to him the last six of the Commandments he answered, "All these have I kept from my youth up"—outwardly, his life was blameless. He was fearless, for he sought not unto Christ "by night" as Nicodemus did, but openly and publicly. He was no dilatory seeker, for he had come "running" (Mark x, 17). He was humble and reverent, for "he kneeled to Him"—how few young men bow the knee to Christ, especially when the eyes of their fellows be upon them! He came to Christ inquiring the way of salvation: "What good thing shall I do that I may have eternal life?" What more could be required of him? There was a fatal defect, for the sequel informs us that he turned from Christ, and "went away grieved." What was wrong with him?

"One thing thou lackest: go thy way, sell whatsoever thou hast and give to the poor . . . come, take up the cross, and follow Me. And he was sad at *that* saying." There was a struggle between his convictions and his corruptions: he desired to serve two masters—God and mammon; and when Christ told him that was impossible he was chagrined. His fatal deficiency may be described in a variety of ways. He had no conviction that he was a ruined, lost and Hell-deserving sinner, no consciousness that he was a spiritual leper in the sight of God, no realization of his utter helplessness to better his condition. Though religious, he was still in nature's darkness, and therefore his affections were not raised above the vanities of this world. There was no love for God within him, and consequently he was unwilling to deny himself, abandon his idols, and give God His rightful place in his life—serving, pleasing, and enjoying Him. He lacked a real and unreserved surrender of his heart to God. Reader, is that the case with you?

"One thing I know" (John ix, 25). That was the confession of one upon whom our Lord had wrought a miracle of grace, namely, the man who was "blind from his birth," to whom the Saviour gave sight. But no

(continued on back page)

Important Notices

Please advise promptly of change in address, otherwise copies will be lost in the mails.

We are glad to send a sample copy to any of your friends whom you believe would be interested in this publication.

This magazine is published as "a work of faith and labour of love," the editor and his wife gladly giving their services free. There is no regular subscription price, as we do not wish the poor of the flock to be deprived. This does not mean that those looking for something for nothing may "help themselves." Those getting this magazine who are financially able and who receive spiritual help from its pages, are expected to gladly contribute towards its expenses; otherwise their names are dropped from our list.

Will those forwarding International Money Orders please have them made out to us at Stornoway, Isle of Lewis, Scotland. Checks (Cheques—Eng.) made out on U.S.A. Banks are not negotiable here, so please do not send them.

All unsigned articles are by the Editor.

CONTENTS

THE PRAYERS OF THE APOSTLES

47. II Thessalonians i, 11, 12

It is both interesting and instructive to compare and collate the different things Paul prayed for on behalf of the several assemblies. For the Roman saints he asked that they might be "like-minded one toward another" and be "filled with all joy and peace in believing" (xv, 5, 13). That the Corinthians might "come behind in no gift and be confirmed unto the end" (i, 7, 8). That the Ephesians might have "the eyes of their understanding opened" so that they might apprehend the wonders of God's great salvation (i, 18-23), and be so "strengthened" by the Holy Spirit as to experimentally possess their possessions (iii, 16-21). That the love of the Philippians might be regulated by knowledge (i, 9-11). That the Colossians might "walk worthily of the Lord unto all pleasing, being fruitful in every good work" (i, 9-12). How rarely these blessings are made the burden of public prayers! There was no petition for justification!

For the Thessalonian saints the apostle first besought their entire sanctification. *Their* spiritual condition was much above the average, as is evident from the whole of the opening chapter of the first epistle, and for them he made an unusual request. They had progressed far in the school of Christ, and the apostle longed that they should attain unto the highest grade of all. Their case illustrates the principle that it is not those Christians who give the least promise at the outset who develop the least favourably, as those who make the best beginning do not always end well. In Acts xvii, 10, 11, we read that those in Berea "were more noble than those in Thessalonica, in that they received the Word with all readiness of mind and searched the Scriptures daily." Yet we are not told of a church being organized there, in fact no further mention is made of them in the New Testament; whereas two epistles are addressed to the church of the Thessalonians! So too of the churches of Galatia: time was when they "did run well," but they ceased to do so (verse 7).

As to exactly what the apostle prayed for in this particular one, there is considerable difference of opinion among the commentators, nor did our translators seem to have been very sure, as appears from the words in italics. It needs to be borne in mind that the Reformers and Puritans were but gradually and in part purged from the errors of Rome. Even the one who annotated this epistle in M. Henry's commentary, after alluding to the heavenly inheritance of the saints, wrote: " Now if this be our calling, our great concern should be *to be worthy of it* or meet and prepared for this glory: and because we have no worthiness of our own, but what is ours through the grace of God, we should pray that He *would make us worthy,* and then count us worthy, of this calling, or that He would *make us meet* to be partakers of the inheritance of the saints in light. (Col. i, 12)." That is nothing better than diluted Romanism, and there is quite a little of that noxious poison still at work even in orthodox sections of Protestantism.

The clear teaching of the New Testament is quite otherwise. In the case of all regenerate souls God already " *hath wrought them* for the self same thing" (II Cor. v, 5), i.e. for their " house not made with hands, eternal in the heavens " (verse 1). The meritorious and imputed righteousness of Christ has obtained for them an indefeasible *title* to everlasting glory, and the regenerating work of the Spirit in their souls has experimentally *fitted* and qualified them for the same, as is clear from the case of the dying thief. Therefore, instead of striving to be worthy, or praying for God to make them so, it is their grand privilege and bounden duty to be daily " Giving thanks unto the Father which *hath made us meet* to be partakers of the inheritance of the saints in light " (Col. i, 12), to praise Him for what His grace has effected for and in us. And second, to diligently and constantly seek enabling grace that we may " *walk* worthy *of* the vocation wherewith we *are* called " (Eph. iv, 1). that is, that our conduct accord with our high privilege, that our daily lives be such as become those so marvellously favoured.

" Wherefore also we pray always for you, that our God would count you worthy of *this* calling and fulfill all the good pleasure of *His* goodness, and the work of faith with power" (verse 11). The two words in italics have been supplied by the translators, but as is so often the case they serve to obscure rather than elucidate. On this verse Bagster's Interlinear (which preserves in English the order of words in the Greek and gives a literal translation) is to be preferred: "For which also we pray always for you, that you may count worthy of the calling of God, and may fulfill every good pleasure of goodness and work of faith with power." Not only is that far truer to the original, but it is much sounder doctrine, besides being more intelligible. It should also be pointed out that " may count worthy " is a single word in the Greek, and is not a forensic one, being quite different from the one rendered " counted " (i.e. legally accounted) in Rom. iv, 3, 5 and " imputed " in Rom. iv, 8, 11. The Greek word in our text is " axioo " and is found again in Luke vii, 7, I Tim. v, 17, Heb. iii, 3 and x, 29, where in each place it has the force of " deemed " or " esteemed."

Now whenever a verse presents any difficulty our initial concern should be to carefully ponder its context. That is particularly incumbent upon us here, for our verse opens with the word "wherefore." Let us then consider first *the occasion* of this prayer, for that will throw light upon its meaning. Verse 4 is the key to all that follows to the end of the chapter. There the apostle declares " So that we ourselves glory in you in the churches of God, for your patience and faith in all your persecutions and tribulations that ye endure" or " are bearing." They were being hotly assailed by the Enemy and were passing through " a great fight of afflictions." So nobly had they conducted themselves that Paul had held them up as a pattern to other assemblies. And now he seeks to comfort and strengthen them. First, by pointing out the present advantage of their severe trials. Their fortitude and faith supplied " a manifest token of the righteous judgment of God, that ye may be counted worthy of the kingdom of God, for which also ye suffer " (verse 5)— a statement the force of which none of the commentators seem to have grasped.

The Greek word for " manifest token " occurs again only in II Cor. viii, 24: " the *proof* of your love." The word for " righteous judgment " is the same as in " Judge not according to the appearance, but judge righteous judgment " (John vii, 24): that is, determine not your estimate of others on superficial and surface grounds, but let your decision or evaluation be a fair and impartial, an adequate and equitable one. Thus, taking verses 4 and 5 together the meaning of the latter should be obvious: by their becoming conduct in the furnace of affliction the Thessalonians had clearly attested themselves to be among the effectually called—their " patience and faith " as surely evidenced their regeneration as did the bounty of the Corinthians give proof of their love. Consequently, their bringing forth that fruit in such an unfavourable season was proof of the just verdict of God in accounting them worthy or meet of His kingdom, for which they suffered. In other words, Wisdom was justified of her children: their deportment made it evident they bore the image of God—" that ye *may* be the children of your Father which is in Heaven " (Matt. v, 45) signifies, that ye *manifest* yourselves as such, by doing what is enjoined in verse 44.

Next, the apostle assured them that God, in His righteousness, would both deal with those who troubled them and exonerate His people at the revelation of the Lord Jesus from Heaven (verses 6-10). Their Redeemer Himself would take vengeance on those who knew not God and obeyed not the Gospel of His Son; whereas He would be " glorified in His saints " and admired in all them that believe." Here then was solid consolation for them: in due time their persecutors should be punished, while they should be richly rewarded and fully vindicated. Therein we are shown one of the many practical advantages of the " blessed hope " of our Lord's return. Instead of making that glorious event the subject of acrimonious controversy, it should be a means of comfort (I Thess. iv, 18) and an incentive to piety (I John iii, 2, 3). The second coming of the Lord and the glorification of His entire Church at that time should be constantly viewed by the redeemed with the eyes of faith, of hope, and of love. The more it is so, the greater will be its holy influence upon their character and conduct; especially will it enable them amid tribulation to rest in the Lord and wait patiently for Him.

" For which also we pray always for you." The correctness of our analysis of the context is here borne out by the word " also." In addition to the grounds of consolation set forth by me as pertinent to your suffering (which the opening " for which " looks back to), I would assure you that I make your case the subject of earnest prayer: the " always " meaning frequently. And *for what* would we here expect the apostle to make request? That they might be delivered from their persecutions and tribulations? No indeed, that had been a carnal or natural desire, but not a spiritual one. Paul had previously informed them that God's people " are appointed thereunto " (I Thess. iii, 3), knowing that " we must through much tribulation enter into the kingdom of God " (Acts xiv, 22): the members of Christ's mystical body are first conformed to their Head in suffering, before they are "glorified together" (Rom. viii, 17). Our prayers must be regulated by the revealed will of God (I John v, 14) and not by the promptings of mere flesh and blood, which are generally contrary thereto. Let us then now turn and consider

Second, *the petitions* of this prayer, using the more accurate rendering of the Interlinear. "That you may count worthy of the calling our God." Three things require elucidation: what is here signified by "the calling"? what is meant by "that you may count worthy of" the same? why Paul made such a request for them? In Eph. i, 18 the apostle prayed that those saints might know "the hope of *His* calling"; in II Pet. i, 10 all Christians are exhorted "make *your* calling and election sure": it is one and the same "calling," of which God is the Author and we are the subjects. It is our call to Christianity. The same Greek word is rendered "walk worthy of your *vocation*" or occupation (Eph. iv, 1). The artist's vocation is to paint pictures, the wife's vocation is to look after her home, the Christian's vocation is to serve, please, and glorify Christ. He is to make holiness his trade; his business is to "*show forth* the virtues of Him who hath called him out of darkness into His marvellous light" (I Pet. ii, 9), and thereby "adorn the doctrine" which he professes.

The Christian calling is described by a double attribute: "Who hath saved us and called us with a *holy* calling" (II Tim. i, 9), and "Wherefore, holy brethren, partakers of the *heavenly* calling" (Heb. iii, 1). The former relates to the way, the other to the end: therefore it is said, "He hath called us *to* glory and virtue" (II Pet. i, 3), meaning by "glory" our eternal inheritance, and by "virtue" grace and holiness: the latter being the way and means by which we arrive at the former. Both are to be viewed first as they are represented in the Gospel offer: "God hath not called us to uncleanness, but to holiness" (I Thess. iv, 7), and our daily work is to make holiness the business of our lives. So also God has "called us unto His eternal glory by Jesus Christ" (I Pet. v, 10)—so far from suffering loss by accepting the Gospel offer, we become incomparably the gainers. Second, our calling is to be considered as it is impressed upon us by the mighty operation of the Spirit. It is by *His* power that we truly respond to the Gospel and are effectually called from death unto life.

This designating the Christian's life by a "calling" or vocation denotes there is work for him to do, duties to be performed. It is not a life of daydreaming and emotional rapture to which he is called, but rather to the carrying out of tasks which are neither easy nor pleasant to the natural man, though pertaining to and delightful for the spiritual nature—such as the mortifying of his lusts and the cultivation of practical godliness. Hence also again, it is represented as a "race" which has to be run—demanding the forthputting of all our energies; and to a long "journey" which is both arduous and dangerous for it lies through the Enemy's territory (I John v, 19), and therefore is it one beset with many perils. Severe trials have to be endured, temptations resisted, powerful foes overcome, or we shall be overcome by them and perish in the conflict. The Christian career, then, is a persevering in grace, a holding on his way along the highway of holiness, which alone leads to Heaven.

Much grace then is needed by the Christian that "having put his hand to the plough," he does not look back and become unfit for the kingdom of God (Luke ix, 62); that having enlisted under the banner of Christ, he does not yield to temptation and become a deserter because of the fierce opposition he meets with from those who hate him and would fain bring about his utter ruin. This brings us to our second question: what is meant by " that you may count worthy of the calling our God "?—a harder one to answer! All the prayers of the apostle may be summarized as a making request for supplies of grace, but more specifically, for some particular grace suited to the case and circumstances of each company for whom he petitioned. Bearing in mind that these Thessalonians were enduring a great fight of afflictions, it is evident that the principal blessing he would seek on their behalf would be the grace of perseverance, that they might hold out steadfast under all their " persecutions and tribulations " and endure unto the end of the conflict.

Paul had recently sent Timothy to establish and comfort them: " that no man should be moved by these afflictions " (I Thess. iii, 3). In his former prayer he had made request that they should be " preserved blameless " (I Thess. v, 23), and here he intimates *how* this was to be accomplished. These Thessalonian Christians had begun well, for which he thanked God (verse 3), and now he makes supplication that they may end well; particularly in view of what they were suffering at the hands of their opponents. Calvin (in his " Institutes ") refers this as a prayer for " the grace of perseverance." Gill wavered, but inclined to " perseverance in the grace by and to which they were called," yet including also " the ultimate glory itself which the saints are called unto." That it *was* their perseverance in faith and holiness which the apostle here had in view is definitely confirmed by each succeeding clause of this prayer, as we hope to make clear in our exposition of them.

" That you may count worthy of the calling our God." There is no idea whatever here of anything entitled to reward: it is not the worthiness of condignity, but of congruity: that is, it is something which evidences meetness, and not that which is meritorious; as patience under sufferings makes it manifest there has been that wrought in us which qualifies or fits us for the glory which is to be revealed. The Greek word for " may count worthy " is rendered " desire " in Acts xxviii, 22: " We desire to hear of thee what thou thinkest ": that is, we deem it right or meet to give thee a fair hearing. So its negative form occurs in " But Paul *thought not good* to take him with them "—we have referred to these passages to enable the reader to form his own judgment of what is admittedly a difficult word. In I Thess. ii, 11, 12 we read the apostle had " charged every one of you, as a father his children, that ye walk worthy of God (suitably, becomingly), who hath called you unto His kingdom and glory "; and here in our text Paul prays that they would be moved to do so by highly *esteeming* their calling and *acting* accordingly.

The apostle was making request for God's work of grace to be continued and completed in their souls, and more particularly, that they might be stirred to discharge their responsibilities in connection with the same. The Greek word occurs again, in an intensified form (" kataaxioo "), in " they which should be accounted worthy (adjudged fit) to obtain that world, and the resurrection from the dead " (Luke xx, 35), which denotes a sentence of approbation passed in their favour. And again in " Take heed to yourselves, lest at any time your hearts be over-charged with surfeiting and drunkenness, and cares of this life, and that Day come upon you unawares. For as a snare shall it come on all them that dwell on the face of the whole earth. Watch ye therefore and pray always that ye may be *accounted worthy* to escape all those things that shall come to pass " (Luke xxi, 34): which clearly implies some difficulty in realizing it and some danger of coming short. As the seed sown, so the harvest: if we " sow to the spirit " then we shall " of the spirit reap life everlasting," but not otherwise.

THE LIFE AND TIMES OF JOSHUA

27. Circumcision

That which is to engage our attention on this occasion, as in the article following, is still concerned with what was preparatory to the real task awaiting Israel, and is found in what, strictly speaking, belongs unto the introductory portion of Joshua, rather than to the body of the book, where Israel's conquest and occupation of Canaan is the distinctive subject. Yet it is in these opening chapters that the Holy Spirit has (in typical form) revealed the fundamental secrets of success in the Christian warfare and their present enjoyment of the heritage which Christ has procured for them. It is therefore all the more needful for us to proceed *slowly* and seek to thoroughly assimilate these initial truths if we are to obtain the richest benefit from them. The first thing absolutely indispensable to Israel's possession of Canaan was their crossing of the Jordan. That, as we have shown, was a figure of the Christian's passing through death and judgment in the person of his Surety and then his entrance into " life." It is only one who is on *resurrection ground* that is qualified to overcome the foes which would prevent him possessing his possessions. Equally essential is it for the Christian to experience in a spiritual and practical way that which marked Israel's history at Gilgal.

"At that time the Lord said unto Joshua, Make thee sharp knives, and circumcise the children of Israel the second time " (v, 2). With those words chapter 5 ought to begin, for verse 1 in our Bibles obviously concludes the preceding one. Here in verses 2-9 the Holy Spirit has recorded what took place in Gilgal, namely, the circumcising of Israel. The narration of that important event is introduced by informing us *when* it occurred—a detail which must not be overlooked when seeking the spiritual application unto ourselves. "At that time," i.e., first when the Lord their God had so signally shown Himself strong in their behalf by performing a miracle of mercy for them. Second, when they had just passed through the river which spake of death and judgment. Third, as soon as they had set foot within the borders of their promised inheritance. Fourth, four days before the passover, as a necessary pre-requisite and qualification for them to participate in that feast. Fifth, ere they began the real task of possessing their possessions—by vanquishing those who would seek to prevent their enjoyment of the same. We shall ponder first the literal or historical meaning of this for the natural Israel, and then its application unto and significance as it respects the spiritual Israel, the Church of Christ.

The "circumcise the children of Israel the *second time* " requires a word of explanation. It should be apparent at once that the reference is not unto a repetition of a painful operation upon those who had previously been circumcised, but rather in contrast from a *general* circumcising of Israel on an earlier occasion. In the light of Josh. xxiv, 14, Ezek. xx, 7, 8 and xxiii, 3 it is clear that during their lengthy sojourn in Egypt the children of Israel departed grievously from the revelation which God had made unto their fathers, and the statutes (Gen. xxvi, 5) He had given them; and judging from the case of Moses' own son (Ex. iv, 24, 25), there is little doubt that the ordinance of circumcision had been generally, if not universally, neglected and omitted by them. The words "God *remembered* His covenant with Abraham, with Isaac, and with Jacob" (Ex. ii, 24, and vi, 5) imply that Israel had *forgotten* it. The express prohibition that none should partake of the passover, save those who were circumcised (Ex. xii, 48, 49), and the added statement, " Thus *did* all the children of Israel: as the Lord commanded Moses

and Aaron, so did they," denotes that circumcision had at last been administered—probably at the beginning of the " thick darkness which was upon all
Egypt " for the " three days " (Ex. x, 21) that preceded the pass-over
night,

Verses 4 to 7 (of Josh. v) tell us what it was that required such a wholesale
circumcising of the male Israelites—adults as well as children—on this
occasion: " Now all the people that came out were circumcised, but all the
people that were born in the wilderness by the way as they came forth out
of Egypt, them they had *not* circumcised " (verse 5), which in view of Genesis
xvii, 9-11, was a startling omission. There has been considerable conjecture
as to why Israel had failed to administer this essential rite for so many years.
Thos. Scott says, "The reason for this omission is not so manifest." John
Gill, "because of their frequent journeying, and the inconvenience of performing it, being always uncertain when they pitched their tents how long
they should remain and when they should remove . . . it was not safe to
administer it." But the most popular explanation is that of *sinful neglect*.
Yet even though that were the case with the great majority, would not the
pious among them have complied? If rank disobedience was the cause, why
is there no record of Moses rebuking them for such a grave sin? And why had
not Joshua insisted upon it while they tarried in the plains of Moab, instead
of waiting till the Jordan was crossed.

Matthew Henry came very much nearer the true explanation, though he
states it rather vaguely and with some measure of uncertainty. The real
reason, we submit, was what occurred at Kadesh-barnea. It was there the
murmuring and unbelief of Israel reached its awful and fatal climax, when
they hearkened to the evil report of the ten spies and refused to go forward
into the land of Canaan, saying " Let us make us a captain, and let us return
to Egypt"; and when Joshua and Caleb expostulated with them " all the
congregation bade stone them with stones" (Num. xiv, 1-10). It was then
that Jehovah swore in His wrath that they should not enter into His rest
(Psa. xcv, 11). It was then that He declared " But as for you, your carcases,
they shall fall in this wilderness. And your children shall wander in the
wilderness forty years, and *bear your whoredoms,* until your carcases be wasted
in the wilderness. All the number of the days in which ye searched the land,
forty days, each day for a year, shall ye bear your iniquities forty years, and
ye shall know *My breach of promise* " (Num. xiv, 32-34)—their apostasy and
breaking of the covenant releasing Him from His engagement to bring them
into Canaan. *There* is the key to Joshua v, 5!

When Israel, after repeated provocations, at length consummated their
rebellion by despising the promised land and refused to advance beyond
Kadesh-barnea, God swore that only two of that generation should enter it,
the remainder being condemned to perish in the wilderness. Thus for thirty-
eight years (Deut. ii, 14) Israel was in a state of *apostasy,* and during that time
their children bore the reproach of the same by being *denied* the " token " or
" sign of the covenant " (Gen. xvii, 11)—wrongly termed by men " the *seal* of
the covenant," for circumcision never " sealed " anything to anyone saving
only to Abraham (Rom. iv, 11). While the awful sentence of Numbers xiv,
32-34, lasted, Israel was a rejected people, and therefore their children were
not entitled to bear the mark of covenant-relationship to God. But for the
sake of their children, He did not withdraw every token of mercy from that
generation, but provided sustenance and guidance throughout their journeys:
the daily supply of manna, the pillar of cloud and fire, the erection of the

tabernacle, etc., were so many intimations that God's favour would yet return unto Israel, though He had cast off their fathers.

The miraculous passage of the Jordan gave clear proof that Israel was once more *restored* unto the Divine favour, that Jehovah had resumed His covenant relationship with them, that in emerging from the river of death, judgment was behind them; that His sentence upon their fathers had been completed.   That miracle showed unmistakably that Jehovah now owned Israel as His people, and therefore were they fit subjects again to receive the sign of the covenant upon their bodies.   Circumcision was the token of the Abrahamic covenant (Gen. xvii, 11).   That ordinance was the mark by which the natural seed of Abraham was distinguished from all other nations as a people in covenant with Jehovah, and which bound them by a special obligation to obey Him.   It was the sign of the promissory part of the covenant which secured to Abraham's seed the land of promise (Gen. xvii, 8).   Thus it was fitting that this second generation should *now* be circumcised.   Moreover, the restoration of circumcision was to be accompanied by a revival of other institutions which had lapsed in the wilderness—such as the passover feast, for which circumcision was a prerequisite.   Upon Israel's entrance into Canaan they came under a stricter discipline than hitherto (Deut. vi, 1; xii, 1, 8).

"At that time the Lord said unto Joshua, Make thee sharp knives and circumcise again the children of Israel the second time."   At the very time when Israel had entered that land whose inhabitants their unbelieving fathers had reported to be "strong" and "the cities are walled, and very great," yea, "all the people we saw in it are men of a great stature" (Num. xiii, 28, 32).   What a testing of Joshua's faith was this: that all the males of Israel should now, for several days, be thoroughly incapacitated for fighting (Gen. 34, 25)!   But God intended it should be made manifest that the camp of Israel was governed by Himself, and not by any worldly policy.   "What general ever opened a campaign in an enemy's country in the manner that Joshua did?   On such occasions, all attention paid to the exercises of religion is too generally considered as a needless waste of time.   Yet if indeed the help of God be the best security for success, and if His anger is more to be feared than the sword of any enemy, it will be found true policy to begin every expedition with repentance of sin, and attendance on the solemn worship of the Lord, and with using every method of securing *His* protection, though to a carnal eye it may appear unfavourable to success" (T. Scott).

"And Joshua made him sharp knives and circumcised the children of Israel" (verse 3).   Severe as was this testing of his faith to thus handicap his fighting forces, yet counting upon the Lord's protection, his confidence in Him triumphed over it.   We need hardly say that such a vast undertaking was not performed by him in person, but is attributed unto Joshua because the operation was carried out under his order and observation—just as we read that "Jesus made and baptised more disciples than John.   Though Jesus Himself baptised not, but His disciples" (John iv, 1, 2).   Not only was this command of God's a severe test of Joshua's faith, but of the people's too: their submission would evidence whether they owned the verity of that Divine promise (Num. xiv, 7, 8) which their fathers had disbelieved.   Moreover, their submitting unto circumcision was designed as a test of their *obedience*, for their conquest of Canaan was conditioned upon their punctillious compliance with all that God had commanded through Moses (i, 8).   Their willing compliance was a fulfilment of the promise which they had made unto Joshua in i, 17, 18, and afforded a further demonstration that *they* were the best of all the generations of Israel—in answer to the prayer of Moses (Psa. xc, 13-17).

"And it came to pass, when they had done circumcising all the people, that they abode in their places in the camp till they were whole. And the Lord said unto Joshua, This day have I rolled away the reproach of Egypt from off you. Wherefore the name of the place is called Gilgal [or "rolling"] unto this day" (verses 8, 9). The commentators are strangely "at sea" concerning the significance of that expression "the reproach of Egypt," most of them regarding it as a reference to the stigma incurred by Israel when they were the slaves of the Egyptians. But surely *that* reproach was for ever rolled away when Jehovah delivered His people from Egypt by a high arm, brought them safely through the Red Sea and there destroyed Pharaoh and his hosts. No, rather is it an allusion to Egypt's taunt of Exodus xxxii, 12. During the thirty-eight years when Israel was *rejected* by God there appeared ground for Egypt's sneer that they would perish in the wilderness; but all occasion for such a reproach had now been removed by the Lord's return unto Israel, and by restoring the token of the covenant He gave intimation that He had resumed His mighty works on their behalf, that they were His people and He their God.

But we must turn now and consider the application of this unto ourselves, for like all the ceremonial rites and institutions of the Old Testament times, circumcision is, antitypically, a real and substantial thing unto New Testament saints. Stating it first in a brief sentence, circumcision respected the *mortification of sin*, the putting off of the filth of the flesh. But that statement calls for explanation and amplification, for the great majority of Christians have very low and defective thoughts on this subject—inherited as they have been from the errors of Rome. Far too many of God's children today suppose that "mortification" signifies a dying to some specific acts of sin, the overcoming of this or that particular corruption. But that is a serious mistake. Watching against, offering stern resistance unto, and obtaining the victory over some particular acts of sin, falls far short of real mortification. That is evident from the fact that none of that is beyond what persons in a state of nature may do, and not a few *have* actually done. Men and women whose hearts know nothing whatever of the power of Divine grace have, nevertheless, succeeded in gaining the mastery over an unruly temper, and of denying their craving for strong drink.

Again, let it be granted that, as the result of a course of strict self-discipline, a Christian has overcome some besetting sin; or, putting it on a higher ground, that by Divine enablement in answer to prayer, he has become dead to some particular lust; nevertheless, the evil nature, the root, the filthy fountain from which such foul streams proceed, the whole body of sin, still remains within! No, Christian mortification consists of something much better, something far greater and grander than anything poor Papists are acquainted with. To be mortified unto sin is a higher and holier mystery than to be delivered from any mere acts of sin. It consists of having union and communion with Christ in *His* death unto sin (Rom. vi, 10, 11). It is the effect and fruit of Christ's death for us, and of Christ's death in us by the power of the Holy Spirit, whereby we live upon and enjoy fellowship with Him in His death, and are made partakers of "the power of His resurrection." As faith is exercised upon Him as our Head, we experience the virtue and efficacy of His death and resurrection in our hearts and lives.

That which was shadowed forth by circumcision, namely the putting off of the filth of the flesh, all believers find the substance of in *Christ,* and the same is made good *in their souls*—in measure here, but perfectly so at death. In order to obtain a complete view of the Christian's circumcision, we need to consider it federally and judicially, then spiritually and experimentally, and then practically and manifestatively. First, then, all believers are *legally* circumcised in Christ. That which circumcision prefigured was the removal of the pollution of sin, and that was accomplished for believers judicially in the death of their Head. Circumcision symbolized the entire mortification of sin, and that is the effect and fruit of Christ's death for His people. "Ye are complete in Him [Christ], which is the Head of all principality and power. *In whom* ye are circumcised with the circumcision made without hands, in putting off the body of the sins of the flesh by the circumcision of Christ" (Col. ii, 10, 11). There we have the blessed fact stated, that in Christ their federal Head His redeemed are already, truly legally circumcised. It is said to be "without hands" to distinguish it from the physical circumcision of the type, and to show that it is the result of no attainment of ours. Colossians ii, 11, is a statement which is addressed to our *faith*, for it refers to something outside of our actual experience, to something which we have in Christ.

The apostle was moved by the Holy Spirit to employ quite a variety of terms to express the same fact. In Romans vi, 2, he said of all believers "we died unto sin." In I Corinthians vi, 9, "but ye are *washed*, but ye are sanctified, but ye are justified in the name of the Lord Jesus." In Galatians ii, 20, he declared—as the representative of all saints—"I am *crucified* with Christ." Here in Colossians ii, 11, he affirms, "In whom also ye are *circumcised*," which signifies that in the sight of God's Law and justice the total pollution and defilement of sin (as well as its guilt and criminality) has been for ever removed. "I have blotted out as a thick cloud thy transgressions" (Isa. xliv, 22). "Thou art all fair My love, there is no spot in thee" (Song of S. iv, 7). "And you that were sometime alienated and enemies in your mind by wicked works, yet now hath He reconciled in the body of His flesh, to present you holy and unblameable and unreprovable in His sight" (Col. i, 21, 22). Those scriptures bear witness that Christ and the Church are federally and legally *one*: that God the Father accepts them and views them in the Beloved as both righteous and holy; that He now sees them as without spot or wrinkle or any such thing; that He pronounces them eternally cleansed and blessed.

The faith of many of God's people apprehends the blessed fact that the guilt and condemnation of their actual transgressions was perfectly atoned for by Christ, but the faith of very few apprehends that their evil nature itself and all their corruptions have been made *a legal end of* by the sacrifice of Christ. They recognize by faith that God views them as cleansed from the curse of the Law, that there is "no condemnation" resting upon them; but they fail to perceive that the justice of God regards them as purged from the very presence and defilement of sin in their natures, that there is no filth within them. Yet the latter is just as true of them as is the former. Their "old man was crucified with Christ" (Rom. vi, 6). They were circumcised in Christ, which is described as a "putting off the body of the sins of the flesh." Indwelling sin is called a "body" because it consists of various parts and members, and that "body of sin" has been "put off," yea, "destroyed" or "annulled" as the word used in Romans vi, 6 signifies. Not only so, but the holiness of Christ has been imputed or placed to the account of their souls, so that God Himself declares, "the King's daughter is *all* glorious *within*" (Psa. xlv, 13), and not merely "without"—as covered with the robe of Christ's righteousness.

We say again that Colossians ii, 11, is a Divine declaration (as is Song of Solomon iv, 7, and Psalms xlv, 13, quoted above) which is addressed *to faith*, and is not a description of Christian experience; though in proportion as faith really appropriates it, we experience the comfort and joy of it.   Alas that some of our readers are likely to refuse that comfort and joy through suspicion and fear that a belief of the same might lead to carelessness and low views of sin.   When God bids His children to "reckon ye also yourselves to be dead indeed unto sin" (Rom. vi, 11)—which means exactly the same as "Reckon ye also yourselves to be circumcised indeed in Christ, in putting off the body of the sins of the flesh"—He certainly is not bidding them do anything which has a dangerous tendency.   He exhorts them to so regard themselves because they have good and solid ground *for* doing so.   They had a representative being and existence in their Head when He suffered and died to remove both the guilt and the defilement of their sins.   Unless we were one with Christ in His death, there could be no pardon or cleansing for us. The saints then are to regard their state before God to be what Christ's is: delivered from sin's dominion, accepted in the Father's unclouded favour.

DIVORCE

That to which we have called attention in the last three paragraphs supplies a forcible illustration and an unmistakable demonstration of the imperative need for the child of God to subject himself unto the written Word, and to be regulated by its teaching in all the practical concerns of his life.   The utter inadequacy of his own understanding (even now that it has been renewed by the miracle of regeneration) and the definite insufficiency of his "new nature" to serve as his monitor, appears no more plainly than in the inability of each to solve this problem according to the mind of God. It might be supposed that "sanctified common sense," and still more so, "the spiritual promptings," of a born-again Arab or Jap would intimate that it was his bounden duty to separate from a heathen wife who positively refused to give the Gospel a hearing and who was determined to remain an idol worshipper.   Nevertheless, such a decision would be the very opposite of what God has prescribed in I Corinthians vii, 12: "If any brother hath a wife that believeth not, and she be pleased to dwell with him, *let him not* put her away"!   Learn, then, dear reader, your imperative need of having a "thus saith the Lord" for your Rule.

But we must turn now to an examination of the apostle's language here. We will not dwell upon I Corinthians vii, 1-9, where Paul was replying to the question, Should a young Christian remain single or marry? further than to say a few words upon verse 6.   From his "I speak this by permission, not commandment" some have drawn the erroneous inference that Paul was not here writing by inspiration of God, but was merely recording his own personal opinion.   The reader will find it easier to follow the apostle's line of thought if he places verses 3-5 in parentheses, for it is evident that verses 7-9 are a continuation of verse 2, and therefore the "this" of verse 6 looks back to what had been said in verse 2—confirmed by the opening "for" of verse 7. The contrast between "permission" and "commandment" in verse 6 is not that of Paul writing as a private individual and as an inspired apostle (as verse 40 shows), but rather that marriage itself is a thing allowable, but *not ordered* by God—as the extreme Jewish element taught.   God has neither forbidden nor commanded His children to marry: it is optional.   **Whichever** you decide upon, you sin not. He who marries does well, he who marries not, does better—provided he has the gift of continency.

From verse 10 to the end of verse 17 the apostle deals with the matter of a believer who is already married to an unbeliever, and in the case of the Gentile Corinthians, of a believer who previously was a heathen, and whose mate is still an avowed idolater. "And unto the married I command, yet not I, but the Lord. Let not the wife depart from her husband" (verse 10). The apostle deals first (as what follows makes clear) with the case of those saints which, in the circumstances described above, contemplated the taking out of a divorce. And he tells them that, so far as *this* matter was concerned, there was no need for them to apply unto him for instruction: Christ Himself had already authoritatively declared that the marriage covenant could not be broken at the option of either of the parties, nor even by mutual consent. Except for the one sin of adultery, the wife had no right to leave her husband under any circumstances whatever, nor was the husband permitted to repudiate his wife for any cause. This the apostle, as His ambassador, emphatically enforces, as his "I command" unmistakably shows. His "yet not I, but the Lord" means, such a binding statement originates not from me: rather is it a maintaining of what the Lord Jesus laid down before me.

"Let not the wife depart from her husband" (verse 10) signifies let her not be unfaithful to her marriage vows, nor under any pretence desert her husband. Difference of religion is not to cause a separation. No divorce is permissible save for the one cause which Christ specified. "The Christian calling did not dissolve the marriage covenant but bound it the faster by bringing it back to the original institution, limiting it to two persons, and binding them together for life" (Matt. Henry). Even though the husband be an infidel, a persecutor and a blasphemer, nevertheless it is the Christian wife's duty to still live with him and meekly bear his taunts and opposition. The trial of such a union is to be patiently endured and the duties thereof cheerfully performed, and thereby she would adorn her profession, and honour and magnify her Saviour. Such a trial, sore and protracted as it may be, affords opportunity for her to prove the sufficiency of Divine grace. If God, in His sovereignty, be pleased to bless her kindness and good example, and hear her fervent prayers, the unbelieving husband may first be ashamed, and then "won," and his heart brought to seek and find Christ for himself (I Pet. iii, 1).

"But, and if she depart, let her remain unmarried, or be reconciled to her husband; and let not the husband put away his wife" (verse 11). This is not said as countenancing such a departure, but rather is giving directions what each party is required to do where such a thing had happened. If the wife, upon being made a partaker of the saving grace of God, has hurriedly or rashly forsaken her heathen partner, yet such a procedure has not annulled the marriage, and therefore she is not free to wed a Christian. She must either remain in the separate-but-married state, or "be reconciled to her husband": that is, seek him out, acknowledge her fault in leaving him, ask his forgiveness, and avow her willingness to live with him in peace. That was her bounden duty. First, because of her marriage vows; and second, to prevent reproach being brought upon the Gospel; and however humbling it might be unto pride to own her mistake, and though against her spiritual inclinations, yet she must spare no effort to re-establish normal relations with the one who was still her husband.

Widening the scope from this particular case of a Christian woman united to a heathen, let us consider that of a Christian woman whose husband is *not* an idolater, but yet a godless man who mistreats his wife. It has been said, "There are cases undoubtedly which justify a woman in leaving her husband, which do not justify divorce. Just as there are cases which justify a child leaving, or being removed from the custody of a parent" (C. Hodge). We agree, yet must add, such cases are not common, and plainness of language is needed to specifically define them—otherwise too wide a door will be opened, and many not warranted to do so will consider themselves entitled to avail themselves of it. Nothing can possibly justify a man in separating from his wife nor a woman from her husband, be either one a believer or an unbeliever, except such things as really make it impossible for them to dwell together: neither dislike, differences of opinions, wasteful extravagance, nor even drunkenness and abuse, warrant one to forsake another whom he or she has solemnly promised to love and live with "till death do us part."

"We can only conceive of two cases which would warrant a wife's leaving her husband. (1) If he be abandoned to the vilest profligacy. He may be unfaithful to her, but unless sunk in shameless profligacy, we do not think even that a sufficient cause for her leaving him. But if he bring prostitutes to his house, live in shameless adultery with the servant under her own roof, or by his base conduct entail on her personal suffering, we think she may, after every exertion made to reclaim him, leave him; but even then, not fully, nor finally, but be willing to return and forgive him if he be really reclaimed from his base ways and is desirous for her to come back. (2) Where violence is pushed to the edge of cruelty and life endangered . . . where there is a continued course of cruelty, an attempt made upon life or limb, and from abandoned drunkenness or insanity, the wife's life is really in danger, and she cannot procure protection from the law, or from any other quarter; then, we think, she may leave her husband, for who would counsel her to stay to be murdered?" (J. C. Philpot, *Gospel Standard,* 1855, page 384.) But even should he spend his remaining years in prison or in an insane asylum, she is still his wife, and is *not free* to marry another.

"But to the rest speak I, not the Lord" (verse 12). We are not acquainted with any commentator who appears to have apprehended the force of the first four of those words. All whom we have consulted assume that the apostle is addressing himself to precisely the same class as he did in verses 10 and 11; yet one had thought the language here used was sufficiently explicit to preclude that idea. In the two preceding verses Paul was giving counsel to those who wondered if it was their duty to obtain a divorce from their heathen partners. That is clear, first, from his "I command, yet not I, but the Lord" (verse 10), for the only relevant matter upon which Christ had legislated or adjudicated was that of *divorce.* Since nothing but adultery was a just ground for a divorce, "let not the wife depart from her husband." Second, from the disjunctive "But" at the beginning of verse 12, and "to the rest [i.e. whose particular problem was not contemplated in verses 10 and 11] speak I" shows that a different class is about to be addressed.

The added words, "speak I, not the Lord" supply further confirmation that he is taking up another subject or dealing with a separate problem. Before considering the same, however, let us free that clause from a misconception which some have entertained of it. In their hostility to the doctrine of the verbal inspiration of the Scriptures, enemies of God have searched diligently to find something in the Word which seemed to militate against that vital truth, and their *wish* being "father to the thought" led them to conclude they had found what they were looking for in the sentence now before us, i.e. that here the apostle acknowledged, in this place at least, he was giving out his *own* thoughts, that it was not the Lord who was speaking by him; which goes to illustrate the trite saying "The Bible can be made to prove anything." So it can, if we fail to understand *what* it says, if we suffer ourselves to be misled by the sound of its words, instead of going to the pains of ascertaining their sense; if we come to the Bible with our minds already made up of what it reveals, instead of humbly approaching it with the sincere and earnest prayer, "that which I see not teach Thou me."

Nor is it only the more-or-less open enemies of the Truth who have wrested such statements as occur in I Corinthians vii, 12, etc., for some who, in the main, were sound in their teaching, have erred grievously thereon. One such commentator, who exercised considerable influence in the second half of last century, interpreted the apostle to mean, "I do not claim, in this advice, to be under the influence of inspiration," which at once repudiates II Timothy iii, 16. But when the apostle declared, "to the rest speak I, not the Lord," he was not drawing an antithesis between what is inspired and what is uninspired, but rather between what the Lord Jesus had taught while He was here on earth, and what His servant was now "moved by the Holy Spirit" to give out. "The Lord" is not the equivalent of "God," but of the Mediator (viii, 6)—compare vii, 22; x, 21, 22; xi, 23; where in each instance the reference is clearly unto *Christ*. On the subject of divorce the Lord Jesus had given express commandment (verse 10), but upon the wider problem which the apostle was now taking up, He had said nothing. Since there was not anything in Christ's teaching which met this particular case, Paul was now authorized by Him to give His people that necessary instruction which met the exigences of their trying situation.

Under the Mosaic economy the Lord had expressly forbidden His people to wed any of the heathen: "Neither shalt thou make marriages with them: thy daughter thou shalt not give unto his son, nor his daughter shalt thou take unto thy son" (Deut. vii, 3). Because some of them had defied that statute in Babylon, upon the return of the remnant of Israel unto Palestine, Nehemiah "contended with them and reviled them, and smote certain of them" (xiii, 23-25), and Ezra the priest (vii, 12) gave orders "separate yourselves from the people of the land and from the strange wives," and accordingly "they gave their hands that they would *put away* their wives, and being guilty, they offered a ram of the flock for their trespass" (x, 11, 19). Though silent thereon after His incarnation, through Ezra and Nehemiah the Lord had revealed His will. It had therefore been the very height of presumption had Paul here given such directions without Divine warrant. "It would amount to the most outrageous blasphemy if the apostle had not felt that in using this language he was the mouth of God, and had he ventured to say of his own proper authority, 'It is not the Lord, it is I! I, I say, and not the Lord'" (L. Gaussen, *Theopneustia*).

Here, then, is a contrast between the requirements of the two dispensations. Under the Old Testament economy one of God's people who wedded an idolater must put her away; under the milder regime of the Gospel, he is not to do so. In His earthly ministry, Christ confined Himself to Palestine and restricted His teaching unto those who were under the old covenant. It was therefore fitting that His apostle unto the Gentiles should be His mouthpiece in resolving this difficulty for the Corinthian saints. Having solemnly ratified, as God's messenger, the primitive ordinance of marriage and asserted its unalterable validity (verses 10, 11), he turned to consider a case of lesser gravity, namely, whether a voluntary separation was proper, yea, advisable, where one party was a Christian and the other was not so. In the apostle's "I command, yet not I, but the Lord" (verse 10) and his "But to the rest speak I, not the Lord," we have indubitable proof that he was dealing with different cases. In both instances he was addressing married people, in both instances where one was a believer and the other an unbeliever; but in the former, where a *divorce* was contemplated; in the latter, where a *separation* only was in question.

"If any brother hath a wife that believeth not, and she be pleased to dwell with him, let him not put here away" (verse 12). The Corinthian, like most of the first Christian churches, was comprised of believing Jews and believing Gentiles. Some of those Jews had before conversion adhered more or less strictly to the Mosaic law, but others of them were lax (as many of their descendants today) and had "learned the ways of the heathen," and had taken wives from them. But now, with the fear of God in their hearts, they too would be most uneasy, apprehensive that probably they must do as their forebears did in the days of Ezra and Nehemiah. No, says the apostle, such a drastic course is not now required, nor is even a separation called for. Christianity requires no believer to turn away from his wife though she be unconverted. On the contrary, if she still loves him and desires to live with him, the Lord Jesus permits her to do so. Christianity is not intended to overthrow the natural relations of life, but to strengthen, to enrich, to elevate them.

"And the woman which hath a husband that believeth not, and he be pleased to dwell with her, let her not leave him" (verse 13). The apostle puts the case both ways, so that there might be no uncertainty. There was also a needs-be for him to do so, for since the husband be "the head of the wife" (I Cor. xi, 3; Eph. v, 23), her "lord" (I Pet. iii, 6), she is required to be in loving subjection. The wife, recently converted, might think that her unconverted partner no longer *had* any authority over her, and that she was at full liberty to follow her own inclinations. Not so; even though her husband be destitute of faith, if he is willing for her to remain with him, she must do so. The marriage vows are to be held sacred, and not broken because any difference of religious opinion or experience has arisen. When the love of God is shed abroad in the heart, its favoured recipient will not be less but far more solicitous for the welfare of those near and dear unto them. A Christian wife whose husband is an unbeliever, has a God-given opportunity to let her light shine before him and to commend unto him the excellency of Christ. Then let her by affection, kindness, patience, and prayer seek to win him.

"For the unbelieving husband is sanctified by the wife, and the unbelieving wife is sanctified by her husband: else were your children unclean; but now are they holy" (verse 14). Care needs to be taken to interpret this verse in strict accord with its context, and not read into it what is entirely foreign to the subject under discussion. To make it teach the eligibility of such children for Christian baptism, is to *force* into it what is far removed from the matter which the apostle was speaking of, as some pedo-baptists have themselves honestly admitted. In this fourteenth verse, as its opening "For" intimates, the servant of Christ was pointing out the *needlessness* of any separation, since the unbelieving one is "sanctified" by the believing partner And second, he shows how *disastrous* would be the consequence if the idea were entertained that the conversion of one makes the marriage void and requires that they should part: if such were the case, then it would necessarily follow that the children born unto them were "unclean." The precise meaning of the words "sanctified," "unclean" and "holy" in this verse, we must now endeavour to show.

Bearing carefully in mind the nature of the particular case the apostle was here dealing with—that of a Christian united to a heathen—it is clear that in this fourteenth verse he was anticipating an objection.   In the preceding verse he had bade the believing wife to remain with her unbelieving husband. By so doing, her conscience was likely to demur and say, Shall I not be spiritually polluted by maintaining such a connection? Shall I not incur moral defilement in the sight of God by continuing to live with one who is an open idolater? If an Israelite during the Mosaic economy who had married a heathen became legally defiled, and his offspring were legally "unclean"—as is obvious from Ezra x, 3—then will not *my* children be in the same deplorable case? No; the cases are by no means parallel. Those Israelites had contracted unlawful marriages. But your case is otherwise: the matter upon which you have sought my counsel is one where the conversion of one has occurred *after* a legal marriage. That is easily resolved: the sanctity of the marriage relationship still obtains.

"For the unbelieving husband is sanctified by [or "to," as the same Greek preposition is rendered in the next verse] the wife, and the unbelieving wife is sanctified by [" to "] the husband." First, let us point out what these words *do not* signify. They cannot mean that God regards the unbeliever as a Christian, merely because he is united to a wife who has become such; nor that he is internally sanctified, for that is effected only by the operations of the Holy Spirit. It does not mean that her having become a believer has brought the husband into a holier relationship, or (as one expresses it) has "diffused a kind of holiness over the unbelieving partner." There is no reference either to moral character or ecclesiastical status. He or she is "sanctified" *only* in connection with that which is here under discussion: they are "sanctified" *maritally*. The unbelieving member is "sanctified" to the purpose of the marriage relation—otherwise conjugal contact could not be maintained.   Since marriage is a Divine institution, cohabiting therein is a holy thing, sanctioned by God Himself. In His sight the twain are "one flesh," and therefore by continuing in the marriage state it is "sanctified" to *both* of them.

The word "sanctified" is by no means used uniformly in the Scriptures, but instead, in a variety of senses. It rarely expresses any subjective or internal change. Occasionally it imports the bare separation of one thing or person from others; but much more frequently, the setting of it (or him) apart unto God, for His service. "The unbelieving husband is sanctified by the wife" neither means that he is made inwardly holy nor "federally holy," but that he is sanctified unto her *as an instrument* for a holy purpose. Marriage is as sacred as the sabbath: by continuing in the marriage relationship, it was sanctified to each of them. Though an unbeliever, nevertheless, the husband is sanctified to his wife for a sacred *end*—for the lawful enjoyment of marital privileges. The question at issue was, is it proper for such a couple to continue living together? The answer is Yes, because they were, and still are, indissolubly united by the holy ordinance of God.

In *proof* thereof, the apostle points out by logical inference what the other alternative would necessarily entail: "else [otherwise] were your children unclean": not spiritually so (for all are "shapen in iniquity" and "conceived in sin") nor ceremonially so; but *legally*. If your connection has become unlawful and an abomination before God, then your children are bastards. If you take the ground that a separation is now necessary, then you are saying to the world that your marriage is no longer valid, that it has become improper for you to remain with your husband, and thereby you expose your children to the stigma of disgrace. "But now [rather] are they holy" shows the error of such a supposition: therefore a continued cohabiting with your husband must be sanctioned by God. "But now are they holy" means in the *same* sense that the parents are "sanctified," i.e. in a legal and civil way: your children are *legitimate* offspring. They are "a godly seed" (Mal. ii, 15), that is, they are reckoned by God as being born in lawful wedlock.

THE DOCTRINE OF REVELATION

11. The Holy Bible

At the close of our last it was pointed out that our knowledge of and belief in all those events of the past which we did not personally behold are based upon the testimony of witnesses, and that we who live in this twentieth century have far better and surer evidence—judged from an historical stand-point—to be assured that Jesus Christ was an historical reality, than we have for believing that Julius Caesar existed. The only objection made against that fact which has even the appearance of substance is, that whereas the history of Julius Caesar followed the ordinary course of events, that of Jesus Christ was radically different, so much so that the latter makes a far greater demand upon our credence than does the former. Those who preceded us have shown that this objection, so far from presenting any real difficulty, only serves to render our belief easier, for it calls attention to just what should be expected in such a case, thereby rendering it more credible. Had the career of Jesus Christ flowed in normal channels, were there no extraordinary features to mark it, then we should indeed have good reason to suspect the records of it.

If Jesus Christ was the Son of God incarnate then we should naturally expect Him to be born in a way none other ever was. If He came here on a unique mission, of supreme importance to the whole human race—a Divine mission, having for its purpose a climacteric display of God's perfections, and the saving of His people with an everlasting salvation—then His life would obviously be without any parallel, yea characterized by the supernatural. The very nature of His mission required that miracles should attest His teaching. Yet those very miracles being matter of fact, evident to the senses of those who witnessed them, of such a nature they could not be misunderstood, were, equally with common occurrences, the subject of *credible testimony*. They were not of a momentary nature, but permanent in their effects. They were not performed in secret, but in broad daylight in the midst of multitudes. They were not few only, but numerous. They were not performed only in the presence of friends but before enemies, and under a government and priesthood which bitterly hated their Performer and the doctrine they supported.

The miracles wrought by the Lord Jesus were, both in their beneficent character and in their wondrous nature, worthy of Him who did them and of the mission which engaged Him. They were not performed as spectacular displays of power, but directed to such gracious and practical ends as feeding the hungry and healing the sick. Moreover, it is to be carefully borne in mind that those wonders were specifically *predicted* centuries before He was

born at Bethlehem.   Wrought as they were in the open, before friends and
foes alike, had there been any deception practised it must have been detected.
But the fiercest of His detractors were compelled to acknowledge their reality
(John xi, 47; xii, 18, 19), though ascribing them to a diabolical influence.   It
is an historic fact that Christ's miracles were not denied in the age in which
they were performed, nor for many centuries afterwards.   They are related
to us by eye-witnesses and are inseparably connected with the rest of the
history of which they form a part.   They are in perfect accord with what the
rest of the Bible reveals of the power and goodness of God.

When Moses beheld the bush burning and not consumed, and heard the
voice of the Lord speaking to him thereout, not only were his senses convinced, but the awe-inspiring effect upon his heart was self-attesting evidence
that the living God was there revealed to him.   But those to whom he related
that startling experience, especially when he declared he had then received
a Divine commission to act as their leader, would require some convincing
proof that God had indeed spoken to him.   When the Lord bade him return
into Egypt and inform the elders of Israel that the God of their fathers had
appeared unto him in Horeb, Moses was fearful that his report would be
received with scepticism, saying, "they will not believe me, nor hearken to
my voice."   Whereupon the Lord, in His condescending grace, told him to
cast his rod on the ground, and it became a serpent; and take it by the tail,
and it became a rod in his hand; so that repeating these miracles "they may
believe that the Lord God . . . hath appeared unto thee" (Ex. iv, 1-5).
Thereby the mission which God had entrusted unto Moses would be *confirmed* beyond all dispute.

Upon this particular point we know of none who has written more
lucidly and convincingly than Mr. J. C. Philpot, from whom we shall now
quote and paraphrase.   "In such a matter as Divine revelation, which, as
being supernatural, is to fallen men naturally incredible, there is a necessity
that the ordinary evidence of human testimony should be as it were backed
and supplemented by extraordinary evidence, that is, the evidence of miracle
and prophecy. . . . Let us see the combined effect of testimony and miracle
when Moses goes to execute his mission.   "Moses and Aaron went and
gathered together all the elders of the children of Israel.   And Aaron spake
all the words which the Lord had spoken unto Moses, and did the signs in
the sight of the people.   And the people believed: and when they heard that
the Lord had visited the children of Israel, and that He had looked upon
their affliction, then they bowed their heads and worshipped" (Ex. iv, 29-31).

"First, there is *testimony*: 'And Aaron spake all the words which the
Lord had spoken unto Moses.'   Next there is *miracle*: 'And did the signs in
the sight of the people.'   Thirdly, there is *belief*: 'And the people believed.'
Fourthly, there is *worship*: 'they bowed their heads and worshipped.'   Thus
we see that the weakness of testimony ["weak" under *such* circumstances as
those—a single weakness unto an unexpected and unprecedented occurrence:
A. W. P.] is made up for and supplemented by the strength of miracle.
Without testimony miracle would be purposeless; without miracle testimony
would be inefficacious.   Testimony is to miracle what Aaron was to Moses—
'instead of a mouth'; and miracle is to testimony was Moses was to Aaron—
'instead of God' (Ex. iv, 16).   But why should miracle possess this peculiar
strength?   For this simple reason: that it shows the special interposition of
the Almighty.   Thus the magicians, when baffled and confounded, confessed
to Pharaoh, 'This is the finger of God' (Ex. viii, 19)."

Another instance of the place and value of miracles in connection with testimony is found in I Kings xviii. Half a century before, ten of Israel's tribes had revolted from the throne of David. Jeroboam their king had set up the worship of the golden calves in Dan and Bethel, which marked the extremities of his kingdom. Two generations had grown up in idolatry and "for a long season Israel [in contradistinction from Judah] had been without the true God, and without a teaching priest, and without law" (II Chron. xv, 3). But in the days of the wicked Ahab, God raised up the prophet Elijah, and His messenger announced that "there shall not be dew nor rain these years, but according to my word" (I Kings xvii, 1), and for three years there was an unbroken drought (James v, 17), which resulted in famine and great distress. Yet when the Lord's hand was lifted up in such manifest judgment "they would not see" (Isa. xxvi, 11), but Jezebel slew the prophets of the Lord (I Kings xviii, 13), while Ahab vowed vengeance upon Elijah himself. Nor did the common people evince any sign of repentance.

Elijah gave orders that all Israel should be gathered together unto mount Carmel, with the four hundred and fifty prophets of Baal and the four hundred prophets of the grove. He then came unto the people and said, "How long halt ye between two opinions: if the Lord be God, follow Him; but if Baal, follow him. And the people answered him not a word" (I Kings xviii, 22)—apparently because they were nonplussed, perceiving not how the controversy might be determined. Whereupon the servant of God proposed, "Let them therefore give us two bullocks: and let them choose one bullock for themselves, and cut it in pieces, and lay on wood, and put no fire under; and I will dress the other bullock, and lay it on wood, and put no fire under. And call ye on the name of your god, and I will call on the name of the Lord: and the God that answereth by fire, let Him be God. And all the people answered and said, It is well spoken" (verses 23, 24). The controversy should be decided by *a miracle!* Nothing could be fairer than what Elijah proposed; no test more convincing than the one here put to the proof. The people unanimously assented, and forthwith the trial was made.

For hours the prophets of Baal called upon their god to answer by fire, but there was no response; they leaped up and down at the altar, cutting themselves with knives till the blood gushed out upon them, but there was not "any that regarded"—the desired fire fell not. After their vain pretensions had been fully exposed, Elijah, to make more evident the miracle that followed, called for four barrels of water and poured it on the bullock which he had cut up and upon the wood until "the water ran round about the altar, and he filled the trench also with the water." Then Elijah prayed unto the Lord God of Abraham, Isaac and Jacob saying, "Let it be known this day that Thou art God in Israel, and I Thy servant, and that I have done all these things at Thy Word. Hear me, O Lord, hear me, that this people may know that Thou art the Lord God, and that Thou hast turned their hearts back again" (verses 36, 37). Nor did the prophet supplicate in vain. "Then the fire of the Lord fell and consumed the burnt sacrifice, and the wood, and the stones, and the dust, and licked up the water that was in the trench. And when the people saw they fell on their faces, and they said, The Lord He is the God; the Lord, He is the God."

Now what we would particularly note in that memorable scene on Carmel is the light which it casts upon the evidential value of miracles. That was made unmistakably plain in Elijah's prayer. The supernatural fire which came down from heaven in the sight of that vast assembly, consuming not only the bullock but the very stones on which it was laid, and the water in the trench round about the altar, was designed to make manifest, first, that Jehovah was God in Israel.   Second, that Elijah was His authorized servant. Third, that his mission and work was according to the Word of the Lord. Fourth, that God still had designs of mercy in turning the hearts of Israel back again unto Himself.   Here, then, is another case in point where the evidence of testimony was ratified by the evidence of miracle.   The mission of Elijah was authorized by the miracles performed in answer to his prayers: the special interposition of God attested the Divine origin of his message, for obviously the Lord would not work such wonders in answer to the petitions of an impostor.   God was pleased to perform those prodigies to testify His approbation of those who served as His mouthpieces, thereby leaving "without excuse" all who turned a deaf ear unto them.

Herein we may at once perceive how futile and senseless is the method followed by the "Modernists" and "Higher Critics." They are obliged to acknowledge the canonicity of the books of the Bible, for the whole of the Old Testament was translated into the Greek more than two hundred years before Christ, while there is independent evidence for the existence of the books of the New Testament from a very early date in the Christian era; yet they refuse to believe the miracles recorded *in them*.   But that is utterly irrational.   One has but to read attentively either the Pentateuch, the four Gospels, or the Acts, to discover that their historical portions and their miraculous portions are so intimately related we cannot logically accredit the former without accrediting the latter.   They necessarily stand or fall together: if the history is true, so also are the miracles; if the miracles be spurious, so is the history.   We could not delete the miraculous plagues upon Egypt and the supernatural destruction of Pharaoh and his hosts at the Red Sea without rendering completely meaningless the historical portions of the book of Exodus.   The same holds good of the book of Acts: abstract the miracles recorded therein, and much of the narrative become unintelligible.

The same feature obtains in connection with the wonders wrought by the Saviour. "Take, for instance, the raising of Lazarus from the dead. How can we separate the narrative from the miracle, or the miracle from the narrative? To see this more clearly, let us look at the narrative as distinct from the miracle. How simply, and so to speak naturally, is it related, and with what a minuteness and particularity of circumstances, which could not from their very nature have been invented. The name of the sick and dying man; the place where he lived, not far from Jerusalem, and therefore open to the closest investigation and examination; the names of his two sisters; the absence of Jesus at the time; the deep grief of Martha and Mary, and yet the way in which it was shown, so thoroughly in harmony with their characters elsewhere given (Luke x, 38-42); the arrival of Jesus; His conversation with them; His weeping at the tomb, and the remarks of the bystanders—what an air of truthfulness pervades the whole! There is nothing exaggerated, nothing out of place, nothing but what is in perfect harmony with the character of Jesus as reflected in the mirror of the other Gospels.

"But this narrative portion of the sickness and death of Lazarus cannot be separated from the miraculous portion—the raising of him from the dead. The first precedes, explains, introduces, and harmonizes with the second. Without the narrative the miracle would be unintelligible. It would float on the Gospel as a fragment of a shipwrecked vessel on the waves of the sea, furnishing no indication of its name or destination. So without the miracle the narrative would be useless and out of place, and of no more spiritual value than the sickness and death of a good man who died yesterday. But narrative and miracle combined, interlaced and mutually strengthening each other, form a massy web which no infidel fingers can pull to pieces. What we have said with respect to the miracle wrought at the grave of Lazarus is equally applicable to the other miraculous works of our blessed Lord. Narrative introduces the miracle, and miracle sustains the narrative—their combined effect being to prove that Jesus was the Son of God, the promised Messiah of whom all the prophets testified" (J. C. Philpot).

To the miracles which He wrought the Lord Jesus again and again appealed as evidence of His Divine mission. Thus, His forerunner, while languishing in prison and dismayed by his non-deliverance therefrom, sent two of his disciples unto Him with the inquiry, "art Thou He that should come, or do we look for another?" To which our Lord made reply, "Go and show John again those things which ye do hear and see; the blind receive their sight, the lame walk, the lepers are cleansed, and the deaf hear, the dead are raised up, and the poor have the Gospel preached unto them" (Matt. xi, 4, 5). The Lord there authenticated the Gospel which He preached by the supernatural works He performed: those displays of Divine goodness and power being the plain and irrefragable evidence that He was the Messiah "who should come," according to the unanimous declarations of the Old Testament prophets. On another occasion, after mentioning the testimony which John had borne unto Him, the Redeemer said, "But I have greater witness than of John: for *the works* which the Father hath given Me to finish, the same works that I do bear witness of Me, that the Father hath sent Me" (John v, 33, 36).

When the unbelieving Jews came and said unto Him, "How long dost Thou make us to doubt? If Thou be the Christ, tell us plainly. Jesus answered them, "I told you, and ye believed not; *the works* that I do in My Father's name, *they* bear witness of Me" (John x, 24, 25). If it be asked, How could any eye-witnesses of those mighty works refuse to believe if they were indeed proofs of His Divine mission? Because, since they rejected His *teaching*, God blinded their eyes and hardened their hearts (John xii, 37-40). But others *were* convinced. "Many believed in His name, when they saw the miracles which He did" (John ii, 23); and on the feeding of the great multitude with five loaves and two small fishes, we are told, "Then those men, when they had seen the miracle that Jesus did, said, This is of a truth that Prophet that should come into the world" (John vi, 15). Said Nicodemus, "We know that Thou art a Teacher come from God: for no man can do these miracles that Thou doest, except God be with Him" (John iii, 2): such displays of Divine power demonstrated that His mission and message was Divine.

Another striking illustration and exemplification of the value of miracles authenticating one employed upon a Divine mission is found in Acts ii. Less than two months after the death and resurrection of the Lord Jesus, and His subsequent departure from this world, we find the apostle Peter declaring openly, "Ye men of Israel, hear these words: Jesus of Nazareth, a man approved of God *among you* by miracles and wonders and signs, which God did by Him *in the midst of you* as ye yourselves also know" (verse 22). This was not said to a company of Christians in private, but to a vast "multitude" in Jerusalem (verses 5, 6). It formed part of an appeal made to the whole mass of the Jewish populace, and it was not contradicted by them, as it most certainly had been if Peter was making an empty boast. The apostle was reminding them that Christ had dispossessed demons, raised the dead, not in a corner but in the most public manner. Those miracles were incontestable, and the significance of them could not be gainsaid: they were so many testimonies from God of His approbation of the One who wrought them. They declared and demonstrated that Jesus Christ was the promised Messiah and Saviour. They certified His mission and doctrine. Much failure attaches to *us* at every point. Our paramount desire to enjoy intimate and unbroken fellowship with the Lord, though sincere, is neither as intense nor as constant as it should be. Our efforts after the realization of that desire, our use of those means which promote communion with Him, are not as diligent and wholehearted as is incumbent upon us. Our pressing forward unto the mark set before us is often most feeble and faulty. But there is no failure with our God: His purpose will be accomplished, He *will* perfect that which concerneth us (Psalm cxxxviii, 8).

(continued from back page)

such as the Word of God, His manifold mercies, our past sins and failures—that a due recollection of them may humble us in the present and for the future. But there are other things which, in a certain sense, the believer needs to forget, namely, his past services unto the Lord, his attainments in grace, his victories over temptation—so that they be not made a matter of complacency nor rested in as a substitute for present exertion. The Christian should ever be conscious of his imperfections and seek to rectify them, and so far from being content with his present knowledge, grace, and love, must press after a higher measure thereof. Are you, my reader, intent upon this one thing? and diligently attending unto the same?

"But, beloved, be not ignorant of this one thing: that one day is with the Lord as a thousand years, and a thousand years as one day" (II Peter iii, 8). It would be outside our present scope and design to attempt an exposition of this verse, rather would we point out the practical lesson which it inculcates for each of our hearts. As the Christian strives after a closer communion with Christ and a fuller conformity unto His image, it appears to him that his efforts meet with little success, and that his pressing forward unto the things before is most tardy. As he cries unto God for more grace, He seems very slow in responding. But, beloved, "be not ignorant of this one thing": God's measurement of time is very different from ours, nor does He ever delay a moment beyond His appointed hour. As the next verse assures us, "He is not slack concerning His promise." To our short-sighted impatience He seems to delay, when in reality "He waits to be gracious" (Isa. xxx, 18). Be not stumbled by His seeming slowness, but patiently wait for Him.

"Not one thing hath failed of all the good things which the Lord your God spake concerning you: all are come to pass unto you, not one thing hath failed thereof" (Josh. xxiii, 14). Those words, it seems to us, form a fitting climax to all that has been before us. They were the words of Israel's leader unto them after their occupation of the promised inheritance. It was a tribute to the unfailing faithfulness of their covenant God. And will not the antitypical Joshua say unto those whom God has given Him, when they are all settled in their eternal Rest, "Not one thing hath failed of all the good things which the Lord your God" promised you!

sooner was he made the recipient of that great mercy than he encountered opposition. First, some of his neighbours doubted his identity; but he reassured them. Then the Pharisees challenged him, but his parents avowed he was their son, and that his eyes had been opened. Then the Pharisees told him that his Benefactor was "a sinner." To which he replied, "One thing I know: that, whereas I was blind, now I see." That is the averment, or at any rate should be, of every truly regenerated person. Though unable to refute the sophistries of those who oppose the Truth, he may appeal to his actual experience and the great change which God has wrought in him—a change apparent to those best acquainted with him. He cannot explain the process, but he is sure of the effects. He may not know the time when he passed from death unto life, but he does know that once he was blind to the glory of God, his own depravity, the suitability of Christ; but he is so no longer. His eyes have been opened to see the sinfulness of sin and the sufficiency of Christ's atoning blood. Is that the case with you, my reader?

"One thing have I desired of the Lord, that will I seek after; that I may dwell in the house of the Lord all the days of my life, to behold the beauty of the Lord, and to inquire in His temple" (Psa. xxvii, 4). That expresses the paramount longing and dominant aim of each renewed soul, while his case remains a normal and healthy one. All his yearnings are concentrated into this, and after the attainment thereof all his energies are directed, for that which is ardently desired will be diligently sought. "That I may dwell in the house of the Lord all the days of my life" is but the Old Testament way of saying, That I may enjoy unbroken and close communion with Him. That desire evidences his love to God: "as the hart panteth after the waterbrooks, so panteth my soul after Thee, O God" (Psa. xlii, 1). Previously, the majesty and almightiness of God terrified him, His sovereignty and justice repelled His holiness and immutability were distasteful; but now the one quickened by Him exclaims, "My soul followeth hard after Thee" (Psa. lxiii, 8), esteeming fellowship with Him far above all the pleasures and treasures of this perishing world. Is that the case with you, dear reader?

"But one thing is needful" (Luke x, 42). We may regard these words as the Lord's intimation of how the desire of Psa. xxvii, 4, may be realized. They were spoken first to the restless and feverish Martha, who was "cumbered (weighted down) by much serving" and was "careful and troubled about many things." What that "one thing" was, Christ explained in the words at once following: "Mary hath chosen that good part, which shall not be taken away from her." That "good part" was that she "sat at Jesus' feet and heard His word." "But one thing is needful": how that would banish care did we but apprehend it! How many distractions would our hearts be freed from if we bowed to our Lord's dictum! There are a great many duties which the Christian has to perform, but Christ would bring our hearts from everything else simply to this: to be absorbed with Himself, to receive from His fullness, to commune with Him, to be instructed by Him. That is the one thing needful for a God-honouring, fruitful, happy life. Have you, my reader, been let into that secret experimentally?

"This one thing I do: forgetting those things which are behind and reaching forth unto those things which are before, I press toward the mark for the prize of the high calling of God in Christ Jesus" (Phil. iii, 13, 14). That expresses the practical outworking of what has been before us above. **There are many things that we are obligated to hold in our remembrance:**

(continued on preceding page).

XXVI	DECEMBER 1947	No. 12

STUDIES IN THE SCRIPTURES

"Search the Scriptures." John v, 39

Publisher and Editor—ARTHUR W. PINK,
29 Lewis Street,
Stornoway, Isle of Lewis,
Scotland.

ALL THINGS

Those two words supply an example of something to which we allude in these pages every once in a while, and which requires to be frequently emphasized in this age of shallowness, namely, the danger there is of being misled by the *sound* of certain expressions in the Scriptures through failing to ascertain their real *sense*. Among professing Christians there are not a few superficial people who imagine that the bare quoting of a verse is sufficient to prove their point and silence an opponent, whether that verse be relevant or no, whether the letter of it accord with or contradict other passages. There are others who, in a mistaken zeal for the integrity and authority of the Word, suppose it would be a perversion or denial of it to place a different meaning upon what appears to be its obvious signification. Luther's tenacious insistence that Christ's words concerning the sacramental bread " this is My body " must be understood literally, is a case in point. In like manner, it is supposed that when a verse says " *all* men " or " all things " it " means what it says " and is to be understood universally.

" Behold I have foretold you *all* things." (Mark xiii, 23): surely it is obvious that those words are not to be taken without any limitation. " Come, see a Man, which told me all things that ever I did " (John iv, 29) is not to be understood absolutely. " All things are lawful unto me " (I Cor. vi, 12) would flatly contradict many passages if it were regarded without any qualification. When the apostle said, " I am made all things to all men " (I Cor. ix, 22) his words must be explained in the light of what immediately precedes. " But ye have an unction from the Holy One, and ye know all things " (I John ii, 20) surely does not mean *everything* knowable, for if it did, it would be affirming that those Christians were omniscient. The words " all thngs," like all others in Scripture, require *interpreting* !

" With God all things are possible " (Matt. xix, 26). Doubtless it will appear to some of our readers that we rob the statement of much of its preciousness if we affirm that it cannot be taken without any limitation, yet such is the case. God himself has plainly told us in His Word that there are some things which He cannot do. " God *cannot* be tempted with evil " (James i, 15), He cannot deny Himself (II Tim. ii, 13), He " cannot lie " (Titus i, 2), and

(continued on back page)

Important Notices

Please advise promptly of change in address, otherwise copies will be lost in the mails.

We are glad to send a sample copy to any of your friends whom you believe would be interested in this publication.

This magazine is published as " a work of faith and labour of love," the editor and his wife gladly giving their services free. There is no regular subscription price, as we do not wish the poor of the flock to be deprived. This does not mean that those looking for something for nothing may " help themselves." Those getting this magazine who are financially able and who receive spiritual help from its pages, are expected to gladly contribute towards its expenses; otherwise their names are dropped from our list.

Will those forwarding International Money Orders please have them made out to us at Stornoway, Isle of Lewis, Scotland. Checks (Cheques—Eng.) made out on U.S.A. Banks are not negotiable here, so please do not send them.

All unsigned articles are by the Editor.

CONTENTS

THE PRAYERS OF THE APOSTLES

48. II Thessalonians i. 11-12.

In all of his prayers for the saints Paul sought from God further supplies of grace on their behalf, and this in order that they might be the more fully furnished and stirred up unto the performing of their duty. God has called His people unto a life of holiness, requiring them to be so " in all manner of conversation " (I Peter i, 15). At regeneration He imparts to them a holy nature or principle, and then bids them to " now yield your members servants to righteousness unto holiness " (Rom. vi, 19). Yet that holy nature or principle, is but a *creature*, and therefore far from being a self-sufficient entity. Like all other creatures, it is dependent upon God: for its life, development, and motions. But like all other rational creatures, its possessor is endowed with the instinct of self-preservation and therefore is he responsible to use all suitable means and measures for its well being. Nevertheless that responsibility can only be effectually discharged by Divine enablement, and therefore it is both our duty and privilege to seek from God all needed grace, and trustfully count upon His goodness supplying the same. The particular grace needed will be determined by our varying cases and circumstances.

In our last we saw that the Thessalonians were being sorely oppressed by their enemies: so much so that Paul had sent Timothy to establish and comfort them concerning their faith, and to urge " That no man should be moved by these afflictions, for yourselves know that we are appointed thereunto " (I Thess. iii, 3). Note well that holy balance: though God had ordained those trials, their spiritual father did not conclude there was no reason for him to be concerned about the outcome: rather did he deal with them as moral and accountable agents. So too though they had exercised much patience and faith " in all their persecutions and tribulations " (verse 4), yet the apostle was mindful of their frailty and the very real danger of them wavering and backsliding, and therefore he prayed much that persevering grace might be granted them; that they might walk worthy of their calling, hew steadfastly to the line of God's revealed will, and thereby glorify their Master. Such supplication on their behalf was intensified as he eyed the Day of punishment and reward (verses 6-9).

If any readers experience a difficulty in our statement that the apostle here prayed for persevering grace to be granted those sorely-tried saints, seeing that the eternal security of all Christians is infallibly guaranteed by the Divine promises, then it is because of their one-sided and defective views of the subject. And since we shall not be able to complete our exposition of this prayer in the present article we propose to devote our remaining space to showing that difficulty is a fancied rather than a real one. Before proceeding further let us point out that by " persevering grace " we intend Divine quickening, strengthening, empowering, to enable the Christian to hold on his way and run the race which is set before him—without which he would make total shipwreck of the faith and be eternally lost. Thus, in seeking from God food for the soul, deliverance from temptation, the help of His Spirit to mortify our lusts, that is, really, asking Him for grace to enable us to persevere in faith and holiness.

There has been a deplorable lack of Scriptural *balance* in the presentation of this subject. Calvinists have thrown their emphasis almost entirely upon God's preservation of His people, whereas Arminians have insisted only upon the necessity for their persevering. Since the great majority of our readers have been influenced far more by the former than the latter, let us point out, first, that God's Word teaches *both*. While it must be insisted upon that it is the power of God, and that alone, which preserves the saints from apostasy (total and final), and not in any degree their own grace, wisdom, strength or faithfulness, yet we must not fail to press the fact that Christians are responsible to keep themselves: that is, to avoid and resist temptations, abstain from everything injurious, and make a diligent use of all those means which God has appointed for their well-being. The Christian is exhorted to *"keep himself* unspotted from the world" (James i, 27). We are bidden " keep yourselves from idols " (I John v, 21), yea, to " abstain from all appearance of evil," and " keep yourselves in the love of God " (Jude xxi). It is criminal for preachers to ignore such passages as these.

God's Word not only enjoins the saints to preserve themselves, but the Holy Spirit has not hesitated to affirm they actually *do so*. He moved David to aver " by the Word of Thy lips I have kept me from the paths of the destroyer " (Psa. xvii, 11). " I kept myself from mine iniquity " (Psa. xviii, 4). " I have refrained my feet from every evil way " (Psa. cxix, 101). Those were not the boastings of self-righteousness, but rather testimonies to the sufficiency of God's enabling grace. The apostle Paul, jealous as he ever was of the glory of God, after exhorting the saints " so run that ye may obtain " (the " incorruptible crown ") and pointing out that the mastery over physical lusts calls for being " temperate in all things," affirmed " I therefore run, not as uncertainly; so fight I, not as one that beateth the air. But *I keep* under my body and bring it into subjection, lest that by any means, when I have preached to others, I myself should be a castaway " (I Cor. ix, 26, 27), While another wrote " he that is begotten of God keepeth himself " (I John v, 18).

But it may be objected. Does not this attribute too much to the creature, and divide the honours, by ascribing the work of preservation partly unto God and partly unto ourselves? Our first answer is, God's Word is to be received with childlike simplicity, and not quibbled over: received as a whole, and not merely those parts which appeal to us or accord with our own views. We have not set forth our *personal ideas* in the last two paragraphs, but have quoted the Scriptures—verses which alas have no place whatever in the preaching of most Calvinists today. If the reader be unable to fit those verses into his doctrinal system, then it is evident there is something wrong with his system. But our second answer is an emphatic denial of such an imputation. For, *our use* of the means God has appointed, our greatest diligence and efforts will all be unavailing, unless *God blesses* the same; yea, our utmost watchfulness and industry would avail us nothing whatever if God left us to ourselves.

Our own wisdom and strength, even as Christians, is altogether inadequate for the task assigned to us, and unless the Holy Spirit Himself energized us and afforded success to our efforts. our case would be like unto Gehazi's, who laid his staff upon the dead child (II Kings iv, 31)—but there was no quickening until his *master* came and acted! Though Christians do indeed keep themselves (and to deny that is to repudiate the passages quoted above), nevertheless, it is wholly from and by the power of God, so that they freely acknowledge " by the grace of God I am what I am " (I Cor. xv, 10). Yet observe well, the apostle added " and His grace was not in vain, but I laboured more abundantly than they all ": nevertheless he disavowed all credit for the same— " yet not I, but the grace of God which was with me." So again, " I also labour, striving according to His working, which worketh in me mightily " (Col. i, 29). Grace is given us to make use of, yet grace is required *to* use it.

We must therefore press upon another class of professing Christians, that we are entirely dependent upon God: we can only work out our own salvation with fear and trembling, as He works in us " both to will and to do of His good pleasure " (Phil. ii, 12, 13). The axe cannot cut unless it is wielded. The keeping ourselves from evil and destruction is not a distinct and separate work from God's preserving us, but a subordinate, though a concurrent one. It is not as though He were one partial cause and we another—as when two persons unite in lifting one burden; but our keeping is from Him, by Him, and under Him, as the little child writes as the hand of his teacher guides his. Therefore there is no ground for boasting, no occasion for self-gratulation; all the praise belongs alone to our Enabler. Thus, while the responsibility of the Christian is duly enforced and his accountability preserved, yet the glory of our preservation belongs entirely unto God.

As the miraculous power of God is absolutely necessary to the beginning of a work in any one's soul, so it is equally necessary for its continuation and progress. Unless God renewed the Christian daily he would perish eternally. Only its Giver can " hold our soul in life " (Psa. lxvi, 9). God preserves His people by breathing into them holy thoughts and quickening meditations, which keep them in His fear and love. By stirring up His grace in us, so that we are moved to holy action. By drawing us, so that we run after Him. By inclining our hearts to love His law and walk in its statutes. By giving us a spirit of prayer so that we are moved to seek fresh supplies of strength from Him. By restraining us from sin and delivering out of temptations. By working in us godly sorrow and causing us to penitently confess our sins. By His consolations when we are cast down, which puts new heart into us. By granting us foretastes of the glory awaiting us, so that the joy of the Lord energizes us (Neh. viii, 10).

If unfallen Adam was incapable of keeping himself, certain it is that *we* cannot do so independently of God: indwelling sin is too potent, Satan too powerful to overcome in our own strength—our falls demonstrate the need of God's preserving us. Nevertheless, Adam was responsible for keeping himself, and was justly condemned because he did not do so. Likewise, believers are responsible to avoid every path which leads to death, and steadfastly tread to the very end that narrow way which alone leadeth unto life. As a rational creature is morally responsible to shun known danger, to abstain from poisons, and to eat nourishing food for the sustaining of his body; so a spiritual creature is accountable to do likewise concerning his soul. If he is to guard against the spirit of self-confidence and self-sufficiency, so also he is to beware of acting presumptuously. When the Devil tempted Christ to cast Himself down from the pinnacle of the temple, assuring Him that the angels would preserve Him, He immediately denounced such recklessness with "thou shalt not tempt the Lord thy God."

We must never divorce the precept from the promise or what God requires from us and what He has purposed for us. God has inseparably connected means and ends, and woe be unto us if we put them asunder. The same God who has predestinated a certain end shall be accomplished, has also predestinated it shall be accomplished via the employment of certain means. Thus His people are told "God hath from the beginning chosen you to salvation through (1) sanctification of the Spirit and (2) belief of the Truth" (II Thess. ii, 13). Our "sanctification of the Spirit" is by His own operation, but "belief of the Truth" is the act required *of us*, and we are not saved, nor ever will be, till we perform it. Likewise we are told that the saints "are kept by the power of God," yet not to the setting aside of their concurrence, for it is at once added "through faith" (I Pet. i, 5). The duty of keeping his faith healthy and vigorous devolves upon the Christian—seeking from God its strengthening, feeding upon suitable food. The duty of exercising that faith rests upon him: "whom resist [the "roaring lion" who seeks to devour him] steadfast in the faith" (I Peter v, 8, 9,).

There is a deadly and damnable heresy being widely propagated today to the effect that, if a sinner truly accepts Christ as his personal Saviour, no matter how he lives afterwards, he cannot perish. That is a satanic lie, for it is at direct variance with the teaching of the Word of Truth. Something more than believing in Christ is necessary to ensure the soul's reaching Heaven. "If ye *continue* in My Word, then are ye My disciples indeed" (John viii, 31). "My sheep," said Christ, "hear [heed, obey] My voice, and they *follow* Me. And I give unto them eternal life, and *they* [those who plainly evidence themselves to be of His 'sheep' by yielding to His authority and following the example which He has left them—and none others] shall never perish" (John x, 27, 28). It is not honest to generalize the promise of verse 28: it must be restricted to the characters described in verse 27! "If ye continue in the faith grounded and settled, and be not moved away from the hope of the Gospel" (Col. i, 23) was how the apostle guarded and qualified his statement in verse 22!

Different far from the soothing opiates now being ministered by the false prophets was the holy balance of Truth preserved by that prince of theologians among the Puritans, John Owen. Yea, far more candid and faithful was he than those hyper-Calvinists who profess to admire his teachings. Said he, when exposing the sophistries of one who opposed the certainty of God's preservation of His people unto eternal glory, on the ground that it encouraged loose living: "Doth this doctrine promise, with height of assurance, that under what vile practices so ever men do live, they shall have exemption from eternal punishment? Doth it teach men that it is vain to use the means of mortification because they shall certainly attain the end, whether they use the means or no? Doth it speak peace to the flesh, in assurance of blessed immortality, though it disport itself in all folly in the meantime? . . . The perseverance of the saints is not held out in the Scriptures on any such ridiculous terms: carry themselves well, or wickedly miscarry themselves; but is asserted upon the account of God's effectual grace preserving them in the use of the means and from all such miscarriages."

On Hebrews iii, 14 Owen said, " Persistency in our subsistence in Christ unto the end is a matter of *great endeavour and diligence*, and that unto all believers. This is plainly included in the expression here used by the apostle: ' If we hold the beginning of our confidence steadfast unto the end.' The words denote our utmost endeavour to hold it fast and keep it firm. Shaken it will be, opposed it will be, kept it will not, it cannot be, without *our* utmost and diligent endeavour. It is true, persistency in Christ doth not, as to the issue and event, depend absolutely on our diligence. The unalterableness of our union unto Christ, on the account of the faithfulness of the covenant of grace, is that which doth, and shall eventually secure. But yet our own diligent endeavour is such an indispensable means for that end, *as without it*, it will not be brought about."

Finally, in his remarks on Hebrews x, 23: Owen said, " The apostle spends the whole remainder of the Epistle in pressing and confirming of this exhortation, on a compliance wherewith the eternal condition of our souls *doth depend*. And this he doth, partly by declaring the means whereby we may be helped in the discharge of this duty, partly by denouncing the eternal ruin and sure destruction that will follow the neglect of it, and partly by encouragements from their own former experiences and the strength of our faith, and partly by evidencing to us in a multitude of examples how we may overcome the difficulties which would occur to us in the way." How far removed from this teaching is that of those who pass for " high Calvinists " today! How little or how much of it is made plain and emphatic in their sermons, we must leave the reader to judge. Owen would now be denounced as an Arminian in many a so-called " place of Truth."

It may be thought that we have wandered far from the subject of our opening paragraphs. But have we? Our endeavour has been to demonstrate the very real need there is to *pray for persevering grace*, both for ourselves and for our brethren. Some ask, Why should we, since God has solemnly promised the eternal security of all His people? First, because our great High Priest has taught us (by His example) to do so: " Holy Father, *keep* through Thine own name those whom Thou hast given Me . . . I pray not that Thou shouldest take them out of the world, but that Thou shouldest *keep* them from the evil " (John xvii, 11, 15). Second, as an acknowledgment of our dependency and a confession of our helplessness. Third, as our concurring with God's revealed will, seeking grace to use the appointed means. We place a very large question-mark after the Christian profession of any man who is unconscious of his frailty and who deems not such a prayer as " Leave me not, neither forsake me, O God of my salvation " (Psa. xxvii, 9) as unsuited to *his* case. The present writer frequently cries " hold Thou me up, and I shall be safe " (Psa. cxix, 117), knowing that the converse would be, Leave me to myself, and I shall assuredly perish.

N.B.   A more detailed exposition of II Thessalonians i, 11, 12, follows (D.V.) in the January and February issues.

THE LIFE AND TIMES OF JOSHUA

28. Circumcision.

In our last we pointed out that the circumcising of all the male Israelites at Gilgal was a type of the circumcision of the Church. First, that all believers were *legally* circumcised in Christ: that at the cross the " body [or totality] of the sins of the flesh " was put off, completely and forever removed from the sight of God's law and justice; for such is the blessed meaning and teaching of Colossians ii, 11. God's elect had a federal being, a representative existence in their Head, so that when He died unto sin, they died unto sin; and it is both the duty and privilege of faith to appropriate that truth, and rest upon that fact. Therein we have revealed the Gospel method of mortifying sin—in blessed contrast from the fleshly devices of the Papists. It must flow from our union and communion with the Lord Jesus in His death, and faith's receiving of the virtue and efficacy of it. The fountain of all true and spiritual mortification was opened at the Cross and God is very jealous of the honour of the person and work of His beloved Son, and every departure from Him and it, every attempt of the carnal mind to devise some other remedy for any of the wounds which sin has inflicted upon and within us, is doomed to certain failure. Christ alone must be looked to for deliverance, not only from the guilt of sin, but from its power and pollution; yes, and from its presence too.

But it must now be pointed out that as Christ is the federal Head of His people, so also is He their vital or life-giving Head. As the natural head of the physical body influences all its members, imparting life and motion to them (for when one side of the brain becomes paralyzed, one whole side of the body does too), so Christ imparts life unto and influences the members of His mystical body, the Church. This He does by sending down His Spirit into their hearts, who communicates *to* them what Christ did and purchased *for* them. Thereby they are " circumcised" *spiritually and experimentally*. That brings us to the second branch of our subject. "For he is not a Jew who is one outwardly, neither is that circumcision which is outward in the flesh. But he is a Jew who is one inwardly, and circumcision is that of the heart; in the spirit, and not in the letter; whose praise is not of men, but of God " (Rom. ii, 28, 29). There is much of deep importance in those two verses yet they are little understood today, especially by Dispensationalists and writers on " Prophecy "; but it would be outside our present scope to give an exposition of them, or even show the apostle's line of argument in that passage; rather we must confine ourselves to that in them which bears directly upon our present theme.

"Circumcision is that of the heart: in the spirit, and not in the flesh." There we are plainly taught that real " circumcision," the circumcision which God most approves, is an *internal* one. Even that is little understood by our moderns, and has no real place in their teaching. We wonder how many of our own readers have any definite and clear-cut conception of what is meant by *spiritual* " circumcision." Very few, we fear. All the more need then for us to take up this subject here, instead of seeing how swiftly we can get through the book of Joshua by merely offering generalizations upon its contents. It should be apparent to all who have read the Scriptures with any degree of attention and care that He who " desires Truth in the *inward* parts " (Psa. li, 6) required very much more from Israel even in Old Testament times than obedience to the outward ordinance of circumcision. The call " Circumcise therefore the foreskin of your heart, and be no more stiffnecked " (Deut. x, 16) is too plain for misunderstanding. It is quite clear from Leviticus xxvi, 41 and the last clause of Jeremiah ix, 26 that the Lord punished Israel because they were " uncircumcised in heart." The same fault Stephen charged upon the Jews of his day (Acts vii, 51).

"Circumcise yourselves to the Lord and take away the foreskins of your heart " (Jer. iv, 4) was His just demand. John Gill acknowledged that " men are exhorted to this " (alas that so many of his admirers refuse to do so), though he rightly added " yet elsewhere He promises to do this for them." God has ever required reality and not simply outward profession, inward and moral purity and not merely external and ceremonial. " O Jerusalem, wash thine heart from wickedness " (Jer. iv, 14). This spiritual circumcision, or cleansing of the heart, is the negative side of regeneration, or as the older writers more aptly expressed it " the privative " side. Strictly speaking there is no English word which accurately defines it, but " privative " is the nearest —that which results in a privation through the absence of something, the withholding or taking of it away. This is one aspect or part of " the great change " which takes place in a person when he is made the subject of a miracle of grace. Since we recently dealt with that in considerable detail, there is the less need to be lengthy on this occasion; but as spiritual circumcision is included in the general term " regeneration," we must not altogether ignore it.

As we emphasised in our articles upon " The Great Change," far too many writers when treating of regeneration confine their attention unto but a single aspect of the same—the communication of a new life or " nature." But *that* contemplates only one angle of it even from the positive side. There is a negative or privative side too. There is travail and pain in connection with a birth. Perhaps the reader will find it easier to grasp what we are saying and the better understand our terms when we remind him that justification has *two* parts to it: a privative and a positive—something removed and something bestowed. The cancellation or removal of the guilt and penalty of all sins is the privative side of justification, for remission (forgiveness) means " sending away." The imputation of the meritorious obedience of Christ to the account of the believing sinner is the positive side, for " justify " signifies to declare a person (not merely innocent, but) *righteous*. The two things are brought together in that lovely type in Zechariah iii, 4, " Behold I have caused thine iniquity to pass from thee "—that is the privative side; " and I will clothe thee with change of raiment " (the " best robe " of Luke xv) is the positive.

Now at regeneration something is *removed*, as well as something imparted: " I will *take away* the stony heart out of your flesh, and I will give you a heart of flesh " (Ezek. xxxvi, 26). Though that be metaphorical language, yet is the figure easily understood. The affections are divorced from evil and united to that which is good. By the miracle of grace, God takes away the love of sin and implants a love of holiness. And how is fallen man's radical and inveterate love of sin removed from him? By the Holy Spirit's illumination, revealing to him the exceeding sinfulness of sin; by His convicting him of the enormity and heinousness of sin, striking his conscience with terror and horror at having waged war against the Almighty; by bringing him to realize that it was *his* sins which caused the Lord of glory to bleed and die. Then it is that the love of sin receives its death-wound in his soul. Then it is he is " pricked in his heart " and cries out in anguish and

despair " what shall I do? " (Acts ii, 37). Which is only another way of saying,
Then it is that his soul is spiritually and experimentally *circumcised*; when
so far as his love of it is concerned, he puts off " the body of the sins of the
flesh " (Col. ii, 11).

The work of the Holy Spirit within the saint is many-sided, but its grand
design and accomplishment is to make good *unto* him what Christ did *for*
him: or to state it in other words, the Spirit imparts to the soul an actual
acquaintance and effects with it a spiritual experience of what he has in Christ
federally and legally. Christ died unto sin, for He was " made sin [judicially]
for us," and His death was the penal death of our sin. Consequently, when
the Holy Spirit is given to us He first works death in our hearts: that is, He
both slays our self-righteousness, and gives a death-wound to sin in our
affections. As the apostle tells us when relating one aspect of his own conversion, " when the commandment came, sin revived, and *I died*" (Rom.
vii, 9). That is, when those words " thou shalt not covet," thou shalt not
even lust after or desire any unlawful object, was applied in Divine power
to his soul, the awful nature and extent of his sin became a living reality in
his conscience, and he died to all good opinions of himself. By the spiritual
slaying of our self-righteousness and making us loathe sin, the soul is experimentally " made conformable unto Christ's death " (Phil. iii, 10).

" The Lord thy God will circumcise thine heart, and the heart of thy
seed [which is to be taken *generally* as " all " and " the world " in the New
Testament] *to* love the Lord thy God with all thine heart " (Deut. xxx, 6).
There we have the two principal aspects of regeneration or the miracle of
grace brought together: the privative side, the circumcising of the heart, when
it is made willing to part with its cherished sins, when its affections are severed
from all evil. That is in order to the positive side, namely, the heart's being
brought to love the Lord with all its faculties and strength. That love to God,
John Gill rightly pointed out is " the duty of every man," and thus of the unregenerate: so, contrary to his followers, Gill not only taught " duty faith,'
but " *duty* love " ! Nevertheless, none performs this duty until God Himself
circumcises the heart. Then it is that the soul of the elect is transformed from
a natural man into "a new creature " (Gal. vi, 15). That moral change of
" putting off the old man with his deeds" (Col. iii, 9) was prefigured by the
fact that literal circumcision was required to be performed on the " *eighth
day* " (Lev. xii, 3)—the numeral which always signifies a new beginning, and
thus of " the new creature."

There is yet another aspect of this subject which calls for careful attention, namely, that circumcision of the Christian which is *practical and manifestative*. What Christ accomplished for His people, His Spirit effects within
them, and they are required to make the same apparent in their daily lives
and actions. Our federal and legal circumcision in Christ was in order to our
vital and experimental circumcision, for by His meritorious work on their
behalf the Lord Jesus procured the gift and grace of the Spirit unto His
people (Gal. iii, 13, 14). Our inward circumcision by the operations of the
Spirit unto His people was in order to the better qualifying us for the discharge of our responsibility and the glorifying of our God. While at regeneration the Spirit gives a death-wound unto sin in the affection of its favoured
subject, and while at the same time He implants in his heart an imperishable
love of and longing for holiness, yet He does *not* then remove from him the
evil principle—" the flesh " remains in his soul unto the end of his earthly
pilgrimage. Consequently, there is now a ceaseless conflict within him (Gal.

v, 17), and therefore he is henceforth called upon to " fight the good fight of faith ": to swim against the stream of his corruptions, deny self, mortify his members which are upon the earth.

The foes against which the Christian is called to wage conflict are mighty and powerful. That evil trinity, the flesh, the world, and the Devil, are relentlessly determined to destroy him. How then is he to successfully engage them in mortal contest? A great variety of answers have been returned to that question, all sort of rules and regulations prescribed; but most of them proceeded from " physicians of no value." It is too generally overlooked that *this* is " the fight of *faith*." The Devil can only be successfully resisted as we remain " steadfast in the faith " (I Peter v, 9). " This is the victory that overcometh the world—our faith " (I John v, 4). And there can be no victory over indwelling sin except by the actings of faith. And faith, my reader, always has to do with Christ: *He* is its grand Object (Heb. xii, 2), its Sustainer (Phil. i, 21), its Strengthener (Phil. iv, 13). That is according to the appointment of the Father, who has determined that His people should be beholden to His beloved Son for everything, that they may ascribe their all unto Him, that they may place the crown of honour and glory upon His Head. Christ is the alone Saviour not only from the guilt and pollution of sin, but likewise from its power and ragings within us.

In this matter of practical circumcision, our mortifying of sin, man's thoughts and ways are as far below God's as in everything else—as far as the earth is below the heavens. Man supposes he must do this in order to obtain that, avoid this in order to enjoy that, abstain from evil so as to enter into good. But he knows not where to obtain strength *for* the doing! Contrastively, God's way is to furnish that which equips for the performance of duty: to bestow freely, that gratitude will respond gladly; to lavish love upon us, that we cannot but love Him in return; to make known what He has made Christ to be unto us, and then bids us walk worthily of such a Saviour. He first makes us " light in the Lord," and then bids us " walk as children of light " (Eph. v, 8). He first makes us saints, then bids us act " as becometh saints " (Eph. v, 3). He makes us holy, then calls us " to be in behaviour as becometh holiness " (Titus ii, 3).

Immediately after Christians are bidden to likewise reckon ye also to have died indeed unto sin, but live unto God in Christ our Lord, they are exhorted " Let not sin therefore reign in your mortal body, that ye should obey it in the lusts thereof " (Rom. vi, 11, 12). Though they have died unto sin legally, sin is far from being dead within them. Though they are no longer " in the flesh " (Rom. viii, 9) so far as their standing before God is concerned, yet " the flesh " is still in them. Though Christ has put away the whole of the guilt and pollution of their sins, He has not yet fully delivered them from its power—that they might prove the sufficiency of His grace, the marvels of His forbearance, and the reality of His keeping power; and that there might be opportunity for the trial, exercise, and development of their graces. But though the evil principle (or " nature ") be not eradicated, the Christian is exhorted " Let not sin therefore reign in your mortal body." In that " therefore " we have an example of the apostle's evangelical method when urging Christians to perform their duty: not in order to obtain some further blessing, but because of what they already have in Christ.

That " therefore " looks back generally over the whole preceding section (from v, 1), but has a more particular reference to vi, 10, 11. The " Let not therefore sin reign " is far more than an appeal for us to exercise our wills:

it is a call for faith to make one's own all that standing and state which is ours by virtue of our legal and vital union with Christ. Faith is urged to apprehend and appropriate our sinlessness in Christ by our death and resurrection in Him. *That* is the only right way of approach unto gaining the victory over sin in our daily lives. God will set no premium upon unbelief, but He will honour *faith*. Faith is called upon to recognize and reckon that sin was vanquished by Christ, and therefore it has no right to lord it over us. We are to refuse obedience to its desires and behests. We are to yield no subserviency unto the dethroned adversary of Christ, but strive constantly against every effort it makes to gain the ascendancy over us. And in order unto strength *for* such striving, we are to draw motives and encouragement from the love of Christ, who suffered and died for us. Strength to resist sin comes from faith's eyeing Christ and love's drawing from Him incentives to mortify that which slew Him.

It is "the love of Christ" which is ever to *constrain* the Christian in all things. But I must first be assured of His love for me, before my affections will flow out to Him in grateful submission and service. Any service which issues from fear or is prompted by reward, is either legal or mercenary, and unacceptable to Him. Without a realization of pardoning mercy in the soul, we can gain no victory over indwelling sin. In Christ we are not only dead to sin legally, but victors over it. As faith beholds sin perfectly conquered by Christ judicially, it seeks to have fellowship with Him therein in a practical way. To repudiate long-cherished sins, relinquish beloved idols, is a cutting and painful experience to nature, and therefore is it designated a circumcision and mortifying of our members; yea, so distressing is such work, our Lord likened it unto plucking out a right eye and cutting off a right hand (Matt. v, 29, 30). Yet such is not only a needful and profitable duty, but it becomes a desirable and *longed-for* one by those who truly love the Lord. The more their minds be spiritually occupied with Christ's love, the more are their affections drawn forth unto Him, and the more are their hearts brought to hate sin; and the more we hate sin, the more are we *dying to* it in our affections!

In our last, we pointed out the importance of observing the opening words of Joshua v, 2 when seeking the spiritual and practical application unto ourselves of what God required from Israel at Gilgal. "At that time": as soon as they had passed through that river which spoke of death and judgment they were required to be circumcised. Likewise it is immediately after the Christian is assured of his union with Christ in death and resurrection that he is enjoined "Let not sin therefore reign in your mortal body." It is by faith's realization of that union we draw motives to resist sin's solicitations and derive strength against it. And as stated in our last we cannot serve God trustfully and joyously unless we are assured we are forever beyond condemnation (Rom. viii, 1), so it must now be added, there can be no progress in the Christian life unless we heed Romans vi, 12. That is amplified in the next verse: "Neither yield ye your members as instruments of unrighteousness unto sin; but (1) yield *yourselves* unto God as those that are alive from the dead and (2) your *members* as instruments of righteousness unto God." Because you have been "made alive," put away all the trappings of death, put off the old man, mortify the lusts of the flesh. Give up yourselves to God without any reserve.

Yet we repeat, obedience unto Romans vi, 12, 13, is possible only as we maintain the assurance of our perfect standing in Christ (verse 11), drawing

motives and strength thereform for practical holiness, and by constantly seeking help from Christ by drawing upon His fullness (John i, 16). That is ever
the evangelical order, " Be ye kindly affectioned one to another, tender-hearted,
forgiving one another, even as God for Christ's sake *hath* forgiven you " (Eph.
iv, 32). " Set your affection on things above, and not on things on the earth."
Why? " For ye died, and your life is hid with Christ in God . . . *mortify therefore* your members which are upon the earth " (Col. iii, 1-5). " Put off all these:
anger, wrath, malice, blasphemy, filthy communications out of your mouth;
lie not one to another." Why? " Seeing that *ye have* put off the old man with
his deeds " (Col. iii, 8, 9). " Behold! what manner of love the Father hath
bestowed upon us that we should be called the sons of God . . . when He
shall appear we shall be like Him; for we shall see Him as He is." And what
is the effect of faith's appropriation thereof? This, " And every one that hath
this hope in him *purifieth himself* [not merely ought to do] even as He is
pure " (I John iii, 1-3).

But, says the Christian reader, notwithstanding my best efforts to keep my
heart occupied with Christ and my faith fixed steadfastly on Him, sin daily
gets the better of me. And what is the effect upon you? Are you pleased
thereby? No, the very reverse; you are cut to the quick. That too is an integral
part of practical " circumcision." Not only is every denying of self, every
striving against sin, an element of mortification or practical circumcision, but
equally so is all godly sorrow, all evangelical repentance, all contrite confession of sin. Blessed are they that " mourn " over their backslidings and falls,
for it evidences they belong to those " whose circumcision is that of *the heart,
in the spirit and not in the letter* " (Rom. ii, 29)—real and effectual, in contrast
from the formal and ceremonial.

DIVORCE

" But if the unbelieving depart, let him depart. A brother or a sister is not
under bondage in such cases; but God hath called us to peace " (I Cor. vii, 15).
So far as we are aware, this is the *only* verse in all the Bible appealed unto
by those who insist that the case of desertion or abandonment constitutes a
valid ground for divorce. It therefore calls for the closest scrutiny, in order to
determine whether there be anything in it which obliges us to take such a
view, or even offers weighty support thereto. Before recording our own understanding of its terms, let the reader give the verse a careful perusal and seek
to supply his or her own answer to the question, What is there in it which
definitely and unequivocally favours such an idea. We say " definitely and
unequivocally," for surely something more solid and satisfactory than uncertain conjectures or vague interferences are required in such a solemn and
radical matter—a matter which involves pitting the teaching of the apostle
against that of the Lord Jesus! Be not carried away by what any " great and
godly men " have said thereon, but form your own judgment of what the verse
really teaches.

Above, we have said, that to make I Corinthians vii, 15 mean that desertion severs the marriage tie, sets the apostle at direct variance with the ringing
declaration of his Master, and so far as we are concerned, that single consideration settles the question, and compels us to reject the common interpretation
of that verse. The words of Christ are too plain to be misunderstood: " But
I say unto you [against all who aver otherwise], that whosoever shall put away

his wife, *saving* [only] for the cause of fornication [adultery], causeth her to commit adultery [should she cohabit with any other man]; and whosoever shall marry her that is divorced [on any other ground], committeth adultery" (Matt. v, 32). He repeats the same thing in Matthew xix, 9. Christ is both the Prophet and the Head of His Church, and beyond *His* authoritative decision there is no appeal. That is abundantly clear from the commission which He has given His servants: " Go ye therefore and make disciples of all nations, baptizing them in the name of the Father, and of the Son, and of the Holy Spirit. Teaching them to observe *all* things whatsoever I have *commanded* you" (Matt. xxviii, 19, 20).

But again; the popular view of I Corinthians vii, 15 is entirely against the scope and method of the passage in which it occurs. In the preceding paragraphs we have been at some pains to make clear Paul's line of thought therein, and have considered, first, his directions unto those who were contemplating a divorce (verses 10, 11), affirming that being united unto an idolater did not constitute a ground for such. And second, that such a situation did not even call for a separation (verses 12-14). Thus, to regard verse 15 as treating of something which supplied cause for a *divorce,* is to suppose the apostle guilty of a literary lapse, and what is worse, make verse 15 flatly contradict what he said in verse 11. But the apostle is to be charged with no such confusion as that: it is the minds of his expositors which are befogged. In verse 15 Paul does *not* go back to the matter dealt with in verses 10 and 11, but instead, continues and completes the subject under discussion in verses 12 to 14.

The question resolved in verses 12 to 15 is, Does a Christian married to a heathen call for a separation, as is clear from the apostle's " But to the rest speak I, not the Lord "—i.e. Christ Himself had given out no decision thereon. In verses 12 and 13 orders were given that where the unbelieving partner *is willing* for the Christian mate to continue cohabiting, there must be no separation. In verse 14 he amplifies that injunction. First, by showing that a separation is needless; and second that it would be disastrous for the children. Then in verse 15, he contemplates the other alternative, namely, Suppose the idolater is *unwilling* for the Christian mate to remain, then what shall the latter do? Most probably there were cases where a devout heathen was bitterly opposed to Christianity, and therefore, violently hostile to the idea of continuing to live with a husband or wife who had become an avowed Christian. When this was the case, and no appeal of either reason or affection had any effect, then what policy ought the believing partner to adopt? *That* is the question to which the apostle here furnishes answer, nor does there appear to us the least ambiguity in his language.

" But if the unbelieving depart, let him depart." If he has deliberately deserted you because of a difference of religion, you must bow to the will of God. If it has not pleased Him to subdue the prejudice of your husband and to soften his heart toward you, you must acquiesce with the Divine providence. The onus rests upon him, and you must accept the situation with good grace. " A brother or a sister is not under bondage in such cases " is explained by the words that immediately follow: " but God has called us *to peace.*" In such a case, the believing wife is not to have recourse unto litigation and insist that the deserter be compelled by law to return unto her. The Christian wife is under no moral bonds to pursue her husband into the courts and demand that he make provision for her support, for that would be to follow a policy the very reverse of that " peace " which God has enjoined upon His children (Rom. xii, 18; xiv, 19; Heb. xii, 14). Believers are " the sons of peace " (Luke x, 6), followers of the Prince of peace, and where no principle is involved, they must avoid all contention and strife.

Not a word does the apostle say in I Corinthians vii, 15 about desertion dissolving the marriage tie, still less that in such a case the believer is free to marry again—that is *man's* presumptuous *addition* to the Word of God. Furthermore, that which immediately follows militates against such an idea. " For what knowest thou, O wife, whether thou shalt save thy husband? or how knowest thou, O man, whether thou shalt save thy wife? " (verse 16). The opening " for " obviously has the force of " because " and introduces an important consideration to *deter from* all precipitate and extreme action. Unmistakably it makes directly against the erroneous view taken of the preceding verse, for if the wife *has* divorced the husband, what hope could there be of God making use of her in winning him! Verse 17 supplies an additional reason why neither divorce nor separation should be insisted upon: " But as God hath distributed to every man, as the Lord hath called every one, so let him walk. And so *ordain I* (proving it was far more than a mere personal advice which the apostle was here proffering!) in all the churches." Paul was averse from breaking up the conjugal relation or any social position the Christian had occupied before conversion Christianity is not a revolutionary and disorganizing element, but is designed to promote the general good. Loyalty to Christ does not forbid, but requires, husbands and wives to dwell together in peace, servants to obey their masters, subjects to honour the king.

It is little to be wondered at that the profane world now entertains such lax views on the sanctity of marriage, when so many professing Christians advocate such an anti-Scriptural sentiment as the permissibility of divorce merely for desertion. It is greatly to be regretted that so many good men during the last three centuries taught that error, for they but paved the way for the well-nigh total moral breakdown which obtains today. When the leaders of Christendom sowed such seed, no other harvest could be expected. Better taught were the early Puritans. One equal in spirituality and scholarship to any member of the Westminster Assembly wrote fifty years earlier, " A man with a good conscience cannot give a bill of divorcement for any cause but adultery, and therefore those laws which permit divorce for other causes are greatly faulty before God. If any should ask whether men's laws may not make more causes of divorcement than this one? I answer, No, for marriage is not a mere civil thing, but partly spiritual and Divine, and therefore God only hath power to appoint the beginning, the continuance, and the end thereof " (W. Perkins, 1587).

Turning now to the last division of our subject. When the marriage bond has been broken by one party, is the innocent one, after a divorce has been obtained, free—in the sight of God, we mean—to marry again? Or is he or she shut up unto a life of celibacy? This question need not detain us very long, yet it is one that calls for a brief consideration at least, for Christendom by no means returns a uniform answer thereto. Probably many of our readers are aware that one of the errors of the Mother of harlots concerning marriage is, that it is *unlawful* for a man who has repudiated his wife for adultery to marry again. Nor is that view entirely peculiar to Romanists, for some Protestants have entertained the same idea, being misled by our Lord's words in Mark x, 11, " Whosoever shall put away his wife and marry another committeth adultery against her," regarding that as an unqualified and absolute restriction. But that is a mistake, through failing to read this verse in the light of Matthew v, 32 and xix, 9.

Scripture must be explained by Scripture, and briefer statements read in the light of fuller ones, and never must one be pitted against the other. Particularly is this the case with the first three Gospels; parallel passages should be consulted, and the shorter one read in the light of the longer one. Thus, when Peter asked Christ, " How often shall my brother sin against me, and I forgive him? till seven times? " our Lord's answer " Until seventy times seven " (Matt. xviii, 21, 22) must not be taken to signify that we are to condone wrongs and exercise grace at the expense of righteousness, for He had just previously said, " If thy brother shall trespass against thee, go and tell him his fault between thee and him alone : if he shall hear [heed] thee, thou hast gained thy brother (verse 15). No, rather must His language in Matthew xviii, 22, be interpreted by His amplified declaration in Luke xvii, 3, 4, " If thy brother trespass against thee, rebuke him: and *if he repent,* forgive him. And if he trespass against thee seven times in a day, and seven times in a day turn again to thee, saying, I repent; thou shalt forgive him " ! God Himself does not forgive us until we repent (Acts ii, 38; iii, 19). While we must not entertain any bitterness or malice in our hearts against those who wrong us, yet not until they acknowledge their offence are we to fellowship them as if no offence had been committed.

So too in order to obtain a right conception of the great commission which the Redeemer has given to His ministers, we need to bring all three accounts thereof together, and not confine ourselves unto only one of them: " that *repentance* and remission of sins, should be preached in His name " (Luke xxiv, 47), is equally essential as bidding sinners " believe in the Lord Jesus Christ." Thus with the matter we are now discussing: Mark x, 11, is to be interpreted by Matthew v, 32. " Whosoever shall put away his wife, saving for the cause of fornication, causeth her to commit adultery; and whosoever shall marry her that is divorced [for any other cause] committeth adultery " —repeated by Christ in Matthew xix, 9. In those words Christ propounded a general rule [" *Whosoever* putteth away his wife causeth her to commit adultery, and he that marrieth her committeth adultery "], and then He put in *an exception*, namely, that for adultery he *may* put her away, and such a one *may* marry again. As He there teaches the lawfulness of divorce on the ground of adultery, so He teaches it is lawful to marry again after such a divorce, without contracting the guilt of adultery.

In his comments on Matthew xix, 9, rightly did John Owen point out, " Hence it is evident, and is the plain sense of the words, that he who putteth away his wife for fornication and marrieth another *does not* commit adultery. Therefore the bond of marriage in that case is dissolved and the person that put away his wife is at liberty to marry. While He denies putting away and marrying again for every cause, the exception of fornication allows both putting away and marrying again in that case. For an exception always affirms the contrary unto what is denied in the rule, whereto it is an exception; or denies what is affirmed in it in the case comprised in the exception. For every exception is a particular proposition contradictory to the general rule: so that when the one is affirmative, the other is negative; and on the contrary. The rule here in general is affirmative: he that putteth away his wife and marrieth another committeth adultery; the exception is negative: he that putteth away his wife for fornication and marrieth another does not commit adultery."

Consider the alternative. If the husband prove unfaithful to his marriage vows, is it in accord with God's revealed character of righteousness and mercy to penalize the innocent wife to remain in the single state the rest of her life? If she has divorced her husband, does God now inflict upon her the sentence of perpetual widowhood because of the infidelity of her partner? For her to be deprived of her right by the sin of another is against the very law of nature, and in such case it would lie within the power of every wicked husband to deprive his wife of her natural right. The right of divorce specified by Christ for the injured party to make use of, is manifestly designed for his or her liberty and relief; but on the supposition that he or she may not marry again, then it would prove a snare and a yoke. As Owen also pointed out concerning such a supposition, "It may, and probably will, cast a man under the necessity of sinning. For suppose he has not the gift of continency, it is the express will of God that he should marry for his relief." Surely I Corinthians vii, 2 and 9 make it clear that God would not have the injured one exposed to a life of immorality.

THE DOCTRINE OF REVELATION
12.   The Holy Bible.

If the Bible be the Word of God, if it immeasurably transcends all the productions of human genius, then we should naturally expect it to be attested by marks which evince its Divine origin. That such an expectation is fully realized we shall, at some length, seek to show. Those marks are of no vague and uncertain kind, but definite and unmistakable, and are of such a character as man could not be the author of them. The indications that the Bible is a Divine revelation are numerous, various, and conclusive. They are such as appeal severally to those of different tastes and temperaments, while taken together they present a case which none can invalidate. The Bible is furnished with such credentials as only those blinded by prejudice can fail to recognize it is a messenger from Heaven. They are of two kinds. extraordinary [miracles and prophecies] and ordinary, and the latter may be distinguished again between those which are objective and subjective—the one addressed to reason, the other capable of verification in experience. Each has the nature of a distinct witness. yet there is perfect agreement between them; united, yet independent.

1.   *Man's Need.* We may well draw our first argument *for* an intelligible and authoritative revelation of God *from* our imperative requirement of the same. In earlier articles we have presented evidence to show God exists, that He created man a rational and moral being, endowed with the power to distinguish between good and evil, and therefore that he was [originally] capable of knowing God, obeying Him, and worshipping Him. But man could neither intelligently obey nor acceptably worship God unless he first had a direct revelation from Him of *how* He was to be served. In order for there to be intercourse between man and his Maker, he must first receive from Him a communication of His mind prescribing the details of his duty. Accordingly we find that immediately after the creation of Adam and Eve God gave them a particular statute. He first informed them what they might do (Gen, ii, 16), and then specified what they must not do. Thus, from the outset, was man made dependent upon his Creator for a knowledge of His will, and thus too was his fidelity unto Him put to the proof.

If such was the case with man in his pristine glory, as he was made in the moral image of God, how much greater is his need of a Divine revelation since he has left his first estate, lost the image of God, and become a fallen and depraved creature! Sin has defiled his soul: darkening his understanding, alienating his affections, vitiating all his faculties. Should a critical objector here say, But you are now *assuming* what has not yet been proved, for you are taking for granted the authenticity of Genesis iii [wherein the defection of man from his Maker is recorded], it should be sufficient reply at this stage to ask, What other alternative remains? Only this: that God created man in his present woeful plight, that he has never been in any better condition. But is not such a concept abhorrent even to reason? Surely a perfect God would not create so faulty a creature. Could One who is infinitely pure and holy make man in the awful state of iniquity in which we now behold him ? How, then, has man become such a depraved being?

Why is it that, the world over, mankind are so intractable and wayward, that so many are regulated by their lusts rather than reason, that if the restraints of human law and government were removed and every one given free rein, the earth would speedily become a charnel-house ? During the first half of this twentieth century, despite our vaunted education and civilization, enlightenment and progress, we have witnessed the most appalling proofs of human depravity, and that on a scale of enormous magnitude. So far from beholding any indication that man is slowly but surely *ascending* from the ape to the Divine, there is abundant evidence to show that the larger part of our race has *descended* to the level of the beasts. But how comes this to be, if man at the beginning was a sinless and holy creature ? Apart from the Bible, no satisfactory answer is forthcoming: neither philosophy nor science can furnish any satisfactory explanation. Here again we see the urgent need of a revelation from God: that Divine light may be cast upon this dark mystery, that we may learn how man forfeited his felicity and plunged himself into misery.

What has just been pointed out makes manifest yet another aspect of man's deep *need* of a plain revelation from God. Man is now a fallen and polluted creature—no one who reads the newspapers or attends the police courts can question that. How, then, do the ineffable eyes of God regard him? How is it possible for fallen creatures to regain their former glory? Reason itself tells us that one who has rebelled against God's authority and broken His laws cannot at death be taken into His presence, there to spend a blissful eternity, without his sins being first pardoned and his character radically changed. The convictions of conscience reject any such anomaly. But apart from Divine revelation, how are we to ascertain what will satisfy the thrice holy God ? In what way shall a guilty soul be pardoned, a sinful soul be purified, a polluted creature made fit for the celestial courts ? All the schemes and contrivances of human devising fail utterly at this vital point: at best they are but a dream, a guess. Dare you, my reader, risk your *eternal* welfare upon a mere peradventure ?

Turning back from the future to the present: how is God to be *worshipped* by man ? Such a question is necessarily raised by the being and character of God and of man's relationship to Him as His creature. That the Deity should be acknowledged, that homage ought to be rendered unto Him, has been owned by the majority of our fellows in all climes and ages. True, their conceptions of Deity have varied considerably, and so too their ideas of how to honour Him; yet the conscience of all nations has convicted them that some form of worship is *due* unto God. It has been generally felt and avowed that there should be an acknowledgment of our dependency upon God, that supplications for His favour should be offered, that confessions of sin should be made, that thanksgivings for His mercies should be returned. Low as man has fallen, yet until he be steeped in vice, the dictates of reason and the promptings of his moral nature have informed him that God ought to be worshipped. Yet without a special revelation from God, how is it possible for any man to know that he worships *aright,* that his efforts to honour God are *acceptable* to Him ? The crude and debasing idol woship of those who are ignorant of or have spurned God's Word will clearly evince the need for such a revelation.

From the works of creation, the voice of conscience, and the course of Providence, we may learn enough of God and of our relation to Him as to make us the accountable creatures of His government, but of that knowledge which is necessary to our *salvation,* we can discover nothing whatever. Unwritten revelation is inadequate to meet the needs of a sinner. We need a further revelation in order to learn our real character and ascertain how we may be acceptable unto God. Creation as such exhibits no Saviour, announces no redemption, and supplies not the least indication that the forgiveness of sins is possible, much less likely. If we break the laws of nature we must suffer the penalty. Ignorance will not exempt us nor will penitence remit the suffering. Nature's laws are inexorable and are no respecter of persons. A child falling into the fire will be burned as surely as the vilest criminal. If we had nothing more than the visible world from which to draw our conclusions, we could never infer a hope of mercy for the transgressor of law. Nor would our moral instincts hold out any prospect of future relief for conscience condemns us and informs us that punishment is just.

Religion [from *re-ligo* " to bind back "] must have something to tie to. It must have a foundation, a basis, an ultimate appeal. What is that appeal ? Many say *tradition*: to the teaching of " the Fathers," to the decree of Councils, to an authority lodged in the Church as a Divine corporation, indwelt and made infallible by the presence of the Holy Spirit. That is the doctrine of Rome—a doctrine which binds to a system assumed to be supernatural, but which is " as shifting as the decrees of councils have shifted, contradictory as the statements of church fathers have been conflicting; blind and confusing; a congeries of truths and errors, of affirmations, and denials, of half lights and evasions from Origen to Bellarmine " (G. S. Bishop). The Papacy's claim to be the seat of Divine authority is refuted by historic fact and personal experience. Her career has been far too dark and chequered, her influence on human life, liberty and progress, much too unsatisfactoy, for any impartial investigator to be deceived by such an arrogant pretention.

Others make their own *instincts* the supreme arbiter. That which commends itself to their " intuitions " or appeals to their sentiments is accepted, and whatever accords not therewith is spurned. But since temperaments and tastes differ so widely, there could be no common standard to which appeal may be made, and by which each one might test the rightness or wrongness of his preferences. Each separate individual would become a law unto himself: nay, if nothing be right or good save what I approve of, then I am my own God. This may be termed the religion of nature, and it accounts for every vagary from the myths of Paganism to the self-delusion of mis-called " Christian Science," for everything put forth from Homer to Huxley. Such self-limitation exposes its utter poverty. Self cannot advance beyond the bounds of an experience which is limited by the present. How can I know anything about the origin of things unless I be taught by One who existed before them. Apart from a special revelation from God, what can I possibly know of what awaits me after death ?

Human reason is the ultimate court of appeal for the majority of this generation. But reason is not uniform: what appears to be logical and credible to one man, seems the very opposite to another. Most of what was pointed out in the last paragraph, obtains equally here—reason can know nothing of what it has no experience. The great subject of controversy between infidels and Christians is whether reason [the intellect and moral faculties] be sufficient to enable us to attain all that knowledge which is necessary for bringing us to virtue and happiness. That question is not to be answered by theorizing but by experiment; not by conjectures, but facts. It must be submitted to the test of history. What conclusions did the reason of the ancient Egyptians, Greeks and Romans arrive at ? So far from formulating any adequate conception of Deity, they worshipped birds and beasts, and invented Gods of the most revolting character. There was no agreement among their most renowned thinkers. Their systems of moral philosophy were woefully defective and their framers notoriously profligate. Even today where the Bible is rejected reason rises no higher than agnosticism: *I know not*— whether there be a God, a soul which survives the death of the body, or what the hereafter may hold.

If it be asked, What purpose does reason serve in connection with spiritual things ? We answer, first, its province is to form a judgment of the evidence of Christianity: to investigate and to estimate the grounds on which it claims to be a Divine revelation. Its duty is to weigh impartially and determine the force of such arguments as we have advanced in the preceding articles and those we purpose presenting in future ones. Second, its office is to examine carefully the contents of Scripture, to acquaint ourselves with its teachings, to attentively consider the demands they make upon us—which we could not do if we had no more understanding than the irrational beasts. Third, its function is to subordinate itself unto the authority of Divine revelation—the absurdity of the opposite is self-evident. Reason is certainly *not* to constitute the judge of what God says, but is rather to consider and test the evidence which demonstrates that He *has* spoken. The wisdom of God is not placed on trial before the bar of human foolishness. Man is the scholar, and not the Teacher; his reason is to act as a servant and not a lord. We act most *reasonably* when we thankfully avail ourselves of the light which God has vouchsafed us in His Word.

Having shown the limitations and inadequacy of man's own faculties— manifested everywhere in the records of history, both ancient and modern— we return to our opening postulate: man's *need* of a special and infallible revelation from God. He needs such in order to deliver him from a state of spiritual ignorance—a state which is fraught with the utmost peril to his soul. Consider how prone is the mind of man to embrace error, how ready and fertile to invent new religions. Even when unfallen, man required that his path of duty be made known to him by his Maker. Much more so does man, considered as a fallen creature, require an unerring Mentor to instruct him in spiritual things, one outside himself, infinitely above him. In a world of conflicting opinions and ever-changing theories, we must have a sure Touchstone, an unvarying Standard, an ultimate Authority to which appeal can be made. Amid all the sins and sorrows, the problems and trials of life, man is in urgent need of a Divine Guide to show him the way to present holiness and happiness and to eternal glory.

2. *A presumption in its favour*. This follows logically from all that has been before us above. Since man sorely needs such a revelation from God, and He is able to furnish it, then there is a strong probability that He *will* do so. He who endowed man with his intellectual faculties, is certainly capable of granting him a further degree of light by some other medium. " Revelation is to the mind what a glass is to the eye, whether it be intended to correct some accidental defect in its structure, or to enlarge its power of vision beyond its natural limits " (Professor Dick). To argue that we should be *uncertain* whether such a revelation be genuine or no, would be tantamount to saying that because there is so much imposture in the world, therefore there is no truth; that because so many are deceived, none can be sure that he is right. It is both presumptuous and unreasonable to affirm that God is unable to supply a communication unto mankind which is lacking in those marks that would authenticate it as coming from Himself. Cannot Deity legibly inscribe His signature on the work of His own hand ?

We might indeed draw the conclusion that since man is so vilely apostatized from his Maker that God will justly abandon him to misery. Yet we perceive that, notwithstanding the criminal conduct of His creatures, God still makes His sun to shine and the rain to fall upon them, providing them with innumerable blessings. Thoroughly unexpected as it might well be, we behold God exercising *mercy* unto the sinful sons of men, ameliorating those evils which they have brought upon themselves, and providing means by the use of which their sufferings are much alleviated. Though we could not from those things warrantably draw the conclusion that God would proceed any further in our behalf, yet if He should be pleased to extend His care unto our souls as well as our bodies, it would only be an enlargement of the scope of that benevolence already displayed in His provisions for us. It would be in perfect accord with the method He *has* employed with His creatures, if He further interposed to rescue fallen men from ignorance, guilt and perdition.

" From man at the head of creation, down to the lowest organized structure, there is not a necessity for which provision has not been made, and that in exact proportion to its wants. You yourself came into this world a poor, helpless, naked infant, full of necessities, and must have perished from the womb unless provision had been made for them. Who filled for you your mother's breast with milk and your mother's heart with love ? But you have a soul as well as a body—no less naked, no less necessitous. Shall then the body have its necessities, and those be provided for; and shall the soul have its necessities too, and for them there be no provision made ? Is there no milk for the soul as well as the body ? no ' sincere milk of the Word ' that it may grow thereby? " (J. C. Philpot). The goodness of God, the benevolence of the Creator, the mercy of our Governor, all point to the likelihood of His ministering to this supreme need of ours, without which ministration every one of us must assuredly perish.

The writer last quoted draws a further argument in support of this conclusion from the relations which God sustains to us as our sovereign Master and our Judge, pointing out that a master's will must be known before it can be obeyed, that a judge's law must be declared before it can be transgressed. Why are theft and murder punished ? Because the law of the land expressly forbids those crimes under a prescribed penalty; but since no human statute prohibits ingratitude, none are penalized in human courts for the same. It is a recognized principle that " where there is no law there is no transgression " (Rom. iv, 15). Then does it not clearly follow from this that God will give unto us His laws—direct, positive, authoritive law, binding upon us by Divine sanctions ? How could He justly punish what He has not forbidden ? And if He has forbidden sin, how and when has He done so ? Where is the statute book, written by His dictation, which makes known His will to us ? If it be not the Bible, we are left without any!

If it would be a far greater tax upon our credulity to believe that the universe had no Maker, than that " In the beginning God created the heavens and the earth "; if it involves immeasurably greater difficulty to regard Christianity as being destitute of a Divine Founder, than to recognize that it rests upon the person and work of the Lord Jesus Christ; then is it not far more unreasonable to suppose that God has left the human race without a written revelation from Him, than to believe the Bible is such ? There are times when the most thoughtful are uncertain as to which is the right course to pursue, when the most experienced need a guide their own wisdom cannot supply: will the One who furnishes us with fruitful seasons deny us such counsel ? There are sorrows which rend the hearts of the stoutest: will He who has given us the beautiful flowers and singing birds to regale our senses, withold that comfort we so much need in the hour of bereavement ? Which is the more reasonable: that the Maker of sun and moon should provide a Lamp for our feet, or leave us to grope our way amid the darkness of a ruined world!

OUR ANNUAL LETTER

" Thou hast dealt well with Thy servant, O Lord, according to Thy Word " (Psa. cxix, 65). There are times when such language as that fitly expresses even our natural feelings, when sight and sense have no difficulty in perceiving that God has ordered things favourably for us; and at such seasons we may not be slack in owning the Hand which has provided so freely for us. But there are other occasions when the sun is hidden, dark clouds mask the sky, and our frail barque is tossed upon a heavy sea, and then we are apt to imagine God is dealing ill with us. Yet it is not so, nor should the Christian ever give place to such evil thoughts, still less to murmuring. Instead of judging the Lord by feeble sense, he should confide in His love and trust in His unerring wisdom. Nor should the voice of praise be stilled: " Giving thanks *always* for all things unto God and the Father in the name of the Lord Jesus Christ (Eph. v, 20).

" Forget not all His benefits " both in grace and providence. But the saint should do more than remember, he should bear testimony to them and record God's goodness unto him. Gratitude is to be expressed. " Thou hast dealt well with Thy servant, O Lord " is the language of a thankful soul, sensible of God's kindness to him, and making hearty acknowledgment of the same. However adverse circumstances appear to be unto carnal reason, if faith be in exercise, this will be its testimony. When death suddenly smote the young son of the woman who had befriended Elisha, and she was asked " Is it well with the child," she answered " It is well " (II Kings iv, 26). That was not merely the language of resignation, but of undiminished confidence in the Lord's goodness. If our hearts be right with God we shall have no hesitation in saying " He hath done all things *well*." Grace triumphs over the flesh and can produce songs of praise even in a dungeon (Acts xvi, 25).

"Thou hast dealt well with Thy servant, O Lord, *according unto Thy Word*." God has engaged Himself to do so: "there is no want to them that fear Him. The young lions do lack and suffer hunger, but they that seek the Lord shall not want any good thing" (Psa. xxxiv, 9, 10). He has declared that all things shall work together for good unto those who love Him. Make much of God's promises, Christian reader, for they are exactly suited unto all the circumstances in the personal history of each saint. Act like those of Hebrews xi, 13. God is faithful and makes good His promises, but faith must be in operation if the comfort of them is to be enjoyed, if the heart is to be sustained while awaiting their fulfilment. The Divine promises are a sure foundation for faith to rest upon, for God cannot belie them. Plead them in prayer, and then bear testimony to God's fidelity as He makes them good unto you.

As we come to the close of still another year, the above Scripture is our own witness. God has dealt well with us: mercifully, favourably, bountifully. He has borne with our waywardness and has been patient with our infirmities. He has heard our cries and made good His Word. No good thing have we lacked. Through another twelve months He has granted both of us a goodly measure of health and strength. Once more He has furnished Seed for the sower. Funds have come in freely, so that every bill was promptly paid. Our circulation has again shown a slight increase. Despite paper shortage and labour difficulties, though the first four copies were very late, we have been privileged to send the twelve issues again to our readers. Many have lovingly remembered us at the throne of grace, though we wish more would pray about paper, the printing, and an increased number of readers. Thanksgiving is due unto God for the much improved service by our new printers.

In such evil days as these, when so many empty professors have discarded their religious masks and appeared in their true characters, and not a few of God's own children are in such a sad case spiritually that they prefer what is either soothing or sensational to that which searches the heart and calls to a closer walking with the Lord, it is "marvellous in our eyes" that the One whom we are seeking to serve still provides sufficient readers to enable us to continue this magazine. Nevertheless, since this be a "work of *faith*," faith has to be tested, and it is no small trial having to cut down our wee mailing-list so drastically when preparing the new one for next year. Though it stands at less than *one* thousand at the close of 1947, more than two hundred now upon it will be dropped unless we have word from them to the contrary. That means that at least an equal number of new ones are required during the next few months to replace the dropped ones if we are to continue publishing. We have no doubt whatever that God will, in answer to believing and importunate prayer, supply them. Yet, it is also our responsibility to beg every interested reader who has, under God, received real help from these pages to prayerfully consider if there are any Christians known to him or her who would be likely to welcome the "Studies," and if so to kindly drop a few lines urging them to write us for them—this is more effectual than *our* sending sample copies to those unacquainted with us.

The series on "The Prayers of the Apostles" has already extended beyond our original intention, but since we know of nothing more needed today by the members of the household of faith, we purpose prolonging them for another year. Our progress in Joshua has been slow, though no slower than the vitality important contents of its opening portion called for: the next few chapters contain that which is likely to be of more general interest, and better pace is expected to be made. We purpose continuing for some months to present more of the varied and convincing evidence that the Bible is Divinely inspired, so let us hear from you before the January and February 1948 issues are exhausted: though they will not be printed before March 1. God willing, the bound volumes will again be available (in January) to those who took last year's issues in their loose form, and through the generosity of a few friends, they are sold at below cost price—7s. 6d. ($1.75) each, post paid. Heartily thanking all our friends for their prayer help and financial fellowship, yours by God's abounding mercy, A. W. and V. E. Pink.

P.S.   The second half of Matthew xxviii, 20, will be our motto text (D.V.) for 1948.

(continued from back page)

(I Cor. vii, 31). "Life" is theirs, in contrast from the unregenerate who merely exist (I Tim. v, 6). "Death" is theirs for it gives entrance into unclouded bliss. "Things present or things to come" are theirs (I Tim. iv, 8).

"For of Him, and through Him, and to Him, are all things: to whom be glory for ever. Amen" (Rom. xi, 36). This is one of the few passages where "all things" is to be understood without any restriction. That is not an arbitrary assertion of ours, but one required by the general tenor of Scripture and by the immediate context. In Romans ix-xi God is set forth as the sovereign Determiner of all creatures and events and the supreme Disposer of them, "working all things after the counsel of His own will" (Eph. i, 11). Everything that happens in the universe is of God's ordination, is through His operation, and is unto His glory in its termination. As Creator God is the originating cause of all creatures, as Provider their sustaining cause, as Governor the determining cause of their end.

"Be obedient in all things" (II Cor. ii, 9): do not pick and choose between God's commandments, but "have respect unto all of them" (Psa. cxix, 6). "Grow up into Him in all things, which is the Head, Christ" (Eph. iv, 15): be symmetrical Christians, flourishing in *every* grace: in knowledge, faith, love, humility, meekness, patience, self-denial, gentleness, temperance. "Giving thanks always for all things unto God" (Eph. v, 20): happily recognize and gratefully acknowledge that the very things which cross our wills and which nature dislikes are appointed by unerring Wisdom and infinite Love. "I can do all things—appointed by God—through Christ which strengtheneth me" (Phil. iv, 13): His grace is sufficient for every need.

How much confusion is avoided, how many erroneous understandings obviated, if we only go to the trouble of ascertaining the subject under discussion, attend carefully to the context, and, especially, compare one part of Scripture with another. To cite only one more case in point: "What things soever ye desire, when ye pray, believe that ye receive them, and ye shall have them" (Mark xi, 24). They are sadly mistaken who suppose that promise has no restrictions: it must be qualified by James i, 6, 7; iv, 3; I John iii, 22; v, 14.

thankful we are that He cannot. That He is unable to do so only demon-trates His ineffable holiness and absolute perfection. "With God all things are possible" is the same as "Is anything too hard for the Lord?" No, it is not. Nothing can baffle His wisdom, nothing can impede His power, nothing can prevent the outworking of His eternal purpose. The context is speaking of the difficulty of a rich man entering the kingdom. But God can change the heart of a miser, incline the will of the covetous. No sinner is beyond the reach of His grace.

"And we know that all things work together for good to them that love God" (Rom. viii, 28). That too must be understood in the light of its con-text. From verse 16 to the end of the chapter Paul showed that the *afflictions* to which the saints are exposed in this life are in no wise incompatible with the favour of God unto them. Their sufferings bring them into fellowship with Christ (verse 17). There is no proportion between them and the future glory (verses 18-25). Suitable aids are furnished them (26-27). They con-tribute to our weal. They do not and cannot separate from the love of God. (29-39). Thus the "all things" has reference to the "sufferings of this present time." "God hath not made a promise that all the *sins* of believers shall work for their good" (Manton)—to have done so had opened a wide door for carelessness and presumption. Such would be contrary to the analogy of the Word, where threatenings are uniformly made against sin. It would be op-posed to the qualification here: "love to God" is our duty and is exercised in obedience and not in sinning. As a fact, the sins of believers *are not* always overruled for "good." (Jer. v, 24; I Cor. iii, 15).

"He that spared not His own Son, but delivered Him up for us all, how shall He not with Him also freely give us all things" (Rom. viii, 32). God has not only given His own Son *for* His people to discharge their obligations, but He has also given Him *to* them (as the "with Him" clearly implies) to enrich them. They are made partakers of His life (Col. iii, 4), of His righ-teousness (Jer. xxiii, 6, Rom. v, 19), of His Spirit (Rom. viii, 9). Christians are "accepted in the Beloved" (Eph. i, 6) and have been given Christ's own status and standing before God (I John iv, 17). Christ is the Heir of all things" (Heb. i, 2) and believers are joint-heirs with Christ (Rom. viii, 17). God has given Christ to us as a "Covenant," as a "Head" of influence, as our great High Priest. Christ is both the security and the channel of every mercy: God supplies our every need "according to His riches in glory by Christ Jesus" (Phil iv, 19). The "all things" of Romans viii, 32, is the "all things that pertain to life and ungodliness" (II Peter i, 3). Of Christ's fullness "have all we received, and grace for grace" (John i, 16). We shall yet share His "glory" (John xvii, 24).

"All things are yours: whether Paul or Apollos or Cephas, or the world, or life, or death, or things present, or things to come: all are yours, and ye are Christ's" (I Cor. iii, 21-23). The Corinthians had yielded to a narrow and sectarian spirit and were pitting one apostle against another, when in reality their respective ministries were designed for the good of all God's people alike (Eph. iv, 11-13): the epistles of "Cephas" (Peter) are as truly the property of the Gentile saints as those of Paul's belong to Hebrew believers. From that the apostle proceeds to make a larger inventory of the Christian's riches. Not only are all ordinances and the ministries of all God's servants the common property of His whole family, but so is "the world," for it exists for their sakes (II Cor. iv, 15) and is to be "used"—though not "abused"—by them

(continued on preceding page)